Human Rights in the 21st Century

Human Rights in the 21st Century

Continuity and Change since 9/11

Edited by

Michael Goodhart

and

Anja Mihr

palgrave
macmillan

First published 2011 by
PALGRAVE MACMILLAN

Palgrave Macmillan in the UK is an imprint of Macmillan Publishers Limited, registered in England, company number 785998, of Houndmills, Basingstoke, Hampshire RG21 6XS.

Palgrave Macmillan in the US is a division of St Martin's Press LLC, 175 Fifth Avenue, New York, NY 10010.

Palgrave Macmillan is the global academic imprint of the above companies and has companies and representatives throughout the world.

Palgrave® and Macmillan® are registered trademarks in the United States, the United Kingdom, Europe and other countries.

ISBN. 978–0–230–28099–1 hardback

This book is printed on paper suitable for recycling and made from fully managed and sustained forest sources. Logging, pulping and manufacturing processes are expected to conform to the environmental regulations of the country of origin.

A catalogue record for this book is available from the British Library.

A catalog record for this book is available from the Library of Congress.

Printed and bound in Great Britain by
CPI Antony Rowe, Chippenham and Eastbourne

Contents

List of Illustrations   ix

Notes on Contributors   x

Acknowledgements   xiv

Introduction   1
Michael Goodhart and Anja Mihr

Part I   Perspectives

1   International Human Rights Since 9/11:
    More Continuity Than Change   13
    Jack Donnelly

2   Why Human Rights Will Prevail in the War on Terror   30
    Morton Winston

3   The War on Terror through a Feminist Lens   49
    Julie Mertus and Tazreena Sajjad

Part II   Human Rights Discourses

4   Reverting to Form: American Exceptionalism and
    International Human Rights   65
    Michael Goodhart

5   Continuity and Change in the Russian Federation's
    Human Rights Policies in the Fight against Terror   86
    Lauri Mälksoo

Part III   Change? Transatlantic Responses to 9/11

6   The High Price of American Exceptionalism:
    Comparing Torture by the United States and
    Europe after 9/11   107
    Jamie Mayerfeld

7   Europe's Human Rights Regime after 9/11:
    Human Rights versus Terrorism   131
    Anja Mihr

 8 Terror Blacklists on Trial: Smart Sanctions
    Challenged by Human Rights   150
    Patricia Schneider

 9 Human Rights and Counterterrorism:
    The Case of the Netherlands   166
    Peter R. Baehr

10 Caught in the Storm: Middle Powers as Barometers for
    the West's Changing Attitude toward Security and
    Human Rights after 9/11   183
    Yan St. Pierre

Part IV   Continuity? Global Trends

11 Transnational NGOs and Human Rights in
    a Post-9/11 World   203
    Hans Peter Schmitz

12 Disaggregating the Effects of 9/11 on NGOs   222
    Lena Barrett

13 Business As a New Actor in the Human Rights Regime   237
    Brigitte Hamm

Conclusion   256
Michael Goodhart and Anja Mihr

Bibliography   271

Index   301

List of Illustrations

Tables

1.1 Freedom House rankings   15
1.2 Global performance, 1989–2007   16
1.3 a. Post-Cold War trends (I): The pre-9/11 baseline;
     b. Post-Cold War trends (I): Before and after 9/11   18
1.4 Trends (II): performance as a ratio of
     the average for the three preceding years   20
1.5 Regional human rights performance, 1999–2007   22
1.6 Selected South and Central Asian countries   23
1.7 Selected Middle Eastern countries   25
4.1 Style and orientation of US international policy   73

Figures

10.1 Level of respect for human rights, Canada (1998–2006)   187
10.2 Level of respect for human rights, Western comparison   187

Notes on Contributors

Peter R. Baehr[†] studied political and social sciences at the University of Amsterdam and Georgetown University, Washington DC. He was Professor of International Relations, University of Amsterdam; staff director (later member) of the Scientific Council for Government Policy (WRR), The Hague; Professor of Human Rights and Foreign Policy, Leiden University; Professor of Human Rights and Director of the Netherlands Institute of Human Rights (SIM), Utrecht, Netherlands. He has published, in Dutch and English, on the United Nations, human rights, and foreign policy.

Lena Barrett began working with the Irish Refugee Council in 1996 while qualifying as a barrister in Ireland. She went on to work with refugee organizations in Europe and Africa over much of the next decade, before returning to the academic world to complete a European Master's in Human Rights and Democratization in 2007, with a thesis focusing on international remedies for torture. She is now based at the Centre for Applied Human Rights at the University of York, UK, where she runs a Fellowship scheme for Human Rights Defenders at risk.

Jack Donnelly is the author of three books and over 60 articles and book chapters on the theory and practice of human rights, including *Universal Human Rights in Theory and Practice*, 2nd edn (Cornell University Press 2003). He has also published in the area of international relations theory, including *Realism and International Relations* (Cambridge University Press 2000) and "Hierarchy in Anarchy and Sovereign Inequalities" (*European Journal of International Relations* June 2006).

Michael Goodhart is Associate Professor of Political Science and Women's Studies at the University of Pittsburgh and was a Humboldt Foundation Research Fellow and Visiting Professor at the Hertie School of Governance, Berlin, in 2008–9. His research focuses on democracy and human rights in the context of globalization, and he has written numerous articles on these themes. He is author of *Democracy As Human Rights: Freedom and Equality in the Age of Globalization* (Routledge 2005) and contributing editor of *Human Rights: Politics and Practice* (Oxford University Press 2009). His current research focuses on problems of global injustice.

[†] See dedication, page v.

Brigitte Hamm is Senior Research Fellow at the Institute for Development and Peace (INEF) at the University of Duisburg-Essen, Germany. She earned her Ph.D. in Political Science and conducts research in the fields of human rights and the private sector, of economic and social rights, and of the measurement of human rights. She is a member of the working group "Business and Human Rights" of the German Forum Menschenrechte and a member of FIAN.

Lauri Mälksoo is Associate Professor of International Law at the University of Tartu, Estonia. He was educated at Tartu University (LL.B. 1998), Georgetown University Law Center (LL.M. 1999), and Humboldt University, Berlin (Dr iur 2002) and carried out postdoctoral studies and research stays at New York University School of Law (2004–5) and Tokyo University Faculty of Law (2006–7). He is a part-time adviser for international law at the Chancellor of Justice of the Republic of Estonia (since 2002) and a member of the EU Network of Independent Experts on Fundamental Rights (2003–6).

Jamie Mayerfeld is Associate Professor of Political Science and Adjunct Associate Professor of Law, Societies and Justice at the University of Washington. He is writing a book which argues that constitutional democracy is incomplete unless domestic human rights institutions are bolted into a system of international guarantees. His recent articles have discussed the justification of international human rights law and international criminal law, the democratic contribution of the International Criminal Court, and the origins of the US torture policy.

Julie Mertus is Professor and Co-Director of Ethics, Peace and Global Affairs at School of International Service, American University. She has written widely on human rights and gender, conflict, the Balkans, U.S. foreign policy and U.N. institutions. She is the author or editor of ten books, including *Bait and Switch: Human Rights and U.S. Foreign Policy*, which was awarded the "Human Rights Book of the Year" by the American Political Science Association, and most recently *Human Rights Matters: Local Politics and National Human Rights Institutions* and *The United Nations and Human Rights*. Her book *War's Offensive on Women* is generally considered to be one of the first on topic. Before entering academia, she worked as a researcher, writer and lawyer for several human rights and humanitarian organizations and governments, including Human Rights Watch, the Open Society Institute, the Nations High Commissioner on Refugees (UNHCR), and Woman Waging Peace. Recently, she has been specializing in creating human rights education materials and in program evaluations, conducting evaluations in such disparate areas as Ethiopia, Albania and South Africa.

Anja Mihr is Associate Professor at the Netherlands Institute for Human Rights (SIM), University of Utrecht, Netherlands. Previously she was a Visiting Professor for Human Rights at Peking University Law School, China and worked for the Raoul Wallenberg Research Institute on Human Rights, Lund University. From 2006 to 2008 she was the European Program Director for the European Master's in Human Rights and Democratization at the European Inter-University Centre for Human Rights (EIUC) in Venice, Italy, where she remains a Senior Fellow. In her latest research she focuses on Transitional Justice, Reconciliation, Human Rights, and Democratization (www.anjamihr.com).

Tazreena Sajjad is completing her doctoral degree at the School of International Service, American University. Her dissertation looks at the question of impunity and the role of non-state actors in transitional justice in Afghanistan and Nepal. Her research interests also include gender in countries transitioning out of conflict. She is a recipient of the De Witt scholarship, Gandhi Memorial Scholarship for Peace, the Abdul Aziz Said Scholarship, the Dean's Dissertation Fellowship, and the Institute for Inclusive Security Fellowship. Prior to beginning her doctoral studies, she worked as a human rights practitioner in countries transitioning out of conflict, including in Afghanistan. Her publications include *Rape on Trial? The Promise of International Jurisprudence, the Perils of Retributive Justice and the Realities of Impunity* (forthcoming); *Mind the Gap: Questioning the Normative Good in the Rule of Law and Transitional Justice: Afghanistan and Beyond* (forthcoming); *and These Spaces in between: The Afghanistan Independent Human Rights Commission and its Work on Transitional Justice.*

Hans Peter Schmitz earned his Ph.D. in Political and Social Sciences from the European University Institute in Florence. He is Associate Professor of Political Science at the Maxwell School of Citizenship and Public Affairs, Syracuse University. He is the author of *Transnational Mobilization and Domestic Regime Change: Africa in Comparative Perspective* (Palgrave Macmillan 2006). His research appeared in *Comparative Politics, Human Rights Quarterly*, the *International Journal for Human Rights, International Studies Review, Monday Developments*, the *Handbook of International Relations*, and the *Zeitschrift für Internationale Beziehungen* (http://faculty.maxwell.syr.edu/hpschmitz/).

Patricia Schneider studied Political Science and Economics at the Universities of Bamberg, Galway/Ireland, and Hamburg. She is senior fellow at the Institute for Peace Research and Security Policy at the University of Hamburg (www.ifsh.de), academic coordinator of and lecturer in the postgraduate Master's program Peace and Security Studies, manager of the "Academic Network South East Europe", cofounder and coeditor of the book series "Frieden durch Recht" (Peace through Law) as well as chief editor and copublisher of the quarterly journal *S+F. Sicherheit und Frieden – Security and Peace* (www.security-and-peace.de/).

Yan St. Pierre is a native of Montreal, Quebec. He is a graduate of the Université de Montréal as well as of the Université Paris VII – Denis Diderot, where he obtained his Master's and wrote his dissertation on the evolution of terrorism and the discourse of terrorism novelty. He is currently working on a Ph.D. thesis analyzing the impact of liberal thought on the elaboration and application of counterterrorism measures in the West.

Morton Winston is Professor of Philosophy and Chairman of the Department of Philosophy and Religion at The College of New Jersey. His areas of specialization include human rights, ethical theory, political philosophy, and philosophy of technology. In 2007, Professor Winston was the Danish Distinguished Chair of Human Rights and International Relations at the Danish Institute of Human Rights in Copenhagen, Denmark.

Acknowledgements

We have incurred numerous debts in the preparation of this volume. An initial expert workshop held in Berlin in March 2007 was sponsored by the Deutsche Forschungsgemeinschaft (German Research Council) and by the Faculty of European Anthropology at Humboldt University. We are grateful to those institutions, and to Caroline Philipp, our Student Assistant in Berlin, whose efforts were essential to making that meeting a success. We also thank Jessica Almquist, George Andreopoulos, Zehra Arat, Karl Peter Fritzsche, Mark Gibney, Günter Nooke, Karen Schlüter, Johannes Thimm, and Andreas Vasilache for their participation in that meeting.

A second conference in Pittsburgh, held in April 2008, was sponsored by the University of Pittsburgh's European Union Center of Excellence, School of Arts and Sciences, Department of Political Science, School of Law, and Graduate School of Public and International Affairs. We thank those units, as well as the staff in the European Union Center, especially Karen Lautanen and Timothy Thompson, for all of their labors on our behalf. We are grateful to Alison Brysk, David Chandler, Alberta Sbragia, and Charles Swift for their support and participation. Thanks are also due to Global Solutions Education Fund, Pittsburgh and the Law School's Center for International Legal Education.

Finally, we appreciate the efficient and supportive efforts of the editorial and production staff at Palgrave Macmillan. Jef Croonen, Student Assistant in Utrecht, helped us tremendously with editing the text.

Michael Goodhart was supported by a research fellowship from the Alexander von Humboldt Foundation in 2008–2009, during which time much of the editorial work was undertaken; in addition, we have received support from the Richard D. and Mary Jane Edwards Endowed Publication Fund at the University of Pittsburgh, and we gratefully acknowledge that support here.

Introduction

Michael Goodhart and Anja Mihr

The terrorist attacks of September 11, 2001 in the United States and subsequent attacks in Madrid, London, and beyond have made combating terrorism a chief priority on both sides of the Atlantic. In the wake of these attacks and the wider "war on terror" they triggered, governments adopted many policies – including detention and interrogation practices and domestic security legislation – that raise serious human rights concerns. Moreover, in implementing these policies some governments committed gross human rights abuses, as at the infamous Abu Ghraib prison near Baghdad or the rendition flights in Europe that led to serious acts of torture and ill-treatment. It is easy to conclude from these straightforward facts that the events and aftermath of 9/11 marked a significant change in the international human rights regime, and many scholars and commentators have reached precisely this conclusion.

Despite the obvious and important concerns raised by these policies, however, the assumption that they represent significant or lasting damage to the international human rights regime is too quick. It relies on inferences about the regime based primarily on national behavior and concerning a relatively narrow range of human rights, and it ignores the resilience of the regime and its capacity for correction and adjustment. In fact, there has been very little systemic analysis of how policies and practices implemented in conjunction with the "war on terror" since 9/11 have affected the broader international human rights regime. This volume fills that gap, addressing questions about continuity and change in the human rights regime from a variety of national and methodological perspectives and at multiple levels of analysis. We adopt a transatlantic approach to these questions, with authors from Europe and North America reflecting on different issues and institutions from a variety of country and methodological perspectives. Our focus is on the national and regional practices of these two continents, which are similarly situated with respect to the threat of global terrorism and similar in their forms of government and levels of development. Historically, they have also been the central players in structuring and maintaining the international human rights regime. Thus while a transatlantic perspective is inherently limited and partial, it is also essential to evaluating the regime.

Quite simply, the aim of the book is to assess the impact of the terrorist attacks of 9/11 and the ensuing "war on terror" on the international human rights regime – without taking the nature or extent of that impact for granted. We are particularly interested in identifying areas of continuity as well as of change and in trying to account for the differences. This aim has only become clear with time and hard work. That last point is important. The initial pilot workshop for this project, held at Berlin's Humboldt University in April 2007, was entitled "Transformation of the International Human Rights Regime After 9/11" – a title which, while productively provocative, assumed what it should have questioned: that there *was* indeed widespread and significant change and that this change was attributable to the terrorist attacks on the United States and their aftermath. After a great deal of passionate debate, we concluded that this way of approaching the topic raised more questions than it answered. What exactly is the international human rights regime? What significant changes has it undergone since 9/11, and (how) can those changes be attributed to events related to 9/11? How do obvious changes in national policy (foreign and domestic) impact the regime? How do these changes differ in Europe and North America, and how do the differences play out internationally? Does 9/11 provide a useful analytic frame for thinking about human rights and about changes in the human rights regime?

Following these fruitful discussions in Berlin, a follow-up conference was held at the University of Pittsburgh in April 2008. This time the focus was different, with participants focused on analyzing and challenging the widely held assumption that 9/11 and related events "changed everything" while also exploring some of these more specific questions in more depth and with greater nuance. This volume continues in the same trajectory, assessing continuity and change since 9/11 in connection with a range of different actors and institutions from a variety of perspectives. While the individual contributions for the most part focus on specific national, regional, institutional, or sectoral questions, the volume as a whole seeks to provide a balanced and diverse assessment of the important larger questions with which the research program began.

The international human rights regime

According to the classic definition, a regime is "[a set] of implicit or explicit principles, norms, rules, and decision-making procedures around which actors' expectations converge in a given area of international relations" (Krasner 1982, 186). In the case of the international human rights regime, the relevant principles, norms, and rules are those expressed in the Universal Declaration of Human Rights (UDHR) of 1948, the International Covenant on Civil and Political Rights (ICCPR), and the International Covenant on Social, Economic and Cultural Rights (ICSECR), both from 1966, and other declarations, conventions, and treaties, as well as the legal and institutional mechanisms developed to guide states and treaty parties to implement and safeguard human rights around the world. Seven of the main international treaties include mechanisms that ask signatory states to report regularly on and explain the human rights situation in their countries.

Today, the International human rights regime comprises more then 190 states which, as members of the United Nations, have agreed to respect the UDHR – even though it is not legally binding. Indeed, some scholars now maintain that the UDHR and the two Covenants, as well as perhaps some of the other important UN treaties and conventions, have attained the status of customary international law. Ratification of these treaties varies from nearly universal acceptance among European countries to very limited acceptance in the United States and some other countries (which put the United States in rather unflattering company).

In addition to these global arrangements, a variety of regional institutions, such as the Council of Europe (CoE), the Organization of American States (OAS), the African Union (AU), the European Union (EU), and the Organization for Security and Cooperation in Europe (OSCE), also shape human rights norms and standards, as do nongovernmental human rights organizations (NGOs) and other activists and scholars working in the area of human rights. In some cases regional mechanisms are better developed and more effective than international institutions. Europe's highly elaborated and diverse regional human rights arrangements with the European Court of Human Rights and the European Court of Justice stand out in this respect. Even within regions there is considerable variation, however; some OAS mechanisms are quite well developed, but the United States has refused to accept their jurisdiction, which has undermined their effectiveness.

There is also a great deal of variation among global and regional arrangements with respect to compliance and implementation. In some cases international human rights institutions have relatively little success; they are frequently ignored by member states and fail to achieve progress on respecting, protecting, and fulfilling the common human rights standards at their core. In other cases human rights institutions enjoy widespread support and command significant legal and moral authority. While the UN treaty committees tend to be weak and relatively ineffective, for example, decisions of the European Court of Human Rights (ECHR) are almost always implemented.

These differences help to explain why various components of the international human rights regime reacted differently to the challenges posed by 9/11 and also shed light on the responses of particular countries to challenges such as balancing counterterrorism and human rights. Moreover, while American policy in the years following 9/11 was broadly unilateralist and largely subordinated human rights concerns to national security, Europeans tried to lead in a different direction, relying on international law and their vaunted regional arrangements in defining an approach to counterterrorism issues that eschewed the excesses of the American "war on terror."

Assessing continuity and change

To effectively assess the impact of 9/11 on the international human rights regime, it is necessary to have some baseline of comparison. The contributors to this volume take the post-Cold War human rights regime of the 1990s until 9/11 as their key point of reference. The period between 11/9 in 1989 with the fall of the Berlin wall and 9/11 was one of remarkable change in the regime. Many states initiated or increased their involvement with global institutions during this period, resulting in an increase both in the number of international human rights treaties and mechanisms and in rates of ratification and participation in these international institutions. Regional institutions, especially in Europe, expanded dramatically as well. This process is ongoing.

Meanwhile, there was a veritable – and well-documented – explosion in transnational civil society activity around human rights and humanitarian issues, with human rights NGOs and transnational social movements with human rights concerns becoming increasingly important in shaping the agenda and – in an unprecedented development – winning an official seat at the table in negotiations on human rights issues. Whether it is the landmine ban or human rights education as part of the formal school curricula worldwide, many such issues that put human rights on the top of political agenda have been widely credited to transnational civil society efforts. NGOs began more closely to partner with the United Nations, with regional organizations, and with states in helping to monitor human rights standards and even in delivering humanitarian and development aid directly. Amid this period of remarkable development, two events from 1993 deserve special mention. First, in 1993 the Vienna World Conference on Human Rights affirmed the universality of the rights declared in the UDHR and launched an ambitious Plan of Action for achieving greater fulfillment of human rights around the world. Also in 1993 the EU with the treaty of Maastricht came into being and subsequently developed into one of the world's leading promoters of human rights – internationally and among its own member and would-be member states. Indeed, the 1990s were also notable as a decade of "domestication of human rights" around the world, with a great deal of progress made in transforming international commitments into domestic legal and political realities. It seems safe to say that at no other time have human rights received so much attention or recognition.

Prior to the 9/11 attacks, three main issues had emerged on the international human rights agenda. The first was institutional reform. In the late 1990s the UN member states agreed that reform of the UN Human Rights Commission was necessary in order to meet new and expected challenges. In addition, the wars in the former Yugoslavia from 1988 to 1999 and the genocide in Rwanda in 1994 led to the establishment of International Tribunals for Yugoslavia (ICTY, 1993) and Rwanda (ICTR, 1994). These institutions, in turn, inspired the creation of a permanent international court with jurisdiction over war crimes and crimes against humanity and made such an institution seem possible. In 1998 the Rome Statute of the International Criminal Court (ICC) was opened for ratification, the culmination of determined leadership and lobbying on the part of the Court's advocates – including, crucially, the NGO community. The second important issue to emerge on the international human rights agenda, following directly from the Vienna Conference and Plan of Action, was implementation of economic, social, and cultural rights. The NGO community again played a key role in pushing this issue, given a crucial lift by Vienna's affirmation of the interdependence and indivisibility of human rights. Some of the traditional human rights organizations wrestled with whether to expand their focus to include these rights, while organizations in the humanitarian and development sectors were already pushing ahead. Finally, combating racism was an important priority for human rights advocates on the eve of the 9/11 attacks. Only weeks before, a major international conference against racism kicked off in Durban, South Africa.

The attacks of 9/11 had an immediate and significant impact on this agenda. Within days of the attacks, counterterrorism displaced social and economic human rights and racism from the top of the political agenda. While this change was neither complete nor permanent, it continues to be a central fact of human rights discourse since 9/11. Perhaps the most notable changes were in American attitudes toward and participation in the regime, with the United States increasingly marginalizing itself through its own political posturing and through its numerous abuses of international and human rights law carried out in the name of the "war on terror." Yet despite these developments, the international human rights regime continued to function and develop – though now without US participation or cooperation. Institutional reform continued apace, with the Rome Statute going into force in 2002 and the new Human Rights Council, established by the UN General Assembly in 2006, holding its first meeting in 2007 (again without US participation or support). One result of these changes was a default to European leadership throughout the regime. Europe, despite its own failings associated with "counterterrorism," was widely seen as a "Western stronghold for human rights," and European countries and organizations struggled to find a new orientation and new strategy for safeguarding human rights in the post-9/11 world.

To a large extent, they have relied on the core idea advanced in Vienna in 1993 – that a culture of respect for human rights is only possible when human rights standards everywhere are respected and implemented. The debates about how best to address the challenge of terrorism while respecting human rights have contributed to increased awareness of human rights worldwide and to new forms of civic engagement. Efforts continue to bring human rights to the people, to embed them in local politics and practice, and to increase participation from the developing south and the BRIC countries in standard-setting and implementation. In short, efforts continue to make more governments and stakeholders accountable for their human rights performance. These efforts have been shaped by the 9/11 attacks and subsequent political and discursive changes, but not derailed by them.

Overview of the book

We imposed few constraints on the authors, asking only that they be clear about their subjects and the scope of their analyses, that they locate their arguments with respect to broader questions about the international regime, and that they say something about the 1990s as a baseline of comparison. Through the pursuit of different types of question using different methods and from differing perspectives, we can get a clearer picture of developments as they affect the regime as a whole. In the contribution the reader will find many familiar and predictable patters that apply to pre- as well as post-9/11. America's exceptionalism and Europe's "warmer embrace" of human rights norms prior to 9/11 have guided and shaped their antiterror policies after the attacks. European states are primarily more accustomed to external legal scrutiny and adhere to it more then other states with a less strong regional human rights regime. But specific country case studies in Europe and North America highlight the fact that even though norms can be high on the agenda, human rights implementation and practice depend very much on a general human rights culture, civil society engagement and the functioning of democratic institutions. Thus, wherever institutionalized independent courts and a strong civil society were effectively working, the regimes suffered fewer negative effects. In total the international human rights regime has been rather resilient. In retrospect the changes made following 9/11 appear necessary and perhaps inevitable.

The chapters are organized, loosely, according to their breadth of analysis. The first chapter, on perspectives, assesses the broad change in the regime as a whole. Jack Donnelly offers a broad empirical assessment of respect for human rights throughout the international regime, arguing that, despite some high-profile exceptions, "the negative changes since 9/11 have been largely incremental" and expressions of already-existing problems. This finding, Donnelly maintains, has important implications for how we think about the medium-term future of human rights. Morton Emanuel Winston contends that, despite a moral slide in the democratic countries on counterterrorism issues and a failure of US leadership, the leadership of global civil society is strengthening the human rights ethos and will ultimately see human rights emerge triumphant in the "war on terror." Julie Mertus and Tazreena Saijad show how the apparent attention to women and their rights in the "war on terror" masks a much more complex – and depressing – reality.

The next two chapters deal primarily with the discourse of human rights. Michael Goodhart argues that the terrorist attacks against the United States triggered a reversion to Cold War form with respect to human rights. This renewed period of messianic American engagement in international affairs threatens to erode the important moral and discursive progress on human rights achieved during the 1990s. Lauri Mälksoo highlights the fact that Russia's human rights policies have hardly changed, but rather the nation has continued to follow its hard line against inner state terrorism. Russian government has been seeing 9/11 as a welcome excuse to exempt the Russian case from the developments in the rest of Europe and beyond. On the one hand, Russian leaders see the US "war on terror" as a vindication of their own approach in dealing with secessionist movements in Chechnya and with the related threat of fundamentalist Islamic terrorism. On the other hand, Russia is coming under growing pressure to live up to its commitments under the CoE, with several ECHR judgments on Chechnya causing the Russian political establishment to reevaluate its approach just as it feels vindicated in it.

So is there any change, and if so, how does it manifest itself? The next chapter highlights the contrast between European and American experiences in dealing with the human rights challenges posed by counterterrorism efforts. Jamie Mayerfeld seeks to understand why torture became institutionalized in the United States after 9/11 but not in Europe. His answer emphasizes Europe's tighter legal and institutional rules, its greater commitment to criminalization of torture and other war crimes in domestic law, and its much greater internationalization of oversight, inspection, and enforcement of its torture regime. Greater internationalization, Mayerfeld shows, made a crucial difference in preventing systematic abuses in Europe. Anja Mihr argues that, while European countries also reacted aggressively to the threat of terrorism, the main European human rights actors, as well as an active NGO community, proved sufficient to counterbalance the threat of severe erosion. In particular, she shows how cooperation among Europe's key human rights actors created a crucial set of checks that permitted effective policies to emerge while blocking any systematic erosion of human rights standards. Patricia Schneider looks at the complex interactions between European and UN human rights mechanisms. Using the issue of terror "blacklists," she considers the delicate problem of finding ways to abolish tensions and disjunctions between major pillars of the international legal system in ways that are supportive of international law. This challenge has important legal and institutional as well as policy implications for the future development of human rights law and mechanisms. Peter Baehr and Yan St Pierre look at two traditional middle powers with longstanding reputations as stalwart supporters of the international human rights regime, the Netherlands and Canada. Baehr, focusing on the Netherlands, provides a comprehensive overview of that country's policies since 9/11, finding worrying signs that its characteristic commitment to human rights might be suffering as a result of fears about the threats posed by international and domestic terrorism. St Pierre reaches similar conclusions about Canada, though he attributes the erosion more to international pressure from the United States than to domestic fears regarding terrorism. These studies raise important questions about the role of middle powers as supporters of the regime and engines of its further development.

How much continuity do we find in the global human rights trend? The final chapters outline different perspectives on nonstate actors who at the same time have continuously increased their relevance within the regime since the 1990s. Hans-Peter Schmitz argues that while the Bush Administration's response to the 9/11 attacks had important negative repercussions for the NGO sector, 9/11 was not a major turning point. Rather, it served to highlight a profound crisis that had been increasingly apparent since the end of the Cold War: the limits of the advocacy approach utilized by NGOs to "name and shame" governments that violate their citizens' human rights. Lena Barrett contends that to understand the effects of the "war on terror" on NGOs, it is important to disaggregate that category according to the nature of the issues an organization works on and the regime-type of the countries in which it operates. Doing so, she finds that NGOs working on terrorism-sensitive issues in authoritarian countries have been very severely impeded, while some others have in fact been invigorated by the new challenges they face, and still others have been only marginally affected. Brigitte Hamm shows that both discourse and institutional development in the area of private sector responsibility for human rights has been largely unaffected by the events of 9/11. Her analysis indicates that different human rights discourses, while clearly related, remain distinct from one another, suggesting that general conclusions about human rights or the human rights regime after 9/11 must be made and interpreted with caution.

In the Conclusion, we return to a broad focus on the regime, drawing on the individual chapters in revising some of the important analytic and substantive questions raised at the outset. While we express cautious optimism about how the regime has fared since 9/11, we also stress points of concern and indicate areas where further research is required.

Part I
Perspectives

1

International Human Rights Since 9/11: More Continuity Than Change

Jack Donnelly

It is often argued that "everything changed" on 9/11. As Vice President Cheney put it on *Meet the Press*, "the theme that comes through repeatedly for me is that 9/11 changed everything" (2003). By early 2003, this was already being described as a cliché (McGeary 2003).

In the case of human rights, no one has suggested that *everything* changed. It is, however, widely believed that respect for human rights has deteriorated dramatically. Such arguments come in many forms, most, from human rights advocates, condemning the change, a few justifying it as a regrettable necessity. See, for example, Brown 2003, Fain 2003, Lawyers Committee for Human Rights 2003, Schulz 2003, Darmer et al. 2004, Hoffman 2004, Webb 2007, Bullard 2008, and Farer 2008. On torture in particular, see Levinson 2004, Roth and Worden 2005, Forsythe 2006, Nowak 2006, and Rejali 2007. For example, William Schulz, the Executive Director of Amnesty International USA, titled his book *Tainted Legacy: 9/11 and the Ruin of Human Rights* (Schulz 2003). This, I will argue, is largely inaccurate. The "war on terror" certainly has harmed human rights, both directly and indirectly, in intended and unintended ways. The global state of human rights, however, has not changed fundamentally.

The global human rights regime

It is hard to find even minor systematic negative effects of the "war on terror" on multilateral human rights institutions and activities. The norms of the global human rights regime have continued to be elaborated and extended. For example, the International Convention for the Protection of All Persons from Enforced Disappearance[1] and the Convention on the Rights of Persons with Disabilities[2] were opened for signature and ratification on December 20, 2006 and March 30, 2007, respectively. And on September 3, 2007, after more than 20 years of discussion, the Declaration on the Rights of Indigenous Peoples was adopted by the General Assembly.

Even more importantly, efforts to create antiterrorism norms that undermine established principles of international human rights law have failed dismally. For example, the Human Rights Council, reflecting the often-stated views of most states, at its second session strongly reaffirmed the applicability of all provisions of international human rights and humanitarian law to those deprived of their liberty in the context of antiterrorism measures.[3] Repulsing this aggressive normative challenge by the world's strongest state has, I would argue, not only reaffirmed but strengthened international human rights norms.

Multilateral institutions likewise show no evidence of decline. The biggest change in the multilateral machinery since 9/11 has been the replacement of the United Nations Commission on Human Rights with a new Human Rights Council. The worst that one can say about the Council's record to date is *plus ça change*; certainly there has been no serious deterioration. The new system of universal periodic review[4] has modestly increased the level of multilateral international scrutiny.

The budget of the Office of the High Commissioner for Human Rights continues to grow, substantially (Office of the High Commissioner for Human Rights 2010, 136–8). In 2008, thematic and country rapporteurs and experts undertook 53 fact-finding visits to 48 different countries, made 135 reports to the Human Rights Council and 19 reports to the General Assembly, and sent over 900 communications to 118 countries, dealing with over 2,000 individuals (Office of the High Commissioner for Human Rights 2009, 32). The expert bodies that monitor state implementation of international human rights treaties have evidenced no negative effects. For example, the Human Rights Committee in the period 1997–2001 registered an annual average of 62 new cases and concluded 49 cases. For 2002–8, the comparable averages were 113 and 80.[5]

Regionally, the European Court of Human Rights remains the "gold standard" of multilateral human rights bodies and the European regional regime against torture remains unrivaled in authority, scope, and impact. In the Americas, the rhetoric of antiterrorism has not been used in official regional bodies to justify infringements of human rights. Quite the contrary, since its 2002 report "Terrorism and Human Rights,"[6] the Inter-American Commission on Human Rights has emphasized the importance of protecting human rights in the course of antiterrorist activities. The democracy norm remains sufficiently strong to deter the United States from supporting coups against governments it does not like. The African regional regime, although by far the weakest of the three, may actually have increased its activity, professionalism, and impact in the past several years. (There are no formal regional regimes for Asia or any Asian subregions, although ASEAN is in the early stages of developing a human rights mechanism.)

Global trends in national human rights practice

Turning to national practice, the available data indicate fundamental continuity in the level of respect for civil and political rights, the rights most often presented as victims of the "war on terror."

Freedom House's annual *Freedom in the World* report assesses overall national performance on civil and political rights on a seven-point scale. Countries are rated "Free" (1.0–2.5), "Partly Free" (3.0–4.5), or "Not Free" (5.0–7.0). Table 1.1 shows the number and percentage of countries in each category.

No global deterioration of any sort is evident.

The Cingranelli-Richards (CIRI) Human Rights Data Project[7] allows for more detailed and variegated assessments. Two summary measures, the Physical Integrity Rights Index (computed on a scale of 0 [lowest] to 8) and the Empowerment Rights Index (scaled 0 to 10), are constructed from separate scores on, respectively, torture, political imprisonment, disappearances, and extrajudicial executions and political participation, workers' rights, and freedoms of movement, speech, and religion.

Table 1.2 presents the data from 1989 through 2007, the latest available when this chapter was completed.

Table 1.1 Freedom House rankings (in %)

	Free		Partly free		Not free	
1974 (n = 152)	41	27	48	32	63	41
1984 (n = 162)	53	32	59	35	55	33
1994 (n = 191)	76	40	61	32	54	28
2001 (n = 192)	85	44	59	31	48	25
2002	89	46	55	29	48	25
2003	88	46	55	29	49	25
2004	89	46	54	28	49	26
2005	89	46	58	30	45	24
2006 (n = 193)	90	47	58	30	45	23
2007	90	47	60	31	43	22
2008	89	46	62	32	42	22

Source: www.freedomhouse.org/uploads/fiw09/CompHistData/CountryStatus&Ratings Overview 1973–2009.pdf

Table 1.2 Global performance, 1989–2007

	1989	1990	1991	1992	1993	1994	1995	1996	1997	1998	1999	2000	2001	2002	2003	2004	2005	2006	2007	2002–07	02–07/99–01
Physical integrity rights index (8 max.)	4.68	4.37	4.64	4.88	4.79	4.87	4.81	4.85	4.81	4.80	4.75	4.53	4.85	5.06	4.72	4.79	4.75	4.66	4.66	4.77	1.01
Torture (2 max.)	0.77	0.71	0.81	0.86	0.77	0.72	0.70	0.79	0.71	0.72	0.66	0.62	0.62	0.66	0.54	0.62	0.61	0.61	0.59	0.61	0.96
Political imprisonment (2 max.)	0.93	0.89	0.99	1.09	1.17	1.10	1.07	1.20	1.14	1.11	1.18	1.14	1.23	1.30	1.28	1.22	1.16	1.12	1.12	1.20	1.01
Disappearances (2 max.)	1.60	1.55	1.57	1.66	1.62	1.70	1.67	1.61	1.62	1.67	1.63	1.62	1.68	1.73	1.69	1.72	1.75	1.71	1.75	1.73	1.05
Arbitrary execution (2 max.)	1.38	1.21	1.27	1.26	1.22	1.32	1.37	1.25	1.34	1.31	1.29	1.16	1.31	1.37	1.21	1.21	1.22	1.20	1.20	1.24	0.99
Empowerment rights index (10 max.)	5.77	5.62	6.02	6.00	6.21	6.14	6.23	6.37	6.34	6.39	6.29	6.16	6.18	6.24	5.24	5.86	5.59	6.13	*	5.81	0.94
Movement (1 max.)	0.73	0.73	0.67	0.68	0.71	0.73	0.70	0.75	0.73	0.72	0.70	0.69	0.70	0.71	0.57	0.65	0.68	0.78	*	0.68	0.97
Speech (2 max.)	0.94	0.90	1.20	1.15	1.07	1.08	1.07	1.09	1.15	1.19	1.10	1.10	1.15	1.13	1.01	0.95	0.87	0.96	0.89	0.97	0.87
Elections (2 max.)	0.86	1.01	1.15	1.09	1.14	1.13	1.13	1.23	1.23	1.21	1.26	1.18	1.32	1.34	1.18	1.28	1.25	1.33	1.25	1.27	1.01
Religion (1 max.)	0.73	0.63	0.67	0.70	0.70	0.72	0.70	0.69	0.68	0.68	0.61	0.62	0.61	0.62	0.54	0.65	0.58	0.64	*	0.61	0.99
Workers' rights (2 max.)	1.06	0.90	1.07	0.99	1.03	0.95	0.95	1.03	1.13	1.23	1.17	1.21	1.10	0.80	0.75	0.78	0.74	0.73	0.79	0.77	0.66
Modified empowerment index (6 max.)	2.69	2.90	3.42	3.37	3.43	3.36	3.47	3.54	3.53	3.55	3.59	3.43	3.62	3.64	3.34	3.48	3.25	3.49	3.35	3.43	0.97
Speech (2 max.)	0.94	0.90	1.20	1.15	1.07	1.08	1.07	1.09	1.15	1.19	1.10	1.10	1.15	1.13	1.01	0.95	0.87	0.96	0.89	0.97	0.87
Elections (2 max.)	0.86	1.01	1.15	1.09	1.14	1.13	1.13	1.23	1.23	1.21	1.26	1.18	1.32	1.34	1.18	1.28	1.25	1.33	1.25	1.27	1.01
Association (2 max.)	0.89	0.99	1.07	1.13	1.22	1.15	1.27	1.22	1.15	1.15	1.23	1.15	1.15	1.17	1.15	1.25	1.13	1.20	1.21	1.19	1.01

The average Physical Integrity Rights Index for 2002–7 is 101 percent of that of 1999–2001. The Empowerment Rights Index, however, shows a clear decline. The 2002–6 average – CIRI changed its Empowerment Index for 2007, making it not directly comparable to earlier years – is only 94 percent of 1999–2001.

The CIRI data on workers' rights, though, is problematic. The 27 percent drop in 2002 is a year-to-year change completely unparalleled anywhere else in this massive data set – and unconnected to any events in the world. Therefore, I have constructed a Modified Empowerment Index, made up of freedoms of speech, association, and electoral participation. (This also allows us to extend the post-9/11 comparisons to 2007.) As Table 1.2 shows, this index experiences a similar, although somewhat smaller (3 percent), post-9/11 decline.

Freedom of speech has suffered a particularly substantial decline, due in part to "the war on terror." Protection against torture deteriorated modestly, as did freedom of movement. But the average level of performance on political imprisonment, arbitrary execution, electoral participation, freedom of religion, and freedom of association has remained essentially unchanged (the 2002–7 average being within 1 percent of the 1999–2001 average). Protection against disappearances has improved modestly.

Comparison with the immediately preceding years, however, might obscure important trends. For example, a slight decline following a decade of steady improvement has a different significance than the same decline from a static baseline or a declining trend.

Table 1.3 shows that the substantial progress of the early post-Cold War years leveled off in the five years prior to 2001, with integrity rights showing no improvement at all. The (modest) post-9/11 downturn thus did not reverse a positive trend.

Table 1.4 tells a similar story. Each cell records the global average as a percentage of the average of the three preceding years. (This evens out year-to-year fluctuations while still allowing for a relatively close and detailed observation of trends.) This data clearly shows large improvements in the period 1990–4, a peak in 1996–8, and stability in 1999 and 2000. It also suggests that the post-9/11 decline set in only in 2003, and has varied considerably from right to right.[8]

Although the "war on terror" had some negative impact, other factors were also probably involved. The leveling off in the late 1990s suggests that most of the relatively "easy" progress had already been made and that even without 9/11 we could have anticipated a certain degree of backsliding as some success stories of the 1990s faced increasing strain. Whatever the cause, though, the above data suggest that while the years

Table 1.3   Post-Cold War trends (I)

a. The pre-9/11 baseline

	1989	1991–5	Ratio	1989	1996–2000	Ratio	1991–5	1996–2000	Ratio
Physical integrity	4.68	4.80	1.03	4.68	4.75	1.01	4.80	4.75	0.99
Modified empowerment	2.69	3.41	1.27	2.69	3.53	1.31	3.41	3.53	1.04
Torture	0.77	0.77	1.00	0.77	0.70	0.91	0.77	0.70	0.91
Political imprisonment	0.93	1.08	1.16	0.93	1.15	1.24	1.08	1.15	1.06
Elections	0.86	1.13	1.31	0.86	1.22	1.42	1.13	1.22	1.08
Speech	0.94	1.11	1.18	0.94	1.13	1.20	1.11	1.13	1.01
Association	0.89	1.17	1.31	0.89	1.18	1.33	1.17	1.18	1.01

b. Before and after 9/11

	1991–2000	2002–7	Ratio	1995–2000	2002–7	Ratio
Physical integrity	4.81	4.72	0.98	4.76	4.77	1.00
Modified empowerment	3.46	3.43	0.99	3.52	3.43	0.97
Torture	0.76	0.59	0.78	0.70	0.61	0.87
Political imprisonment	1.11	1.18	1.06	1.14	1.20	1.05
Elections	1.16	1.27	1.09	1.21	1.27	1.05
Speech	1.13	0.89	0.79	1.12	0.97	0.87
Association	1.17	1.19	1.02	1.20	1.19	1.00

after 2001 have not been good for human rights, the decline from post-Cold War highs has been modest, uneven, and incomplete.

Regional patterns

Global averages may mask important regional variations. Table 1.5 reports the CIRI data by region.[9]

As a rough and ready measure, we might define "significant" regional change as more than 2 percent from the 1999–2001 baseline. Of the 16 comparisons in Table 1.5, four show improvement, six show deterioration, and six show no significant change. Variation across regions appears largely unconnected with the "war on terror."

The Western democracies

In the United States, the Patriot Act, warrantless searches, and similar abuses are reflected in a dramatic decline in the Physical Integrity Rights

Index. The declines in Canada and New Zealand, however, have been modest and have left those countries at relatively high levels of performance. (Australia remains constant across the whole period.) Neither index has changed significantly for Northern and Western Europe. Every violation of every right is a matter of legitimate concern. Even modest and limited infringements merit strong opposition by human rights advocates and concerned citizens. Nonetheless, the retrenchments since 9/11 do not add up to even a modest *systematic* pattern of deterioration. The Western liberal democracies remain deeply committed to internationally recognized civil and political rights and retain generally effective practices to implement them.

South and Central Asia

The geographic heart of the global "war on terror" has been in South and Central Asia. Physical integrity rights, however, have not suffered: the 2002–7 average is 2 percent above that for 1999–2001. The improvement in empowerment rights is a quite substantial 11percent.

Even the regional level of aggregation, though, may mask important variations. Table 1.6 therefore looks at four countries deeply affected by struggles against national or international terrorism, namely, Afghanistan, Pakistan, Uzbekistan, and Sri Lanka, plus two "control" cases, Bangladesh and Tajikistan, and India, the leading regional power.

Pakistan's decline in respect for physical integrity rights, as well as the more modest deterioration in empowerment rights, can reasonably be attributed to the "war on terror." Afghanistan, however, shows a clear improvement.

In Uzbekistan, the protection of physical integrity rights declined significantly after 2001 and respect for empowerment rights dropped from dismal to abysmal. A link to the "war on terror," however, is hard to sustain. The data bottom out in 2004 and 2005, precisely when the United States suspended aid in protest against increasing Uzbek repression and then stuck to its harshly critical policy even as it was evicted, in retaliation, from Kharshi-Khanabad Air Base, a major staging station for operations in Afghanistan.

In Sri Lanka, protection of physical integrity rights improved substantially following the government's 2002 ceasefire with the Tamil Tigers. Conversely, the deterioration in 2006 and 2007 reflects the unraveling of that ceasefire. The global "war on terror," however – in contrast to Sri Lanka's often terroristic response to separatist terrorism – had either no effect or a modest positive effect (if we attribute the Tigers accepting the ceasefire in part to the post-9/11 delegitimation of terror as a tactic).

Table 1.4 Trends (II): performance as a ratio of the average for the three preceding years

	1985	1986	1987	1988	1989	1990	1991	1992	1993	1994	1995	1996	1997	1998	1999	2000	2001	2002	2003	2004	2005	2006	2007
Physical integrity rights index (8 max.)	4.97	5.20	4.76	4.90	4.68	4.37	4.64	4.88	4.79	4.87	4.81	4.85	4.81	4.80	4.75	4.53	4.85	5.06	4.72	4.79	4.75	4.66	4.66
Torture (2 max.)	0.91	1.02	0.89	0.89	0.77	0.71	0.81	0.86	0.77	0.72	0.70	0.79	0.71	0.72	0.66	0.62	0.62	0.66	0.54	0.62	0.61	0.61	0.59
Political imprisonment (2 max.)	0.96	0.99	0.80	0.90	0.93	0.89	0.99	1.09	1.17	1.10	1.07	1.20	1.14	1.11	1.18	1.14	1.23	1.30	1.28	1.22	1.16	1.12	1.12
Disappearances (2 max.)					1.60	1.55	1.57	1.66	1.62	1.70	1.67	1.61	1.62	1.67	1.63	1.62	1.68	1.73	1.69	1.72	1.75	1.71	1.75
Arbitrary execution (2 max.)					1.38	1.21	1.27	1.26	1.22	1.32	1.37	1.25	1.34	1.31	1.29	1.16	1.31	1.37	1.21	1.21	1.22	1.20	1.20
Empowerment rights index (10 max.)					5.77	5.62	6.02	6.00	6.21	6.14	6.23	6.37	6.34	6.39	6.29	6.16	6.18	6.24	5.24	5.86	5.59	6.13	*
Movement (1 max.)					0.73	0.73	0.67	0.68	0.71	0.73	0.70	0.75	0.73	0.72	0.70	0.69	0.70	0.71	0.57	0.65	0.68	0.78	*
Speech (2 max.)					0.94	0.90	1.20	1.15	1.07	1.08	1.07	1.09	1.15	1.19	1.10	1.10	1.15	1.13	1.01	0.95	0.87	0.96	0.89
Elections (2 max.)					0.86	1.01	1.15	1.09	1.14	1.13	1.13	1.23	1.23	1.21	1.26	1.18	1.32	1.34	1.18	1.28	1.33	1.33	1.25
Religion (1 max.)					0.73	0.63	0.67	0.70	0.70	0.72	0.70	0.69	0.68	0.68	0.61	0.62	0.61	0.62	0.54	0.65	0.58	0.64	*
Workers' rights (2 max.)					1.06	0.90	1.07	0.99	1.03	0.95	0.95	1.03	1.13	1.23	1.17	1.21	1.10	1.07	0.67	0.79	0.68	0.76	0.79
Modified empowerment index (6 max.)	2.70	2.80	2.65	2.68	2.69	2.90	3.42	3.37	3.43	3.36	3.47	3.54	3.53	3.55	3.59	3.43	3.62	3.64	3.34	3.48	3.25	3.49	3.35
Speech (2 max.)	0.93	0.96	0.88	1.01	0.94	0.90	1.20	1.15	1.07	1.08	1.07	1.09	1.15	1.19	1.10	1.10	1.15	1.13	1.01	0.95	0.87	0.96	0.89
Elections (2 max.)	0.92	0.96	0.93	0.84	0.86	1.01	1.15	1.09	1.14	1.13	1.13	1.23	1.23	1.21	1.26	1.18	1.32	1.34	1.18	1.28	1.25	1.33	1.25
Association (2 max.)	0.84	0.88	0.84	0.83	0.89	0.99	1.07	1.13	1.22	1.15	1.27	1.22	1.15	1.15	1.23	1.15	1.15	1.17	1.15	1.25	1.13	1.20	1.21
Integrity				0.98	0.94	0.91	1.00	1.07	1.03	1.02	0.99	1.01	0.96	1.00	0.99	0.95	1.03	1.07	0.98	0.98	1.01	1.03	0.98
Torture				0.95	0.83	0.84	1.03	1.03	1.13	0.89	0.99	1.08	0.96	0.98	0.89	0.89	0.93	1.04	0.85	1.02	1.01	1.03	0.96
Imprisonment				0.98	1.04	1.02	1.09	1.16	1.18	1.02	0.96	1.08	1.01	1.01	1.03	1.00	1.08	1.10	1.05	0.96	0.96	0.92	0.96
Modified empowerment			0.99	0.99	1.08	1.24	1.12	1.06	0.99	1.02	1.04	1.02	1.01	0.96	0.96	1.03	1.03	0.94	0.98	0.93	0.92	1.04	0.98
Speech		1.09	0.99	0.95	1.26	1.13	0.99	0.95	0.97	1.02	1.06	1.06	0.96	0.96	1.01	1.01	0.90	0.87	0.90	1.00	0.99	1.08	0.97
Elections			0.90	0.95	1.15	1.27	1.08	1.05	1.00	1.01	1.09	1.06	1.01	1.08	1.08	1.07	1.01	0.92	0.90	0.99	0.99	1.08	1.01
Association					0.97	1.05	1.16	1.18	1.15	1.15	1.01	1.09	1.01	0.95	0.95	0.98	0.98	0.99	1.02	0.95	1.01		

Improvement

	1985	1986	1987	1988	1989	1990	1991	1992	1993	1994	1995	1996	1997	1998	1999	2000	2001	2002	2003	2004	2005	2006	2007
Integrity				0.98	0.94	0.91	1.00	1.07	1.03	1.02	0.99	1.01	0.99	1.00	0.99	0.95	1.03	1.07	0.98	0.98	0.98	0.98	0.98
Modified empowerment				0.99	0.99	1.08	1.24	1.12	1.06	0.99	1.02	1.04	1.02	1.01	1.01	0.96	1.03	1.03	0.94	0.98	0.93	1.04	0.98
Torture				0.95	0.83	0.84	1.03	1.13	0.97	0.89	0.89	1.08	0.96	0.98	0.89	0.89	0.93	1.04	0.85	1.02	1.01	1.03	0.96
Imprisonment				0.98	1.04	1.02	1.09	1.16	1.18	1.02	0.96	1.08	1.01	0.98	1.03	1.00	1.08	1.10	1.05	0.96	0.92	0.92	0.96
Speech				1.09	0.99	0.95	1.26	1.13	0.99	0.95	0.97	1.02	1.06	1.08	0.96	0.96	1.02	1.01	0.90	0.87	0.84	1.02	0.96
Elections				0.90	0.95	1.15	1.27	1.08	1.05	1.00	1.01	1.09	1.06	1.01	1.03	0.96	1.08	1.07	0.92	1.00	0.99	1.08	0.97
Association				0.97	1.05	1.16	1.18	1.15	1.15	1.01	1.09	1.01	0.95	0.95	1.05	0.98	0.98	0.99	0.99	1.08	0.95	1.02	1.01

Deterioration

	1985	1986	1987	1988	1989	1990	1991	1992	1993	1994	1995	1996	1997	1998	1999	2000	2001	2002	2003	2004	2005	2006	2007
Integrity				0.98	0.94	0.91	1.00	1.07	1.03	1.02	0.99	1.01	0.99	1.00	0.99	0.95	1.03	1.07	0.98	0.98	0.98	0.98	0.98
Modified empowerment				0.99	0.99	1.08	1.24	1.12	1.06	0.99	1.02	1.04	1.02	1.01	1.01	0.96	1.03	1.03	0.94	0.98	0.93	1.04	0.98
Torture				0.95	0.83	0.84	1.03	1.13	0.97	0.89	0.89	1.08	0.96	0.98	0.89	0.89	0.93	1.04	0.85	1.02	1.01	1.03	0.96
Imprisonment				0.98	1.04	1.02	1.09	1.16	1.18	1.02	0.96	1.08	1.01	0.98	1.03	1.00	1.08	1.10	1.05	0.96	0.92	0.92	0.96
Speech				1.09	0.99	0.95	1.26	1.13	0.99	0.95	0.97	1.02	1.06	1.08	0.96	0.96	1.02	1.01	0.90	0.87	0.84	1.02	0.96
Elections				0.90	0.95	1.15	1.27	1.08	1.05	1.00	1.01	1.09	1.06	1.01	1.03	0.96	1.08	1.07	0.92	1.00	0.99	1.08	0.97
Association				0.97	1.05	1.16	1.18	1.15	1.15	1.01	1.09	1.01	0.95	0.95	1.05	0.98	0.98	0.99	0.99	1.08	0.95	1.02	1.01

No Significant Change

	1985	1986	1987	1988	1989	1990	1991	1992	1993	1994	1995	1996	1997	1998	1999	2000	2001	2002	2003	2004	2005	2006	2007
Integrity				0.98	0.94	0.91	1.00	1.07	1.03	1.02	0.99	1.01	0.99	1.00	0.99	0.95	1.03	1.07	0.98	0.98	0.98	0.98	0.98
Modified empowerment				0.99	0.99	1.08	1.24	1.12	1.06	0.99	1.02	1.04	1.02	1.01	1.01	0.96	1.03	1.03	0.94	0.98	0.93	1.04	0.98
Torture				0.95	0.83	0.84	1.03	1.13	0.97	0.89	0.89	1.08	0.96	0.98	0.89	0.89	0.93	1.04	0.85	1.02	1.01	1.03	0.96
Imprisonment				0.98	1.04	1.02	1.09	1.16	1.18	1.02	0.96	1.08	1.01	0.98	1.03	1.00	1.08	1.10	1.05	0.96	0.92	0.92	0.96
Speech				1.09	0.99	0.95	1.26	1.13	0.99	0.95	0.97	1.02	1.06	1.08	0.96	0.96	1.02	1.01	0.90	0.87	0.84	1.02	0.96
Elections				0.90	0.95	1.15	1.27	1.08	1.05	1.00	1.01	1.09	1.06	1.01	1.03	0.96	1.08	1.07	0.92	1.00	0.99	1.08	0.97
Association				0.97	1.05	1.16	1.18	1.15	1.15	1.01	1.09	1.01	0.95	0.95	1.05	0.98	0.98	0.99	0.99	1.08	0.95	1.02	1.01

Table 1.5 Regional human rights performance, 1999–2007

	1999	2000	2001	2002	2003	2004	2005	2006	2007	2002–7	02–07/01	02–07/99–01	Change
Africa													
Physical integrity (8 max.)	3.93	3.95	4.00	4.22	4.04	4.37	4.07	3.83	4.08	4.10	1.03	1.04	3.96 +
Modified empowerment (6 max.)	2.89	2.70	2.85	2.89	2.63	2.63	2.54	2.87	2.59	2.69	0.91	0.96	2.81 –
East and Southeast Asia													
Physical integrity	4.25	3.75	4.13	4.50	3.93	3.81	3.88	3.75	3.75	3.94	0.95	0.97	4.04 –
Modified empowerment	2.75	2.44	2.88	2.88	2.56	2.19	2.06	2.56	2.25	2.42	0.84	0.90	2.69 –
South and Central Asia													
Physical integrity	2.77	2.15	3.08	2.92	2.75	2.73	2.85	2.67	2.46	2.73	0.89	1.02	2.67 =
Modified empowerment	1.77	1.38	1.61	2.00	1.42	1.83	1.61	2.15	1.54	1.76	1.09	1.11	1.59 +
Western Asia													
Physical integrity	4.27	3.93	4.44	4.81	4.87	4.40	4.19	4.38	3.94	4.43	1.00	1.05	4.21 +
Modified empowerment	2.20	1.53	2.25	2.06	1.53	2.00	1.94	2.19	2.06	1.96	0.87	0.98	1.99 =
Eastern and Southern Europe													
Physical integrity	5.95	5.32	6.26	6.45	5.55	5.60	6.32	6.04	6.13	6.02	0.96	1.03	5.84 +
Modified empowerment	4.37	4.32	4.78	4.65	4.35	4.40	4.14	4.04	4.33	4.32	0.90	0.96	4.49 –
Northern and Western Europe													
Physical integrity	7.35	7.29	7.41	7.59	7.18	7.29	7.29	7.41	7.12	7.35	0.99	1.00	7.35 =
Modified empowerment	5.59	5.65	5.59	5.59	5.53	5.65	5.35	5.29	5.24	5.48	0.98	0.98	5.61 =
Latin America and Caribbean													
Physical integrity	4.63	4.58	5.04	5.13	4.59	4.50	4.75	4.67	4.83	4.73	0.94	1.00	4.75 =
Modified empowerment	4.79	5.00	5.04	4.96	4.59	4.63	4.50	4.79	4.79	4.69	0.93	0.95	4.94 –
Canada, Australia, New Zealand													
Physical integrity	7.67	7.33	7.67	7.00	7.00	7.00	6.67	7.00	7.00	6.93	0.90	0.92	7.56 –
Modified empowerment	6.00	6.00	6.00	6.00	6.00	6.00	5.67	6.00	6.00	5.93	0.99	0.99	6.00 =
USA													
Physical integrity	7.00	7.00	5.00	6.00	6.00	4.00	4.00	4.00	5.00	4.80	0.96	0.76	6.33
Modified empowerment	6.00	6.00	6.00	6.00	6.00	6.00	6.00	6.00	6.00	6.00	1.00	1.00	6.00

Table 1.6 Selected South and Central Asian countries

	1992	1993	1994	1995	1996	1997	1998	1999	2000	2001	2002	2003	2004	2005	2006	2007	1999–2001	2002–2007	02–07/99–01	Change
Afghanistan																				
Physical integrity					0	0	0	0	0	0	3	–	–	4	4	4				+
Modified empowerment					2	0	1	1	0	0	2	–	–	2	2	2				+
Pakistan																				
Physical integrity	3	2	3	1	2	2	3	2	1	1	2	1	1	1	0	0	1.33	0.83	0.63	–
Modified empowerment	4	4	3	1	2	2	3	3	3	3	2	1	3	2	3	2	3.00	2.17	0.72	–
Sri Lanka																				
Physical integrity	0	2	2	0	0	1	1	2	0	2	3	4	5	4	2	0	1.33	3.00	2.25	+
Modified empowerment	6	6	6	6	6	6	6	4	4	3	4	3	2	3	4	2	3.67	3.00	0.82	–
Uzbekistan																				
Physical integrity	5	4	5	3	5	2	4	3	2	3	3	2	1	1	3	4	2.67	2.33	0.88	–
Modified empowerment	4	3	5	3	2	4	2	0	0	1	0	0	0	0	0	0	0.33	0.00	0.00	=
Bangladesh																				
Physical integrity	1	5	3	3	3	4	3	4	2	4	1	0	1	0	1	0	3.33	0.50	0.15	–
Modified empowerment	5	6	7	7	7	7	6	3	1	2	3	2	3	4	4	2	2.00	3.00	1.50	+
India																				
Physical integrity	0	0	0	0	0	0	0	1	0	0	0	1	0	0	0	0	0.33	0.17	0.50	=
Modified empowerment	6	8	9	9	10	10	7	3	3	4	4	5	4	4	4	4	3.33	4.17	1.25	+
Tajikistan																				
Physical integrity	2	0	0	0	0	1	2	1	2	4	3	5	4	5	3	4	2.33	4.00	1.71	+
Modified empowerment	6	4	5	4	4	3	0	1	1	0	1	1	1	1	3	2	0.67	1.50	2.25	+

In the other three cases – which I chose for loose similarity, before looking at the data – respect for physical integrity rights improved in one country, deteriorated in another, and remained roughly constant in the third. Bangladesh's dismal performance – it starts out well above Pakistan (3.33 versus 1.33) but drops below even Pakistan's deteriorated level (0.5 versus 0.83) – is completely unconnected to the "war on terror."

The regional pattern in South and Central Asia seems largely driven by factors internal to individual countries, with the external impact cutting in both directions. A major negative impact of the "war on terror" simply cannot be found. Even in Pakistan, which probably represents the best case for the position I am arguing against, the impact has been modest.

Western Asia

Western Asia experienced a 5 percent average improvement in protection of physical integrity rights while respect for empowerment rights has remained essentially constant. Table 1.7 reports data on seven individual countries of interest: Iraq, Israel, Lebanon, and Turkey, which have all faced significant terrorist threats; Saudi Arabia and Kuwait, which have received substantial American support; and Egypt, added to the list from North Africa.

Israel suffered a notable drop in respect for personal integrity rights. Comparable decline is evident in Egypt. In both cases, American support in general and the "war on terror" in particular almost certainly have facilitated intensified violations.

Saudi Arabia and Kuwait, however, do not show much change – although both are below the regional average and an argument of American toleration in return for political support is certainly plausible. In Turkey, respect for personal integrity rights improves – as in Sri Lanka, probably in part because of the delegitimation of terror as a tactic after 9/11. The decline in respect for empowerment rights, however, was driven by longstanding internal Turkish struggles over the role of religion in politics.

Iraq and Lebanon are in different ways special cases that defy analysis before and after 2001. Civil and political rights in Lebanon, however, seem not to have suffered from the "war on terror." (The consequences of the 2006 "July War" with Israel would not be expected to show up in this human rights data.) As for Iraq, perhaps the fairest assessment is that it is hard to argue that the human rights situation has been systematically worse than during Saddam Hussein's rule.

Table 1.7 Selected Middle Eastern countries

	1999	2000	2001	2002	2003	2004	2005	2006	2007	2002–2007	02–07/99–01	Change
Egypt												
Physical integrity (8 max.)	3	4	3	2	2	2	3	3	3	2.50	0.75	3.333333 –
Modified empowerment (6 max.)	2	1	2	1	2	0	2	2	3	1.67	1.00	1.666667 –
Iraq												
Physical integrity	0	0	0	0	–	–	1	1	0	–	–	0 +?
Modified empowerment	0	0	0	0	–	–	3	3	3	–	–	0 +
Israel												
Physical integrity	3	3	2	2	2	2	2	2	2	2.00	0.75	2.666667 –
Modified empowerment	4	4	5	5	5	5	3	3	4	4.17	0.96	4.333333 –
Kuwait												
Physical integrity	5	5	6	6	6	6	5	7	6	6.00	1.13	5.333333 +
Modified empowerment	1	1	1	1	1	1	1	2	3	1.50	1.50	1 +
Lebanon												
Physical integrity	–	–	4	5	4	4	4	6	4	4.50	–	4
Modified empowerment	–	–	3	3	1	1	3	3	3	2.33	–	3
Saudi Arabia												
Physical integrity	5	5	5	5	5	4	5	4	3	4.33	0.87	5 –
Modified empowerment	1	1	1	1	0	0	0	0	0	0.17	0.17	1 –
Turkey												
Physical integrity	1	2	2	2	3	3	2	3	3	2.67	1.60	1.666667 +
Modified empowerment	4	2	4	4	2	2	2	3	2	2.50	0.75	3.333333 –

Taken as a whole, these cases may suggest some negative impact of American support. But even here, deteriorations take the form of modest increases in existing levels and types of violation. They are restricted to individual countries rather than the region as a whole – where respect for civil and political rights has improved modestly since 2001.

Conclusion

Similar accounts could be developed for the other regions. Deteriorations are driven largely by country-specific internal forces. The "war on terror" has in several particular cases provided additional support for intensified forms of well-established violations. No systematic negative impact, however, can be found in the regional data.

Additional dimensions

A more comprehensive account would look at the impact of the "war on terror" on bilateral foreign policy, the activities of human rights NGOs, responses to genocide and humanitarian crises, and the development of international humanitarian law. Although space does not allow even a superficial consideration of these topics, I would suggest that similar patterns can probably be discerned here as well.

US foreign policy does suffer a major systematic deterioration that can unquestionably be attributed to the "war on terror." Bush Administration policies both directly violated human rights (and humanitarian law) and, on the basis of a shared fight against terrorism, provided support for rights-abusive regimes. But even setting aside the Obama Administration's return to policies much closer to those of the Clinton Administration – not to mention the fact that European international human rights policies were not substantially altered in the pursuit of antiterrorism objectives – we must not exaggerate the baleful human rights effects on or of American foreign policy.

With the notable exception of Iraq, the United States typically has not directly produced, or even actively encouraged, human rights violations. Rather, it has failed to resist violations as steadfastly as human rights advocates have demanded. Even in Pakistan, the United States has exerted considerable influence to restrain the nature and scope of violations. We must remember that the pre-9/11 American record in Pakistan was hardly very encouraging (Newberg 2004).

Furthermore, bad behavior in high-profile cases has not been uniform – consider Uzbekistan, noted above – nor has it spilled over into day-to-day diplomacy. Throughout the Bush Administration, human rights remained on the American agenda in its bilateral relations with most countries. Elections were stressed pretty much across the globe. Initiatives continued to be taken on behalf of dissidents and human rights defenders. Civil society support remained substantial. On a few particular issues, especially religious liberty, slavery, and human trafficking, American policy actually became substantially more aggressive under Bush. And, perhaps most importantly, human rights has remained an essentially nonpartisan element of American foreign policy.

Turning to NGOs, national human rights organizations in some countries certainly have suffered. In general, though, freedom of association has not been victimized in the name of antiterrorism. And although some American human rights NGOs moderated some of their rhetoric against some "front line" countries, the activity of international human rights NGOs has generally remained as robust as prior to 9/11 (although there is nothing like quantitative data that could be used to support this impressionistic assessment).

International action against genocide made considerable progress in the 1990s. The limited response in Darfur thus has certainly been deeply discouraging. The "war on terror," however, has had only an indirect impact, largely by tying down resources in "the war in Iraq" (which in its genesis had nothing to with antiterrorism). Neither the lack of European leadership nor Russian and Chinese resistance to military action has had anything to do with antiterrorism.

As for international humanitarian law, the Bush Administration failed to convince *any* other leading state that its Guantanamo policy was anything other than a clear and egregious violation of international law. The Obama Administration has brought the United States largely back into the fold. Much the same is true of Bush policy on "extraordinary renditions."

Conclusion

Given this data, how can we explain the commonly held view that the "war on terror" has had significant systematic negative human rights consequences?

First, there are indeed striking cases that rightly cause concern, even anguish. Both the media and foreign policy typically respond to particular issues of pressing concern, rather than reflect on broader patterns. Second, the United States was from Carter through Clinton the world's most vocal supporter of international human rights – at least in so far as they applied to other countries. The irrational exuberance of the Bush

Administration's "war on terror" has called into question this longstanding and important American commitment and contribution. In addition, abuses such as Abu Ghraib, Guantanamo, and clandestine renditions have eroded American moral leadership what remained. (Obama's considerable personal popularity seems not to have been translated, at least yet, into renewed American leadership.)

Third, many Americans have been justifiably concerned by the assaults of their government on their own civil liberties, as symbolized in the Patriot Act. We must not overgeneralize from this relatively unusual case, and we must not lose sight of the fact that national deteriorations in human rights practices have largely been matched by improvements in other countries.

Bad things did happen to human rights, and are continuing to happen, as a result of the American-led "war on terror." The result, however, has not been a general human rights disaster. There has been no global, or even regional, rollback of the progress of the 1990s.

As I argued in an article written in 2003 (Donnelly 2004), when the evidence was much less clear, human rights have not suffered an *absolute* decline in the foreign policy of the United States or other Western powers. There has been no decline either in the absolute importance attached to human rights by global or regional institutions. The *relative* place of human rights, however, has declined, especially in American foreign policy. This movement of antiterrorism to or near the top of the list of priorities – in a clumsy and heavy-handed way in the United States, and in a more nuanced and less destructive way in most other Western countries – has undoubtedly had real negative consequences.

There is good reason to believe, though, that many of these reverses will be short-lived. For example, in the United States the relatively hysterical pursuit of the "war on terror" appears largely to have passed. The American Congress, the American military, and the American public all support an absolute ban on torture. Even the extremely conservative Supreme Court forced the Bush Administration to back off from some of its more outrageous claims and practices. The Obama Administration's decision to close Guantanamo has received fairly widespread bipartisan support, and the debacle in Iraq seems to have convinced most Americans that fighting "them," "over there," needs to be done in a thoughtful, measured way as a part of a broader American foreign policy that pursues a wide range of objectives. This was the position of all three major American presidential candidates in 2008 and has been the practice of the Obama Administration.

The rollback from the 1990s has been limited, as has been the preemptive power of antiterrorism, especially compared to anticommunism. Therefore, it seems to me likely that the international human rights situation should return in the next few years to something like the late 1990s (although freedom of speech is likely to lag behind). Barring another disaster with the psychological impact of 9/11, I suspect that in 10years we will look back on the post-9/11 years as a relatively brief and modest deviation rather than a fundamental reversal of the human rights progress of the 1990s.

Notes

1. www.ohchr.org/english/law/disappearance-convention.htm, accessed November 8, 2010.
2. www.un.org/disabilities/convention/conventionfull.shtml, accessed November 8, 2010.
3. See http://ap.ohchr.org/documents/sdpage_e.aspx?b=10&se=63&t=3, accessed November 8, 2010.
4. A single website assembles state, NGO, and Commission materials, plus press commentaries. See www.upr-info.org/. The official UN site is www.ohchr.org/EN/HRBODIES/UPR/Pages/UPRMain.aspx, accessed November 8, 2010.
5. Computed from A/64/40, para. 106; A/61/40 para. 97; A/55/40 para. 539.
6. www.cidh.oas.org/Terrorism/Eng/toc.htm, accessed November 8, 2010.
7. CIRI data is publicly available at http://ciri.binghamton.edu/index.asp, accessed November 8, 2010. The dataset, however, was expanded for the years after 2000 by nearly 30 small countries (see http://ciri.binghamton.edu/documentation/new_countries_december_2004.pdf, accessed November 8, 2010) that as a whole have a significantly higher than average level of performance. In order to avoid overstating the post-9/11 level of performance, the data presented below excludes these countries.
8. The improvement in 2006 is interesting. Until we have data from 2008, and probably 2009 as well, we will not be able to say whether performance bottomed out in 2005.
9. For regional codings, see http://ciri.binghamton.edu/myciri/my_ciri_select_countries.asp, accessed November 8, 2010.

2
Why Human Rights Will Prevail in the War on Terror

Morton Winston

The standard view, held by many human rights scholars, is that the attacks of September 11, 2001, the initiation of the War on Terror, and the subsequent US-led invasions of Afghanistan and Iraq, have been very bad for human rights. These events marked the beginning a of moral slide in which internationally recognized human rights norms, for instance, concerning torture, arbitrary imprisonment, and fair trial, came increasingly under attack from democratic states seeking to protect their citizens from future terrorist attacks. On this view, the security and counterterrorism policies adopted by the Bush Administration and some other governments have undermined the integrity of the entire post-Second World War human rights framework.

Against this standard view, I shall argue that the years since 9/11 have witnessed a reassertion and strengthening of the human rights paradigm. The policies of the Bush Administration with regard to torture of detainees, arbitrary indefinite detention, and secret prisons, rather than delegitimizing the human rights framework, have themselves been delegitimized by it. While this may indeed be a bad thing from the point of view of "brand USA," it is a good thing from the point of view of the global human rights movement because it demonstrates the robustness of the current global consensus on human rights. Furthermore, the abdication of moral leadership on human rights by the United States helps counteract the sense of hypocrisy many people feel when listening to pronouncements about their devotion to human rights by officials in the American government. It is going to be difficult for the United States to restore its credibility as a global leader in human rights, but this also may not be a bad thing.

In order to gauge the impact of post-9/11 developments on human rights, it will be useful to begin by placing the contemporary post-9/11 period in historical perspective and describing the human rights regime as an ethico-legal paradigm. This analytical framework will provide a critical perspective from which I will defend the view that the contemporary human rights paradigm has not been significantly undermined by the War on Terror but may in fact have been strengthened.

The human rights paradigm

Harold Hongju Koh, Dean of the Yale Law School, has outlined four phases the development of modern international human rights law has passed through since the end of the Second World War:

> (1) In the early years, an era of "universalization" of human rights norms; (2) in the second phase, an era of "institutionalization," in which human rights institutions were created: governmental, intergovernmental, and nongovernmental; (3) a third era of "operationalizaton," starting roughly with the Helsinki Accords in 1976, whereby a human rights compliance process became operationalized and the institutions and norms began to work together to produce results; and (4) the era in which we now live, the age of "globalization." The first period of this current era – running from the fall of the Berlin wall to the fall of the Twin Towers – was a period of global optimism, where we saw that globalization could be a tool for the transformation of the economy, rights, and global governance. But then five years ago, with the dawn of the War on Terror, we commenced an era of global pessimism that stays with us today. (Koh 2007)

Before commenting on Koh's characterization of the post-9/11 period, I want to comment on this analytical framework. Koh's schema for understanding the human rights regime seems to me to omit a crucial element, namely, the "domestication" of human rights norms and values within the domestic laws and the ethical cultures of diverse societies. Domestication is a measure of how deeply and thoroughly the idea of human rights has taken root in the ethical cultures of particular societies. While it is sometimes difficult to measure, polling results, which I will discuss later, suggest that the process of domestication of human rights norms and values has continued to progress globally despite, and perhaps even because of, the War on Terror.

The domestication of human rights has been led largely by nongovernmental human rights organizations and national human rights institutions, which have been working steadily over many decades to bring the idea of human rights into the consciousness and discourse of global civil society.[1] The increased internalization of human rights norms and values within the ethical culture of global civil society has supplemented the legalistic and state-centric approach to human rights by the United Nations, which relies on national governments which are state parties to human rights covenants and treaties to enforce the compliance of other state parties with their solemn commitments. There has always been a problem with this horizontal approach in that it makes nation states, which are the main violators of human rights, also their main protectors. Any enforcement scheme that makes the poachers also the gamekeepers is fundamentally flawed. The domestication of human rights has added a second kind of vertical enforcement mechanism, that of world public opinion, which has worked effectively in at least some cases to shame offending governments into better compliance with internationally recognized human rights norms.

The global human rights movement has strengthened the human rights paradigm by privatizing certain crucial functions, like the monitoring and documenting of human rights violations and abuses, as is done, for instance, by Amnesty International and Human Rights Watch, and by working though the media to bring egregious patterns of human rights violations to public attention. These efforts to reinforce and internalize international human rights norms and values within global civil society represent a crucial missing element in Professor Koh's scheme for understanding the history of the contemporary human rights paradigm. While the degree to which human rights norms are institutionalized within national legal systems is an important measure of their penetration, such institutionalization cannot happen without there first being a high degree of domestication of human rights norms and values within the ethical culture.

Rather than understanding human rights wholly in terms of their legal embodiments, as members of the legal academy tend to do, I understand the human rights paradigm as an ethical-legal hybrid which has arisen historically as a normative response to experiences of oppression. The human rights system as a whole is a historically evolved, socially constructed normative paradigm whose primary purpose is to ameliorate and prevent widespread, systematic or institutionalized forms of oppression. Human rights norms begin as moral claims advanced by a few people of conscience that are then carried forward by social movements, such as the antislavery movement, the women's movement, the humanitarian movement, the anticolonial movement, the trade union movement, and similar transnational social movements, which gradually win social legitimacy (Winston 2007).

In some cases, these social movements have succeeded in legitimizing some of their moral claims by turning them into law. Enactment and codification of human rights norms as national and international law marks an important milestone on the path to creating a mature human rights system because it recruits the sovereign law-making authority of states, along with their executive and police powers, and their power of judicial review, to the cause of protecting human dignity by preventing oppression. These kinds of legal institutions are supposed to provide safeguards that prevent countries from backsliding when human rights norms and values are under threat. In order for this to happen, that is, for human rights to become operational, it is necessary to develop effective institutions at the local, national, and international levels of governance that discharge the responsibilities required for the effective protection of human rights, and to provide these institutions with adequate funding and resources with which to effectively fulfill their respective roles in protecting human rights.

The processes of domestication, institutionalization, and operationalization of human rights have progressed at very different paces in different national societies. In some countries, for instance, in states such as Norway, Sweden, Denmark, Finland, the Netherlands, and a few others, there is a high degree of domestication and institutionalization of the human rights paradigm. But in many other nations, including the United States of America, the level of domestication and institutionalization of human rights remains relatively weak as compared to that found in Western Europe and several other countries. The very different responses to the security threat posed by international terrorism by the United States, and most of the countries of the European Union (EU), is explained in my view by the greater degree of domestication and institutionalization of the human rights paradigm within European societies. The European human rights system, which is generally recognized as the most developed in the world, by and large functioned effectively to prevent serious backsliding on human rights in the face of the terrorist threat.[2] However, the constitutional system of checks and balances in the United States did not. This failure underscores the need to strengthen the domestication and institutionalization of human rights in the United States.

Despite some serious failures of implementation and operationalization of human rights norms internationally, however, the overall trajectory of human rights has been progressive over the past 60 years, and we have been moving steadily, if slowly, toward greater inclusiveness and greater effectiveness in realizing the promise of "All human rights for all." There have been many victories and successes in those nations where human rights have been institutionalized in domestic law and effectively implemented. The human rights ethos also played an important historical role in bringing down the Berlin Wall, and in ending apartheid in South Africa. Another major achievement took place in July of 2003 with the establishment of the International Criminal Court (ICC) in the Hague, with jurisdiction to try persons accused of war crimes, crimes against humanity, and genocide. So the overall picture over the past 60 years is not really all that bleak and there is still reason to believe that the human rights paradigm is making progress in the world.

As Koh notes, the period from the fall of the Berlin Wall to the fall of the Twin Towers (from 11/9 to 9/11) was a period of relative optimism. The end of the Cold War, the demise of apartheid, and the synergies of global communication and transportation technologies, unleashed economic forces that gave hope to billions of people in the former Eastern European and Soviet states and in the Global South that they might be lifted out of poverty and oppression. But since 9/11 this mood of optimism has been replaced with a sense of fear and insecurity, because of the upsurge in international terrorism, but also in part because of the counterterrorism policies and practices of many nations.

While I will focus my discussion primarily on the impact of state-sponsored counterterrorism policies on human rights, I wish to make it clear that acts of terrorism that deliberately target of civilians in order to induce fear in a larger population are among the most serious violations of human rights. Terrorist acts are human rights crimes and those that are widespread and systematic constitute crimes against humanity. Terrorism, whether practiced by states or by non-state actors, deserves universal condemnation, and the victims and survivors of terrorism deserve our solidarity and support.[3] However, the most effective and ethical ways to counter terrorism are not by committing human rights violations oneself. This is a fundamental lesson of the failure of the Bush Administration's counterterrorism policies.

The human rights record of the Bush Administration

The conventional view held by most members of the international human rights community is that the Bush Administration's response to the events of 9/11 has been very bad for the human rights regime. This is true, of course, if one judges this in terms of the number and kinds of human rights violations committed by the government of the United States. There is no doubt that these American human rights violations and abuses have been very bad for their victims, and nothing that I say here should be interpreted as suggesting that these violations were not serious and systematic. It is also true that some other countries have emulated America's bad example and have adopted security and counterterrorism measures that limit or invade the civil liberties of their own citizens.[4] In some cases, security measures have been adopted that have been used to repress internal political dissent. It also is fair to say that there has been a general weakening of the rule of law worldwide as the result of 9/11 and that civil rights and liberties in many nations are in a more precarious position now than they were before the terrorist attacks on New York and Washington, London, Madrid, Istanbul, Mumbai, and other cities. So there has been a crossing of moral boundaries, a moral slide, which in some cases has meant that the solemn commitments designed to prevent the abuse of government powers have been abrogated.

The list of human rights violations and abuses that can be laid at the feet of the Bush Administration is long and includes: the "disappearance" of suspected terrorists into CIA-run secret prisons; the denial of the right of habeas corpus of detainees; the use of "enhanced" interrogation methods, otherwise known as torture, such as water-boarding, sleep deprivation, and auditory stimulus overload by military interrogators and the CIA; the indefinite detention without charges or trials of suspected terrorists at Guantánamo; the construction of the concept of "unlawful enemy combatants"; the use of Predator drones to assassinate suspected terrorists; the detention of an American citizen, Jose Padilla, without charges or trial for more than three years; the irregular renditions of persons such as Maher Arar to countries such as Syria, Egypt, and Yemen, where they have been tortured; the torture of persons such as Khalid Al Masri in secret CIA prisons; the ill-treatment and death of detainees held at Baghram airbase in Afghanistan; and the secret and illegal eavesdropping on American citizens by the National Security Agency in violation of the Foreign Intelligence Surveillance Act, among others.

A number of these abuses have been the subject of several high-level special reports on US human rights violations prepared by the charter-based bodies of the United Nations. In the report dealing with respect for civil and political rights while conducting counterterrorism, the Special Rapporteur for the Mission to the United States of America, Martin

Scheinin, identified "serious situations of incompatibility between international human rights obligations and the counter-terrorism law and practice of the United States. Such situations include the prohibition against torture, or cruel, inhuman or degrading treatment; the right to life; and the right to a fair trial" (Scheinin 2007a). He has also identified deficiencies in US law and practice pertaining to: "the principle of non-refoulement; the rendition of persons to places of secret detention; the definition of terrorism; non-discrimination; checks in the application of immigration laws; and the obtaining of private records of persons and the unlawful surveillance of persons, including a lack of sufficient balances in that context." This report and many others dealing with the human rights record of the Bush Administration, both by agencies of the United Nations and by human rights nongovernmental human rights organizations, both in the United States and abroad, demonstrate beyond a shadow of doubt that senior officials of the government of the United States conspired to systematically abuse international human rights obligations, suspend the rule of law, and authorize the commission of war crimes.

It is clear that Bush Administration officials conspired to break the law, and also that the Department of Justice and the Congress were complicit in these crimes and their cover-up. The *New York Times* stated unequivocally that "some of the very highest officials of the land not only approved the abuse of prisoners, but participated in the detailed planning of harsh interrogations and helped create a legal structure to shield from justice those who followed orders," and this was done "with President Bush's clear knowledge and support" (April 20, 2008). The President's top national security advisors, Vice President Dick Cheney, Secretary of Defense Donald Rumsfeld, National Security Advisor Condoleezza Rice, Secretary of State Colin Powell, and Director of Central Intelligence, George Tenet, held dozens of meetings in the White House Situation Room to organize and give legal cover to enhanced interrogation methods, including brutal methods of abuse that all civilized nations consider to be torture (Jordan and Hess 2008). A (partially redacted) report issued by the Senate Armed Services Committee on December 11, 2008, the day after the 60th anniversary of the passage of the Universal Declaration of Human Rights (UDHR), concluded that,

> the authorization of aggressive interrogation techniques by senior officials was both a direct cause of detainee abuse and conveyed the message that it was okay to mistreat and degrade detainees in U.S.

custody...The abuse of detainees in U.S. custody cannot simply be attributed to the actions of "a few bad apples" acting on their own. The fact is that senior officials in the United States government solicited information on how to use aggressive techniques, redefined the law to create the appearance of their legality, and authorized their use against detainees. (Levin 2008)[5]

Although the use of torture and other violations of human rights went unchecked during the initial stages of the War on Terror, the disclosure of the abuses at Abu Ghraib and subsequent revelations generated a massive backlash against these policies.

Beginning in 2004 and continuing until the present, the outcry from legal scholars, academics, human rights advocates, public officials, military leaders, journalists, and informed citizens condemning these abuses and calling for the government of the United States to observe international human rights and humanitarian standards has overwhelmed the attempts by apologists to defend these policies. The revelation of the abuses at Abu Ghraib led to a public conversation about the use of torture, the practice of indefinite detention, and other human rights abuses that opened the eyes of the American public and provided a "teachable moment" in which to explain what the relevant international human rights standards are and why they remain important. The opportunity to explain why, for instance, the prohibition on torture should be absolute, or why the right of habeas corpus should be extended to prisoners at Guantánamo, helped to strengthen the domestication of the human rights ethos both in the United States and abroad, and the turning tide of public opinion led to the widespread rejection of these Bush Administration policies.

In the first two years following the attacks of 9/11, as the outlines of the Bush Administration's policies became apparent, there was good reason to be worried about the impact of the War on Terror on the international human rights framework. Paul Hoffman, who was at the time Chair of the International Executive Committee of Amnesty International, wrote that Amnesty's view was that, "the way in which the 'war on terrorism' has been waged threatens to undermine the international human rights framework so painstakingly built since World War II" (Hoffman 2004). He quite rightly pointed out in this article that it is possible for there to be effective security and counterterrorism tactics that do not abuse human rights; that the commission of human rights violations in the name of security against terrorism is counterproductive; and that Bush's policies were distracting attention from other serious human rights problems, like eradicating poverty or stopping the genocide in Darfur, while diverting vast resources toward an ill-conceived War on Terror.

But the backlash against Bush's security and counterterrorism policies from the global human rights movement, from leading international human rights NGOs such as Amnesty International and Human Rights Watch, and from domestic civil and human rights NGOs such as the American Civil Liberties Union (ACLU) and Human Rights First, has been vigorous and largely successful in discrediting these policies.[6] The legal academy, both in the United States and elsewhere, has responded as well, and there are now scores if not hundreds of articles in law reviews and in the more general scholarly literature condemning the Bush Administration's antiterrorism policies. Self-correction has also come from the US Supreme Court, which has rebuked the Bush Administration's Guantánamo detention policies in four important cases: *Hamdi v. Rumsfeld* (2004), *Rasul v. Bush* (2004), *Hamdan v. Rumsfeld* (2006), and *Boumediene v. Bush* (2008). Legal opinion both in the United States and around the world has firmly rejected the specious arguments put forward by Bush Administration lawyers such as David Addington, John Yoo, Jay Bybee, and Alberto Gonzalez, that the inherent powers of the president as commander in chief of the armed forces place him above the law and justify the violation of the Bill of Rights, the separation of powers, the Uniform Code of Military Justice, and international human rights and humanitarian law.

The *Hamdan v. Rumsfeld* decision of the US Supreme Court was a major setback for the plan to shield members of the Bush Administration from legal accountability. In a 5–3 decision the court held that the Bush Administration violated the separation of powers in setting up military commissions to try terrorist suspects held at Guantánamo, finding that only the Congress had the authority to amend the Uniform Code of Military Justice. However, with the passage of the Military Commissions Act of 2006 (MCA), the 109th Congress itself became complicit in these crimes and their cover-up. Section 5 of the MCA, which was signed into law by President Bush on October 17, 2006, effectively revoked US ratification of the Geneva Conventions by explicitly prohibiting "any person from invoking the Geneva Conventions in any habeas corpus or other civil action to which the United States, a current or former officer, employee, or member of the Armed Forces, or other agent of the United States is a party as a source of rights in any court of the United States or its states or territories." And it also "makes the provisions of this section effective upon enactment, and applicable to all cases, without exception, pending on or after enactment which relate to any aspect of the detention, transfer, treatment, trial, or conditions of detention of an alien detained by the United States since September 11, 2001."

The MCA was designed to shield senior officials of the Bush Administration from any legal accountability in US courts by granting both those who designed the torture policies as well as those who carried them out retroactive legal immunity. The Bush Administration's earlier decision to "unsign" the Rome treaty creating the ICC, and the passage of the American Service-Member's Protection Act of 2002 (otherwise known as the Hague Invasion Act) protects US military personnel and other elected and appointed officials of the US government against criminal prosecution by an ICC to which the United States is not party.

Thus it is unlikely that there will be any legal accountability in US courts or international tribunals for these crimes. The constitutional remedy for such violations of the rule of law by senior officials of the government of the United States is impeachment. Only the US House of Representatives can draw up articles of impeachment, but the 110th Congress, which came under the control of the Democratic Party in the 2006 elections, declined to do so. This whole shameful episode in the history of the United States thus exposes a serious and fundamental failure of the system of checks and balances in the US Constitutional system. Both the executive branch and the Congress failed to uphold the Constitution. Only a series of narrow decisions by the US Supreme Court, decisions that, save for the votes of a few justices that could easily have gone the other way, prevented the United States from giving legal authorization to war crimes and violations of fundamental human rights. Unless the present Congress and President Obama create institutional safeguards to prevent the subversion of the rule of law such as took place under George W. Bush, there is no guarantee that it will not happen again.

Shifts in world public opinion

Critics of my argument might suppose that while "liberal elites" may have rejected the Bush Administration's policies, popular support for them, particularly among Americans, remains strong. But a review of the evidence provided by public opinion polls suggests otherwise. The rejection of Bush's policies has not been restricted to elite opinion. In the past several years both editorial opinion in the press and world public opinion has turned sharply against the human rights policies of the Bush Administration. The election of Barack Obama as the 44th President of the United States also provides evidence that the majority of Americans have rejected these policies.

Public opinion polls conducted in Europe, Asia, Africa, Latin America, and in the United States itself demonstrate that global public opinion has firmly rejected the policies of the Bush Administration regarding human rights. For instance, a poll conducted by the BBC of more than 27,000 people in 25 countries found that the majority believe that torture is not justified even if it is used to obtain information that could save innocent lives from terrorist attacks (World Public Opinion 2006b). Other polls found that two in three Americans say the United States should change the way it treats detainees at Guantánamo Bay as prescribed by the UN Commission on Human Rights (World Public Opinion 2006a, 2008a), and that a sizable majority of Americans oppose the rendition of suspects to countries that practice torture and reject the argument that terrorists should not have the same due-process rights as US citizens (World Public Opinion 2007b). Another poll conducted in 2006 showed that a large majority of Americans believe that the United States is viewed more negatively by people in other countries as a result of the policies of the Bush Administration (World Public Opinion 2007c). The same poll found that 73 percent of Americans were somewhat or very worried that the United States might be losing the trust and friendship of people in other countries. This belief was confirmed by another poll in 2007 that found that in 20 of 26 countries surveyed the most common view is that America is having a mainly negative influence on the world. In his testimony before the House Foreign Affairs Committee in March 2007, Steven Kull, director of the Program on International Policy Attitudes at the University of Maryland, testified that during the 1990s similar polls were predominantly positive toward the United States of America, but in recent years, under the Bush Administration, "favorable views of the United States have dropped in the UK from 83 percent to 56 percent, in Germany from 78 percent to 37 percent, in Morocco from 77 percent to 49 percent, in Indonesia from 75 to 30 percent, in France from 62 to 39 percent, from Turkey from 62 to 12 percent and in Spain from 50 to 23 percent. Only Russia has held steady" (World Public Opinion 2007a).

Polling data collected after Bush's reelection in 2004 suggest that negative attitudes toward the United States, while significant, are not as strong as those for Bush and his policies. Doug Miller, President of GlobeScan, one of the leading global polling agencies, commented that, "Our research makes very clear that the re-election of President Bush has further isolated America from the world. It also supports the view of some Americans that unless his Administration changes its approach to world affairs in its second term, it will continue to erode America's good name, and hence its ability to effectively influence world affairs" (World Public Opinion 2005). Clearly, the Bush Administration did no such thing during its second term.[7] The major US corporate-owned news media rarely report such findings, but even their pundits have acknowledged that under the Bush Administration the United States has lost its moral standing in the world. While this decline in the esteem with which America is regarded in the world is due to several factors in addition to the poor human rights record of the Bush government, for example, the war in Iraq, its support for Israel, and its bellicose posture toward Iran, and so on, it is clear that its flagrant disregard for international human rights norms has played a significant role.

Further confirmation that support for human rights remains strong globally despite the War on Terror comes from a poll on public attitudes toward human rights released on the 60th anniversary of the signing of the UDHR. This study, which surveyed opinions of over 47,000 respondents about human rights in 25 countries, attempted to "understand the role of human rights as it plays out at the deepest level – the convictions of individuals living in various countries around the world" (World Public Opinion 2008b). That is, it attempted to measure what I have been calling the domestication of human rights. In the words of this report's authors, "the prognosis for the principles of the UDHR is good" (8).

> The basic finding of the study is that the norms of the UDHR receive robust support throughout the world. Stated in general terms, they are endorsed by majorities in every country. However in a minority of nations, when it comes to situations where there are risks of political instability or where civilians may be at risk, publics sometimes back away from the broadest application of the principles. (7)

Large majorities in all countries surveyed expressed support for religious freedom, freedom of expression, media freedom, and equal rights for women and for racial and ethnic minorities. All publics also endorsed the view that governments should be responsible for ensuring that their citizens enjoy basic social and economic rights to food, education, and health care. In general, large majorities in all nations rejected the use of torture; however, pluralities in Kenya and India favored making an exception in the case where terrorists have information that could save lives (28), a view that was also supported by 31 percent of Americans.

These polling data show that the norms embodied in the contemporary human rights paradigm have not been weakened or delegitimized by their being violated, even by one of the most powerful nations. Human rights, particularly civil and political rights, function as a shield against tyranny and the abuse of power by governments. They are designed to thwart systematic or institutionalized oppression by state authorities, and as such, the fact that they are violated or ignored does not undermine their validity as moral and legal norms. Instead it highlights and reinforces the perception of why the effective protection of human rights is necessary and why the selective application of human rights standards by states must be firmly resisted, even, and perhaps especially, when the state that selectively violates them is a "superpower."

The contemporary international human rights paradigm has proven more robust and resilient than many people feared. In the confrontation between the policies of the United States of America – the nation that liberated Western Europe from Nazi oppression in the Second World War; the nation which played a central role in the creation of the United Nations; whose former first lady, Eleanor Roosevelt, chaired the Human Rights Committee which produced the *UDHR*; the nation based on the Enlightenment principles of liberty and equality for all, one whose constitution and Bill of Rights served as a model for many modern liberal democracies, and which calls itself the leader of the "free world" – and the contemporary human rights paradigm, the United States lost and human rights won.

The loss of US credibility as a human rights promoter

The standard view of the human rights record of the Bush Administration is that it was a tragic case of America failing to live up to its own ideals and highest values. However, there is another, darker, but more historically accurate view, that holds that the human rights crimes of the Bush Administration have only put the final nail in the coffin of the image of the United States as the world's champion of human rights. That the United States had long ago lost the mantle of moral leadership for human rights was already apparent to most careful observers of the history of American foreign policy. Despite a brief and ineffectual attempt to make human rights the cornerstone of American foreign policy during the Carter Administration (1977–80), the trajectory of US policy since the beginning of the Cold War in 1949 has been largely in conflict with the values, goals, and aspirations of the global human rights movement. American governments, whether led by Republicans or Democrats, have placed US national security and economic interests above those of human rights with few exceptions.

As Michael Sullivan has documented, "the primary *strategic* goal of the United States since 1945 has been to supplant the major imperial powers of the pre-Second World War era – the United Kingdom, France, Germany, and Japan – as the sole economic hegemon of the global capitalist system." The motive of US foreign policy during the past 60 years "has primarily been to make the world safe *not* for democracy, but rather for capital" (Sullivan 2008). The victorious Allied powers at the end of the Second World War, including the United States, earned a huge amount of moral capital by having the vision to create the United Nations and commit it to the promotion (but alas not the protection) of human rights and fundamental freedoms. But the United States has squandered a great deal of its moral capital in the ensuing decades and can no longer rest on its laurels. The erosion of the United States' status as a leader of the global human rights movement began to be apparent as early as 1953 with the "McCarthyism" and "Brickerism" that took hold on American foreign policy during the first phases of the Cold War and which began the pattern of American exceptionalism and detachment from the international human rights system. America's anticommunist crusade during the Cold War (1949–89) led to the CIA-sponsored overthrows of democratically elected but leftist governments in Iran (1953), Guatemala (1954), Indonesia (1965–6), Chile (1973), Nicaragua (1981–8), and elsewhere. Add to this its illegal and immoral war in Vietnam (1961–75); US support for repressive military dictatorships and kleptocracies in the Philippines, Indonesia, Congo, and elsewhere; its unflagging support for the racist and antidemocratic regimes in Rhodesia and South Africa; US interventions into the domestic politics of countries such as Greece (1947–9), Lebanon (1958), British Guiana (1961–6), Laos (1961–73), Angola (1975), El Salvador (1979–92), and elsewhere; and numerous other instances in which the US government conducted its foreign policy contrary to the principles of international law and the core values of the international human rights movement – and it is easy to see why many of those who have carefully examined the historical record have come to regard the United States as morally challenged in the field of human rights (Chomsky 1998).

Critics of this view are likely to object that I have painted an unduly negative caricature of the human rights record of the United States. While it is true that the United States has ratified several important human rights conventions, such as the International Covenant on Civil and Political Rights, the Torture Convention, and the Genocide Convention (albeit with reservations in each case), and it played an important role in establishing the Ad Hoc Tribunals for the Former Yugoslavia and Rwanda, American foreign policy has never given human rights concerns real priority despite the desire of many Americans that it should. The United States remains largely isolated from the international human rights system; it has failed to ratify many key conventions and even in those cases in which it has ratified these instruments, it has done so with reservations which are designed to prevent these ratifications from having any effect on US domestic law. The doctrine of constitutional supremacy effectively detaches the US legal system from international accountability for human rights, and as a result internationally accepted human rights norms are far less institutionalized in the United States than they are in many other countries.

The US government tends to use the rhetoric of human rights and democracy in much the same way as the princes and kings of medieval Europe used the religious authority of the Holy Roman Church to lend a aura of legitimacy to their regimes, or in the way in which contemporary theocracies, such as those in Saudi Arabia and Iran, use Islam as a means of garnering popular support for their authoritarian and oppressive systems of government. The lip-service American politicians give to their devotion to human rights and democracy plays a similar function in the context of US foreign policy. Under George W. Bush this hypocrisy was brought into sharp relief. As Shirin Ebadi, the Iranian human rights lawyer who won the 2003 Nobel Peace Prize, has dryly put it, "it is not hard to see the Bush administration's focus on human rights violations in Iran as a cloak for its larger strategic interests" (Ebadi 2005).

While human rights violations and abuses by themselves do not undermine the legitimacy of the human rights paradigm, hypocrisy and double standards can. Ordinary people in many countries who see that they have been or are being oppressed by the foreign policies of the United States, and who hear American politicians claim that they are doing so in the name of human rights and democracy, quite understandably draw the conclusion that human rights and democracy are a tools of oppression. But, if so, then the loss of the US government as a credible spokesman for human rights helps avoid this sense of hypocrisy. If no one can any longer seriously believe that when US government officials talk about the importance of human rights they really mean it, then their pronouncements on this subject are more readily discounted as propaganda. The fact that the policies of the Bush Administration have been discredited in large part because they violated important norms of international human rights and humanitarian law shows that people are now able to distinguish hypocrisy about human rights from authentic commitment. This is a boon for the global human rights movement.

Regaining America's moral stature

The loss of America's moral stature and leadership in the global human rights movement, while regrettable, is not irreversible. There is some chance that the Obama Administration and the Democratic Congress will begin to take steps to restore America's tarnished image and reassert its moral leadership in the field of human rights.[8] The Obama Administration made a good start by announcing that it intended to close the detention center at Guantánamo, end the use of torture, and stop using the term "War on Terror." But despite this positive rhetoric regarding human rights, many in the US human rights community are becoming increasingly dismayed by the lack of political will within the Obama Administration to translate words into deeds. Obama's "look forward, not back" posture has prevented the investigation and prosecution of those responsible for ordering torture and other crimes under Bush's administration. He has continued Bush's policy of detaining terrorism suspects without charges or trails, and has retained military commissions for problematic cases. There has been no indication that the Obama Administration is planning to ask Congress to repeal the Military Commissions Act and the American Service-Man's Protection Act, or to ratify the 1998 Rome treaty that created the ICC, the 1997 Landmines Treaty, or even the Convention on the Rights of Children. As Kenneth Roth, the Executive Director of Human Rights Watch has observed

> From a human rights perspective, there is no doubt that the Obama White House has done better than the Bush administration. As one would expect from so eloquent a president, Obama has gotten the rhetoric largely right. The challenge remains to translate poetic speeches into prosaic policy – and to live up to the principles he has so impressively articulated. (Roth 2010)

In other words, there has been no fundamental change in the US posture regarding human rights; American governments whether Democratic or Republican tend to talk the talk but not walk the walk on human rights. Given its long record of hypocrisy, restoring America's credibility with regard to human rights will not be easy. In fact, America's credibility as a human rights champion was lost long ago.

For the time being, then, the traditional human rights promoting states, such as the Netherlands and the Nordic States, must take on the role of leading the global human rights movement and defending the international human rights framework. Despite the widespread rejection of Bush Administration antiterrorism policies, human rights are, I would argue, less well domesticated in the United States than they are in the countries of Western Europe. In the United States, most issues concerning the responsibility of the state to its citizens are still framed in terms of civil rights, and domestic social issues such as gay and lesbian rights, access to health care, unionization and collective bargaining, social security, and other matters are rarely framed in terms of human rights. This difference in domestication helps account for the rather different responses to the threat posed by terrorism by the nations of Western Europe. The European attitude toward the ICC, toward the United Nations, and toward the best methods of defending themselves against terrorism, has been markedly different than that of the United States, even before the Bush Administration took office. Indeed, respect for human rights, and the pursuit of international cooperation for their universal protection and enjoyment, has been a cornerstone of European policy, both foreign and domestic, since at least the signing of the Helsinki Final Act in 1975. European security and counterterrorism policies adopted in the aftermath of 9/11 have differed significantly from those of the Bush Administration (with the partial exception of the United Kingdom), and public opinion in the EU has been consistently and strongly opposed to the human rights violations and abuses authorized by the Bush Administration.

The more moderate, lawful responses to the threat of further terrorist attacks adopted by European states is, I believe, largely accounted for by the greater degree to which human rights are domesticated in European societies. The European human rights system is generally regarded as the most developed in the world, and in this case, it worked well to prevent the kinds of serious human rights abuses that the American constitutional system failed to prevent.

However, I would also argue that the Council of Europe and the EU has had its own reputation tarnished by its acting as an enabler to much of what is worst in American foreign policy. This is evidently true of the United Kingdom, whose "special relationship" with the United States misled Tony Blair into believing that going along with Bush's Iraq fiasco would allow him greater influence over decision making in Washington DC. The other major Western European powers, such as France and Germany, although they refused to take part in the invasion and occupation of Iraq, did little to prevent their British and American allies from invading a sovereign nation without just cause. Official criticism of the invasion of Iraq coming from the EU was muted and ineffectual. Few Europeans take seriously the notion that the EU should take on the role of a "Second Superpower" and use its political muscle to restrain the United States from any more reckless misadventures. As a result, the EU has functioned as an enabler of the US misbehavior, standing passively by while its ally continues to play the role of a rogue state. Perhaps one lesson of the Bush years is that Brussels needs to chart a course that is more independent from Washington DC.

Conclusion

The War on Terror has not been as bad for human rights as many people feared. The more moderate, but lawful and effective, responses to terrorism by the EU, and the rejection of the misguided policies of the Bush Administration have shown that the global consensus on human rights is strong and indeed may be more robust than many people thought. There is still good reason to believe that the human rights agenda is progressing in the 21st century despite the setback of the Bush Administration. The explanation for the robustness of the human rights paradigm is that it is the result of the progressive domestication and internalization of human rights norms and values into the ethical cultures of many more societies. The main drivers of this process of domestication are not states, but rather the thousands of human rights NGOs that now operate in virtually every country. The increasing domestication of international human rights norms and values into the ethical cultures of diverse societies represents the silver lining behind the dark cloud of fear that obscured hopes for a more just and peaceful world in the 21st century following the horrific terrorist attacks of September 11, 2001.[9]

Notes

1. On the important role of human rights NGOs, see Korey 1998; Welch 2001. On the role of national human rights institutions, see Pohjolainen 2006.
2. The main exception to this generalization is the United Kingdom, which because of its special relationship with the United States and its lack of a written constitution, slid further than its European neighbors.
3. There has been some debate on whether non-state actors can commit human rights violations. For a brief review of this discussion and a conclusion that agrees in its essentials with mine see Scheinin 2007b, 11–18.
4. Amnesty International, Human Rights Watch and other human rights NGOs have documented many other nations who have adopted draconian national security laws after 9/11. The United Kingdom now grants law enforcement authorities greater scope to detain suspects without timely or meaningful civilian judicial review. Belarus passed a law in December 2001 that could have been lifted from the Patriot Act which allows the authorities to search homes or other locations without notice and seize things without a judicially approved search warrant. Still other countries, like Malaysia and Sudan, resurrected old security laws to crack down on peaceful dissenters or journalists. Liberia, Zimbabwe and other countries have applied the United States'

"enemy combatant" label in order to detain journalists and members of the political opposition.

5. In April 2009 the Obama Administration released previously classified Justice Department memos, one from 2002 and three from 2005, which demonstrate that the use of interrogation methods involving torture and other forms of cruel, inhuman, and degrading treatment was cleared by lawyers in the Office of Legal Counsel. Additional documentary evidence for the claim that a torture policy was approved at the highest levels of the US government can be found in sources such as Hersh 2004, Danner 2004, Greenberg et al. 2005, and Mayer 2008, among others.

6. Amnesty International's Secretary General, Irene Khan, drew flack when she called Guantánamo the "gulag of our times" in June 2005. Vice President Dick Cheney stated at the time that, "For Amnesty International to suggest that somehow the United States is a violator of human rights, I frankly just don't take them seriously." But the public relations campaign using retired military officers as TV experts that the Bush Administration and the Pentagon launched to discredit Amnesty and justify Guantánamo was later revealed to be a staged public relations exercise. See Barstow 2008.

7. In its World Report 2008, Human Rights Watch found there was no improvement in the human rights situation in the United States despite attempts by the democratically controlled Congress to end abuses carried out in relation to its war on terrorism. It also upbraided the EU for tolerating sham elections, stating, "It seems Washington and European governments will accept even the most dubious election so long as the 'victor' is a strategic or commercial ally" (Human Rights Watch 2008d).

8. See Schulz 2008.

9. Research for this chapter was begun while the author was serving as the Danish Distinguished Chair of Human Rights and International Relations at the Danish Institute for Human Rights in Copenhagen, Denmark. The chapter was revised following the International Human Rights Regime since 9/11 conference held on April 17–19, 2008 at the University of Pittsburgh, and revised again in December 2008. I am grateful to Morten Kjaerum, former director of the Danish Institute for Human Rights, for his comments on an earlier draft of this chapter. I also benefited from comments and suggestions from Chip Pitts and William Schulz, as well as my fellow participants in the University of Pittsburgh conference.

3

The War on Terror through a Feminist Lens

Julie Mertus and Tazreena Sajjad

This chapter offers a feminist perspective for analysis of post-9/11 changes in international human rights theory and practice. In so doing, it suggests not a singular *perspective*, but the expansion of the international relations (IR) analytical toolbox informed by various feminist theories and their methodologies. A primary goal of this approach is to unpack the power dynamics within international relations and to expose the gender assumptions in traditional models of state security. At the same time, the chapter suggests a methodology that is also central to ethical human rights practice: honoring the individual narratives of those labeled as "victims," and uncovering and valuing their roles as "subjects" (Tickner 2001, p. 47).

While feminist approaches vary, they do share a common political agenda: advancement of the human rights and political and social status of women. As Spike Peterson observes: "...while feminist theories are in the first instance about analyzing the world more adequately than mainstream theory, they are at the same time about enabling a world with more equitable sex/gender relations" (Peterson 2004, p. 35). In this sense they are self-consciously "political," though the ideology and politics they espouse may vary considerably. We believe that drawing attention to the lived experiences of women has become an imperative for well-informed, effective, and just decision making in the human rights field. Moreover, this perspective is consistent with respect for and observance of core human rights principles such as nondiscrimination, participation, and inclusion.

We have divided this chapter into three main parts. First, we provide a brief explanation of what it means to apply feminist perspectives to international relations problems generally. Second, we review specific examples of how responses to September 11 were variously framed as a war *for* women, or a war *against* women. In our analysis we ask questions largely unexamined by many of our peers, including the following queries: Where are the women? How are gender roles constructed? Who has the power? Who wins and who loses in seemingly gender-neutral interventions, post-conflict peace-building and political restructuring? These questions may not necessarily lead to new answers, but they do support new ways of thinking about post-9/11 developments.

On using a feminist lens

What are "feminisms" and how might exploring them contribute to this study of the post-9/11 practice of human rights? Feminism is a historically constituted, local and global, social and political movement with an emancipatory purpose and a normative content. It posits a subject (women), identifies a problem (the subjection and objectification of women through gendered relations), and expresses various aims. As a movement, it is geared toward action coordination and social transformation, interrogating existing conditions and relations of power with a view toward not only interpreting but also changing the world. Feminist analysis of international relations is not new. Over the past few decades, feminist scholarship has perpetually used gender lenses to question the establishment and naturalization of the domain of the "masculine" and the "feminine." Dichotomies and their attendant positivist ahistorical and reductionist commitments, which dominate key postulations about the debates on war/peace, international/domestic, realism/idealism, politics/economics, are parameters that map a hostile terrain for feminist thinkers. Critical feminist scholarship creates the space to challenge these largely uncontested gendered assumptions of public premises.

Contemporary feminism engages with the praxis of identity and gender construction, state and interstate relations, the global political economy, the politics of difference and solidarity, decolonization and democratizing practices, the role and contribution of feminist knowledge and scholarship to transnational organizing, and the creation of alternative discourses on community. Central tasks for feminist scholars have been both deconstructive and reconstructive: focusing on revealing through critique the masculinist limitations of mainstream approaches to the field, while also investigating political and economic processes in which women and men are engaged. Such works illustrate how an emphasis on gender has generated an increasing focus on masculinity, its multidimensionality, on the diversity of women's lives, identities, and strategies, and on the power differentiations among women as well as between them and men, and among men (Youngs 2004, p. 77).

Each strand of feminism offers its own particular critique of the dynamics within international relations (Sylvester 2002). The liberal feminist, for example, draws on the traditional themes of liberal theory, stressing the importance of individual rights, the rule of law, and other supportive institutional mechanisms (Ramazanoglu 1989; Tong 1998). The standpoint feminist stresses the inherent differences between the men and women (Hartsock 1998; Naples 2000). The socialist/Marxist feminist attributes women's marginalization to the capitalist/private property system, emphasizes the economic value of women's labor, and argues for the restructuring of the economic system (Weeks 1998). The radical feminist discerns and analyzes the patriarchal nature of society and, in keeping with the socialist feminist, emphasizes the need for dramatic social change in order to achieve genuine equality for women (Whelehan 1995, p. 73). The cultural feminist seeks to understand women's social locations in society by concentrating on gender differences between women and men and holds that these essential differences form the foundation of women's subordination in society (Blumenthal 1997; Alcoff 1998). The third wave feminist focuses on action and embraces diversity as central to social change and, in so doing, it offers a strong critique of what is usually identified as the first two waves of feminist struggle and warns against a single feminist agenda (Gillis et al. 2005).

Still other scholars adopt a feminist approach that seeks to move beyond "adding women" and finds that the orienting assumptions of international policy analysts – their very way of being in the world – is distorted in a manner that privileges men. Thus, Marysia Zalewski has observed that the issues deemed important and relevant in international relations, assumptions about who and what counts and how the game is played, reflect the interests of the powerful (i.e. the masculine) while the less powerful (i.e. the feminine) are pushed to the margins (1995, p. 350). The explanation for this problem of ontology is the use of a "male" or "masculine" lens that accepts differences as natural and overlooks the deeply embedded impact of patriarchy. "That there are these differences [between men and women] is undeniable," Zalewski urges, "but what really matters, in terms of effects on people's lives, is how these differences are interpreted and acted upon" (1995, p. 344).

The use of a feminist perspective thus "can be used to challenge dominant assumptions about what is significant or insignificant, or what are central or marginal concerns" (Steans 1998, p. 5). The typical top-down analysis focuses on states, sovereignty, security, power, and conflict and overlooks individuals, social movements, cooperation, and human relations. At the same time, the significance of these constructs in relationship to women's subordination is obscured. The explanation for the shortcomings, Tickner has asserted, is that "[k]nowledge constructed in terms of binary distinctions such as rational/emotional, objective/subjective, global/local, and public/private, where the first term is often associated with masculinity, the second with femininity, automatically devalue certain types of knowledge" (Tickner 2001, p. 133). The goal of this more radical feminist analysis is to transform epistemological orientations and in so doing uncover *and challenge* sites of power and domination (Hirschmann 1992).

In crafting their analysis, feminists also reject the binary categories of subject and object. This allows the researcher to value the knowledge held by the participant as being expert knowledge. Although feminists remain interested in the exercise of power at the "top" of the international arena, we understand world events by listening to local narratives and drawing lessons from "below." A paradigmatic example of this scholarship is Anne Cubilie's forceful book, *Women Witnessing Terror* (2005). Her work introduces the voices of women witnesses and continually returns to those voices as it makes an informed case for thoughtful and strategic interventions. Narrative, contextual reasoning, and multi-perspectivity allows for these voices to be heard. This method is valuable because, drawing from the lived experience of women through their own voice, women tell "a different kind of war story" (Nordstrom 2007), highlighting the gendered dynamics and experiences of political violence and transitional efforts for peace-building in the aftermath.

Feminist methodology often includes personal experience as its theoretical starting point. Accordingly, in their response to 9/11, instead of focusing on such "big" actors and structures at the "top" – like the commanders of United States military, the members of the United Nations Security Council, and the judges of the International Criminal Court or the Yugoslav Army – feminists tend to look at the "little" actors and structures at the "bottom" – village women leaders, grassroots anti-conscription organizations and shoestring humanitarian efforts (e.g. Mertus 2003). One illustration of this phenomenon is the efforts of feminist academics to support public forums in which Afghan women could speak for themselves (see, for example, Mills and Kitch 2006) and the increasing attention paid to "women's voices" by mainstream human rights organizations (see, for example, Horsbrugh-Porter 2009).

In sum, employment of a feminist lens differs greatly according to the type of feminism informing the inquiry. At their core, however, feminist analysts share the concern that they are "responsive to women, reflect their experiences, and seek to transform their lives in a manner that recognizes individual agency and corrects disproportionate power imbalances" (Slaughter and Ratner 1999, p. 416). It is with this in mind that we apply a feminist lens to what has been variously described as the war *for* women and the war *against* women.

Application of a feminist lens to framings of post-9/11 responses

The concept of "framing" refers to the attempt of government policymakers and advocacy NGOs (of all political persuasions) to create "patterns of understanding" that influence the way problems are understood and addressed (Lissack 2004). Frames call attention to an issue and refract it through a particular lens – here, a feminist lens – that suggests certain understandings and outcomes. The "war on terror" may be framed in different ways, with dramatically different results. Here we consider two seemingly dichotomous framings, namely, the portrayal of the response to 9/11 as a war either *for* or *against* women.

Framing the conflict as a war for women's human rights

In rallying the troops for war, the treatment of women in Afghanistan became a politically salient way to identify the enemy as being barbaric and themselves as (women)'s liberators. First Lady Laura Bush and Secretary of State Colin Powell were also conscripted to mobilize support to liberate Afghan women (Hunt 2006). In a radio address to the nation, Laura Bush told the American public that "they have an obligation to speak out against the Taliban's treatment of women" (Laura Bush 2001). She argued, "the people in the civilized world must act swiftly, because in Afghanistan, we see the world the terrorists would like to impose on the rest of us" (Laura Bush 2001).

Politicians, journalists, and political pundits alike, of all ideological stripes, seized on the Taliban's abuse of women's human rights as justification for intervention in Afghanistan. This portrayal of women as victims became an increasingly important component of the post-9/11 discourse, evoking at one level the need for a "perfect victim" and on another the need to legitimize military and civil interventions in Afghanistan. Nowhere is this depiction and rhetoric more striking than in the evocation of the vulnerable and systematically victimized blue, burqa-clad Afghan woman, quintessentially compelling a rescue mission from the highly misogynistic regime of the Taliban.

In the immediate aftermath of 9/11 the conflation of the woman's body as a marker of oppression or liberation became blatantly clear in the discourses surrounding Afghan women and their "freedom" from the Taliban. The burqa, the heavy garment that covers the entirety of a woman's body with only a narrow mesh screen for vision, has become the universal symbol of women's oppression in Afghanistan (Abu-Lughod 2002, p. 785). There is ample documentation that discloses women in Afghanistan being beaten simply for accidental exposure of an inch or two of skin (Iacopino et al. 1998, p. 52; Amnesty International 1999; United Nations 2000, p. 7). Less clear in the public discourse is that the Taliban's misogyny neither began nor ended with the imposition of the burqa. Oppressive policies and rampant human rights abuses were perpetrated by all sides involved in the three decades of conflict in Afghanistan. Violations against women were gender-based but were also rooted in their religious beliefs, political affiliations, or class, resulting in multidimensional discrimination. Nevertheless, the general and dominant refrain placed the burqa at the forefront of all forms of violence and as the key indicator and marker of oppression against Afghan women (and later Muslim women generally). Consequently, the fall of the Taliban was directly associated with greater freedom for Afghan women, and their "liberation" from the burqa and subsequent empowerment.

Ayotte and Husain suggest that those representations of Afghan women as oppressed, disempowered, and in need of "saving" by the West constituted epistemic violence, and served to obfuscate or altogether erased women as *subjects* in international relations. They further observe "in claiming to secure Afghan women from the oppression of the Taliban, the United States has reinscribed an ostensibly benevolent paternalism of which we should remain wary" (Ayotte and Husain 2005, p. 113). "The image of Afghan women shrouded in the burqa and the injustices leveled against them became symbolic justification for military intervention several times" (Chenoy 2002, p. 229).

The long-term persecution of women in Afghanistan has, over the course of time, served as the primary symbols of difference, of "otherness," defined and victimized by their religion and "lack of civilization." Yet in their demarcation, they were useful – politicians and colonels alike employed them to enact the romance of a rescue mission, involving "our" men, to rescue "those" women from "their" men. The myth of protection foists upon men responsibilities of soldiering and on women the function of being those for whom men must fight, underlining men as agents and women as passive pawns in international politics, regardless of what individual men and women are doing (Petman 2004, p. 89).

Just as the oppression of women was invoked as a justification and rationale for "the war on terror," during the late 18th and early 19th century heads of state attempted to justify imperial expansion through appeals to the need to save these "irrational, irresponsible, unbusinesslike, unstable, childlike" people (Rosenberg 1991, pp. 31–5). The discourse surrounding the Afghan invasion focused on the "inherent" nature of the male "other" and the need to save their "oppressed, docile" women. Nayak (2006, p. 48) suggests that this form of infantilization is patterned and includes the following elements: descriptions of gender violence are racialized, to underscore that patriarchal violence does not exist in the West and that the only reason a woman may die in a non-Western country is because of a monolithically oppressive, static culture (Narayan 1997); promotion of a militaristic solution to end gender violence; and use of the "progress" of other women in achieving or exercising rights, such as voting, to justify US strategic actions.

Widespread cultural opposition to women in public life created cumulative obstacles for women: their poor representation in key institutions and their more limited access to education and resources stymied their ability to participate and many women who did participate found themselves targets of campaigns against them. The lack of personal security which affected citizens in much of the country disproportionately affected women and consolidated the opinions of many families and communities that it was not appropriate for women to be active outside the home. The Bush Administration took every opportunity to detail the abusive and misogynistic treatment of Afghan women at the hands of the Taliban – abuses that the US government had been aware of for years, but never addressed until al-Qaeda became a target in Afghanistan (Hunt 2002).

This rhetorical construction of Afghan women as *objects* of knowledge legitimized US military intervention under the rubric of "liberation," which made the root causes of structural violence in Afghanistan both invisible and marginal. A feminist analysis would challenge the basis for the intervention by putting Afghan women at the center of the analysis, inquiring whether military intervention serves their needs and responds to their security concerns.

The intervention did not in fact serve women's needs. If the war really was for women, the cause was lost. Despite the 2000 UN Security Council Resolution stressing the importance of including women in peace negotiations, and the Bonn Agreement on Afghanistan which called for the participation of women, only two women were included in the interim administration. At the same time, a meeting of Afghan women in Brussels issued a proclamation which called for gender justice across a full range of issues, beyond those usually labeled as women's concerns (Charlesworth and Chinkin 2002). The brief Allied governments' courting of Revolutionary Association of Women of Afghanistan (RAWA), a feminist group strongly advocating women's rights in Afghanistan and Pakistan, collapsed when they proved ungrateful, political and critical of both Taliban and other women's rights abusers in the region, and of US-led bombing and invasion (Hunt 2002, pp. 116–21).

During the first few months of the new government in 2004, women won their battle to obtain a legal quota of 25 percent of seats in parliament. In other areas of politics, however, any gains for women were small and short-lived. For a short time, three women sat in President Karzai's cabinet: the Ministry of Women's Affairs, the Ministry of Martyrs and Disabled, and the Ministry of Youth (Karzai Administration 2004–2006). All are considered to be second-tier cabinet positions. In 2006, women represented 31 percent of the civil service, a huge gain from the Taliban period, and yet by 2009 that figure had dropped to 21.4 percent. Most women in the civil service are employed in the ministries of women's affairs, public health, education, social affairs and labor, and the civil service commission. Other ministries have as few as 4 percent female employees. The number of women in middle management positions in the civil service is 9 percent, with a disproportionate number of those in the Ministry of Women's Affairs (Human Rights Watch 2010). Given these figures, a strong argument can be made that if the post-9/11 wars are portrayed and justified as wars *for* women, the victory was *de minimus* at best.

Not only did the new Afghan government fail to move forward on women's human rights, on some issues it moved backward. The influence of ultraconservative leaders and warlords in political office and the rise of religious fundamentalism have meant that many official gender restrictions have returned in Afghanistan. Certain warlords who were (and remain) "allies of the U.S. coalition in the war against the Taliban...used their connections with the United States to seize power but then embraced some of the Taliban's most odious restrictions," including curtailing educational opportunities for women, forcing chastity examinations, imprisoning women for refusing to marry or for leaving a marriage ... and blocking redress in cases of state-orchestrated sexual assault.

The Afghan government has done little to shut down the infamous Vice and Virtue Patrol which is well known for beating and harassing women and girls for traveling without male guardians and for even slight infractions of stringent dress requirements. The Patrol continues to operate under the new Ministry of Justice and under the aegis of the Department of Islamic Instruction. Not considering this to be sufficient, in June 2007, Karzai sent the Afghan parliament a proposal for reestablishing the Department for the Promotion of Virtue and the Prevention of Vice. His political future apparently required a demonstration that he would not let society slip into Western immorality.

The deliberations around the passage of the Shiite Personal Status Law (SPSL) (Jones 2009) signed into force by President Karzai in March 2009 further provides "a glimpse of the types of political deal-making that are likely to affect women's rights" (Kandiyoti 2009). Ostensibly giving recognition to the persecuted Shi'ite minorities by according them separate legislation, the restrictions the SPSL introduced on the rights of Shia women led to it being dubbed "the rape law" in the Western media (see Oates 2009). Beyond the *contents* of the law the very *process* through which cross-factional clerical interests asserted their clout over lawmaking, marginalizing due legislative process intimidated women's and human rights activists who protested are highly indicative of the trend in overshadowing women's struggle for substantive achievements in the country. Under these conditions, the argument that the international military and civil intervention in Afghanistan was *for* women cannot be supported.

Framing the conflict as a war against women

An alternative framing of the conflict in Afghanistan is that it was *against* women. This is more plausible because the concerns of women cannot be addressed if women are invisible and branded as hopeless, infantile victims who cannot act on their own. Although some counterexamples exist, for the most part mainstream journalists did not consider and depict women as meaningful, independent actors. On the contrary, the media presented September 11 and its repercussions through a purely masculine lens: "men attacking, saving lives, and responding through further attack" (Charlesworth and Chinkin 2002, p. 602). The images of manly heroic American men "all but eclipsed that of the many heroic women, who rose to the occasion, be they fireworkers or police officers" (Tickner 2002, p. 335).

In the days and months after 9/11, however, women disappeared from the op-ed pages and the nightly news. Conservative pundits like Jerry Falwell and Pat Robertson received considerable airtime when they blamed the terrorist attacks on the American Civil Liberties Union (ACLU) and gays, while women of all political orientations were nowhere to be found. Women were not regarded as authorities having anything to add to the analysis (Petman 2004, p. 85). For example, according to a *Guardian* survey of almost 50 opinion pieces in the *New York Times* in the first six weeks after the attack, only two were by women (Charlesworth and Chinkin 2002, p. 601).

As political analyst Katha Pollit observed

> You could see the gender skew everywhere – in the absence of female by-lines in Op-eds about the war, in the booing of Hilary Clinton during the Concert for New York at Madison Square Garden, in the slavish eagerness of the media to promote the callow and inadequate Dubya as a strong leader whose "cockiness" and swagger are just what America needs in a time of crisis. (quoted in Ruby 2001, p. 178)

A feminist approach poses the question: Where were the women? The good women were doing what all good women should do during war or other periods of large-scale violence: they were standing by their men, patiently supporting them from the sidelines, keeping the home-fire burning. The really, really good women were patriotically waving the flag while shopping at the mall (doing their part in keeping the economy afloat (Mayhall 2009, p. 29). It is quite wrong, however, to suggest that gender had disappeared or even that women were absent in the aftermath of 9/11. Women made their appearance in the media but in ways long embedded in the gendered war story. They appeared alongside men as victims and relatives of victims of 9/11 (Petman 2004, p. 88). When images of women did appear, they were most likely with children.

The presidential elections of 2009 in Afghanistan provide a poignant example of the marginalization and cooption of women. Women received virtually no coverage in news reporting and topics concerning women's rights were rarely featured in the electoral campaign. Their participation as candidates, voters, and administrators of the elections was also severely limited. Two of the 41 presidential candidates in Afghanistan in

2009 were women and 333 women ran for seats on the provincial councils, constituting 10 percent of candidates. This was a slight increase in the national average but in close to half of the country's provinces, the proportion of women candidates decreased. The quota system ensuring a minimum 25 percent of representation by women in provincial councils remains a necessary provision in a context where there is no semblance of a level playing field for men and women. Women's freedoms of movement, association and expression were restricted to an even greater degree than men's and their political participation was specifically targeted in several parts of the country.

In provinces such as Ghazni and Kandahar, women candidates reported that they could not campaign at all due to fears for their safety, while in most parts of the country women carried out only low-profile campaigns close to home. In response to women's security needs, the Ministry of Interior launched a program to provide a bodyguard to each woman provincial council candidate but implementation of the program was so limited that few candidates were able to benefit. In fact, in Herat, female Provincial Council candidates filed complaints that bodyguards previously provided were actually withdrawn (AIHRC UNAMA 2009). Further, according to the joint report by AIHRC and UNAMA (2009), none of the three female Provincial Council candidates standing in Kandahar resided in Kandahar due to security threats; neither did they undertake a public campaign in the province. Death threats to female Provincial Council candidates in the North East caused them to further curtail their already limited campaigns. In the East, female candidates' posters were removed, and in other areas, defaced (AIHRC UNAMA 2009). The office of a female Provincial Council candidate in Kabul was destroyed the week of 27 July. On 30 July, night letters were plastered on buildings in the neighborhood of a female Provincial Council candidate in Takhar warning her to stop campaigning or suffer consequences; on 1 August, her house was fired on at night (AIHRC UNAMA 2009). Overall, female candidates tended to have limited access to funds for their created largely by women's disadvantaged status in the family and community (AIHRC UNAMA 2009). The contextual assessments show that a realistic participation rate for women was significantly lower than 50 percent (EU 2009).

On the day of the elections, difficulties in recruiting sufficient numbers of women as polling station staff and security searchers resulted in an additional deterrent to women voters, as did the location and relocation of some polling stations for security reasons. Hundreds of polling stations for women (stations throughout the country were segregated to keep men and women from publicly mingling) did not even open in some areas where Taliban influence continues to be high, but women also suffered discrimination and intimidation in some places in central and northern Afghanistan. Female candidates received threats and were even largely ignored in news coverage of the elections (Gall,The New York Times, August 22, 2009). The EU and the Election Observation Mission (EOM) received consistent reports about individuals owning several voter cards and voter cards being bought and sold, in some cases quite openly (Preliminary Statement of the Election Observation Mission, 2009).

According to the Free and Fair Elections in Afghanistan (FEFA), the largest Afghan observer organization, at least 650 women's polling centers did not open on the day. The 2009 National Democratic Institute reported that in certain polling centers in the south and southeast of the country almost no women voted (NDI 2009). Yet, in some of the provinces in which women are most restricted, the proportion of women in the registry was over 60 percent. In the case of the highest figures of women voters, the EU preliminary statement noted that a number of those apparently registered are in fact "ghost voters." Cultural and security considerations made it difficult to eliminate the illegal practice of men voting on women's behalf. The intervention of Western democracies in the civil society of Afghanistan did little to support Afghan women in even the most basic democratic act: casting a ballot.

Most recently, discussions about reconciling with the Taliban to end the ongoing conflict have again raised red flags for many Afghan women. On May 13, 2010, Secretary of State Hillary Clinton told three senior female Afghan officials: "we will not abandon you ... [I]t is essential that women's rights and women's opportunities are not sacrificed or trampled on in the reconciliation process" (Clinton 2010). While the question of reconciling with the insurgency has brought about a mixed reaction from the international community and many in the Afghan population, human rights activists, civil society actors, and women's groups have a right to be concerned. Afghan women's groups have continued to raise their voices in public forums such as the recent London Conference in January 2010 and in the June 2–4 (2010) National Deliberative Peace Jirga held in Kabul, urging the importance of protecting the rights and achievements of women since 2001 and advocating specific ways in which women can be included into political and other public spaces in the country. With the discussions about reconciling with the Taliban and other insurgent groups gaining momentum and international interest, the concerns of women's groups have only intensified.

Conclusion

The embedding of the feminist ideology to frame the "war on terror" created the belief among some in the liberal feminist movement that, with the collapse of the Taliban regime, life would return to normal. Women in particular would be able to access the public realm from which they had been so systematically and effectively removed. During the 2002 State of the Union Address, Bush confidently stated: "The last time we met in this chamber, the mothers and daughters of Afghanistan were captives in their own homes, forbidden from working or going to school. Today women are free... " (Bush 2002). The number of girls enrolled in schools was touted in the media to demonstrate the direct correlation between the US invasion and the emancipation of the Afghan women.

The reality on the ground, however, reflects a far grimmer picture, with the Afghan women in particular "enduring" the consequences of Operation Enduring Freedom. The current numbers on Afghan women's progress, highlighted by the Bush Administration, and others that have espoused the success of the liberation project, do not inspire euphoria. Neither do they necessarily inspire sustained and cautious optimism. Afghan women and girls continue to suffer extremely low social, economic, and political status. As Human Rights Watch observed in its 2010 backgrounder on Afghanistan, Afghan women and girls:

> rank among the world's worst off by most indicators, such as life expectancy (46 years), maternal mortality (1,600 deaths per 100,000 births), and literacy (12.6 percent of females 15 and older). Women and girls confront barriers to working outside the home and restrictions on their mobility; for example many still cannot travel without an accompanying male relative and a burqa. While the number of girls in school increased quickly after the fall of the Taliban in 2001, only 35 percent of school-age girls were in school in 2006. (Human Rights Watch 2008)

International feminists have long critiqued the cycle and cost of violence, and now critique the dramatic privileging of hyper masculinity and the prerogative state after 9/11. By that account, the post-9/11 world has not offered something new as a site of feminist engagement, but rather a reiteration of the problematic nature in which conditions of security, state, and interstate relations are constructed and engendered. In the post-9/11 world, these myopic notions of security and state were evident in the foreign policy in Afghanistan, but even included highlighting surveillance and curtailment of civil liberties in the name of homeland security and increasing intolerance and division within those homelands.

The Bush Administration's policies post-9/11 also provided cover for other governments, such as China, Pakistan, Russia, and Egypt, to jettison even a rhetorical commitment to certain human rights in the name of fighting terrorism or providing for national security (Bush 2002). For others, including countries in Europe, these policies served as an opportunity to de-prioritize other human rights concerns, such as racism and violence against women. In some instances, countries have tightened their hold on religion and culture, often resulting in the curtailing of women's rights and mobility. The rise of fundamentalism in all its forms and the narrowing of spaces for a discussion on rights, access, and responsibility is inextricably linked to the "war on terror" (Davis 2002). The feminist project is embracing the new dimensions of these challenges being brought forth in the post-9/11 world where a false binary seems to be easily embraced – universalism versus cultural relativism, globalization versus regressive and revivalist tendencies. With feminists decrying the hijacking of their agenda to justify military means and ends, there appears to be no time or space for complacency or compliance. With added urgency, the work goes on.

Part II
Human Rights Discourses

4
Reverting to Form: American Exceptionalism and International Human Rights

Michael Goodhart

America's "war on terror" and its related policies on human rights have been subjects of intense global controversy since 9/11.[1] The conventional wisdom is that US policy changed radically after the attacks, significantly damaging international human rights. To many observers, these changes reflect a characteristic American exceptionalism, a pattern of arrogance, hypocrisy, and double standards that typifies US attitudes and behavior on human rights (see Ignatieff 2005a). A disturbingly broad range of examples – regularized torture, the unsigning of the Rome Statute of the International Criminal Court (ICC), the suspension of the Geneva Conventions, detention without review in Guantanamo, "preemption" – supports this view.

Too simplistic notions of American exceptionalism can be deeply misleading, however. Most accounts are quite static, attributing American policies to fixed traits, habits, or beliefs. They are thus unable to account for change. I develop a dynamic account of Providential exceptionalism and use it to demonstrate that, in style and substance, American views on human rights have reverted to their Cold War form. Understanding the US response this way deepens our understanding of it and of the threat it poses to human rights. By legitimizing a rival – and largely incompatible – discourse of national security, the American response risks undermining the discursive foundations of the human rights regime.

The chapter begins with a brief critical assessment of American exceptionalism. This discussion clarifies that the changes in American attitudes and behavior after 9/11 cannot be understood without reference to the changes that followed the end of the Cold War. The salience of exceptionalist rhetoric and discourse declined sharply in the 1990s, corresponding with a historic shift in American international policy that enabled rapid and significant development in the international human rights regime during this period. These changes facilitated the emergence of human rights as the preeminent discourse of legitimacy in world politics. The reversion of American discourse and policy to their Cold War form thus threatens to erode the regime's normative foundation.

In focusing on American exceptionalism and on changes in American discourse and behavior, I do not mean to suggest that US action determines outcomes in the international human rights regime. I am focusing on one important factor that *conditions* outcomes, one that has received much global attention and which is, in my view, inadequately understood and often misleadingly employed. By analyzing this phenomenon I hope to improve our understanding of American views and policy on human rights and of the often-neglected normative dimension of the international human rights regime.

Varieties of exceptionalism

Since 9/11, the term "American exceptionalism" has been invoked promiscuously in mainstream and academic discourse to excoriate American policies on human rights, military preemption, and the wider "war on terror." The almost casual use of this term masks a deeper ambiguity about the underlying concept and its explanatory power.

There are at least three distinct scholarly interpretations of American exceptionalism, each of which has divergent (and problematic) implications. *Historical exceptionalism* refers to claims about America's unique historical origins and development. It is anchored in arguments stressing America's lack of a feudal past, its abundant land, diversity among its working classes stemming from immigration, and a variety of other factors (e.g. Lipset 1996). In a critical introduction, Shafer summarizes historical exceptionalism as "the notion that the United States was created differently, developed differently, and thus has to be *understood* differently – essentially on its own terms and within its own context" (Shafer 1991, v). The epistemological thesis underlying this view is problematic: every country has a unique history. Recognizing this, some scholars have suggested the study of "comparative exceptionalism" to understand differences among various exceptionalisms (Kammen 1993). The claim that America is unique and must be understood differently, however, is grossly under-theorized.[2] Moreover, as an explanatory concept, historical exceptionalism is static and rather deterministic.

Behavioral exceptionalism differs in focusing less on the roots of America's distinctiveness than on the fruits of it: its allegedly unique role in international affairs. Michael Ignatieff identifies three types of exceptionalist behavior in the arena of human rights: *exemptionalism*, the American habits of demanding exemptions from agreements and regimes for its citizens and delaying or refusing to ratify conventions or doing so with numerous reservations (Ignatieff 2005b, 4–7);[3] *double standards*, the habit "of [judging] itself by different standards than it uses to judge other countries and [judging] its friends by standards different than those it uses for its enemies" (Ignatieff 2005b, 7); and, *legal isolationism*, the insistence that American jurisprudence should ignore the human rights standards and jurisprudence of other countries and of the international community (Ignatieff 2002, 2005b, 8–11; cf. Koh 2003). Again, however, exemptionalism and double standards are hardly unique to the United States – though they stand out due to American wealth and power. This observation indicates that *American* exceptionalism is difficult to differentiate theoretically from *hegemonic* exceptionalism (Lepgold and McKeown 1995). At any rate, perhaps the only attempt to test behavioral exceptionalism empirically found little supporting evidence (Lepgold and McKeown 1995).[4]

Cultural exceptionalism is the claim that Americans hold distinctive beliefs and attitudes about the world and their place in it. A typical statement is David Forsythe's view that "the belief in the exceptional freedom and goodness of the American people" is the core of American political culture (Forsythe 2006, 161). Like historical exceptionalism, cultural exceptionalism is not uniquely American: every people has beliefs about itself. Such claims typically have very limited explanatory power. Critics of American exceptionalism often cite ingrained arrogance, hypocrisy, and messianic fervor to explain American actions. The problem with cultural exceptionalist claims, like their historical or behavioral analogues, is that fixed traits and beliefs explain variation in policy and attitudes poorly. Perhaps that is why so many critics of exceptionalism see no variation in American behavior.

I maintain that a more nuanced and analytically sophisticated account of American exceptionalism can provide powerful insights into American attitudes and policy, especially on human rights. Such an account relies on historical and cultural observations to explain behavior broadly. To do so, it must be both specific (detailing the relevant features of American history and culture in sufficient detail to avoid triviality) and dynamic (able to explain variations in behavior). I attempt to sketch such an account here, emphasizing the widespread belief among Americans that the United States is a chosen nation, one upon which Providence has bestowed unique blessings of liberty and which therefore has a historical mission to defend and disseminate liberty throughout the world. I call this account *Providential* exceptionalism.

Providential exceptionalism

The idea of America's special role in history has a surprisingly European orientation. The first colonists of Massachusetts Bay perceived that "as Puritans they were charged with a special spiritual and political destiny: to create in the New World a church and society that would provide the model for all the nations of Europe as they struggled to reform themselves" (Madsen 1998, 1–2). The first generation of English settlers understood its "errand" or mission in precisely these redemptive terms.[5] Their colony would be, in John Winthrop's famous metaphor, a "city upon a hill" (Winthrop, in Miller 1956a, 83). Winthrop warned his fellow colonists that their experiment might go wrong: their city on a hill could be a beacon or a warning. The possibility of failure and its apocalyptic consequences always weighed heavily on the Puritans and impressed subsequent generations with the gravity of their mission (Miller 1956b, 13–15). Indeed, a recurring theme of exceptionalist rhetoric is that God uses the enemies of his people as instruments of punishment and correction; America's trials thus confirm its providential character even as they point to its present failings.

The Puritans held a rather strange (to us) view of liberty. The subtleties of this doctrine, a response to the Arminian heresy, lie beyond this chapter's scope, but a brief sketch clarifies something important about the distinctly American understanding of liberty that animates Providential exceptionalism. According to Winthrop, there are two kinds of liberty: natural liberty or license (which humans share with animals), and federal liberty, which "is the proper end and object of authority and cannot subsist without it; and it is a liberty to that only which is good, just, and honest" (Miller 1956a, 92). Federal liberty, put simply, is liberty to do the right thing. Winthrop compares it to a woman's choice to marry: she chooses her husband freely, but in marrying she submits her will entirely to his. Winthrop used federal liberty to justify submission to political authorities; later thinkers, relying on the idea of human reason, turned it in a democratic direction, but they never ceased believing that liberty should be used properly in the fulfillment of God's larger purposes (Miller 1956a, 121–43).[6]

Speeches and sermons dedicated to these themes are ubiquitous, and there is little to gain from multiplying examples. The key point is that by the mid-18th century Puritan ideas about the migration to America had entered mainstream discourse, profoundly shaping the rhetorical context for subsequent political events. As Bailyn (1992, 32) describes, "... in the minds of the Revolutionaries the idea, essentially worked out in the sermons and tracts of the settlement period, [was] that the colonization of British America had been an event designed by the hand of God to satisfy his ultimate aims." This idea was promoted in history books "found everywhere" in the colonies, solidifying the widespread notion "that America had a special place, as yet not fully revealed, in the architecture of God's intent" (Bailyn 1992, 33). Preaching the new democratic interpretation of covenant, the New England clergy fomented sentiment for independence, and this rationale was reiterated by many leading figures in the struggle for independence.[7] The theme of Providential exceptionalism "elaborately orchestrated by the colonial writers, marked the fulfillment of the ancient idea, deeply embedded in the colonists' awareness, that America had from the start been destined to play a special role in history" (Bailyn 1992, 140; cf. Ross 1995, 22). That role was to nurture and defend liberty and promote its diffusion across the globe. By the middle of the 19th century, after the American Civil War – which Lincoln, in his Gettysburg and Second Inaugural addresses, conceived explicitly in terms of Providential exceptionalism – the idea had become thoroughly mainstream and secular (or at least, ecumenical). Thus in a now-famous speech Rabbi Isaac Wise honored Washington and his compatriots as "the chosen instruments in the hands of Providence, to turn the wheel of events in favor of liberty forever ..." (in Bellah 1975, 41).

This brief sketch is intended as a heuristic device; I am not asserting that America actually has a divinely ordained role to play in perfecting and promoting liberty in the world; nor am I making any claims about Americans' religious views. Although Providential exceptionalism developed from the Puritan understanding of a divine mission, the idea has long since been secularized, become part of America's so-called civic religion, complete with the iconography of the city on the hill. Providential exceptionalism is not an ideology: it is more diffuse and less systematic than ideology and lacks its partisan nature. Siobhán McEvoy-Levy (2001, 5ff) describes American exceptionalism as a "collective belief system," and I shall adopt something like that view here. Providential exceptionalism figures prominently in the American political imagination and large majorities of Americans do seem to believe it.[8] This distinctive belief about its own difference is itself a crucial fact of American history (Howe, cited in Kammen 1993, 27–8).

My model leverages the explanatory power of Providential exceptionalism to make sense of American attitudes and policy in international affairs. My method follows that of Stanley Hoffman, who, in a brilliant essay on the "American Style" in foreign policy decision making, defended his approach to understanding the distinctive tendencies, characteristic reactions, and recurrent patterns in the actions and attitudes of a particular country as "a postulate and a construct" that "attempts to establish order in a chaotic mass of features by positing that a nation perceives the world, and its place in it, in a fashion which is never quite that of any other nation ..." (Hoffmann 1968, 362). At the same time, he cautioned that "this way is a procedure of selection, and therefore inevitably one of exclusion, and it is a procedure of distortion, because things that may be important are left out and also because the things selected are refracted through the prism" of analysis (Hoffmann 1968, 362). My approach relies on the simple (selective, distorting) idea that Providential exceptionalism shapes how Americans understand the world and their country's place in it, thus illuminating some important and remarkable features of the "American style" of political engagement.

Terms of engagement

Providential exceptionalism operates in the realm of perceptions, of intersubjective reality. It can be described as a sort of cognitive schema, a filter that colors how Americans see the world and a frame that shapes their responses to it (cf. Holsti 1962). Several powerful insights and conjectures about the American style of engagement in international affairs follow. For instance, Providential exceptionalism helps to explain why Americans tend to evaluate international affairs in moral or moralistic terms.[9] To the American mind, the country's providential role makes world politics inescapably a domain of values and principles; the very point of international engagement is moral reform. The arrogance that often accompanies this attitude (but which is often invisible to Americans) flows from the belief in a special duty to perfect and promote liberty throughout the world.

Another important tendency supported by Providential exceptionalism is that of equating any threat to the United States with a threat to liberty itself, and equating threats to liberty elsewhere as threats to the United States. So, for instance, the terrorist attacks of 9/11 were widely viewed by Americans as attacks on liberty ("they hate our freedom"). This is both implausible and wildly exaggerated, but it helps to explain Americans' subsequent puzzlement about the unwillingness of others, especially some European allies, to join in the "war on terror" and eradicate the threat. (Equally implausible and exaggerated was the view that communist rule in South Vietnam would unleash a "domino-effect.") When such external threats appear grave – an appearance amplified by this tendency of equation – the characteristic American response is a messianic style of international engagement.

I refer to the style and orientation of this engagement as "messianic" in light of certain distinctive qualities and characteristics of the belief in Providential exceptionalism. When threats are grave, engagement becomes obligatory, a necessary sacrifice. The preservation and promotion of liberty become sacred duties entailed by America's special role. This exceptionalist mode of engagement engenders a redemptive outlook for international policy, with American actions conceived not merely as meeting a threat but rather as cleansing and purifying the world of the evil that gave rise to it. Messianic engagement therefore promotes transformative objectives; it aims to refashion the world in America's image, implementing the model of democratic liberty it has worked out in its splendid isolation. Transformation and redemption fit hand in glove: in recreating the world, America simultaneously ensures its own salvation; anything less invites further danger and leaves the mission unfulfilled. Messianic engagement has a moralizing (not just moralistic) and uncompromising tone appropriate to these ambitions, and it deals in stark contrasts – black and white against the diplomat's shades of gray. To be against America is to oppose freedom, to try to turn the "wheel of events" against liberty. "You are either with us or against us."

These tendencies have often been noted. Providential exceptionalism enriches our understanding of them in two respects. First, in tracing them to a common source – Americans' distinctive belief in their country's special role – the concept provides greater explanatory power. It suggests that these tendencies are not merely idiosyncratic traits or reflections of particular political constellations, but rather related to a widely shared belief system that comprises political elites and citizens alike. Put differently, it imposes a coherence on these tendencies that allows us to treat them as theoretically grounded empirical expectations – predictions – about American engagement in international affairs.

This coherence, along with the intersubjective nature of Providential exceptionalism, mean it is open to manipulation (McEvoy-Levy 2001).

Most obviously, threats can be cynically exaggerated or even manufactured: the sinking of the battleship *Maine* in Havana harbor, used by the Hearst corporation to whip up sentiment against Spain; the Gulf of Tonkin incident, used to justify escalation of American involvement in Vietnam; and Colin Powell's presentation on Iraqi weapons of mass destruction to the UN Security Council are (in)famous examples. But manipulation need not be cynical; it can quite plausibly be both sincere and beneficial, used to align values and specific strategies (see McEvoy-Levy 2001, 157). President Kennedy's masterful use of exceptionalist rhetoric during the Cuban Missile Crisis is a good example, as is President Reagan's remarkable call for Soviet Premier Gorbachev to tear down the Berlin Wall. Exceptionalist beliefs can also impede policymakers – at least if we assume that in democracies international policy is broadly constrained by public opinion (Davis and Lynn-Jones 1987). President Johnson's portrayal of the Vietnam conflict as an anticommunist crusade, for example, effectively made the war "unlosable" for him (Hook and Spanier 2000, 131–2). Providential exceptionalism does not, then, generate static or deterministic expectations; whether, how, and how successfully actors manipulate these beliefs leads to widely different outcomes.

The second advantage of this framework is precisely its capacity to account for variation both in outcomes and in the style and orientation of American international policy. Messianic engagement, we have seen, is activated by grave (real or perceived) threats to America and to liberty. When threat levels are perceived as "normal," the style and orientation of American international policy look starkly different. Providential exceptionalism encourages a pragmatic style of engagement, one that encourages a realistic outlook and seeks to advance conventional American interests while avoiding unnecessary conflicts or entanglements, with their corrupting potential. This pragmatism (which Hoffmann identified as a hallmark of his "American style") extends a typically American can-do attitude (and aversion to complexity) to international affairs. The central objective of this pragmatist style is preservation – of American wealth, safety, and separation itself. The tone and rhetoric of policy is moralistic – the habit of viewing international affairs in terms of values and principles remains – but not moralizing; it is more diplomatic and flexible. American leaders and diplomats will always speak in the language of providence, liberty, and democracy that is normal, even expected, by domestic audiences, even as they otherwise operate in a more traditional diplomatic idiom.

These expectations about the style and orientation of US international policy are summarized in Table 4.1.

Table 4.1 Style and orientation of US international policy

	Level of perceived threat	
Aspect of US international policy	Normal	Grave
Style of engagement	Pragmatic	Messianic
Outlook	Realistic	Redemptive
Objective	Preservation	Transformation
Rhetoric/tone	Moralistic/ diplomatic	Moralizing/ uncompromising

Providential exceptionalism allows us to see these very different styles of engagement within a single explanatory framework; America's vacillation between messianic engagement and relative isolationism are two sides of the same coin. Recall that the belief in America's distinctive role in the world is deeply tied up with its geographical and spiritual separation from the rest of the world; it follows that this separation is itself something to be prized and protected. In the era of independence Americans remained convinced that separation allowed their culture of liberty and democracy to flourish, a conviction that, along with the fact of their geographical separation, formed the country's isolationist instincts. Both Washington's famous warning against foreign entanglements and Monroe's determination to protect a sphere of American influence from European encroachment illustrate this inclination. Differentiating between grave and normal perceptions of threats allows for a dynamic understanding of American engagement.

In the second half of the chapter I use Providential exceptionalism to explain certain features of the American response to the terrorist attacks of 9/11 and, more importantly in the context of this volume, to demonstrate their significance for the international human rights regime. Before proceeding to this argument, however, I must again stress that in using the concept of Providential exceptionalism I am not endorsing its core belief or affirming its desirability. I should also reiterate that the analytic framework developed here is a heuristic device, one that treats Providential exceptionalism as a fact about the world from which useful insights can be derived; it is not a causal account.

The Cold War, human rights, and providential exceptionalism

From *before* its beginning, the Second World War had been portrayed by President Roosevelt in terms reflecting a broader redemptive outlook and transformative objective. Allied policy, first outlined in the *Atlantic Charter* during the summer preceding Pearl Harbor, promised civil and political freedoms and freedom from fear and want on a global scale. It foretold permanent peace, decolonization, and international cooperation based on the principles articulated in the Universal Declaration of Human Rights and realized through a variety of new multilateral institutions including the United Nations and the Bretton Woods institutions. These institutions, along with the Marshall Plan, reflected the transformative ambitions of the victorious allies.

Unfortunately, the optimism surrounding an Allied-led unity of nations following victory over the Axis powers began to fade even before that victory was achieved. International communism quickly replaced virulent fascism as an existential threat to liberty, to American ideals, interests, and security. The details and implications of this conflict are familiar and need not be elaborated here. Instead, I want to make two broader observations informed by the analytic framework developed in the previous section. The first concerns the style and orientation of American international policy during this period. The Cold War struggle was typically depicted in world-historical, even apocalyptic, terms. The doctrine of containment remade the prophylactic impulse of American isolationism as an aggressive policy of international engagement in the messianic style. American international policy had a clear redemptive orientation: to purge the evil of "godless communism" from the world and to vanquish its false notions of human freedom. Ultimately, America sought not coexistence but rather the defeat of its global rival, the liberation of Eastern Europe, and the spread of liberal democracy throughout the world. The soaring rhetoric and uncompromising tone of the Kennedy and Reagan years best exemplify this: when Kennedy set out to "let every nation know, whether it wishes us well or ill, that we shall pay any price, bear any burden, meet any hardship, support any friend, oppose any foe, to assure the survival and success of liberty"; when Reagan famously called the Soviet Union an "evil empire," and denounced a "deadening accommodation with totalitarian evil," they were working within a messianic mode of engagement. Both fashioned policies to match their rhetoric.

Of course, American attitudes and behavior during the Cold War often fell short of stated ideals. America allied with unsavory regimes, "friendly tyrants" whose opposition to the greater evil of communism led the United States not only to overlook but to condone, cooperate in, and whitewash their brutality and their abuse of human rights (Pipes and Garfinkle 1991). It did so even while insisting that it was struggling on behalf of liberty against totalitarian evil. These double standards fueled criticism of human rights as mere, as did America's habit of refusing to sign or ratify human rights instruments produced by the very international institutions it had helped to establish.

Both of these tendencies make sense with the analytic framework proposed here. Lipset (1996, 20) has observed that "Americans must define their role in a conflict as being on God's side against Satan – for morality, against evil." So, "if circumstances oblige [the US] to cooperate with evil regimes, they are converted into agents of virtue" (66); take as examples US collaboration in the Pinochet coup or its support for a succession of strongmen in South Korea and South Vietnam. The exemptionalist tendency is to reflect a view that America has perfected liberty. Tellingly, many American reservations to human rights treaties stipulate that the treaties must not contradict, or must be interpreted in light of, the US Constitution. They thus represent less a rejection of human rights than an affirmation of the belief that they are already enshrined in American law. Human rights are for others a template for achieving what Americans have already secured at home. American leadership and laggardness on human rights are, again, two sides of the same coin: America leads because of its special role but hangs back from ratification and implementation out of an impulse to preserve its domestic liberty from foreign contamination.[10]

The second important point to stress about the Cold War concerns its extraordinary length and scope. Unlike previous periods of messianic engagement, which had lasted a few years at most, the struggle against communism endured for some four decades and played out in myriad contexts from proxy wars and an arms race to diplomacy, rival aid programs, and even international sport. This period of engagement spans virtually the entire history of the international human rights regime, making it easy to misinterpret the messianic style of American engagement, especially in the area of human rights, as "normal" or typically American. This is a mistake; as I argue below, this simplistic view of American engagement obscures two crucial shifts essential to understanding the challenges facing the international human rights regime after 9/11.

The long 1990s

Americans greeted the fall of the Berlin Wall on November 9, 1989 with euphoria. Their reaction reflected the symbolic importance of this historic event marking the end of an epic struggle for liberty and heralding a long-awaited redemption and transformation. Francis Fukuyama's (1992) famously influential interpretation of the end of the Cold War as the climax of a Hegelian historical drama with America (and its values) as protagonist captured the zeitgeist. However naive or even silly this notion might have appeared to critics, the prediction that liberalism and democracy would quickly spread around the world was in an important sense merely the logical extension of the Cold War's Providential rationale. Fukuyama's position was not much different from that of President G. H. W. Bush, who, after successfully assembling a global coalition to reverse the Iraqi invasion of Kuwait, described to Congress the

> prospect of a new world order. In the words of Winston Churchill, a "world order" in which "the principles of justice and fair play ... protect the weak against the strong ..." A world where the United Nations, freed from cold war stalemate, is poised to fulfill the historic vision of its founders. A world in which freedom and respect for human rights find a home among all nations.

The dozen years between the fall of the Berlin Wall and the collapse of the twin towers, between 11/9 and 9/11, did represent a kind of new world order – or so I shall argue here.[11] This period, which in homage to Eric Hobsbawm I call "the long 1990s,"[12] saw significant consolidation and expansion in the international human rights regime. Framed by two profound shocks to the international system, the long 1990s represents a period of unprecedented primacy for human rights in global politics, one that I shall argue is importantly linked with a change in the style of American international engagement. Progress in the international human rights regime during this period was enabled and encouraged by key changes in US policy and attitudes. Understanding the long 1990s through the lens of Providential exceptionalism both enhances our understanding of the conditions in which the international human rights regime flourished and clarifies the threat posed to it by America's revision to its Cold War form – to messianic engagement – since 9/11.

Just as our framework suggests, the triumph of 1989 ushered in a more pragmatic orientation toward international affairs. Several structural factors account for this transition (cf. Dietrich 2006). First, the absence of a powerful enemy inaugurated an era of American hegemony in which (the appearance of) grave threats was greatly diminished. Second, the rapid development of global capitalism, driven by American corporate and financial power, augmented this traditional military hegemony. Finally, the ideological victory over Soviet communism cemented the power and appeal of "American" values. Together these structural changes in the geopolitical order after 11/9 gave the United States unprecedented sway globally. In these altered circumstances, the newly pragmatic American orientation to international affairs, and to human rights in particular, led to significant changes in US policy and attitudes and enabled important developments in the international human rights regime.

During the long 1990s the United States ratified three major human rights treaties: the Convention against Torture, the Convention on the Elimination of Racial Discrimination, and the International Covenant on Civil and Political Rights. (Prior to 1989, the United States had ratified only the Geneva Conventions, the Slavery Convention, and the Genocide Convention.) The United States also ratified the Convention on Child Labor and signed the Convention on the Rights of the Child and its Optional Protocol on the involvement of children in armed conflicts. It signed the Convention Relating to the Status of Refugees, and signed or ratified eight other UN conventions. It was instrumental in the creation of the international criminal tribunals for the former Yugoslavia and for Rwanda and supported the negotiations on the Rome Statute of the ICC. Although the United States voted against the final Statute, it nonetheless signed it in December 2000.

Moreover, the United States was active in humanitarian and peacekeeping missions around the world, including in Somalia, Haiti, Bosnia, and Kosovo. A timely shift in US policy cleared the way for East Timorese independence, and America provided significant support for peacekeeping efforts there. The United States played a key role in brokering and monitoring peace in the former Yugoslavia. Further, it significantly curtailed its support for authoritarian regimes, and it became more consistent and more compliant with international norms, laws, and expectations regarding human rights. While human rights had been an important part of the rhetoric of US foreign policy since the Carter Administration, scholars had found little evidence of a coincident change in policy. As this overview indicates, during the long 1990s the policies finally began to match the rhetoric.

Critics – Chomsky is perhaps the loudest – scoff at this notion, claiming that American diplomacy pays only lip service to human rights while pursuing other aims. The 1990s, on this view, are no different – except in so far as American hegemony helped to mask the true nature of American exceptionalism more effectively (see Winston, this volume). One might maintain that American participation in UN humanitarian missions in places like Somalia and Haiti and its lead role in the NATO campaign against Serbia are all best explained in terms of American imperialism or insatiable capitalist appetites, and treat the flurry of ratifications and increased multilateralism as mere rhetoric. I find such arguments highly implausible. Still, they become incoherent when the same critics who make them bemoan a dramatic worsening of US international and human rights policy after 9/11. It is hard to see how things could have become dramatically worse when they have always been perfectly terrible. Let me be clear that I do not imagine that American policy or attitudes underwent a complete transformation in the long 1990s, or that US actions were no longer influenced by economic interests or realpolitik. I also realize that there were significant human rights failures during this era, some attributable to flawed American policies. My point is not that American policy and attitudes were perfect; it is that they were significantly better.

Recognizing this change is important for understanding how it enabled consolidation and development in the international human rights regime. The ideologically charged rhetoric of the Cold War had long precluded any global consensus on the meaning and application of human rights. Indeed, human rights were a major point of contention between the superpowers, with each side accusing the other of ignoring fundamental rights and touting its own preferred interpretation. Without equating them, we can safely say that both sides in this conflict held hypocritical positions on human rights and applied double standards in their assessments of the behavior of allies and enemies alike. These practices undermined the normative standing of human rights by reducing them to mere ideological posturing, rhetorical cover for policy decisions driven by familiar geopolitical concerns. The ideological rivalry also blocked effective functioning of international human rights institutions and of the crucial UN Security Council.

The collapse of the superpower rivalry cleared the way for a remarkable broadening and deepening of the international human rights regime. This change is perhaps best exemplified in the *Vienna Declaration and Programme of Action* agreed at the UN World Conference on Human Rights in Vienna on June 25, 1993. The Conference

> [reaffirmed] the solemn commitment of all States to fulfil their obligations to promote universal respect for, and observance and protection of, all human rights and fundamental freedoms for all in accordance with the Charter of the United Nations, other instruments relating to human rights, and international law. *The universal*

nature of these rights and freedoms is beyond question. (UNGA 1993, emphasis added)

Such an affirmation would have been unthinkable only a few years earlier, and it reflects the rapid ascent of human rights to a position of unrivalled preeminence in global politics. For the first time since the founding of the regime in the 1940s, human rights became the unchallenged standard of global political legitimacy and the dominant discourse of global politics.

This transformation too was matched by changes on the ground. During the long 1990s the number of democratic states grew rapidly. Transnational civil society developed and matured, and nongovernmental organizations (NGOs) concerned with human rights issues came to play an increasingly important role in global politics. The Pinochet case, the evolving doctrine of universal jurisdiction, and the progress toward establishing the ICC – long a dream of human rights advocates – typify the stunning legal developments of this period. On the ground, the regime was also considerably strengthened. The United Nations undertook 38 peacekeeping or humanitarian missions in the 1990s, up from five in the 1980s and three in the 1970s. (It is worth noting that these missions all received Security Council backing.) The establishment, following the Vienna Conference, of the Office of the UN High Commissioner for Human Rights has had a profound impact, helping to coordinate UN activities across a range of institutions and providing a clear moral voice and focal point for human rights in world politics. Again, I am not painting the long 1990s as some mythical golden age: one only need reflect that every peacekeeping or humanitarian mission is an effort to ameliorate a human rights disaster of some kind to recognize that human rights violations remained ubiquitous in the 1990s. From a regime perspective, however, progress was undeniable.

The change in American attitudes and policies brought on by the Cold War's end played a major role in enabling and promoting these developments. As a global economic and military superpower, American support for and endorsement of the regime had considerable influence and played a key role in enforcement (see Meyer 1999). More importantly, many of the advances surveyed here would have been impossible without the aid (or at least the acquiescence) of the United States. The shift from a messianic to a pragmatic style of engagement in American international policy facilitated the emergence and consolidation of human rights principles as guiding norms in global politics. America's exceptionalist behavior improved: it increased its ratification, compliance and cooperation, reduced its hypocrisy and double standards, and took a more active and supportive role in the regime itself. Perhaps most importantly, however, the shift away from messianic engagement helped to defuse ideological controversies over human rights, with the result that constructive American engagement contributed importantly to the consolidation of human rights norms globally.

My argument is *not* that the United States caused, or was chiefly responsible for, the positive developments in the human rights regime during the long 1990s. Numerous factors, including the reintegration of former communist states into Europe and the EU, the expansion of the Council of Europe's human rights mechanisms, the active leadership of many Southern countries and NGOs, and others also proved significant. My contention is only that the change in the American approach to human rights throughout the long 1990s crucially enabled these changes. It would require different analyses to trace the institutional and discursive changes in detail and to determine the relative impact of various factors. My focus on the US role after 11/9 is intended to provide context for America's reversion to its Cold War style of engagement after 9/11 and the implications of this change for the international human rights regime.

Reverting to form: 9/11 and the return to messianic engagement

The breathtaking terrorist attacks of 9/11 brought the era of pragmatic American engagement on human rights to an abrupt end. They signaled, if belatedly, the advent of a new and significant external danger, one seared with sudden and psychologically devastating intensity into the minds of millions as the World Trade Center towers collapsed and the Pentagon smoldered on live television.

American leaders and the American public predictably interpreted these events as a grave threat. Indeed, each of the key geopolitical changes that had facilitated the pragmatic turn in American international engagement during the long 1990s was reversed or revised by the attacks. First, while American hegemony remained unquestioned, the seriousness of asymmetrical challenges to power became painfully evident; hegemony could no longer be mistaken for security. Second, the globalization of capital and markets, while certainly augmenting American hard and soft power in many respects, also turned out to make it easier for states to avoid dependence on American trade and largess. The Kantian ideal of a "commercial peace" – the hope that trade among states would lead to a reduction of conflict and a harmonization of interests around universal liberal values – was cruelly exposed as wishful thinking. Finally, the idea that American values had become universal exploded in a symbolic cloud of toxic dust at Ground Zero.

As Providential exceptionalism would predict, the country quickly lurched back into messianic engagement, and the reversion to Cold War form is eerily complete. The moralizing and uncompromising rhetoric that followed the attacks – of a "war on terror," one in which every country is "for us or against us" – perfectly fit the style of messianic engagement. George W. Bush's much derided "crusade" comment, though lamentable for its syntax, is perhaps most remarkable for its perfect consistency with and expression of a providentialist (not religious) interpretation of 9/11 (attributing recent American behavior to the religious fervor of the Bush Administration distorts more than it clarifies). The "war on terror" has a clearly redemptive outlook and transformative objective; its aim, as articulated by President Bush, is to rid the world of evildoers. Subsequent events have made the practical implications of this plain enough. While Europeans shared Americans' horror – and their fears about radical Islam – they could not identify with American means or ends. This difference is often attributed to Europeans' sobering past experience with terrorism. That seems right, but also incomplete; Providential exceptionalism explains why Americans adopted such far-reaching objectives and extreme policies in the first place.

Following 9/11, America also relapsed into bad Cold War habits, exempting itself from the Geneva conventions, from the UN Security Council's framework for the legal authorization of war, and from its own domestic laws regarding torture and the treatment of detainees. It willingly subverted constitutional protections for human rights in the name of security, even as it framed the larger struggle as a defense of freedom. It once again adopted gross double standards, allying with such human rights-abusive regimes as Pakistan and Uzbekistan and largely condoning Chinese and Russian aggression against nationalist minority groups taken in the name of "counterterrorism" while decrying the human rights abuses of its newfound foes. Finally, America has explicitly rejected the "legalistic" European approach to counterterrorism and pushed the case for legal isolationism – most notably regarding torture – to new extremes. US actions have again provided damning evidence to those who see American rhetoric on human rights as cover for naked imperial ambition – as in the cynical invocation of Muslim women's rights as a pretext for war. Marx said that history repeats itself first as tragedy, then as farce; the American response to 9/11 has managed both at once.

American exceptionalism and the international human rights regime

These observations on US policy are not new. What is new and important is the analytic leverage gained by situating the post-9/11 changes in a framework informed by a dynamic understanding of Providential exceptionalism. This framework reveals that recent American policy and attitudes on human rights represent neither an unprecedented departure from the past nor a seamless continuation of it. Rather, we see a return to familiar and predictable patterns of behavior prompted by a grave threat and a familiar and predictable reaction to it.

The "everything changed" and "nothing changed" perspectives are misleading in precisely the same way. Each ignores the regularity or predictability of American behavior, and each misses that the long 1990s were a period of significant consolidation and expansion in the international human rights regime. As a result, neither perspective permits adequate conceptualization of the link between the two. I have argued that the change in American policy and attitudes after the Cold War, prompted by a return to a pragmatic style of international engagement, was a key factor in enabling and promoting these developments. It remains to consider how this reversion to form jeopardizes that progress.

In many respects, the formal elements of the regime – international law and institutions and human rights performance – remain resilient (see Donnelly, this volume). While there has been a great deal of justified concern about specific policy changes in the United States and globally, these changes probably reflect less about the regime and its stability than about the politics in times of emergency. Meanwhile, UN reform, including the creation of a new Human Rights Council, has continued, new international human rights treaties continue to be negotiated and enacted, and the ICC has taken up its first cases. Viewed institutionally, or in terms of compliance, the impact of 9/11 and subsequent events on the international human rights regime appears rather minimal – at least outside of narrowly restricted domains.

What is worrisome, from the perspective developed here, is the (re) introduction of a security discourse into global politics. This discourse, which has justified and animated the "war on terror" since its inception, threatens to supplant human rights as the dominant normative discourse in global politics (Dietrich 2006; Gearty 2007). The worry is not that human rights institutions will suddenly collapse; it is rather that the shift in American policy and attitudes might slowly undermine the human rights regime through decreased enforcement, diminished capacity, reduced resources, and an erosion of the normative standing of human rights. The security discourse and policies associated with it could slow or even arrest the progress achieved in the long 1990s. Prolonged American rhetorical and material support for security policies that impinge on human rights and detract from the normative preeminence of human rights could eventually destroy the regime's capacity and legitimacy.

Signals from the Obama Administration are mixed. Major news agencies reported last year a decision to drop the language of a "war on terror" in a conscious effort to improve America's image abroad and respond to criticism from human rights groups (Reuters 2009). The administration might well follow through on closing Guantánamo, winding down the war in Iraq, repealing the most damaging Bush-era policies, and working more constructively and enthusiastically with international partners. At the same time, the administration has defended and even embraced flawed policies on detention and interrogation. Its escalation of the wars in Afghanistan and Pakistan indicates that it still sees the terrorist threat in messianic terms.

This might be a political necessity. The architects of the "war on terror," led by former Vice President Cheney, continuously stoke Americans' fears and perpetuate the myth of an existential struggle for freedom and survival. Add to this that the asymmetric nature of the terrorist threat means that attacks will eventually again succeed. The danger remains real that this success will strengthen or reinforce the messianic impulse, especially since Americans may well be unable (or unwilling) to acknowledge the conflicts between their avowed purposes and the policies they adopt in pursuit of them.

We should note several important differences between the Cold War and post-9/11 periods. First, while terrorism and Islamic fundamentalism do pose serious and ongoing threats, they do not present an alternative ideology with global appeal. Second, despite the very real and frightening potential for increasingly sophisticated and deadly attacks, terrorism does not pose an existential threat (breathless claims to the contrary notwithstanding). There is thus no particular danger in prosecuting the campaign against terrorism in a fundamentally different way than that in which the Cold War was fought.

We urgently require a strategy and discourse that effectively reconcile security with human rights without subordinating the latter to the former. This will be difficult to achieve, because the human rights policies likely to make an appreciable difference in combating terrorism – increased security and economic rights for the world's poorest people, genuine democracy (and thus a move away from a carbon economy), equality for women – will take decades to bear fruit. In the meantime, they are easily vilified by those who – cynically or sincerely – continue in a messianic vein.

This raises the crucial question. Is it possible to effect a shift from messianic back to pragmatic engagement – from security back to human rights discourse – without a clear victory of the kind that has previously triggered such shifts (in 1918, briefly in 1945, in 1989)? Can we talk ourselves out of a phase of messianic engagement?

Notes

1. Versions of this chapter have been presented in various forums; I am grateful for the many helpful comments and suggestions I received on these occasions. I owe special thanks to Michael Ignatieff, Siobhán McEvoy-Levy, and Dawid Bartelt. Heather Elko McKibben provided exemplary research assistance and many helpful suggestions; thanks also to Siobhan Dempsey, Audrey Garber, Arielle Juberg, and Patrick Moroney for research assistance. Revisions to this chapter, and work on the entire book, were supported by the Alexander von Humboldt Foundation.
2. It would have to be explained *why* the United States – but not other countries – requires a unique epistemology.
3. Most American reservations specify that the relevant treaties be interpreted in a way consistent with the US Constitution; I return to this theme below.
4. The authors did not examine legal isolationism, but American jurists have been citing foreign and international law for over 200 years.
5. Virginia's "Cavaliers" also saw themselves as "a peculiar people, marked as chosen by the hand of God" (cf. Miller 1956b, 115; John Rolfe, in Bellah 1975, 40). If we have difficulty seeing divine purposes in their venality and slave-trading, the Cavaliers did not; Miller 1956b, 99–140.
6. Some scholars attribute American unwillingness to submit to international laws, treaties, and regimes to a peculiar devotion to popular sovereignty (e.g. Rabkin 1998; Spiro 2000; Ignatieff 2002). Many democratic countries, however, regard popular sovereignty as the appropriate standard of legitimacy but are less hostile to supranational authority than Americans. American reluctance reflects the imperative of using liberty, as expressed through popular sovereignty, to fulfill the nation's Providential purposes. Subordinating popular sovereignty to outside authority jeopardizes this aim – hence America's reluctance to ratify even treaties that clearly reflect its values.
7. For examples see Bellah 1975, Bailyn 1992.
8. In four polls conducted between 1981 and 1990, between 79 and 81 percent of respondents agreed that America has a "special role to play in the world today" (data from the iPOLL Databank provided by the Roper Center for Public Opinion Research, University of Connecticut). Unfortunately, no similar data are available for other decades. This evidence, while hardly conclusive, supports the plausibility of my claim.
9. The implied contrast here is with a European view that regards international politics as a chess match, diplomacy as moves in a great game.

10. One can find this position untenable, even ridiculous, without denying that it might be sincerely held and is logically coherent.
11. James Der Derian (2003, 448, n. 11) attributes this turn of phrase to Thomas Risse.
12. Hobsbawm coined the term "the long 19th century" (1789–1914) to highlight that conventional periodization schemes are often arbitrary and potentially misleading and to show the value of alternate schemes emphasizing continuity and change; Hobsbawm 1989, 1996.

5

Continuity and Change in the Russian Federation's Human Rights Policies in the Fight against Terror

Lauri Mälksoo

The question whether the terrorist attacks of 9/11 had any impact on human rights policies in the Russian Federation reminds me of an anecdote in which representatives of three different European nations were asked to write a book about the elephant.[1] Predictably for this kind of an anecdote, the French representative wrote her book about the love life of the elephant. The German titled her heavy volume "Introduction to the Metaphysics of Elephants. Part I." Finally, the Finn came up with the volume "What does the elephant think about us Finns?"

The joke is about the exaggerated humbleness of small nations who are quite concerned about whether their very existence gets noticed or not. Big nations, in contrast, tend to universalize whatever happens to them and take their own historical importance for granted, even exaggeratedly so. In this sense, there is a certain self-centeredness in the very question "How did something that happened to the US influence anybody else?" The presumption is that 9/11 must have turned things elsewhere, maybe everywhere, upside down. It is suggested that 9/11 did not happen just to the United States, it somehow happened to everyone else too. However, horrible acts of mass violence have happened elsewhere both before and after 9/11. Arundhati Roy has justifiably asked why acts of war or terror outside the West, while not with fewer victims than 9/11, have generated so much less attention and outrage (Roy 2001, 219).

Nevertheless, it makes sense to ask the indicated question – How did the aftermath of 9/11 influence policies elsewhere? To continue with the same metaphor of the elephant, the element of state practice in customary international law has sometimes been compared to a road in the jungle. If a small animal steps aside from the well-established road, he is unlikely to produce a new rule and his steps may be easily condemned as a violation of an existing rule. However, if the biggest animal in the jungle – for example, elephant – decides to make steps in a new direction, it will be more challenging to qualify it a "violation." Chances are that the groundbreaking steps the elephant took may even be interpreted as a basis of the new rule and practice. In this sense it certainly makes sense to study how whatever happens to the biggest player affects anyone else.

The present chapter is divided in four substantive sections. First, I will outline the historical context and compare the differences between Russia and the West before making any points on post-9/11 times and possible shifts in the human rights regime. Second, I will look at the history of and experiences with terrorism in Russia. Third, I will investigate what has changed in respect to human rights in Russia after 9/11. This includes an analysis of international reactions and a survey of some of Russia's judicial leaders' recent pronouncements on human rights in the time of terror. Fourth, I will appraise the jurisprudence of the European Court of Human Rights regarding the Russian Federation. Finally, I will conclude and present my final arguments about the aftermath of 9/11 in Russia.

Russia, the United States and the West: comparisons on terror and beyond

When Alexis de Tocqueville (1805–59) published his "Democracy in America" in 1835, he predicted a big future for both outlier states of the European civilization, the United States and Russia. Yet he simultaneously pointed out important differences between the two countries and even concluded that while in the United States the individual action was based on "liberty," in Russia it was based on "slavery" (Tocqueville 2003). Following these points, many thinkers have emphasized historical differences between the two countries (Krashennikova 2007). It is important to mention some of these differences between Russia and both the West in general and the United States in particular, before we turn to our times.

One difference lies in geography. Historians point out that one reason why Russia has historically felt compelled to expand territorially so much is because it has few "natural" borders (Pipes 1997; Lieven 2000). In the geopolitical literature of the 20th century, much ink was spent on theorizing about antagonism between the sea empire (Britain; the United States) vs the land empire (Russia). The argument was that flexible sea empires preferred trade and indirect control while land empires employed more direct territorial control and conquest.

Irina Suponitskaya has recently compared the history of Russia and the United States and emphasized that quite different value systems have developed in both countries. While the ultimate ideal of the United States has been liberty, Russia has prioritized equality (Suponitskaya 2010). Ideas such as rule of law, private property, and individual rights remained historically alien or at least underdeveloped in Russia (Lukasheva 2009, 18 and 206). One way or another, both the Tsarist and Soviet governments were systematically repressive toward their own "subjects" and citizens. In Stalin's period the internal repressions were so intense that the historian Robert Conquest has use the metaphor of the "Great Terror" to characterize what was going on in the 1930s (Conquest 1990).

In some ways, Soviet Russia only imitated the discourse of rights as it was practiced in the West. On the face of it, Stalin's constitution of 1936 was the most democratic and human rights-oriented text in the whole world. However, state practice highlighted a perennial problem in the Russian history – what President Medvedev has in our time picked on as "legal nihilism." Text and reality were two different things. Text was there as societal ideal, for the image or sometimes even as mockery; real life went on *po poniatiam* (in accordance with unwritten rules) such as knowing one's place in the hierarchy and not daring to question the power of individuals above you.

In any case, internationally the USSR had an ambivalent attitude toward the whole program of international human rights law. The country abstained its vote when the General Assembly adopted the Universal Declaration of Human Rights in 1948. The Soviet leaders felt more animated when the rhetorique of human rights – especially social and economic rights – enabled them to ideologically attack the West.

It took the USSR a long time to recognize that human rights were not entirely within the domestic jurisdiction of the given sovereign nation. Arguably, the symbolic "recognition of human rights in exchange of the inviolability of existing borders" in the Helsinki Final Act of the Conference on Security and Co-operation in Europe in 1975 helped to let the genie of human rights in Russia out of the bottle (Thomas 2001). In any case, leading dissidents such as Andrei Sakharov (1921–89) extensively relied on human rights documents – the Universal Declaration of Human Rights of 1948 and the Helsinki Final Act of 1975 (Lourie 2002).

Thus, what we have had since the collapse of the USSR in 1991 essentially is historically the most far-reaching attempt to modernize Russia in Western terms, to introduce the rule of law, democracy, and human and constitutional rights into Russia's social and political fabric. There have been a few other liberal progressive moments in Russia's history – for example, reforms carried out by Tsar Alexander II (1818–81) or reform plans of former Prime Minister Petr Stolypin (1862–1911). However, for some reason, the liberal rights-oriented program always came to a halt and even turned into resistance. The record of introducing rights in Russia's life has been shaky and ambivalent at best and no "end of history" has been in sight in this sense.

However, once again, it is important to emphasize that the post-Soviet attempt to create a rights-based society is the most far-reaching one in Russia's history. The main symbols of this semantic turn are, first, the liberal (albeit strongly presidential) Constitution of the Russian Federation of 1993, second, the country's ratification of the European Convention on Human Rights (ECHR) in 1998 and third (so far only partly successful), the attempt to create an independent and meaningful Constitutional Court (see Trochev 2008; Nußberger et al. 2009).

This background makes Russia's historical trajectory profoundly different from that of the United States in particular and most of the West in general. Why has the debate about human and constitutional rights in the time of terror been so intense in the West (see for example, Wittes 2008)? It is because people have grown historically accustomed to live with rights and feel uncomfortable when their own rights or the rights of co-citizens get restricted in the light of new policies and/or necessities. The debate on the exact criteria of when and how to restrict such rights – for instance the question of what exactly constitutes torture – is central to systems based on the rule of law and civil rights. The "war on terror" and some policies adopted by the United States have been confronted with so much criticism by important segments of the US society and other liberal democracies because these policies have triggered the uneasy feeling that, in terms of rights, liberal democracies would fall back into a darker age.

In contrast, when the fight against terror emerged in Russia in the 1990s, the culture of human rights was weak to start with. There had been no "golden age of rights" that Russian society could refer back to. Since the Russian state had always been repressive toward its citizens, what was the big deal if it continued to be the same yet again, especially against the terrorists who had turned against the majority of society? When talking about breaks and continuities in Russia, the threat of terror that emerged in the 1990s offered a great justification to those who preferred to conduct state business as usual (even though some of the same people may have actually contributed to political conditions feeding terror).

The experience of terrorism in Russia

Some introductory words should also be said on the history of terror in Russia. In a way, Tsarist Russia was the very birthplace of modern terror. Lenin's brother Alexander was a political terrorist. In the context of the 19th century Tsarist repressions, it was sometimes unclear to the progressive parts of the society whether terrorists – such as Vera Zasulich (1849–1919), for example – represented the evil cause, as the government insisted, or were (maybe simultaneously) legitimately fighting Tsarist injustices.

During the *Pax Sovietica*, there was very little of "terror" in terms of bomb-blasts, kidnappings, etc. However, Soviet history is filled with incidents of repression of whole peoples, especially at the geographical margins of the former Russian Empire (see for example, Mälksoo 2001). Again, it was Stalin's regime that punished, besides many Russians, whole minority nationalities for not being loyal to the Soviet imperial project. This repression by the Soviet state occasionally triggered guerrilla ("bandit") tactics in the Baltic republics, the Ukraine, and Caucasus.

In order to understand the nature of terror that emerged in the post-Communist Russia of the 1990s, we may go back to the geopolitical distinction between sea and land empires. Why did 9/11 hit the United States as such a shock and horrible surprise? It was partly because the United States, being a "sea empire," had mostly managed to keep war and violence outside its borders. The United States had created a different kind of internal coherence, mostly through commerce, prosperity, democratic institutions, and identity. Many people in the Muslim world blamed and continue to blame the United States for its bias and responsibility in the Israeli-Arab conflict but no one could argue that the United States exercised a direct territorial control in Israel and/or Palestine. The historical struggle over who owned the Holy Land – and the terror – took place outside the borders of the United States. In contrast, Russia having historically developed as land empire had conquered vast adjacent territories populated with peoples with separate identities. Such peoples started to reject what they perceived as unjustified dominance by the imperial centre. When they did not get what they wanted – full self-determination or more of it – they sometimes turned to violence.

In the Russian Federation of the 1990s, the problem of separatism/ethnonationalism became linked with the problem of terror. In the mid-1990s and after the Khasavyurt accord of August 30, 1996 between the Chechens and the Russians, there was a window of opportunity in which it might have been possible for the secessionist situation in Chechnya to be resolved without further violence. There was a chance that the independent Chechnen state would emerge along the lines of former Soviet republics that already had separated from Russia in 1991, as a *fait accompli*. One of the reasons why this scenario did not materialize was because the Chechens were unable to successfully construct and consolidate their statehood along the lines of ethnonationalism – like the Baltic republics had done, for example. Instead, the alternative idea of a religious state, "Caucasian kalifate," emerged. If ever there was a theoretical chance that Russia would have recognized the Chechen independence constructed along ethno-nationalist – "European" – lines, the idea of secession based on Islamic fundamentalist ideas would have turned the post-Soviet Russia – a multinational and multi-confessional state – upside down and proved unacceptable even for the weak Russia. The prospect was already demonstrated by radical Chechen warlords such as Shamil Basayev (1965–2006) who resorted to forms and methods of warfare that terrorized civilian population outside Chechnya.

In December 1999, Prime Minister Vladimir Putin started the Second Chechen Campaign to reconquer the separatist region. Unclarified terrorist bombings that were carried out in September 1999 in Moscow and provincial towns of Buinaksk and Volgodonsk served as *casus belli* for the newly installed Putin's government. Thus, in the Russian mind, the issue of "terrorism" became closely interlinked with the problem of Chechnya/North Caucasus as such.

As soon they became known, the Russian Federal forces systematically violated fundamental rules of treaty and customary international law applicable to domestic armed conflicts during the Second Chechen Campaign (see further Gilligan 2010). The combined international humanitarian and human rights law included the distinction between combatants and civilians, the principle of proportionality, prohibition of torture, and "disappearances," etc. Of course, the guerrilla methods used by the Chechen *boeviki* often encouraged these kinds of violations by the federal forces. However, what was politically most problematic was the insistence of the Russian government that whatever was going on in Chechnya was a mere "fight against terrorism." Most of the governments in the West disagreed: the problem of Chechnya could not be reduced to a problem of "terrorism" only, even though that problem was part of it too. Not all Chechen *boeviki* were necessarily "terrorists" – unless the term lost any colloquial meaning. (Of course, for lawyers, the problem with the word "terrorism" is that there still is no legally binding universal definition. However, most analysts tend to think about terrorism as something they "know it when they see it.")

The successful subjugation of Chechnya by the Russian federal forces during the Second Chechen campaign in 1999–2000 did not liquidate the problem of terrorism in the Caucasus region. On the contrary, in some sense, it intensified the problem further – but probably that was the price the Russian government was silently willing to pay for the sake of an arguably even higher historical cause, the preservation of the territorial integrity of the Russian Federation. After the violence of the Second Chechen campaign, Russia *really* found out what terrorism was like. In October 2002, the Moscow Nord-Ost theatre hostage crisis occurred, and in September 2004, the Beslan hostage crisis occurred, both with several hundreds of victims, in the second case predominantly schoolchildren. Five years after Beslan, when Chechnya looked relatively pacified under President Ramzan Kadyrov – a former *boevik* himself – violence and acts of terror had spread from Chechnya to the neighboring Russian Caucasus republics Dagestan and Ingushetia. The two suicide bombings in Moscow in March 2010 were – according to government information – carried out by "black widows" from Dagestan.

The initial Western/international response to the Second Chechen campaign (1999–2000) was negative and condemning. The relationship between the NATO member states and the Russian Federation had already deteriorated considerably when NATO forces bombed Yugoslavia in March 1999 to stop the persecution of Kosovo Albanians by the government of Slobodan Milosevič. In that conflict, Russia vehemently protested against the "aggression" against Yugoslavia and violation of its own procedural rights as Security Council member under the UN Charter. In 2001, it seemed that the West and the Russian Federation were in terms of normative values almost as far from each other as in the time of the Cold War. Then 9/11 happened. As became known through the international media, the President of the Russian Federation, Mr Vladimir Putin, was the first foreign leader to make the support call to the US President George W. Bush after the 9/11 attacks (CNN 10.09.2002). In the next section, I will investigate whether 9/11 had any impact on human rights policies and attitudes in and regarding the Russian Federation.

The impact of 9/11 and its aftermath on human rights policies in Russia

One of the competitive sports that 9/11 triggered among commentators was the rush to answer the question of what would be "Russia's 9/11."

Quite different suggestions have been made – from the terrorist attack on the school in Beslan to the "orange revolution" in the Ukraine (Ivan Krastev). If we, however, take seriously Mr Putin's words that the collapse of the USSR was "the greatest geopolitical catastrophy of the 20th century," we will understand how deeply the Russian political elite felt affected by Moscow having lost significant parts of its Empire in 1991. But even so, the loss of the "independent" Soviet republics was one thing; starting to lose parts of the Russian Federation itself was another. That became the ultimate red line. Thus, I would argue that if ever there was a Russian equivalent to 9/11, it had taken place already before 9/11, and it was the (almost) successful war of secession in Chechnya.

One issue that has animated scholars since 9/11 is whether the United States in particular and the West in general subsequently "traded" Chechnya against Russian support in the war against terror. Emma Gilligan in her book entitled *Terror in Chechnya* asks whether 9/11 and subsequent steps taken by the United States and coalitions led by it such as wars in Afghanistan and Iraq weakened international criticism on human rights in Chechnya (Gilligan 2010, 165).

One of the international bodies where a noticeable shift in opinion took place was the UN Commission on Human Rights. (In 2006, this body was reformed and now bears the name of Human Rights Council.) The UN High Commissioner for Human Rights, Mary Robinson, vigorously pointed out Russia's massive human rights violations in Chechnya. In response to her report, the UN Commission on Human Rights initiated its first formal reproach of a permanent member of the Security Council in its criticism of Russia. The 2000 and 2001 UN Commission on Human Rights resolutions initiated by the EU expressed alarm at the indiscriminate and disproportionate violence of the Russian armed forces and called for a national-based and independent commission of inquiry (Gilligan 2010, 166–7). The 2000 resolution at the Commission on Human Rights was passed with 27 votes for, seven against, and 19 abstentions; and the 2001 resolution with 22 votes for, 12 against, and 19 abstentions. Gilligan further observes

> The resolutions on Chechnya drew to a sudden halt in the aftermath of the September 11 attacks on the United States and a change in one-third of the seats on the commission ... The EU's third resolution on Chechnya was rejected by a vote of 15–16–22. Exploiting the anxiety that emerged after September 11, the Russian Federation networked heavily before the final vote, urging "all those who were against terrorism in all its forms, those who were against armed separatism,

those who did not accept politicization and double standards of the Commission, to vote against this resolution." (Gilligan 2010, 167)

In 2003, the EU resolution on Chechnya was dropped for a second time in the UN Commission on Human Rights and subsequently the topic disappeared from the radar of the over-politicized body.

Shifts in bodies such as the UN Commission on Human Rights can be partly explained by the new broad antiterror alliance that was formed under the leadership of the United States in the UN Security Council. Along with major powers from the EU, the Russian Federation supported far-reaching post-9/11 antiterror measures proposed mostly by the United States.

In the Council of Europe, Russia's voting rights were suspended in April 2000; however, an attempt to completely suspend Russia's membership failed. Russia's voting rights in the Parliamentary Assembly of the Council of Europe (PACE) were restored in January 2001. Thus, in this body one cannot establish a direct link with 9/11.

As far as the United States and 9/11 are concerned, Emma Gilligan made some further pertinent observations. She argued that Russia

...won the propaganda war in Europe and the United States over Chechnya after the September 11 attacks, and, whether or not European and U.S. diplomats, politicians, or the political elite were fully convinced that Russia was fighting international terrorism in Chechnya on a magnitude similar to that which the United States was engaged in, this rationale proved a convenient escape route to sublimate the disturbing stories that continued to come out of the region. (Gilligan 2010, 178)

Gilligan further observes that "the post-September 11 alliance that emerged between the United States and Russia did, however, mark a sudden, if temporary, decline in the number of open critiques on the situation in Chechnya" (Gilligan 2010, 178). Bill Bowring came to an essentially similar conclusion regarding the United Kingdom which, in his words, "has played a questionable role in apparently assisting President Putin to deflect international condemnation of his actions in Chechnya, especially after 11 September 2001" (Bowring 2008, 81).

Facts indicate that Gilligan's observations on the Western shift of mind on Chechnya are largely correct. Criticism on Chechnya weakened after 9/11; the West became more understanding about Russia's position and concerns. The picture that Gilligan provided on the Western change of heart toward Russia's practices should be supplemented by looking at the Russian discourse on human rights and the fight against terror. Was the new opportunity that 9/11 provided for Russia picked up? We could first consult the views of Valery Zorkin, head of the Constitutional Court of the Russian Federation. He has recently published a book on human rights and constitutionalism in Russia (Zorkin 2008). Among other points, Zorkin elaborated on what Russia's lessons in the post-9/11 world might be:

> After the 11th September 2001 laws were adopted in the US and in a number of European countries that contain substantive limitations of the rights and freedoms of citizens in the carrying out of anti-terrorist measures. This concerns the eavesdropping of phone calls, limitations to the banking secret, and creation of information systems for collecting personal data. As such, the adoption of such laws does not, of course, threaten the constitutional foundations of these countries. Apparently, this is a completely adequate reaction to the ever-growing expressions of terrorism.
>
> Another question is: until where may one go with the limitation of constitutional rights? Very different recipes have been suggested. Even an idiosyncratic ideology of the refusal of basic rights has been formulated. For example, in the US, in the book of Alan Dershowitz, former human rights defender, entitled "Why Terrorism Works?" has been published. In this book, the author makes a call to use collective punishment to the families, ethnic and confessional groups of terrorists; use any kind of torture; considerably limit immigration and rights of foreigners, especially coming from specific regions of the world, etc.
>
> These kinds of views are more and more spread also in other countries, including in Russia. And not only among scholars but also among politicians to whom big groups of voters gave their votes.
>
> May specialists in the field of constitutional law ignore such tendencies? Where is the point where restricting certain rights means denying these rights? In the name of what and by whom would such restrictions be made? ... The legal solutions that the contemporary fight against terrorism demands cannot be found in existing legal constructions. This concerns especially these situations that relate to the question of the limitation of human rights. (Zorkin 2008, 90–1)

In this lengthy quotation of Judge Zorkin, post-9/11 developments in the United States serve as a useful model. Compared to radical suggestions made by Alan Dershowitz, any policy shift that Russia may or may not adopt would look pale. No longer being at the forefront of action and attention, Russia was now merely "learning" from far-reaching practices and ideas of others (former criticizers of Russia). However, there is no mention in Judge Zorkin's presentation that such antiterror developments in the West have also been encountered with massive protests and doubts in the general public, nongovernmental sector, or judicial institutions (including the US Supreme Court).

In the end, political philosophies are applied in concrete cases. Judge Zorkin mentions the judgment of the Constitutional Court No 8-П of June 28, 2007, concerning the complaint of Mr Guziev and Ms Karmova regarding the violation of their constitutional rights and freedoms by Article 14 paragraph 1 of the Federal Act on Burials (January 12, 1996). The law provided that terrorists who lose their lives in terrorist attacks would be buried in the way that neither their relatives nor the public generally would know about the location of their graves. The Constitutional Court upheld the constitutionality of this law arguing that it helps to diminish the negative psychological impact caused by the terrorist act to the victims and population at large. According to Judge Zorkin, burying the terrorist in the vicinity of his or her victims "might serve as propaganda of the idea of terror." On the other hand, such ceremonies would hurt the feelings of the relatives of the victims of the terrorist act and are capable to spread ethnic and religious hatred (Zorkin 2008, 91–8).

Judge Zorkin also writes that due to threats such as terrorism people should have an understanding for the restrictions of their rights in the criminal procedure. According to him, working against such threats is "objectively impossible if the police and special services cannot the use a broad range of special means and methods that are situated beyond the usual framework of criminal procedure and that usually have a secret character. Many of these means and methods restrict constitutional rights and freedoms of individuals and citizens, but without their use the fight against criminal phenomena, especially their gravest forms, would lose their effectiveness" (Zorkin 2008, 99).

In the Western constitutional tradition, there is usually a tangible tension between the executive and the judiciary. In the case of the post-9/11 "war on terror" in the United States, it grew into a prolonged legal confrontation between the White House and the Supreme Court (Wittes 2008). However, Judge Zorkin's comments and arguments demonstrate a rather smooth coexistence with the Kremlin and the lack of an open human rights policy debate *between* the constitutional organs since the presidency of Vladimir Putin. The role of the Constitutional Court does not seem to be to challenge the historically over-powerful executive (and by doing so perhaps undermine its "authority") but rather to find legal arguments and provide additional legitimacy for the decisions the executive has already made (see also Mommsen and Nußberger 2007, 20). The Constitutional Court did not find it problematic when, in February 2005, President Putin canceled direct elections for governor in 89 regions of Russia partly using the threat of terrorism as an excuse (Osiatyński 2009, 50).

On April 19, 2010, the Constitutional Court upheld the constitutionality of an amendment made to the Code of Criminal Procedure in 2008 according to which individuals accused of the crime of terrorism were not given the right to jury trial. Only two judges of the Constitutional Court wrote dissenting opinions (Pushkarskaya 2010).

In addition to Judge Zorkin's views, we could also consult a recent book written by Vladimir Ustinov who was the Head State Prosecutor from 2000 to 2006 and the Minister of Justice of the Russian Federation from 2006 to 2008 (Ustinov 2008). This book is specifically dedicated to legal issues concerning terrorism.

Mr Ustinov has carefully studied the antiterrorist legislation and practices in the West, both before and after 9/11. His analysis relies on the experiences of the West, presenting them in the form of "lessons learned" for the Russian Federation. A few passages will sum up the main emphases in the thinking of Mr Ustinov:

> It is evident that in the fight against terrorism even more liberal states often use not only tough measures but also measures that are questionable from the point of view of international standards. It would not hurt to remember this fact in Russia that... constantly looks at the West, being afraid to make any wrong step and with this to trigger dissatisfaction of the foreign teachers-democrats. (Ustinov 2008, 116)

> ...it is not correct to suggest that counter-terrorist activity should be subordinated to abstract-global human rights, under which for some reason usually are understood the rights of the terrorists but not their victims. (Ustinov 2008, 174)

Mr Ustinov also claimed that international governmental and non-governmental organizations often conduct spying missions when officially proclaiming their exclusive concern for human rights:

> It makes sense to learn from the experience of the US that for a long period did not let representatives of influential international organizations (Red Cross Committee, European Commission, etc.) to the territory of the military base in Guantanamo where Taliban prisoners

of war were kept. This is even more appropriate in Russia because the latter has legal reasons for that – as a rule, guaranteeing security to the representatives of different international organizations implies considerable financial expenditures. (Ustinov 2008, 74)

Furthermore, Mr Ustinov quite enthusiastically and supportively recounted how the United States and the Western European governments have restricted individual freedoms and intend to do so even further in the future (Ustinov 2008, 115). However, his reading of the restrictions of civil rights remains critical. Ustinov pointed out an inclination toward "double standards" in the United States:

A consequence of the September terrorist acts was the restriction of the rights and freedoms of the citizens in the US. Its legitimacy was not questioned by the society or the majority of the politicians since in danger was state security but that means the security of every citizen. Right to life comes first, the right of the state and its citizens. Everything else is secondary. By the way, the discussion is not about "general human rights." There are only rights of the US citizens. With respect to the rest, a substantive restriction of the rights and freedoms guaranteed in the Constitution is possible... In this context it is legitimate the question why the US and its partners in the NATO until recently defended the rights of Chechen fighters who, on the one hand do not consider themselves to be citizens of Russia and on the other hand do not recognize the rights of other persons including civilians in Chechnya and its neighboring republics? (Ustinov 2008, 176–7)

One of the merits of the account of Mr Ustinov is that there are no euphemisms. The author did not conduct rhetorical balancing acts but simply told the Russian readers what he really thought. For example, Ustinov agreed with the President of the Society of Veterans of the Antiterror unit, "Alpha," Mr Goncharov:

The first task of the state is to maintain the system of human rights as a whole and in this connection life, health, freedom and property of the citizens. It is only the second task to make sure that in each concrete situation the restriction of concrete rights is minimal. And the state is not obliged to "tremble" in front of imaginary "rights" of the terrorist since the terrorist, both according to his own opinion and as a consequence of his activities leaves the social contract with the state regarding the protection of his rights. (Ustinov 2008, 198)

Finally, Mr Ustinov once again proved that, in terms of "lessons learned," it is particularly the model of the United States after 9/11 that he kept in mind for the Russian Federation. This experience tells Russia that, if required by the interests of the state, certain norms of international law can be violated vis-à-vis the terrorists who conduct asymmetrical warfare:

The experience of the US demonstrates that the state which is under the attack of terrorists ... may consider the guarantees and possibilities of the peaceful resolution of the situation that are foreseen in international law, insufficient and inadequate with respect to criminals – terrorists and their aids. This is the more so since terrorists, as a rule, do not recognize any legal or moral limitations. (Ustinov 2008, 202)

One can only add that the scholarly commentary in Russia seems to largely follow and mirror these positions that in essence hold that human rights should take a step back in the fight against terror. One specific phenomenon in the Russian literature on terrorism and human rights is a certain great power jealousy: how come the world still somehow seems to tolerate the wrong the United States has done after 9/11 but Russia has been harshly criticized for its activities in Chechnya? This is the leitmotif of the talk of "double standards." For example, in a book dedicated to the topic of secret prisons of the CIA, the authors wonder why the PACE has been so critical of the Russian policies in Chechnya while at the same time demonstrating a "high degree of tolerance" toward human rights violations conducted in the CIA's secret prisons in Europe (Bykova and Stepanov 2007, 90).

Another phenomenon that one can observe in at least some of Russia's special literature is the eagerness to treat the problems of terrorism, separatism, and extremism in the same breath as parts of the same problem. This must again be the result of the painful experience with Chechnya. For example, the collective of authors led by the political scientist A. V. Voz'zhenikov devote a book to the phenomenon of terrorism, but the book ends with a chapter on separatism: "Counteracting to the separatism in Russia – an important direction in the fight against terrorism" (Voz'zhenikov 2006, 442). This approach creates the impression that any distinct ethnic group of Russian citizens who might propose separating from the Russian Federation would also be suspect of the crime of terrorism. However, while most terrorists in the Russian context may have been separatists as well, many separatists, even those who took up the fight against federal forces, were not automatically "terrorists."

Finally, a few words must be added on legislative changes concerning terrorism in the Russian Federation. The initial law regulating counter-terrorist activities was the Federal Act of July 25, 1998 No 130-F3 "The Suppression of Terrorism Act." On March 6, 2006, the new Federal Act No 35-F3 "About Counter-terrorist Activities," replacing the 1998 Act, was adopted.

The ideologically most significant Article of the March 6, 2006 Federal Act "About Counter-terrorist Activities" is Article 2, which addresses the fundamental principles of counterterrorist activity in Russia. What is new in the Act is the first principle underlying counterterrorist activities in the country: securing and protecting fundamental human and citizens' rights and freedoms. Recently an authoritative legal commentary on that Federal Act has been published (introduced both by Nikolai Patrushev, director of FSB, and Vladimir Lukin, the human rights commissioner (ombudsman) of the Russian Federation). The commentary argues that the fact that the Act starts with the protection of human rights testifies that the legislature now pays more attention to securing human rights and freedoms in the state's counterterrorist activities (Trunov 2007, 35). However, at the same time, Article 2 para. 3 of the same Act lays out that "priority will be given to the rights and interests of individuals who are endangered by terrorism." As I argued above, sometimes legal texts in Russia refer to human rights for the reasons of image and because the West normatively expects it. In practice, words may be there not only to express but also to hide ideas and cover up practices. In any case, politically the adoption of the new version of the antiterrrorism act in 2006 was triggered both by European pressure to make sure that human rights were not left aside and also because of the need to fight terror more efficiently.

The relationship to the European Court of Human Rights and its regime

The conclusion so far is that 9/11 indeed changed certain aspects about human rights practices and policies in and regarding the Russian Federation. In terms of international criticism, the United States over-reactions in the war against terror led global attention elsewhere and somewhat leveled the moral standing between the West and Russia.

Now everyone's hands were quite full if not occasionally dirty. In terms of its domestic policies and attitudes, the Russian elite could usefully refer to the "Western origin" of the idea that human rights were not meant to slow down the fight against terror.

Although these setbacks from the point of view of human rights were rather noteworthy, they did not necessarily mark permanent shifts in attitudes and policies. No fundamental breaks in the human rights regime can be observed. For the Russian Federation, the human rights regime was largely determined by its participation in the European Court of Human Rights and generally in the Council of Europe.

Some shocking events in recent history – such as the 9/11 terrorist attacks in the United States – may cause huge waves for the country concerned and other countries but are unlikely to entirely change the already chosen path of participants in the international community. A good example would be Russia's participation in the European Court of Human Rights system. Russia's ratification of the ECHR took place in 1998, that is, even before NATO's Kosovo intervention of 1999 and before September 11, 2001. The entry of Russia in the Council of Europe system took place before the Second Chechen campaign and before President Yeltsin had handed over the power to his chosen successor, Prime Minister Vladimir Putin. Had Russia not made this important step in 1998, it would probably have been harder to make in subsequent years.

As far as condemnation of Russia's human rights violations is concerned, the weakening of international standards cannot be observed in the European Court of Human Rights (ECtHR) after 9/11. On the contrary, the "Chechen cases" at the ECtHR have already become classics for their clarity and toughness and the reason that the ECtHR is essentially the only international body which has held Russia accountable (see Gilligan 2010 and Bowring 2008, 69 ff). Rather than weakening the ECtHR's usual standards, one may even speculate whether 9/11 and the US overreaction after the terrorist attacks may not have indirectly led to the judicial consolidation at the ECtHR. By becoming a member of the ECtHR system, Russia and the rest of Europe started to share the Herculean task of improving the human rights record in post-Soviet Russia. The Council of Europe system also constituted at least one dimension where Russia was "together" with Europe – in contrast to security matters where the United States was via NATO in the same boat with the rest of Europe, leaving Russia outside. The more the Bush Administration was criticized by Western countries and governments for its human rights transgressions, the more Russia could find some symbolic and compensatory consolation in "being part of" Europe.

Notwithstanding official political optimism, it was not at all clear from the outset that the ECtHR would be able to efficiently continue its work with problematic new member states such as Russia, at the time. Occasionally, it seemed that the system would not resist built-in pressures such as the decision of the Russian government not to ratify Protocol 14 aiming to reform the ECtHR by simplifying its procedures. (Finally, Russia ratified Protocol 14 in January 2010.) It seemed sometimes like a little miracle that on the one hand the Court has been systematically very critical about Russia's human rights violations and yet on the other hand Russia, although often visibly irritated, continues to operate within the system. It is certainly special from a historical point of view, as before the ratification of the ECHR in 1998, Russia and its legal predecessor, the USSR, never recognized the jurisdiction of international courts over the country's domestic matters (see further Mälksoo 2008).

Some of the Russian cases at Strasbourg really look like cases of restorative or transitional justice – pronounced by "European others" but pronounced nevertheless. Russia's war in Chechnya has figured prominently on the docket of the Strasbourg court. Other cases concerning terrorism and antiterror measures of the government are emerging. In 2010 the ECtHR even accepted the jurisdiction over complaint by victims in the Dubrovka (Nord-Ost theatre) terrorist hostage-taking crisis where the way the government conducted its operations arguably amounted to human rights violations of hostages (Ivleva 2010).

Thus, the ECtHR not only retrospectively corrects some of Russia's gravest misbehavior in Chechnya but also has put the West's response on human rights violations in Russia back on track. The approach has rightly been to depoliticize the issue of human rights in Russia as much as possible and to frame human rights problems and violations in judicial, legalistic, and formalistic terms. It seems that, currently, the depoliticized and legalized language of human rights is the only type Russia would "take" from the rest of the world. Judicial activism regarding Russia can also be observed in other international courts – thus, Georgia initiated proceedings against Russia in 2008 at the International Court of Justice (ICJ), blaming the latter for racial discrimination of Georgians.

Conclusion

The survey of developments regarding human rights policies in the Russian Federation after 2001 offers a mixed picture. Let us start from negative aspects. The events of 9/11 and subsequent policies and exceptions created by the US-led Western coalition offered a much-needed pretext for the conservative state-centered political forces in Russia which did not want the discourse of human rights to intervene in the way they were accustomed to govern the population and conduct state affairs. These forces had never taken human rights too seriously but now they had a moment of special gratification: the "leader of the free world" did not seem to take human rights seriously either. Ergo, human rights talk was all a scam anyway (as they had always argued). Also, another parallel was usefully made: the United States denied human rights to the "others" such as "illegal combatants," "Muslim terrorists," etc. Why then was Russia not entitled to deprive human rights from individuals who, in a similarly hostile way, had defined themselves as "others" vis-à-vis the Russian state? The effects of this thinking have been felt on numerous occasions in domestic political and judicial developments in the Russian Federation.

On the other hand, where the Americans failed or were perceived to fail, the Europeans stepped in to fill the vacuum. Metaphorically speaking, the torch was passed on. After 1945, America taught human rights to Europe or at least reminded the Old Continent of the existence of human rights. Since 1998 when Russia ratified the ECHR, Russia has been struggling to learn respect for human rights with and from Europe. Coincidentally, the Strasbourg Court started to give "feedback" to Russia exactly in the post-9/11 period. Unfortunately, there have already been some setbacks in this process of human rights socialization of post-Yeltsin Russia. Nevertheless, Russia continues to hang on in the Strasbourg system and this looks like a promising sign. Russia will continue to offer an important test of credibility to an optimistic account on the role of international human rights treaties and mechanisms that was recently offered by Beth A. Simmons. Professor Simmons argued that:

> Treaties alter politics through the channel of social mobilization, where domestic actors have the motive and the means to form and to demand their effective implementation. In stable autocracies, citizens have the motive to mobilize but not the means. In stable democracies, they have the means but generally lack a motive. Where institutions are most fluid, however, the expected value of importing external political rights agreements is quite high. (Simmons 2009, 16)

Being now part of the Strasbourg system is perhaps the most important factor that restricts Russia from again becoming a "stable autocracy." At the same time, and to put it euphemistically, Russia has not moved much closer to the ideal of "stable democracy" in the past 10 years. More important may be the catalyzing role of the ECHR and ECtHR. Looking at shelves in Russia's better bookstores or articles in the few critical newspapers, one can see that the interest in and enthusiasm about the Strasbourg Court and its promise is fairly high (Nikitinski 2010). Whether these tendencies have produced positive fruits can be better assessed 10 years from now, when 20 years have passed since the 9/11 attacks, and the fight against terror has hopefully not become the world's daily routine.

Note

1. Research for this chapter has been supported by grants of the European Research Council and the Estonian Science Foundation (No 8087).

Part III

Change? Transatlantic Responses to 9/11

6

The High Price of American Exceptionalism: Comparing Torture by the United States and Europe after 9/11

Jamie Mayerfeld

Introduction

International human rights institutions make a difference.[1] Long before 9/11, European countries bound themselves to a strong transnational regime for the protection of human rights, whereas the United States rejected international supervision of its human rights practices. The divergence helps explain why the use of torture as a counterterrorist strategy following 9/11 met significantly greater resistance in Europe than the United States.

Both Europe and the US claim to honor the international legal prohibition of torture and ill-treatment. The difference is that Europe recognizes a broader, less flexible, and less ambiguous version of the prohibition, and buttresses it with a sturdier system of oversight and enforcement. This policy is anchored in a regional human rights regime that raises the common standard of acceptable behavior and empowers member states to exercise vigilance over each other through the medium of strong supranational institutions.

The United States, by contrast, has refused either to accept strong international oversight of its human rights commitments or to incorporate international human rights law into its domestic legal system. This decision not only made it easier for the Bush Administration to adopt a policy of torture, but has also facilitated the surplus cruelties of America's domestic criminal justice system, which share some features with the infamous abuses of Abu Ghraib and Guantánamo.

Transatlantic differences should not be overstated: Europe has not eliminated torture and abuse in its prisons and police stations; moreover, several of its officials colluded in the US torture regime. Nonetheless, the United States' embrace of torture after 9/11, like its official sanction of harsh criminal justice policies, puts it in a class apart. The Bush torture program – which the Obama Administration has partly but not entirely suspended, and which Obama or future presidents could resume with little difficulty – demonstrates the folly of American exceptionalism on human rights. It underscores deep structural defects in the American legal system that are systematically if imperfectly remedied in Europe. Post-9/11 developments remind us why countries should make the enforcement of human rights a collective enterprise, and not act as judges in their own case.

I do not claim that US marginalization of international human rights law is the sole cause of the torture policy, but instead that it is a significant contributing factor. At work are various cultural, ideological, and political factors, along with the historical accident that brought certain people to power at a certain moment in time, and the way in which America's great power status encourages permissive attitudes about the use of violence. Marginalization of international human rights law accompanies and is nourished by other causes at the same time that it magnifies their impact. One explanation, however, must be discarded – the idea that, as the world's leading power with primary responsibility for maintaining global order in an age of terror, the United States is in some sense acting rationally or even appropriately when it resorts to the use of torture. Torture cannot be normalized, not even by calling it a "rational" response by great powers. Torture is irrational, because it is inhuman; it has no place in any normatively intelligible scheme of action. In any case, its effects in the "War on Terror" have been the opposite of those imputed by its apologists. By inflaming the enemy, deterring voluntary cooperation, and fabricating a pretext for the catastrophic Iraq War (statements extracted by torture were the main basis for a claimed link between Saddam Hussein and Al-Qaeda), it has made the United States and the world more vulnerable to terrorist attack.[2] In the words of the US Senate Armed Services Committee (2008), "the abuse of detainees in U.S. custody ... damaged our ability to collect accurate intelligence that could save lives, strengthened the hand of our enemies, and compromised our moral authority."

Europe and America's contrasting approaches to international human rights law

Global human rights treaties and customary international human rights and humanitarian law receive a warmer embrace in Europe than in the United States (with Russia and Belarus among the notable exceptions). But the principal manifestation of European commitment to international human rights is the development over the past 60 years of a regional system of rights protections that has profoundly shaped national policy in all but the most recalcitrant states. In 1950, the 13 original members of the Council of Europe approved the first human rights treaty in history. Now binding on 47 countries, the European Convention on Human Rights (ECHR) has developed a powerful implementation regime jointly overseen by the Committee of Ministers and Parliamentary Assembly of the Council of Europe, along with the European Court of Human Rights, located in Strasbourg. Currently the Court hears over 1,000 cases each year, almost all brought by individual plaintiffs, though states can also submit complaints against each other.[3] In the 90 percent of cases where the Court rules that a violation has occurred, the Committee of Ministers takes responsibility for ensuring that the violating states pay the ordered restitution and terminate the violation. To date, all fines have been paid, and most though not all states seek to adjust their policies to comply with the Court's rulings.

In addition, the ECHR has inspired the adoption of over 200 additional human rights treaties by its parent body, the Council of Europe, as well as the creation of new Council of Europe institutions dedicated to promoting human rights. Its provisions are reinforced by the human rights principles and programs of the European Union (EU) and Organization of Security and Cooperation in Europe (OSCE). Admission into the EU and the North Atlantic Treaty Organization (NATO), and to a lesser extent the Council of Europe itself, is now made contingent on a demonstrated commitment to human rights – a practice that enhances the clout of the Convention and its Court. In view of the mutually reinforcing contributions of Europe's regional organizations to human rights, alongside the strong commitment of several European countries to the domestic and multilateral promotion of human rights, and the rise of a powerful regional network of human rights NGOs, we can now speak of the protection of human rights in Europe as a collective project, one that has fostered a culture of respect for rights and freedoms across the region.

At the same time that Europe was laying the foundation for a transnational human rights regime, the United States was moving in the opposite direction. In the years immediately following the Second World War, its general policy was to support the creation of new global human rights institutions while preventing them from acquiring too much power (Anderson 2003). The ambivalence of the late 1940s gave way to steady resistance in the 1950s, as Southern segregationists, nativist Republicans, and militant anticommunists joined forces against a common perceived threat. Fear of international human rights led Senator

John Bricker of Ohio to propose a constitutional amendment that would bar international treaties from having domestic legal effect unless implementing legislation was enacted. The amendment failed by one vote in the Senate, but only after President Eisenhower promised not to ratify any human rights treaties.

The "ghost of Senator Bricker" still haunts US policy (Henkin 1995). The Genocide Convention, opened for signature in 1948, was not ratified by the United States until 1988. The United States waited 26 years before ratifying the International Covenant on Civil and Political Rights (ICCPR), 25 years before ratifying the Convention on the Elimination of All Forms of Racial Discrimination (CERD), and ten years before ratifying the Convention against Torture and Other Cruel, Inhuman or Degrading Treatment or Punishment (Torture Convention). It still has not ratified the Inter-American Convention on Human Rights, the Rome Statute of the International Criminal Court (ICC), or major treaties on socioeconomic rights, children's rights, landmines, forced disappearances, and discrimination against women.

Even when it ratifies human rights treaties, the United States attaches "reservations" and "understandings" whose acknowledged purpose is the avoidance of obligations not already enshrined in US law (Mayerfeld 2007, 125–6). Ratification is also accompanied by "non-self-executing declarations" that bar US courts from enforcing the treaties' provisions. (Although no such declaration was attached to the United States' ratification of the 1949 Geneva Conventions, federal appeals courts have found their own reasons to declare the Conventions non-self-executing, and the Supreme Court has not ruled on the question.)

The "reservations, understandings, and declarations" sharply reduce the impact of human rights treaties on US policy and practice. They reflect a belief that the United States has no need of international human rights law because its own rights protections are sufficient. According to this belief, the purpose of US ratification is to encourage human rights improvements in *other* countries. Among Americans, belief in the sufficiency of US rights law is largely unquestioned. The view permeates not only popular culture and political rhetoric, but also scholarly and legal analyses of the United States' relation to international human rights.[4] Thus legal scholar John Rogers (1999, 208) writes: "The protective power of U.S. human rights law is enormous. It is perhaps what we treasure most about our Nation." United States government delegations to human rights treaty monitoring bodies take a similar stand. American officials assured the Human Rights Committee that "fundamental rights and freedoms protected by the [ICCPR] are already guaranteed as a matter of

U.S. law ... and can be effectively asserted and enforced by individuals in the judicial system on those bases."

The Bush Administration's embrace of torture should cast doubt on this view. That the United States' legal institutions permitted this most paradigmatic of human rights violations, coordinated from the highest centers of power and continued long after public exposure, suggests that American rights protections are not all they are cracked up to be. Whether the myth of America as a beacon of rights is dislodged by notorious facts to the contrary or proves impervious to them (as myths sometimes do) remains to be seen. (It is important to add that US involvement in torture predates 9/11, although the torture policy of the Bush Administration introduced a new and in many ways unprecedented chapter of the story. See Harbury 2005; McCoy 2006.)

United States and European torture compared

The story of the Bush torture program is well known.[5] On February 7, 2002, President Bush declared that members of Al-Qaeda and the Taliban were not legally entitled to humane treatment. In the summer of 2002 National Security Adviser Condoleezza Rice approved the CIA's use of so-called "enhanced interrogation" techniques, including water-boarding, sleep deprivation, stress positions, throwing prisoners headfirst into walls, and confinement in coffin-sized boxes. The policy was backed by secret memos prepared by the Office of Legal Counsel (OLC) in the Department of Justice that used a vanishingly narrow definition of torture to authorize the methods in question, postulated a series of blanket defenses that US officials could invoke if criminally charged with torture, and asserted that the president was constitutionally empowered to order torture despite legislation and treaties to the contrary if he deemed it necessary for national security (D. Cole 2009). The methods were used in CIA "black sites" abroad, while similar methods, backed by similar arguments, were approved by the Pentagon for use in Afghanistan, Guantánamo, Iraq, and even the United States. The United States also sent individuals to be tortured by foreign security forces under the so-called extraordinary rendition program. Hundreds if not thousands of people have been tortured under these policies, some of them for months or years at a time. Dozens of detainees have died in US custody as a result of torture or ill-treatment (Human Rights First 2008).

On assuming office, President Obama issued executive orders prohibiting "enhanced interrogation" methods, requiring the shutdown of all CIA detention facilities, and repudiating the Bush Administration interrogation memos. Yet he has blocked important measures that would provide justice for the victims of torture and deter the future use of torture. He has opposed the creation of a truth commission and voiced resistance to prosecutions (Mayer 2009). A "preliminary review" ordered by the Department of Justice in August 2009 to determine whether criminal investigation was warranted into US interrogation practices appeared to exempt all those who acted within the notoriously permissive guidelines set by the Bush-era OLC. Ill-treatment at Guantánamo continued for some time after Obama's inauguration, and is still being inflicted in US prisons in Afghanistan (Baker 2009; Andersson 2010).

The Obama Administration has fought attempts by torture victims to bring suit in US courts, and even pressured British courts to halt lawsuits that would reveal information about the US torture program. It has maintained that persons seized outside combat and shipped across international borders to Afghan prisons may be kept in detention without any access to the courts. In May 2009, Obama announced that some Guantánamo detainees would be tried before military commissions affording fewer due process protections than standard criminal trials, and that some prisoners, deemed "too dangerous to release," would be kept in "prolonged" detention without any trial at all. He supported a congressional amendment of the Freedom of Information Act that permits the suppression of photographs showing US torture. In brief, ill-treatment continues, extrajudicial detention remains in place, torture victims are left without legal remedies, and little has been done to hinder future presidents, or Obama himself, from ramping up torture in the future. Bush set a precedent for officially sanctioned torture; Obama has moderated the policy, but not uprooted the precedent.

Europe shares the United States' vulnerability to international terrorism. The 9/11 attacks took the lives of 111 Europeans, 67 of them British. Hundreds were killed in Al-Qaeda-inspired bombings in Istanbul (2003), Madrid (2004), and London (2005). There have been renewed attacks in Britain, and police have foiled terrorist plots in several European countries. Yet no state in Europe has responded by instituting an interrogation regime remotely comparable in scale or severity to that adopted by the United States. Nor did any European country follow the Bush Administration in openly admitting methods of "coercive interrogation" that constitute torture in all but name. The US embrace of torture sets it apart from Europe, especially the western European states with which it is normally compared.

The contrast should not be exaggerated. Torture and ill-treatment have not been eliminated from Europe. (Amnesty International's annual reports are a quick reminder of the fact.) As in the United States, police brutality is widespread. Russia still practices torture in Chechnya. In several eastern and southeastern European countries, ill-treatment and torture in police custody remain common. Torture in Turkey, having declined significantly since the 1990s, is far from ended (Human Rights Watch 2004).

Ill-treatment has also occurred in the context of national policies introduced to combat international terrorism (Human Rights Watch 2008b). In addition, European officials have lent various forms of assistance to the US torture program (Amnesty International 2006; ECCHR 2009). Several countries granted overflight and refueling privileges to the United States' extraordinary rendition flights. Other assistance has been more direct. Local authorities in Italy, Britain, Sweden, Macedonia, and Bosnia delivered or facilitated the transfer of citizens or temporary residents into the hands of US officials, who sent them overseas for torture or severe ill-treatment. Intelligence officers from Britain, Germany, Turkey, and possibly France traveled to Guantánamo Bay to interrogate their countries' citizens and residents imprisoned there (Geyer 2007).

It is a damning fact that among the overseas "black sites" used by the CIA to torture "high value" Al-Qaeda detainees, some were located in Europe. From 2003 to 2005, secret detention centers in Poland, Romania, and Lithuania were the setting for harrowing abuse such as water-boarding, longtime standing, hypothermia, extreme isolation, and a range of psychological methods intended to cause severe mental regression (Marty 2007; Mayer 2008, 275–7; M. Cole 2009). The interrogators were American CIA operatives, but the premises were supplied and secured by the host governments with the knowledge of high-ranking officials, whether or not they knew the details of the interrogation methods being used.

British complicity runs deep. Despite knowing that the United States subjected detainees to inhumane treatment in violation of international law, British authorities facilitated the rendition of British residents to Guantánamo Bay and Bagram prison in Afghanistan (Amnesty International 2006; ECCHR 2009). Pakistan's notorious intelligence service seized and interrogated British citizens at the request of MI5 and MI6, which met and questioned the detainees but took no action in response to obvious signs that they were being tortured (Human Rights Watch 2009a). British intelligence officials also supplied Moroccan officials with questions for use in the torture of British resident Binyam Mohamed (Rose 2009).

Collusion in American torture policies has led Amnesty International (2006) to describe Europe as "the U.S.A's partner in crime." This is an addition to the fact, noted above, that many Europeans still suffer brutal treatment in the ordinary criminal justice system. If the US record constitutes a failure, the European record can scarcely be termed a success. Nonetheless, several factors should be kept in mind. Where police torture and ill-treatment remain routine, as in much of eastern and southeastern Europe, the problem is largely attributable to the durable legacy of authoritarian rule, weak rule of law, and precarious control over military and security personnel. Nor should we forget the entrenched cruelties of the American criminal justice system, with its soaring incarceration rate, massive use of solitary confinement, prison overcrowding, rampant prison violence, and continued use of capital punishment. Incarceration rates are lower in every European country, dramatically so in those at similar levels of wealth (Forman 2009). In northwestern Europe (if not elsewhere), prison conditions are on the whole much superior to those in the United States, though serious abuses persist in pretrial custody (Whitman 2003, 74–80). Solitary confinement in Europe does not approach, either in intensity or scale, the American practice. The death penalty has ended everywhere except Belarus (which is not in the Council of Europe).

Without excusing European collusion in the Bush torture program, we should nonetheless remember that it occurred mainly at the behest and under the direction of the United States. (Hence the irony that America's human rights exceptionalism exerted a negative influence on *European* behavior.) Knowledge of illegal detention, rendition, and interrogation practices was confined to a much narrower circle of officials in Europe than in the United States. As far as we know, no high-ranking European officials authorized the use of coercive methods by their subordinates. Nor have any European officials lent their public endorsement to the practice. As I discuss below, criminal investigations into torture are more advanced in Europe than the United States.

The US torture program has provoked official condemnation in much of Europe. The Council of Europe commissioned Dick Marty's two monumental investigations into renditions and secret detentions in Europe which it then published in unredacted form. The European Parliament of the EU released its own report, and both the Council of Europe and EU passed resolutions strongly denouncing US abuses and European collusion in them.

Where collusion occurred, it can be understood as the defeat of one kind of multilateralism by another, with European rights protections succumbing to the superior might of transatlantic security and intelligence networks.[6] The second Marty report analyzes in detail the role played by NATO agreements and procedures in facilitating the black sites and extraordinary renditions. The showdown between the two multilateralisms appears starkly in Bosnia, where in October 2001 national police arrested six men at the request of the US embassy. Months later, Bosnian courts ordered the men released (because the US embassy refused to hand over evidence allegedly demonstrating a terrorist plot) and issued an order banning the deportation of four of the men. Nonetheless, on the day of their release, all six were promptly rearrested by Bosnian police and transferred to US NATO troops for shipment to Guantánamo, where they were tortured (Amnesty International 2006).

After 9/11, torture met stronger resistance in Europe than the United States. This is not meant to exonerate Europe or certify its human rights regime as a "success." European human rights institutions did not prevent official complicity in torture. Nonetheless, the fact remains that under stress from counterterrorism campaigns those institutions proved more effective than their American counterparts. I now examine some of the reasons why.

Strengthening versus weakening the prohibition of torture

To understand the divergent responses by Europe and the United States, we must look at the different institutional choices made by each party in the years preceding 9/11. In those years, Europe strengthened whereas the United States loosened the domestic impact of international human rights law. Four differences are salient. Unlike the United States, Europe (1) abstained from adding loopholes to the international legal prohibition of torture and ill-treatment; (2) established judicial oversight of its international human rights commitments; (3) adopted an international inspection regime to monitor compliance with the international prohibition of torture and ill-treatment; and (4) committed itself firmly to the criminalization of torture and other war crimes.

Avoiding legal loopholes

Though torture and ill-treatment are prohibited on both sides of the Atlantic, the version of the prohibition recognized by the United States is looser than that recognized by Europe. In effect, Europe and the United States adopted different laws.

The source of the prohibition in contemporary international law is Article 5 of the Universal Declaration of Human Rights (1948): "No one shall be subjected to torture or to cruel, inhuman or degrading treatment or punishment." This formulation reappears in the ICCPR and the Torture Convention and, except for omission of the word "cruel," in Article 3 of the ECHR: "No one shall be subjected to torture or to inhuman or degrading treatment of punishment." Under all three treaties, the prohibition of torture may never be suspended, even during an emergency that "threatens the life of the nation."

When the United States ratified the ICCPR in 1992 and the Torture Convention in 1994, it limited the prohibition in two ways. First, it attached a reservation to both treaties stating that it was bound by the prohibition on "cruel, inhuman or degrading treatment or punishment" only in so far as this meant "the cruel, unusual, and inhumane treatment or punishment prohibited by the Fifth, Eighth and/or Fourteenth Amendments to the Constitution of the United States." Second, it narrowed the definition of torture. Whereas the Torture Convention defines torture as the intentional infliction of severe pain or suffering, "whether physical or mental," the United States stated that mental pain or suffering constitutes torture only if it inflicts "prolonged mental harm" and results from one of four specified techniques: the threatened or actual use of physical torture, the threatened or actual use of mind altering drugs "or other procedures calculated to disrupt profoundly the senses or the personality," the threat of imminent execution, or the threat that any of the previous measures will be inflicted on another person.[7]

The narrower definition of torture found its way, with minor alterations, into several US statutes. It has been used by US courts to assess allegations of torture in civil and criminal trials, and petitions by foreigners against deportation orders to countries where they face a risk of torture. The redefinition can be seen as an invitation to quibbling, and the Bush Administration took it in that spirit. Administration officials and their backers argued that water-boarding is not torture, since the distress caused is (allegedly) psychological rather than physical, and the particular kind of psychological distress does not satisfy the United States' criteria of mental torture (Mayerfeld 2007, 130–3). This argument is unconvincing on its own terms: water-boarding produces severe physical pain, arouses terror of imminent death, and causes lasting psychological damage (Correa 2007; Rejali 2007, 280–5). But this is a conversation we should not even be having. If water-boarding does not slip past the United States' narrowed definition of torture, other forms of psychological torment may. The US reformulation implies that torment is not torture if the right means of inflicting it are chosen. US interrogators, advised by administration lawyers, took this as permission to inflict a variety of torments, even if in their zeal they sometimes crossed the line into conduct prohibited by the United States' narrower definition.[8]

International law prohibits not only torture, but all cruel, inhuman, or degrading treatment or punishment (ill-treatment for short). The prohibition of ill-treatment, like that of torture, may not be suspended, even during an emergency that threatens the life of the nation.[9] In the reservations noted above, the United States narrowed the prohibition of ill-treatment to conduct prohibited by the Fifth, Eighth, and Fourteenth Amendments to the US Constitution – meaning, in practice, the interpretation of those amendments by US courts. The most relevant constitutional provisions are the Eighth Amendment prohibition of "cruel and unusual punishment," the Fifth Amendment prohibition of compulsory self-incrimination, and the Fifth and Fourteenth Amendment prohibition of the deprivation of liberty without due process of law.

It can be argued that "cruel and unusual punishment," rightly understood, is coextensive with "cruel, inhuman or degrading treatment or punishment." But that is not how the Supreme Court has interpreted it. The Eighth Amendment phrase has been construed far more narrowly, with profound consequences for public policy.[10]

In justifying its treaty reservation, the US government has claimed that the term "degrading treatment" is ambiguous and vague (Mayerfeld 2007, 125–6). This is unconvincing: terms like "cruel," "inhuman," and "unusual" are no more precise. The real objection, thinly veiled by the government's language, is the view that degrading treatment is not always inappropriate. This view has deep roots in America's legal culture. In his magisterial comparison of American, French, and German criminal justice practices, James Whitman (2003) has argued that the stark transatlantic differences derive from an American conviction that punishment *should* be degrading and the equally strong European (or at least French and German) conviction that it must not be. Even if (as Whitman himself argues) this difference has cultural sources deeper than any legal text, it nonetheless makes a big difference that the European commitment to dignified punishment is solemnized in a legal prohibition of "inhuman or degrading treatment or punishment" now binding on 47 countries.

In America there persists a widespread attitude that conditions of confinement not only may but should be shaming. Some prison officials boast openly of employing degrading measures. Inmates have been placed in tents in 110-degree heat, set in chain gangs, shackled, put in fetal restraints, housed naked in outdoor cages, forced to dance naked, and subjected to unnecessary body cavity searches (Forman 2009). Many prisoners endure overcrowding, filthy and unsanitary quarters, severely inadequate health care, the continual threat of violence, and enforced inactivity. Recurrent revelations of severe prison mistreatment arouse little protest. In James Forman's words (2009, 355), "We have allowed this sort of degradation and humiliation to become normal, acceptable, even inevitable. It has become the cost of doing business, a necessary incident to running such a large prison system full of incorrigibles."

Among the most merciless policies is the widespread use of solitary confinement, now imposed on an estimated 25,000 American prisoners (Rhodes 2004; Lobel 2008). The suffering caused is so intense that solitary confinement deserves to be classified as torture (Gawande 2009; Hansen-King 2009). Many of the most disturbing practices at Guantánamo Bay – the confinement of inmates to their cells for 23 hours a day, the deprivation of personal items, the physically violent "extraction" of prisoners from their cells, the indifference to mental illness caused or aggravated by such conditions – are in fact standard procedure at "supermax" facilities throughout the United States. Some American prisoners have been subjected to solitary confinement for over 30 years. We cannot understand the abuses of the "War on Terror" without grasping their connection to the pervasive cruelties of America's criminal justice system.[11]

The Eighth Amendment offers some measure of protection. Some egregious abuses are investigated by the authorities and checked by the courts. In the 1960s and 1970s, state and federal courts ordered the comprehensive reform of a number of prison systems (mostly but not exclusively in the South) that had practiced torture, forced labor, and brutal overcrowding (Feeley and Rubin 1998). But the high tide of judicial protection of prisoners' rights has long since passed. Chief Justice Warren's declaration in 1958 that the Eighth Amendment rests on the "the dignity of man" is rarely cited now.[12] Under current jurisprudence, the test of whether prison conditions constitute "cruel and unusual punishment" is not their objective character, but whether the responsible officials exhibit a "culpable state of mind."[13] Harsh conditions attributable to the "mere negligence" or "error in good faith" of prison officials do not qualify; they must instead result from "deliberate indifference" or "maliciously and sadistically" motivated conduct.[14] Since 1996, moreover, the Prison Litigation Reform Act has hindered the ability of prisoners to seek relief in federal courts (ACLU 2006, 85).

For much of its history, the European Court of Human Rights did little to challenge prison conditions in the region (Murdoch 2006b, 219–20). However, in the past two decades, two major Council of Europe initiatives inspired by Article 3 of the ECHR have sought to improve prison conditions and in the process encouraged greater intervention from the Court (Murdoch 2006b, 46–51 and 220–1). In 1987 and again in 2006, the Committee of Ministers of the Council of Europe issued a set of detailed guidelines for the treatment of prisoners. The European Prison Rules are not legally binding, and conditions in several countries are far from anything approaching compliance. (They are often appalling, as European Court of Human Rights cases like *Kalashnikov v. Russia* (2002) and *Dergoz v. Greece* (2001) attest. See also Cassese 1996.) The Rules nonetheless represent a collective effort to flesh out the meaning of Article 3, and provide a normative standard against which national policies can be assessed. (See, for example, rule 60.5: "Solitary confinement shall be imposed as a punishment only in exceptional cases and for a specified period of time, which shall be as short as possible.") The nine principles that introduce the 2006 Rules deserve particular emphasis, because of their evident commitment to the dignity of prisoners, and because they are trained on the actual circumstances of confinement and not (as in contemporary US Supreme Court jurisprudence) on the mental disposition of prison officials. (See, for example, Principle 5: "Life in prison shall approximate as closely as possible the positive aspects of life in the community.")

A second major initiative was the adoption, in 1989, of the European Convention for the Prevention of Torture and Other Inhuman or Degrading Treatment or Punishment. Now binding on all 47 member states of the Council of Europe, the convention establishes an interdisciplinary committee (known for short as the Committee for the Prevention of Torture, or CPT) with the power to inspect any detention center of its choosing (Evans and Morgan 1998). Following country visits, The CPT communicates its recommendations to host governments in the form of confidential reports, which are now voluntarily published by all Council of Europe countries except Russia and which thus become a resource for human rights advocates. On the rare occasions when the CPT determines that a government is withholding cooperation, either by interfering with visits or refusing to implement the committee's recommendations, it can issue a public statement describing its concerns. Both the CPT and the European Prison Rules have influenced the judgments of the European Court of Human Rights, which since 2001 has acted more assertively to correct abusive prison conditions. Together, the Court, the CPT, and the Prison Rules have formed, in the words of Jim Murdoch (2006b), "a complex scheme of interwoven standard-setting and implementation machinery which draws upon international expectations and domestic practices and is given practical force through state goodwill and, when necessary, by the threat of judicial condemnation."

So long as the US Supreme Court insists on narrow construal of the Eighth Amendment, the ban on "cruel and unusual punishment" grants less protection than the ban on "inhuman or degrading treatment or punishment." The difference proved critical after 9/11. For the Bush Administration, the treaty reservation on ill-treatment was the gift that kept on giving. It implied, according to administration lawyers, that the ban on "cruel, inhuman or degrading treatment or punishment" did not reach US conduct overseas, since the Supreme Court historically did not extend the protection of the Fifth, Eighth, and Fourteenth Amendments to foreigners outside US territory. In response, Congress in December 2005 overcame the concerted resistance of the Administration to pass the Detainee Treatment Act, prohibiting the government from applying "cruel, inhuman, or degrading treatment or punishment" anywhere in the world. But the Act reinscribed the original treaty reservation, repeating that "cruel, inhuman or degrading treatment or punishment" means "the cruel, unusual, and inhumane treatment or punishment prohibited by the Fifth, Eighth and/or Fourteenth Amendments." It was a reckless move, given that the Supreme Court has never ruled on the constitutionality of using painful interrogation methods to prevent terrorism. The Bush Administration was now happy to claim that none of its interrogation techniques, including water-boarding, constituted cruel, inhuman or degrading treatment as understood by the United States. The Eighth Amendment did not apply, it argued, because the techniques were not inflicted as punishment; the self-incrimination clause did not apply, because they were not inflicted as part of a criminal investigation; and the due process clause did not apply, because the use of painful interrogation against a suspected terrorist in order to stop terrorism does not "shock the conscience." Armed with these arguments, Michael Mukasey, President Bush's 2007 nominee for Attorney General, refused to tell the Senate Judiciary Committee whether water-boarding was illegal. The Democratic-controlled Senate confirmed him anyway. These ingenious maneuvers would have been unavailable if, a decade earlier, the United States had simply pledged, without qualification, not to engage in torture or cruel, inhuman, or degrading treatment or punishment.

It may be objected that I have assigned too much importance to the United States' treaty reservations and understandings. The problem (it will be argued) was less the reservations and understandings themselves than the Bush Administration's misinterpretation of them. I agree that the Administration made fallacious arguments about its treaty and constitutional obligations. The question then becomes: How did it get away with such arguments? I now turn to this question.

Judicial oversight

When adopted in 1950, the ECHR established a transnational court and commission to monitor national compliance with its provisions. States originally had a choice whether to allow individuals to bring complaints before the Commission, and whether to recognize the jurisdiction of the European Court of Human Rights. Over time, states increasingly accepted both mechanisms. A 1998 revision to the ECHR abolished the Commission and made jurisdiction of the Court and the right of individual petition (now directly to the Court) obligatory for all member states.

Because the ECHR is now incorporated into the domestic law of all member states, judicial oversight occurs at the national as well as transnational level. In some countries (such as Russia), domestic incorporation exists more in name than reality (Greer 2006, 126–31). But in others, the process is far advanced. National courts frequently apply the Convention as well as rulings of the Strasbourg Court. Several countries also screen proposed legislation for compliance with the ECHR and Strasbourg jurisprudence prior to enactment (Greer 2006, 85). As compliance becomes more automatic, there arises what Fionnualla Ní Aoiláin (2004, 219) calls, with reference to the prohibition of torture and ill-treatment, a "process of circular enforcement":

> As European states have become accustomed to external legal scrutiny, and their legal systems have accordingly bent to preempt and/or accommodate such review, it has become much easier for the Court to extend both the depth and breadth of its jurisprudence in the context of article 3.

Britain illustrates the value of placing international human rights commitments under the oversight of domestic judges. Not until 2000, when the 1998 Human Rights Act (HRA) took effect, was the ECHR incorporated into domestic law. Since 9/11, British courts have used the HRA to limit detention without trial of terrorist suspects, prohibit the use in judicial proceedings of evidence obtained by torture, require government investigation of ill-treatment by British armed forces in Iraq, and block the deportation of terrorist suspects to countries where they run a significant risk of torture (Bonner 2007; Donohue 2008).

The scene in the United States is altogether different. Compliance with the ICCPR and Torture Convention is overseen at the international level by two part-time committees whose views (unlike rulings by the European Court of Human Rights) are not legally binding. The United States chose not to accept the optional provisions granting individuals a right to submit complaints to the committees. The committees' role is thus chiefly limited to that of questioning and commenting on the United States' periodic reports on national compliance. The committees have voiced increasingly stern criticisms, which the United States has felt free to reject. Nor does the United States view itself bound by the general comments periodically issued by the committees on general questions of treaty interpretation.

Any possibility of judicial oversight at the domestic level was barred from the moment of ratification, when the United States declared that the substantive provisions of the ICCPR and Torture Convention (along with those of the Racial Discrimination Convention) were not self-executing, so that, in the words of a recent Supreme Court opinion, the treaties do not "create obligations enforceable in the federal courts."[15] The lack of judicial enforceability gives the treaty obligations something of an ethereal existence, leaving many Americans uncertain whether international human rights law really is law (an attitude far less intelligible in most of Europe). Ordinarily, courts play an important role in transmitting, teaching, and instilling the law, thereby making it seem "real." The non-self-executing declarations bar US courts from playing this role with respect to international human rights law.

The European Court of Human Rights affirmed the absolute prohibition of torture and ill-treatment in the landmark case of *Ireland v. UK* (1978), ruling that Britain's subjection of suspected IRA supporters to the so-called "Five Techniques" violated Article 3 of the ECHR. The Court reversed the unanimous view of the Commission that the techniques constituted torture, but still held them to be inhuman and degrading, and thus forbidden under any circumstances. The ruling established a clear precedent for all members of the Council of Europe that ill-treatment, let alone torture, could never be justified by the exigencies of combating terrorism. It became the foundation of a rich jurisprudence on Article 3 that over time has raised the standard of minimally acceptable treatment owed to detainees. (In a subsequent ruling the Court hinted that if a similar case were brought again, the "Five Techniques" would be considered torture.)[16]

The absolute prohibition has survived the impact of 9/11. In *Chahal v. UK* (1996), the Court had invoked Article 3 to uphold an absolute ban on the repatriation, or *"refoulement,"* of any individuals, including suspected terrorists, to countries where they faced a serious threat of torture or ill-treatment. In the 2008 case of *Saadi v. Italy,* Britain intervened as a third party to argue that the possibility of ill-treatment by a foreign state ought to be weighed against the danger of terrorist attack if deportation is blocked. In a unanimous opinion, however, the 17-judge Grand Chamber declared such balancing inadmissible.

Bush Administration lawyers, by contrast, faced a landscape unencumbered by judicial precedent relating to coercive interrogation. All that stood in the way was a set of treaty obligations rendered largely abstract by the impossibility of judicial enforcement. In this environment, the Administration made what looks like a decision to ignore its treaty obligations, though it never admitted doing so, and though it took the precaution of producing secret memos which argued that actions apparently in violation of those obligations were not what they seemed. If we ask why Bush Administration lawyers advanced such implausible arguments, part of the answer is that they faced little constraint from past US case law and little danger of judicial challenge in the future.[17]

The non-self-executing declarations cover not only the prohibition of torture and ill-treatment, but also numerous treaty provisions designed to give the prohibition practical effect. The Torture Convention, for example, obligates member states to educate public officials about the prohibition of torture and ill-treatment, review law enforcement and military procedures to remove possible sources of abuse, and guarantee the right of individuals claiming to have suffered abuse to a prompt and impartial examination of their complaint. The non-self-executing declaration, however, makes the executive and legislative branches sole judge of their compliance with these obligations.[18]

The marginalization of international human rights law reflects and reinforces a general US trend toward the expansion of presidential power and erosion of judicial oversight (Savage 2008). In matters deemed to affect national security, courts with the encouragement of the president and sometimes Congress have invoked sovereign immunity, state secrets, and the political question doctrine to dismiss a large number of suits brought by the victims of government abuse (Gilman 2007; Davis 2008).[19] Thus an attempt by German citizen Khaled el-Masri to sue CIA director George Tenet for kidnapping and torture was thrown out by federal courts on grounds of the states secret doctrine, and the Supreme Court refused to hear the case on appeal. Obama has been no less vigorous than his predecessor in seeking to block lawsuits by victims of US torture.[20] Presidents fighting judicial oversight are assisted by the nonjusticability of human rights treaties. The right to a remedy for the violation of one's human rights is a bedrock principle of human rights law, affirmed in the above-noted provisions of the Torture Convention as well as the ICCPR, which obligates member states "to ensure that any person whose rights or freedoms as herein recognized are violated shall have an effective remedy, notwithstanding that the violation has been committed by persons acting in an official capacity" (art. 2). Although the United States is bound by this obligation, judges must pretend that it doesn't exist. Thus are domestic checks and balances undermined by the circumvention of international human rights law (see Flaherty 2006).

International inspection

Since its creation in 1990, the CPT has made over 200 visits to the 47 countries in the Council of Europe. Local officials holding detainees in their custody know that they can receive a visit from the CPT at any time (Council of Europe 1999). (Country visits are announced with a few weeks' notice, but committee members can visit detention sites of their choosing without warning.) Of the Council of Europe's 47 countries, 46 voluntarily publish the committee's reports, thus contributing to the process of dialogue and cooperation. Because of the CPT's recommendations, more countries grant detainees prompt access to legal counsel and medical attention, and improvements in the physical accommodation of detainees have been widely adopted (Murdoch 2006a, 140). The CPT helped spur major structural reforms in Turkey from the late 1990s onwards that led to a significant reduction, though far from an eradication, of torture. Less progress was achieved in Russia, however, and a trend in many countries toward higher incarceration rates, with consequent overcrowding, threatens several of the committee's achievements (Murdoch 2006a, 138–42).

Through general reports, in addition to communications with individual governments, the CPT has played a major role in setting regional standards for detainee treatment. It has popularized the formula that three basic rights – access to a lawyer, access to a doctor, and notification of one's detention to a third party of one's choosing – are vital to the prevention of ill-treatment in pretrial detention. To combat the problem of state denial, the committee has spelled out in detail the measures needed for ensuring that apparent cases of ill-treatment receive prompt and impartial investigation. The work of the CPT inspired much of the content of the 2006 European Prison Rules and has exerted a growing influence on the jurisprudence of the European Court of Human Rights (Murdoch 2006a, 134–8).

A major legacy of the European Convention to Prevent Torture is the adoption of the Optional Protocol to the Torture Convention, which set up a similar committee on a global scale. The text of the Optional Protocol borrows heavily from the European Convention for the Prevention of Torture, though with some alterations that result in part from lessons learned by the CPT. One innovation is the creation of national mechanisms within each member state to monitor the treatment of detained or confined individuals on a permanent basis. Adopted in 2002, the Optional Protocol came into effect in 2006, though its committee has yet to initiate the visiting process. Of the 50 member states, 26 are from the Council of Europe.

Unlike Europe, the United States has not welcomed international monitoring of its detention policies. It has neither signed nor ratified the Optional Protocol to the Torture Convention. In much of the United States, monitoring of prison conditions by independent bureaucratic agencies is either absent or under-resourced. In years past, the responsibility for providing effective independent oversight has largely fallen to the federal courts, but that task has been rendered more difficult, as previously noted, by the 1996 Prison Litigation Reform Act.

The Bush Administration did not act on, much less publicize, the blistering reports by the International Committee of the Red Cross (ICRC) of the ill-treatment, including torture, of prisoners in Guantánamo Bay, Iraq, and Afghanistan. It moreover adopted various stratagems to conceal its most brutal practices from the ICRC, and kept some detainees, the so-called "ghost prisoners," entirely hidden.

The European CPT is not a panacea. It bears repeating that prison conditions in several European countries remain abysmal. Russia continues to defy the Council of Europe by practicing torture in Chechnya. The failure of the CPT to smoke out CIA black sites in Eastern Europe is a dramatic illustration of its limitations, and leaves us to wonder what else it may be missing. Nor is it clear what power it has to deter torture and ill-treatment by European officials in operations conducted outside Europe. Its achievements are nonetheless considerable, and offer something to build on. If the United States is serious about prevention of ill-treatment of detainees at home and abroad, it will offer its full and unrestricted cooperation with an international monitoring regime.

Criminalization

"What unites many countries in the world," writes Charles Simic (2009), "both the ones that don't give a fig about human rights and the ones that profess they do, is their unwillingness to punish their war criminals." Recognition of this problem was the main impetus for the Rome Statute of the ICC. The ICC rests on the principle that atrocities are properly prosecuted by the governments whose officials perpetrate them or on whose territories they take place. Only if those governments fail to take action will the ICC launch judicial proceedings. The hope is that governments, fearing ICC intervention, will enforce their own criminal laws, and that would-be perpetrators, aware of this fact, will abstain from committing crimes in the first place.

Torture and inhuman treatment are war crimes under the Rome Statute. The 111 countries that have ratified the ICC Treaty include all 27 EU member states and 40 of the 47 countries in the Council of Europe, but not the United States. Like most countries, the United States makes torture a punishable crime under one or another of its domestic laws. As a state party to the Torture Convention, it has promised to "ensure that all acts of torture are offenses under its criminal law" (art. 4). In partial fulfillment of this pledge, it passed the 1994 Torture Act, making it a federal crime to commit torture outside the United States. The 1996 War Crimes Act made it a federal crime to violate the grave breaches provisions and Common Article 3 of the 1949 Geneva Conventions and selected articles of the 1907 Hague Land War Convention.

In the end, these laws provided little deterrent. With the protection of secret memoranda concluding (however questionably) that none of the painful interrogation techniques violated the Torture Act or the War Crimes Act, Bush Administration officials felt free to proceed. The Detainee Treatment Act, though it banned ill-treatment abroad, appended no criminal penalty, and in fact extended criminal and civil immunity for detention and interrogation practices "that were officially authorized and determined to be lawful at the time they were committed," so long as the agent "did not know" and "a person of ordinary sense and understanding would not know" that "the practices were unlawful." The Administration received a fright when the Supreme Court ruled in *Hamdan v. Rumsfeld* (June 2006) that Common Article 3 covered the treatment of suspected terrorists. By implication, "cruel treatment and torture" as well as "humiliating and degrading treatment" of detainees were now punishable under the War Crimes Act. In response, the Bush

Administration persuaded Congress to adopt language in the 2006 Military Commissions Act that excluded certain violations of Common Article 3 from the scope of the War Crimes Act and made the revision retroactive to 1997. To disguise this shameful operation, the drafters used language so confusing that no one could be sure which coercive methods did and did not fall under the amended War Crimes Act. But the language performed the crucial function of helping potential defendants in future trials say that the law was too unclear to serve as the basis of a conviction. These deliberations, like the torture memos which they partly converted into legislation, took place far from the shadow of international criminal law. Because they immunized actions clearly punishable under the Rome Statute, they would be far less imaginable in countries that had ratified the ICC Treaty.

The torture memos reveal both that US officials were highly motivated to avoid prosecution and that the specter of prosecution could be dispelled. In the end, the memos accomplished their intended purpose of furnishing a "golden shield" to those implicated in the controversial techniques. When the Department of Justice under Obama announced a "preliminary review" to consider criminal investigation into Bush-era abuses, it excluded actions that complied with the memos' legal advice. None of the architects of the torture program have been the subject of a US criminal investigation, much less prosecution. A few dozen mostly low-ranking soldiers have been prosecuted under military law, but most sentences have been light. The harshest punishments have generally been reserved for those whose abuses were made famous by the Abu Ghraib photos, leaving the question whether their real crime was committing the abuses or bringing them to the world's attention.

Criminal proceedings are further advanced in Europe. In 2009 an Italian court convicted 23 CIA officials in absentia for the kidnapping and extraordinary rendition of an Egyptian cleric. Six Bush Administration lawyers who helped authorize the torture program are the subject of a criminal probe in Spain. Prosecutors in Spain and Germany have sought the arrest of CIA officials accused of participating in extraordinary rendition, and Britain has launched a criminal investigation into complicity of its intelligence services in torture.

Conclusion

Europe demonstrates the power of the collective enforcement of human rights. Participation in a strong international human rights regime grants other countries the power to judge the adequacy of one's record. One's policies must satisfy a higher standard of justification, because they are judged by other countries not sharing one's biases and blind spots (at least not to the same extent). But the other countries cannot judge in an arbitrary or capricious manner, since the standards they apply to others will be applied to themselves. If the parties do not really care about human rights, the regime will sink into a meaningless exercise. But if they begin with a measure of genuine commitment, the regime can hold each party to its professed ideals. Mutual oversight and collective decision making, when sincerely undertaken in the service of human rights, can raise the standard of minimally acceptable behavior and generate improved means of enforcement.

The most dramatic symbol of this approach is the European Court of Human Rights. Individuals throughout the continent can challenge the policies of their government before a supranational court. But the Court is only one of several regional institutions in Europe that oblige each country to defend its policies to all the rest. This process, now deeply internalized, has helped make certain kinds of human rights violations unthinkable in most countries belonging to the Council of Europe.

There is nothing to stop the United States from integrating itself more fully into existing international human rights laws and institutions. It can ratify the American Convention on Human Rights and accept the jurisdiction of the Inter-American Court of Human Rights. It can ratify the Optional Protocol to the Torture Convention and the Rome Statute of the ICC. It can withdraw the reservations, understandings, and declarations that dilute the impact of already-ratified human rights treaties. It can implement its human rights treaty obligations through domestic legislation. Most important, it can increase the power of domestic judges to enforce its human rights obligations under international (not to mention domestic) law. Only the will, not the opportunity, has been lacking.

To reject participation in a strong international human rights regime is to make oneself judge in one's own case. When refusal to submit to an impartial judge is combined with hegemonic power, there can arise the arrogance and blindness that Locke diagnosed as the incurable condition of absolute monarchies. The dismissal of international human rights law is anti-constitutional, because it is opposed to fundamental constitutional principles of checks and balances, impartial adjudication, and a guaranteed remedy for the violation of individual rights. In the case of the United States, it has severely undermined the protection of human rights.

It is important not to exaggerate the differences. Ill-treatment is widespread in Europe, and torture retains a stubborn hold on several countries. Leading officials offered crucial assistance to the US torture program. That they left the actual torturing to US and other foreign officials does not absolve them of guilt. Yet European complicity never approached US levels.

In this story, cause and effect are complexly entwined. To a considerable degree, different legal landscapes on either side of the Atlantic reflect different cultural attitudes regarding the appropriate treatment of prisoners and detainees. A more punitive outlook is one reason why the United States, unlike Europe, sought to marginalize international human rights law in the first place. But the laws, once adopted, exert their own power. America's treaty reservations, understandings, and declarations not only reflected but also facilitated a set of harsher policies culminating in torture. Conversely, the European Convention of Human Rights reflected genuine values held by European states, but those states then found themselves constrained in ways they did not anticipate.

My argument has been that post-9/11 differences between the American and European use of torture were largely determined by institutional choices made before 9/11. In this sense, 9/11 did not bring about institutional change, but rather underscored an institutional reality that already existed. Post-9/11 abuses revealed the preexisting weakness of US human rights institutions, their inability to withstand a shock to the system. The United States, if it is serious about respecting human rights, must no longer seek exemption from the international human rights regime.

Notes

1. For helpful comments and advice, I am indebted to Michael Blake, Emilie Combaz, Fiona de Londras, James Forman Jr, Michael Forman, Steven Greer, Joshua Hansen-King, and audiences at the University of Washington, Tacoma, and University of Washington Law School. For excellent research assistance, I would like to thank Julia Abelev.
2. The ineffectiveness of torture as a counterterrorist method has been established beyond doubt. See Rejali 2007, 446–536. For a firsthand account that separates myth from fact about interrogation, see Alexander 2008.
3. Major studies of the Court include Greer 2006 and Goldhaber 2007.
4. Even those critical of the United States' self-declared exceptions sometimes give voice to this belief, when they ask in puzzlement why a country with such a strong commitment to protecting rights would resist the incorporation of international human rights law. This sentiment appears in a number of the essays in Ignatieff 2005.
5. There is now a vast literature. Definitive treatments include Mayer 2008, US Senate Armed Services Committee 2008, and International Committee of the Red Cross 2007.
6. For a discussion of how global security networks have found ways to roll back international human rights protections, see Scheppele 2006.

7. Other reservations and understandings attached to these two treaties also weakened their provisions, for example, an understanding that creates a looser interpretation of the ban on sending people to countries where they face a substantial risk of torture.

8. Extreme isolation, sleep deprivation, blaring music, sensory deprivation, and sexual humiliation, often in combination, were among the techniques used to induce mental regression and learned helplessness Mayer 2008, 148–75. Although these measures caused intense suffering, with some detainees fearing them more than beatings and stress positions, their classification as "torture" could be hindered by the United States' redefinition of the term.

9. See the ICCPR, art. 4(2); ECHR, art. 15(2); American Convention on Human Rights, art. 27(2).

10. For an argument that America's harsh system of criminal punishment is a betrayal of the Constitution, see Kateb 2007.

11. See the powerful arguments of Kaplan 2008; Forman 2009; American Civil Liberties Union (ACLU) 2006; and Dayan 2007.

12. *Trop v. Dulles*, 356 U.S. 86 (1958).

13. *Wilson v. Seiter*, 501 U.S. 294 (1991).

14. The quoted passages originate in *Whitley v. Albers* 475 U.S. 312 (1986), but *Wilson v. Seiter* gave them broader application.

15. *Sosa v. Alvarez-Machain*, 542 U.S. 692, 734–5 (2004).

16. European Court of Human Rights (1999), *Selmouni v. France* no. 25803/94.

17. The lawyers were well aware of this. In his May 30, 2005 memo arguing that water-boarding and other "enhanced interrogation" techniques did not violate the United States' obligation under the Torture Convention to refrain from cruel, inhuman or degrading treatment or punishment, acting Assistant Attorney General Steven Bradbury noted that "we cannot predict with confidence that a court would agree with our conclusion," but added reassuringly that, because of the United States' non-self-executing declaration, "the question whether the CIA's enhanced interrogation techniques violate the substantive standard of United States obligations under Article 16 is unlikely to be subject to judicial inquiry." For good measure, this reassurance is restated in the memo's penultimate sentence; Bradbury 2005, 38 and 40.

18. In its 2006 shadow report to the Committee against Torture, the ACLU (2006, 72–87 and 90–3) argues that the United States has not, in fact, complied with these obligations.

19. The state secret argument has also been wielded by several European governments resisting inquiry into their possible collusion with extraordinary renditions. This use of the argument is strongly criticized in Marty 2007, paragraphs 5–6.

20. Canwest News Service "U.S. opposes Arar appeal on torture," *Edmonton Journal*, May 13, 2010.

7
Europe's Human Rights Regime after 9/11: Human Rights versus Terrorism

Anja Mihr

Since 2001, the European human rights regime has shown more continuity than change. The regime as such is one of the most defined and complex regional regimes in the world. It is mainly composed of three major international organizations and hundreds of different conventions, treaties, protocols, and guidelines for all aspects of human rights and mandates, the European Union (EU), the Council of Europe (CoE), and the Organization for Security and Cooperation in Europe (OSCE). Their overlapping human rights treaties and guidelines have been constantly harmonized before and after the attacks of September 11, 2001. The attacks on 9/11 did have an impact on some human rights policies as well as public awareness among Europeans; however, the structure and functioning of the regime was not affected. Instead, I will argue that 9/11 has triggered a review process among European member states. The attacks have furthermore strengthened the regime, although some human rights guarantees have been jeopardized and eroded since 2001. The events of 9/11 even created a short-term atmosphere for strengthening established regimes; that is to say, when states seem to benefit more from international norms and delegate power to supranational institutions in order to reduce domestic uncertainties (Moravcsik 2000). According to this regime theoretical approach, many European states experienced these uncertainties. They feared a threat to public security at the expense of human rights and the rule of law. It brought political decision-makers to the table to react while delegating power and sovereignty to the regime in order to better deal with political and security issues in their home countries.

From the time of the fall of the Berlin Wall on 11/9 in 1989 to the terrorist attacks on 9/11 in 2001, the European institutions were acting as a key standard-setter for documents, declarations, treaties, conventions, recommendations, and directives that influenced the UN and other human rights regimes worldwide. The European human rights regime always understood itself in the tradition of postwar Europe's joint catharsis. Established, reestablished and newly established democracies jointly aimed at building both legally and politically binding intergovernmental human rights institutions to strengthen their budding institutions and to be better equipped against future domestic conflicts – bearing in mind that, at the time the regime was established in the 1950s, the Cold War between the West and Soviet Union was already underway. The rule of international law was seen as the backbone of the regime when ratifying the 1950 European Convention on Human Rights and Fundamental Freedoms and putting in place the European Court of Human Rights in Strasbourg in 1959. It was again revitalized after 9/11 when the security crisis occurred. Bearing Europe's history in mind, the regime avoided using the term "war on terror" that was launched by the Bush Administration in the United States. Instead, they preferred to title their actions "combating terrorism" or "counterterrorism," due to the sensitivity the term "war" has in Europe.

The 47 member states of the CoE in Strasbourg, the 56 of the OSCE in Vienna, and the 27 of the EU in Brussels – with overlapping memberships – reacted to 9/11 according to their capacities and different mandates. The regime was equipped with a high level of legal enforcement mechanisms including both the European Court of Human Rights and the European Court of Justice (ECJ) in Luxembourg, which was established in 1989. Since the Lisbon Treaty for the EU came into force in 2009, the Luxemburg Court will in the future also take more jurisdiction over human rights as mentioned in the 2000 EU Fundamental Rights Charter. With the two courts on its side, the regime has two major legal institutions that enforce member states – if necessary – to correct, revise, or leverage human rights standards, legislations, and practice in their countries. In the years since 9/11 the regional supranational courts have played a major role in the political discourse about counterterrorism and human rights protection. The nongovernmental organization (NGO) community based in Brussels has struggled accordingly to adapt their policies and strategies to the new priorities set by the European member states to "counterterrorism." They have all worked in the same direction, namely to leverage human security in Europe and safeguard human rights. Nevertheless, some member states and their governments reacted more robustly and more strategically than others.

Immediate reaction

In surveys shortly after 9/11, over 80 percent of EU citizens were very concerned about terrorism attacks and in 2008 the same survey showed that only 5 percent of Europeans think that terrorism and the fight against terrorism is among the important issues that the European governments would face. Instead human rights, peace, and democracy have been equally high on the agenda and reached over 70 percent throughout the years (European Commission 2009, 21). Thus, in public terms the concern about terrorism as a serious threat has changed, but not the question of human rights priorities or democratic standards, despite the terror attacks in Madrid in 2004 and London in 2005.

Although 9/11 marked a major shift in international relations and world order, the issue of human rights erosion through counterterrorism measures soon vanished from the political agenda. Europe had and has no "media attractive Guantánamo" although the issue of rendition flights entered the public human rights debate for a very short while. To better understand the European human rights regime, it is worth taking a brief look at the continuous human rights developments in laws and standards in Europe prior to 9/11.

In the fall of 2001, European governments agreed that the EU and the CoE ought to be the primary institutions to alert its member states if human rights were at stake in the name of counterterrorism. They were empowered to monitor, protect, and promote human rights in different ways while the implementation of the resolutions of the UN Security Council 1368 and 1373 from September 2001 went on to undertake any measure possible to join the worldwide fight against terrorism. Meanwhile, the OSCE, though the largest intergovernmental regional organization in the world followed the policies of the EU and the CoE. Its task was to implement their decisions and those of the UN Security Council in the years to come.

But regardless of the "alert" by the European organizations in Brussels and Strasbourg, most European governments quickly combined all forces to combat terrorism, pass laws, and "antiterrorist packages." Without doubt, some EU member states felt as though they had to react faster than anybody else, in particular Germany and the United Kingdom, since they had hosted some of the terrorists of 9/11. Many European countries were considered gateways for radical Muslims and posed a potential threat to the security of the regime. Right from the beginning, these measures were seen to differentiate Muslims from non-Muslims, terror suspects from ordinary citizens. This had consequences for the other human rights issues in Europe such as discrimination and stereotyping of people with a Muslim or Arabic background. European governments still carried the burden of the fact that some of the terrorists of 9/11 had been under prior observation, but this had not prevented them from planning and conducting the terror attacks in the United States. The terrorist threat, however, was not primarily targeted at the West, as many believed, but rather against the corrupt and authoritarian regimes and countries from which the terrorists were recruited, that is to say mainly Middle Eastern, Southeast Asian and African countries. Nevertheless, "Western values" and their political democratic order also threaten some of the terrorist groups' own narrow values systems – more so in the main countries of origin of Egypt, Morocco, Pakistan, Saudi Arabia, Iraq, or Afghanistan.

The majority of European countries had no intention to go to war with any state or armed group at that time. No state enemy could be clearly identified to justify such a war, as is the requirement under international humanitarian law and the Geneva Conventions when using the term "war." Although some European countries later joined the US wars in Iraq and in Afghanistan under the NATO-SFOR mandate, the heads of European states agreed on three major steps as leading guidelines for their antiterror laws – from which the US administration also benefitted from: first, to control financial transactions of alleged terrorist groups; second, to enter into private data of their citizens; and third, to control weapons transfers.

European leaders are aware that their continent hosts the largest Muslim community outside the Arab world. Europe's borders are closer to the countries involved in organized terrorism and to those that openly supported it. And the fact that a large number of international terror suspects belong to radical Islamic movements has not helped the human rights community to uphold human rights and anti-discrimination. Some of the CoE's or OSCE member states in Southern and Eastern Europe share a border with the countries that were primary suspects of hosting terrorists, such as Afghanistan or Iraq. Member states of the CoE, such as Turkey, Bosnia, and Herzegovina or Azerbaijan are largely Muslim countries and thus the sensitivity within European institutions towards international terrorism driven by Islamic identity is evident. The OSCE had to do more in order to convince its 56 member states, many of them with a Muslim majority, to be part of the alliance to combat terrorism. Among its member states are countries like Tajikistan, Kyrgyzstan, Uzbekistan, and Turkmenistan. They are predominately Muslim states which have to be included rather then excluded in the political decision-making process to combat terrorism. Many of the policies and legal instruments to safeguard human rights in the fight against terrorism within the OSCE participating states are those "borrowed" by the CoE, the UN, or even the EU (OSCE 2005). In the following years, the European regime acted by complementing and coordinating their decisions (Council of Europe 2002; Heinz and Arnd 2005). Some examples:

- September 21, 2001: The EU Council adopted an action plan to fight terrorism.
- October 3, 2001: The EU Commission proposed that the member states should freeze all funds belonging to organizations and individuals suspected of financing terrorist activities.
- November 2001: The CoE set up a plan of action to combat terrorism.
- December 2001: The EU Commission set up a group of scientific experts in the battle against biological and chemical terrorism.
- July 2002: The CoE passed guidelines on human rights and the fight against terrorism concerning police custody, interference with privacy, pretrial detention, or extradition.
- December 2002: The OSCE ratified the Charter on Preventing and Combating Terrorism.
- December 2002: The EU framework decision on terrorism was handed down, stating that violent acts will only be considered as terrorist offences when intentionally committed with a specific terrorist aim.
- 2003: The CoE set the Committee of Experts on Terrorism (CODEXTER).
- 2004: The EU member states adopted the "solidarity clause" thereby committing their countries to assist each other politically, legally, and militarily, if a member state is hit by an act of terror.
- 2004: The EU Commission and the EU Council approved a treaty with the United States of America that requires airlines from EU member states to pass their passenger data to the US Customs Service. The European Parliament opposed this on privacy grounds and took the case to the ECJ. In 2007 EU-US agreement on passenger data exchange (PNR) was signed.
- 2005: The Committee of Ministries of the CoE called for an expert group on "Terrorism and Human Rights" to explore the possibilities for a new instrument in international law to deal with terrorist threats.

- February 2007: European Parliament passed a resolution against CIA rendition flights.
- June 2007: The CoE passed the European Convention on the Prevention of Terrorism.
- September 2008: The ECJ of the EU passed a leading decision against the resolutions of the UN Security Council in 1999 and 2001 concerning targeted or smart sanctions, blacklists of terror suspects and the freezing of terrorist or group accounts with implications for human rights protection.
- April 2010: EU Commission's Terrorist Finance Tracking Program (TFTP) discussed with US authorities.

The attacks in Madrid in March 2004 and in London in July 2005 pressured European leaders once more to confirm their common efforts in the joint battle. Even though major normative steps had already been taken prior to 2004, the attacks in Madrid and London restricted freedom and liberty rights considering the privacy of people and police detention reached a sensitive limit. These new policies culminated in the preemptive detention of terrorist suspects in London who had allegedly planned to take explosive liquids on board an aircraft at Heathrow Airport in 2006. These men were convicted in 2009. As a consequence, within hours after the attempt, in Europe and worldwide, airport security was paralyzed and the new and restrictive EU security guidelines for hand luggage with a maximum capacity of liquids to be taken on airplanes were introduced as a result. Rather than calming air-travelers, these guidelines are a daily annoyance to frequent travelers and tourists, until today. Thus it was once more shown how quickly and jointly the European leaders and the political regime can act, if needed. But these laws also stand symbolically for quick if not overreaching measures that have restricted the freedom of movement and privacy rights of millions of citizens since 2001. It nevertheless remains a sensitive issue, because according to opinion polls what matters to Europeans throughout the aftermath of 9/11 are the stronghold of human rights (37%), peace (35%), and democracy (34%) above any terrorist threat (European Commission 2008, 48).

In the years since 9/11, the European Court of Human Rights (ECtHR), the ECJ, the national constitutional courts, civil society, and NGOs have played a major role in monitoring and safeguarding liberties and human rights. After they intervened, political decisions and law reforms on domestic levels and some of the decisions by the EU council of ministries had to be amended or abolished. Since 2009, the Lisbon Treaty, which includes the European Charter for Fundamental Rights from

2000, is seen as a main threshold for human rights standards today in Europe. Surprisingly, the Charter has not been questioned in the light of 9/11; it has rather been seen as a stronghold of European values. The overlapping membership of most European states in the regime leads sometimes to detrimental or contrary actions within the different organizations. Thus, whenever the EU – the "youngest" player, having entered the arena of human rights only in 1992 – enters the sphere of human rights, it ideally coordinates with the CoE and the OSCE/ODIHR (the OSCE's Office for Democratic Institutions and Human Rights in Warsaw) (Leino 2002, 455–95). The Memorandum of Understanding between the CoE and the EU from May 2007, and the speech by the EU Commissioner for External Relations and European Neighbourhood Policy Benita Ferrero-Waldner at the OSCE Ministerial Council in November 2007, have both underlined the importance of coherence in their human rights work (Council of Europe 2007; Ferrero-Waldner 2007). All three organizations foster, promote, and monitor human rights and democratization processes under different but complementary mandates. That is to say that ideally but not necessarily in reality, they are complementary actors rather than competitors.

Whereas the CoE is seen as the main human rights norm and standard setter (with such documents as the convention on terrorism, the anti-torture convention, anti-trafficking in human beings convention, etc.), the OSCE uses its monitoring and early warning mechanism to watch human rights implementation, development, and abuse and makes the information collected public. With the division of tasks among the three intergovernmental organizations and its political commitment to foster and promote human rights in normative terms and by the number of conventions, treaties, declarations, and agreements, there seems to be no erosion but rather an expansion and review of human rights in Europe since 9/11. In practical terms, however, there are human rights abuses taking place connected specifically to the counterterrorism measures of states, for example, the multiple cases on data protection, ill-treatment and torture, police custody, and the issue of rendition flights. These realities evidence the actual challenges that this human rights regime has been facing since 2001 (Mihr 2008b).

The regime since 9/11

The European Union

After 9/11, the 27 EU member states were aware of the fact that the threat of terrorism would affect all EU countries, and in particular target states like the United Kingdom, France, Germany, and Spain and that these threats could not be combated on the state level alone. The EU made reference to the European Convention for Human Rights and its basic freedom rights catalog. On this basis, the EU ministers developed their first guidelines on "Human Rights and the fight against Terrorism" in 2001. In 2005, the EU counterterrorism strategy followed (European Council 2005). Despite all the shortcomings of national legislation and antiterror laws, human rights have played a pivotal role and were brought up on the agenda of state ministers and heads of states in their periodical meetings in Strasbourg or Brussels. Another motor in this process was the vivid human rights NGOs community with big players in the field such as Amnesty International (Amnesty International EU Office 2005) and Human Rights Watch (Human Rights Watch 2008a) as well as politicians in the various European parliaments who carefully watched the developments on the inter- and intra-state level. Some of their concerns and protests regard terrorist blacklists, pre-charge detention and rendition flights that are generally linked to torture and ill-treatment of suspects. NGOs and EU parliamentarian concerns and appeals have often been approved by the decisions of the ECJ in Luxemburg and the ECtHR in Strasbourg (see Schneider, this volume). The treaty of Maastricht (1992), the Copenhagen Criteria (1993) for accession countries, the treaty of Amsterdam (1997), and the Fundamental Rights Charter (2000) all feed in to the so-called European Instrument for Democracy and Human Rights (EIDHR) with an annual budget of €140 million (European Commission External Relations 2007, 15–20). This instrument summarized at large the objectives and methods of European human rights policies to monitor and safeguard human rights (Nowak 2002, 256). Later this instrument was also added by the Fundamental Rights Agency in Vienna (Bojkov 2004, 323–53).

In theory, the EU member states are obliged to pass only those antiterror laws that are in conformity with human rights and democratic standards, in particular those of the European Convention for Human Rights. But the reality was often different, because in 2002 the EU had already set a definition of terrorism which made the balance between human rights and counterterrorism more difficult than expected. To the present day, it serves as a reference point for police actions, preventive measures, and police detentions which carry potential risk to violate freedom rights. More so, it serves as a reference document for the UN Security Council decisions on counterterrorism. The definition of who is a terrorist allows governments to combat terrorism at many levels including the very private sphere of citizens. According to this, terrorist offenses exist when acts are aimed to seriously damage a country or an international organization and to seriously intimidate a population. The offence has to unduly compel a government or international organization to perform or abstain from performing, or seriously destabilize or destroy the fundamental political, constitutional, economic, or social structure of a country or an international organization.

Persons who are identified as terrorists aim to procure an attack upon a person's life which may cause death; aim to destroy the physical integrity of a person; by kidnapping or hostage-taking; causing extensive destruction to a government or public facility, a transport system, an infrastructure facility, including an information system; by seizure of aircraft, ships, or other means of public or goods transport; the manufacturing, possession, transportation, or use of weapons including biological and chemical weapons; the release of dangerous substances, or causing fires, floods, or explosions that can interfere with supply of water, power, or any other fundamental natural resources, the effect of which is to endanger human life (European Council 2002). Terrorism is – in short – when someone is planning or committing any of these aforementioned acts. Evidently, terrorism covers a range of different cases and situations and can also be defined in a very broad sense. The definition can give a lot of room for interpretation and judgment. Amnesty International and Human Rights Watch have been arguing that under these definitions a large number of citizens can be considered alleged terrorist suspects. And what is of even more concern, they can be quickly put on the so-called terrorist blacklist without prior notice – with severe consequences to their constitutional rights (Amnesty International EU Office 2005).

The drafters of the guidelines did not forget to add that this decision does not alter the obligations to respect fundamental rights and legal principles as enshrined in the Maastricht Treaty or any of the other European treaties. At the end of the day what counts is that each state is individually responsible for applying and implementing this definition in its national legislation. That gave room for many different interpretations and domestic law reforms to combat terrorism in and among European states. The framework decision on terrorism states that the member states will prosecute terrorist acts that take place in their own territories or on board a ship or an aircraft that is registered in that particular state. State security services, military, or police are also competent to act when the offender is one of their own nationals or residents or when a terrorist act is committed against their own institutions or people or against an institution of the EU. The framework decision even gives member states the possibility of declaring themselves competent to investigate terrorist acts that have taken place on the territory of another member state. Moreover, the definition shows to what extent all laws such as refugee and immigration laws, weapons transfers, freezing of accounts, privacy or data control have been linked with "antiterror" laws since 2001. At the same time, the prevention of any of those attempts or intentions led to a number of measures by the EU and the member states that almost automatically had to impact human rights practice. Affected were those freedom and civil human rights that deal with free movement, private travelling, business, credit card accounts, bank transfers, migration, and the private sphere.

The dilemma was clear from the beginning. On the one hand, the heads of states had to satisfy their constituencies and citizens' demands for more security and punishment in order to remain a legitimate actor in promoting the rule of law inside and outside the borders of Europe. On the other hand, governments could only keep their credibility over the long term if they upheld human rights, their standards and personal freedoms that are the basis of European democracies. Thus, in 2004, the EU member states supplemented the 2001 action plan against terrorism and the 2002 terrorism definition again. The new definition realigned them to pursue seven major objectives, which confirmed previous decisions. Among the objectives were to reduce terrorists' access to financial and economic resources, increase the capacity to investigate and prosecute; protect the security of international transport, strengthen the coordination between the member states, identify the factors that contribute to the recruitment of terrorists and finally to encourage third countries to engage more effectively in combating terrorism (European Union 2009a).

In the years since 2004, the EU states have agreed on even more measures, supplements, and framework decisions that often increased the confusion and misinterpretations of the guidelines and directives already in place. Human rights advocates and organizations as well as governments struggled to follow one common guideline. Although the heads of states claimed to not play "security" off against liberty and human rights a clear guideline and balance between security and human rights were not always evident. The main problem of this balance that remains today is how to implement these decisions in day-to-day practice of security forces, administration, border controls, and courts.

Some of these decisions and guidelines were purely political measures to respond to citizens' fears, although they were not needed from a legal perspective. Article 29 of the Treaty of Maastricht from 1992, for example, already refers to terrorism as one of the serious forms of crime to be prevented and combated by developing common action in three different ways: first, closer cooperation between police forces, customs authorities, and other competent authorities, including Europol; second, closer cooperation among judicial authorities; and third, cooperation among other competent authorities of the member states. But before the framework decision from June 2002 was adopted, only seven EU countries (namely France, Germany, Italy, Portugal, Greece, Spain, and the United Kingdom) – those dealing with organized terrorist groups for decades – had specific laws to fight terrorism which varied from one country to another. But instead of drawing new EU guidelines in the aftermath of 9/11, it would have been enough to implement the Maastricht Treaty of 1992 and its security standards.

The Europe human rights regime has been strongly challenged by the unclear and confusing number of guidelines and directives. This was already evident in 2002 when the first cases of unlawful rendition flights by the United States via European and EU countries was made public. More than half of all EU countries were involved in these cases of extrajudicial transfer of persons accused of terrorism. They were transported in so-called CIA flights from one state (where the person had been captured) to another via Europe or from Europe to countries where they were subject to torture or ill-treatment. Among those transfer countries that allowed rendition flights were 15 out of the current 27 EU member states (Austria, Belgium, Cyprus, Denmark, France, Germany, Greece, Portugal, Romania, Sweden, and the closer allies in the "war on terror" Poland, Ireland, the United Kingdom, Italy, and Spain). The practice had been noticed and criticized by the CoE in 2002. By then, the Council's Assembly had already estimated that 100 people had been kidnapped by the US CIA agents to be deported to other countries. Some of these flights went via Europe either to Guantánamo Bay in Cuba or to other Eastern European countries and – at that time – non-EU states. Secret detention facilities were discovered and made public, for example, in Poland and Romania before they joined the EU in 2004. EU countries, being willing servants, claimed to be free of any practices that included torture or arbitrary detention. Their argument was that territory outside of the EU was not under their control and therefore outside of their jurisdiction. In those countries the terrorist suspects were subject to serious violations outside EU border and jurisdiction. Subsequently, most of these cases were later dealt with by domestic courts or the ECtHR (Archer 2000; Leino 2002; Fischer et al. 2007).

While estimations and investigations continued over the years, the EU Parliament launched a full-fledged report in 2007 which detected over 1,200 rendition flights over a period of six years. Thus, the fight against terrorism and the protection of human rights gained a new dimension as a large number of victims of human rights abuse in the name of counterterrorism were detailed. It received some publicity and media coverage but in general it remained at the exclusive level of human rights NGOs, legal experts, lawyers, and politicians. That also explains why the general public did not refer to counterterrorism as a major issue in the opinion polls. Nevertheless, it was a test case for the EU and the CoE on how seriously its member states would take the protection of human rights. Even though the European Convention on Human Rights and Fundamental Freedoms and the Charter of Fundamental Freedoms of the European Union were already in place, the credibility of the legal system and the rule of law were at stake for both the CoE and the EU alike. Because of this, it had to be proven how coordinated and comprehensively the CoE and the EU could work together in the regime. The EU Parliament joined the Council's special investigators and experts. As a result a new resolution was adopted by the parliament in 2007, which asked its member states to initiate investigation in their countries, stop turning a blind eye to CIA flights over their territories with the intention to torture alleged suspects and, in this respect, it also called for the closure of Guantánamo Bay (European Parliament 2007).

Following the resolution of the parliament in September 2008, the ECJ passed a leading decision against the resolutions of the UN Security Council from 1999 and 2001 affecting terror suspects. The court made clear that any resolution by another international organization should always be subject to further scrutiny and checking by the states that are responsible for its implementation. It further decided that "smart sanctions," blacklists of terror suspects and the freezing of terrorists' or groups' accounts would have implications for human rights protection (see Schneider, this volume). As a result, any UN sanction must be checked by the European court to see whether they meet all European human rights standards. In 2008 alone, 46 individuals and 48 organizations were included on such lists in Europe. Many of them appealed successfully to the ECJ to remove them from the list and regain their full sovereignty and privacy (Pfeiffer und Schneider 2008). Thus the ECJ, as the last European supranational institution, called its member states to revise any resolution by the UN or other international organizations and thus revise its antiterror laws and counterterrorism practice in the context of human rights.

With this decision, the EU has shown once more that if there is strong enough political will, the legal enforcement mechanism to protect human rights exists. Because only the EU can apply sanctions and restrictions if a member state fails to comply with norms and standards, charges can be pressed against member states at the ECJ, and penalties or compensation payments to victims of human rights violations might be obtained (Woods 1998, 283–300; Nowak 2002, 253–7). Thus, the EU and its institutions, especially the ECJ, are currently the strongest and most effective enforcement mechanisms of the European human rights regime.

The Council of Europe

The CoE is strong in monitoring treaties and obligations as well as its implementation on the national level. One of its main instruments is the ECtHR. The EU and the OSCE would have not been able to take the necessary steps in combating terrorism on the one side while safeguarding human rights on the other, without the human rights standards, treaties, and backing of the Council. This became evident in 2007 with the aforementioned EU Parliament resolution on rendition flights that was backed by the evidence that the CoE provided.

Two months after the terrorist attacks in 2001, the CoE began to implement its plan of action, which resulted in the adoption of a set of international instruments. Ever since then, the CoE's activities in the fight against international terrorism have been built on three cornerstones; strengthening legal action against terrorism, safeguarding fundamental values, and addressing the causes of terrorism.

Even though the 1951 European Convention on Human Rights and Fundamental Freedoms enshrines only individual rights including the prohibition of torture, the freedom of thought, conscience, religion, or peaceful assembly, the ECtHR is completely overwhelmed, dealing with an average of 30,000 provisional files and about 15,000 applications on an annual basis. Over 90,000 cases are pending. Approximately 1,000 judgments and over 10,000 decisions are issued annually by the court (Buergenthal et al. 2002, 143–54). Besides the tremendous number of pending cases at the ECtHR in Strasbourg, the Council also suffers under the multitude of over 200 conventions which are often not known or simply disregarded by their member states and thus do not protect people under threat. With this number of files, decisions and legally binding documents the Court and the Council are hopelessly overburdened. But interestingly enough, cases that involve alleged terrorist acts or issues connected to terrorism have not significantly risen since 2001 because its instruments to tackle the issues of terrorism and human rights protection are not under the jurisdiction of the ECtHR.

In the aftermath of 9/11, the European governments often overreacted and quickly undertook uncoordinated law reforms that threatened human rights standards. As a consequence, the CoE had to investigate and develop effective measures to safeguard human rights in the area of terrorism. Only a few weeks after the attacks in 2001 an intergovernmental committee of experts (namely the multidisciplinary group on International Action against Terrorism (replaced by the Committee of Experts on Terrorism (CODEXTER) in 2003) was established. Other measures in the years to come were more coordinated and included human rights aspects.

In 2005, all 47 member states decided on the European Convention on the Prevention of Terrorism following the EU framework decision on terrorism from 2002. It was the first convention of its kind worldwide, attempting to define terrorism and legal consequences. After launching the investigations on rendition flights in 2006 together with the European Parliament and the Parliament's decision in February 2007, the convention finally went into force in June 2007. The Convention defines those acts that may lead to acts of terrorism, such as incitement, recruitment, and the training in so-called terror-camps. It also reinforces international cooperation in the prevention of terrorism as already outlined in the EU definition on terrorism. However, the big difference between the EU definition and the Council's convention is the legal character of the convention that makes it binding for all 47 member states – if ratified. It will then be valid in countries in Central Asia and the Caucasus where most of the preventative work against terrorism is conducted (Council of Europe 2005).

Post-9/11, the CoE has enhanced its role in standard setting and giving recommendations for its member states. No less then nine conventions dealing with human rights and counterterrorism went into force prior to 2009, dealing with extradition, suppression of terrorism, mutual assistance on criminal matters among member states, compensations for victims of violent crimes, money laundering, cybercrime, and financing terrorism. These conventions target not only victims of international terrorism but also those of the radical movements within Europe. Some of them are the IRA in Northern Ireland or the ETA in the Spanish Basque Country, even though they have no linkage to radical Islamic groups. In addition to these conventions, 14 other resolutions, declarations, and recommendations passed through the Council's Committee of Ministers since 2001. There is no shortage of principles or standards; rather there is a shortage of implementation and policies. Nevertheless, the CoE's capability of agreeing on these sets of norms, values, and principles, and turning them into standards and conventions, is the backbone of the human rights regime in Europe.

But even the immensely increasing number of resolutions, declarations, recommendations, and conventions in the name of counterterrorism had a stability effect on human rights, even if member states could pick and choose from them as they pleased as they backed their domestic policies. Some governments used this opportunity to reduce domestic political uncertainties and to safeguard the rule of law against all public protests or claims from rather conservative parties to even legitimize and justify torture and other forms of ill-treatment in their combat against terrorism.

Out of the declarations and recommendations member states can pick and choose which ones they like to join and implement in their national law. At the same time, the pure velocity and multitude of documents indicate that earlier legal instruments were not always recognized or implemented by member states. To monitor them all and advise all 47 governments how to implement them overburdens the Council's capacity.

The OSCE

In contrast to the EU and the CoE, the OSCE with 56 member states is a purely politically binding intergovernmental organization. It does not set any legal standards or norms, nor does it have an independent jurisdiction or court to monitor and decide about violations of its mandate. It is thus the practical and technical branch of this human rights regime. The OSCE implements and monitors the standards and policies of others such as the CoE, the UN, and – where applicable – those of the EU. Because of its mandate the OSCE has been able to go into areas and regions in Europe where neither the EU nor the CoE were able to go – in particular in far Eastern Europe and Central Asia, to set up field missions, undertaking antiterror trainings and awareness-raising measures. Here, the OSCE ought to ensure and monitor that human rights are protected alongside the many counterterrorism acts and to ensure that governments undertake active steps to combat racism, discrimination, and other forms of intolerance that are somehow related to the severe measures of some governments in their fight against terrorists.

Since 9/11, the OSCE has enhanced its commitments to prevent and combat terrorism. One of the first documents that outlined its function and work along all other measures undertaken by the UN, the CoE, or the EU was the Bucharest Plan of Action in 2001 followed by the

OSCE Charter on Preventing and Combating Terrorism in 2002 (OSCE 2001). Despite the fact that both documents have no legal implications whatsoever, they state, for example, that the human right to a fair trial, privacy, freedom of association, and freedom of religion or belief are to be upheld by its member states against all odds. Based on these documents, ODIHR has initiated programs intended to promote human rights and has strengthened the rule of law as key components that enable states to address the various social, economic, political, and other factors that engender conditions in which terrorist and extremist organizations may recruit or win support.

Because the OSCE cannot do much more than appeal to state responsibilities and obligations and promote human rights, the language used by the participating states is often emphatic in character (Amor and Estébanez 1998, 273). It also underlines its character not to be in competition with other intergovernmental organizations, like the UN, the EU, or the CoE. Thus in terms of the regional human rights regime before and after 9/11, the OSCE's human rights approach is based on the general European human rights regime assumption that individual human rights are best protected in states that adhere to the rule of law and democratic values (Buergenthal et al. 2002, 213). Thereafter, the OSCE/ODIHR saw its main function as emphasizing the rule of law and training security officers how to deal with terror suspects and concurrently keep human rights standards.

By 2004, ODIHR was mandated to collect and compile antiterrorism legislation from all OSCE participating states (OSCE 2004). Organized by subject and country, the compilation has served as a resource for lawmakers in the OSCE region, but also for the ECtHR and the EU. In consequence, ODIHR has been providing technical assistance to participating states with respect to their implementation of UN Security Council Resolution 1373, and the different international conventions and protocols on counterterrorism of the CoE and others. Under the Bucharest Plan of Action, no limits are set on the variety of actions and the creativity of measurements to implement what its participating states have set on paper. The OSCE has provided technical assistance to member states upon request in support of drafting antiterrorism legislation and strengthening existing legislation. Thus, besides its "soft power" in the field, the OSCE also provides valuable information for further acts and decisions. Consequently, ODIHR has been liaising and coordinating with other governmental and nongovernmental partners in the field to fulfill its mandate (OSCE 2009).

The regime today

The European human rights regime reacted immediately after 9/11 with a number of guidelines, doctrines, and legislative measures. It was strengthened in the sense that it helped member states to fill democratic uncertainties on how to deal with the security threat. Some governments used this threat to revise their policies and thus fill legal and political policy gaps to solve some of their domestic problems, for example when fighting years-long terrorist or separation movements as in Spain, France, Russia, or Turkey that have nothing to do with international terrorism.

Nevertheless, European decision-makers argued that traditional law enforcement methods and the promotion of the rule of law were better equipped to combat terrorism than supplementing the criminal justice model of counterterrorist actions with military actions by the United States of America (Steiner et al. 2007, 453). And despite the fact that the United Kingdom, Spain, Italy, and Poland largely shared the view of the US administration and joined the war in Iraq, the majority of European governments in the EU Council opted for the traditional law enforcement mechanism instead.

Despite that, terrorist attacks have continued on all continents, and abductions, arbitrary killings, bombings, and suicide attacks happen on a weekly – if not daily – basis. The large majority of these attacks takes place outside Europe and the Americas in the Middle East, Africa, and Asian Regions as seen in Mumbai in 2008, in the Swat valley in Pakistan in 2009 and continuously in Afghanistan, Iraq, Saudi Arabia, Yemen, and other parts of that region. States react in different ways and many of their measures go beyond their own legal frameworks and violate basic human rights and humanitarian law around the world. Blacklists of terrorist suspects as published by the UN, renditions flights, torture, extended application of death penalties, illegal imprisonments in Guantánamo and elsewhere are some of the harder countermeasures that have been applied since 2001. The closing of bank accounts of terrorist suspects or the denial of visas, restricted movement, and the violation of the freedom of press, expressions, and assembly are just a few more human rights issues that have been negatively affected.

Even despite this, Europe has been least affected by 9/11 as it reacted the most in normative and legal terms. The European governments and their supranational institutions knew from experience that to combat international terrorism would go beyond their common strategies to fight separatist terrorist groups domestically, like the IRA, the ETA, or the separatist movements in Corsica, for example. Terrorists generally operate across borders. And while the world community quickly passed a number of pieces of antiterror legislation within the first two to three months after the terrorist attacks in New York, human rights activists and governments in the most affected regions and countries in Africa, the Middle East, and the United States did not or could not make use of a functional regional human rights regime that would counteract and revise antiterror measures that restricted basic human rights.

With the shallow "feeling of security" in mind, fewer Europeans today fear terror attacks, while at the same time the majority have welcomed the counterterror measures and packages drawn by their governments. In Brussels and Strasbourg, the heart of the European human rights regime, security talks often take place without the public's being involved. In the focus of these talks are preventative counterterrorism measures and applying a fair and equal justice system and thus the rule of (international) law (Goede 2008). To some extent this is also the result of the public pressure on governmental representatives in the human rights regime. Public voices have often highlighted the fact that human rights norms and standards do not necessarily have to be immolated while at the same time security measures increase.

Conclusion

Since 9/11, the European human rights regime's strongest normative mechanisms have prevailed and been strengthened. But the regime has given state governments lots of room on how to interpret and use its norms. Some states used them to restrict freedom rights and justify human rights violations. It is an open question regarding whether they can be fully restored. Despite the numerous preventive "counterterrorism" measures, the mix of EU, CoE, and OSCE and their different mandates and the cooperation among them, along with the supranational jurisdiction and a vivid NGO community, have been counterbalancing the threat of a severe erosion of the human rights standards in Europe more than in other regions of the world.

Overall, the European human rights regime has succeeded in some cases to safeguard and reinstall norms (e.g. renditions flights and precharges). So far the European regime has been the only one able to clarify the terms "terrorism" and "counterterrorism." But at the same time it failed in keeping up citizens' rights concerning privacy issues, free movement, assembly, or physical integrity.

The regime as such has been strengthened through stronger cooperation and if it keeps up its system of checks and balances and cohesion between the different intergovernmental institutions of the EU, the CoE, and the OSCE, it will manage to deal with other threats and challenges for human rights in the 21st century.

8
Terror Blacklists on Trial: Smart Sanctions Challenged by Human Rights

Patricia Schneider

By targeting individual persons and organizations, the new smart sanctions of the UN terror blacklist represent an innovation in international law. International law as drafted in Security Council resolutions is no longer restricted to managing relations between states, but also has a direct impact on individuals. This new situation makes it necessary to take precautions to protect human rights as part of a post-9/11 human rights regime. However, no such precautions have so far been taken. The major complaint concerns the UN's methods – which have been criticized by courts – of placing people and organizations on and removing them from its blacklist (listing and delisting). Sanctions are increasingly put into effect by the UN member states. Individuals and organizations affected by sanctions sought legal remedy at the European Court of Justice (ECJ) and received it in September 2008. The ECJ ruled that European Union (EU) regulations that had been created merely in order to implement Security Council decisions needed to be reviewed by the courts of the European Community to ensure improved human rights protection for terror suspects. What are the EU's terrorist blacklisting procedures, which have come under scrutiny for possible breaches of basic human rights standards? What are the main problems and what are the results of current developments likely to be? The key challenge is to abolish the disjunction between the two major cornerstones of international law – the functioning of the UN system and international human rights obligations. This is possible, but a great deal of political pressure, strengthened by the ECJ's ruling, will be necessary to achieve it.

Following some background, the second section of this chapter analyzes the UN system of antiterror sanctions in general, while the third takes a close look at the controversial listing procedure. The fourth part considers the details of the ECJ's judgments. In order to understand these, it is necessary to discuss the system of EU terrorist lists, which occupies the fifth section. Besides the proceedings before the European Community courts, a case had already come before the European Court of Human Rights, and it will be discussed in the sixth section. The seventh section deals with complaints brought before national courts. The paper concludes by presenting policy recommendations.

Background

In September 2008, the ECJ passed a landmark decision with major consequences for human rights protection, combating terrorism and the legitimacy of United Nations (UN) Security Council decisions. The cause was a case brought to the court by an individual and an organization that had been placed on the UN "terror blacklist," as a result of a Security Council decision. The ECJ was particularly critical of the fact that there was no opportunity to review the decision's compatibility with the rule of law.

While this ruling strengthened human rights protection, it also called into question a fundamental principle of the UN Charter. According to Article 25, the members of the UN agree "to accept and carry out the decisions of the Security Council in accordance with the present Charter."[1] There is no national or international court with the power to review Security Council resolutions.

The ECJ's ruling asserts, in effect, that decisions of the Security Council can be subject to judicial review by the courts of the European Community where the Security Council has not itself established a suitable review process. This, however, opens the door to a weakening of the international legal order as embodied in the UN, though it also strengthens international human rights obligations. Ultimately, however, this could lead to individual states deciding for themselves – via laws they pass or their influence over national courts – whether they are obliged to implement Security Council resolutions or not. The ECJ is not offering to take over the review process itself, but merely criticizing the fact that none exists.

The weakening of the sanctions regime would be particularly problematic with regard to measures aimed at combating terrorism. It is well known that there are considerable differences of opinion between UN member states both over fundamental questions, such as the definition of terrorism, as well as regarding the status of particular groups and individuals. UN resolutions represent a valuable contribution to international coordination and cooperation in this area.

UN antiterror sanctions

The UN Security Council passed Resolution 1267 on the early date of October 15, 1999. Originally directed at aiding the fight against the Taliban in Afghanistan, it stated that money and other economic resources belonging to individuals and organizations listed in an annex were to be frozen.[2] A UN sanctions committee was established to implement the resolution and relevant additional provisions.[3] Sanctions committees are subsidiary organs of the UN Security Council, and may be established according to Article 29 of the UN Charter. The sanctions committee's constitution reflects the current makeup of the Security Council and the committee is always chaired by a non-permanent member (United Nations 2007). There are currently 11 such committees, dealing with Somalia, Congo, Sudan, and Iran, among others.

The sanctions regime based on Resolution 1267 has been enhanced by means of a large number of Security Council resolutions and is the first to have no geographical focus (in its current form), as sanctions can now be directed against people or organizations that have no connection with Afghanistan.

In the case in question, the sanctions committee is responsible for registering individuals and organizations on the list. Following the attacks of September 11, 2001, the resolution was extended to apply to people and organizations that could be linked to Al Qaeda. The plaintiffs were added to the list on October 19, 2001, on the basis of their alleged links to Al Qaida and the Taliban.

These "targeted" or "smart" UN sanctions are intended to be more effective than general sanctions and to reduce the negative humanitarian impact on innocent populations. While trade and economic embargos were previously directed at states, smart sanctions aim to exert economic and political pressure not only on regimes, but also on individuals (Schmahl 2006, 566 ff.). Alongside the military and political leaders of conflict parties, terror suspects have increasingly been included in such sanctions lists. Smart sanctions should make it harder for targeted individuals to organize. The sanctions urge states to withhold various kinds of support, make travel more difficult, and block access to money by freezing bank accounts. There is no provision for making financial reparations in case of error. Therefore it is imperative that, as Feinäugle formulated: "... the drastic effect the listing has for the individual must be balanced and weighed against the goal of fighting terrorism" (2010, 130).

The complete UN terror blacklist is freely available on the Internet (United Nations 2008c) and openly stigmatizes those placed on it by displaying a number of details like their postal addresses and passport numbers. It contains the names of individuals and organizations, including banks, nongovernmental organizations and charities. The list currently contains the names of several hundred individuals and around 100 organizations that can be linked with the Taliban or Al Qaida.

The controversial listing procedure

While there has been relatively little international criticism of the mere fact that the UN has maintained a terrorist blacklist, the procedure for listing and delisting names has been on the receiving end of fierce criticism from a large number of states, NGOs, the Secretary-General, and the General Assembly.[4] In January 2006, with the support of the governments of Germany, Switzerland, and Sweden, several meetings of experts took place, which led to the publication of a report in March 2006 containing detailed recommendations on how the procedure could be improved (Biersteker and Eckert 2008).

One recommendation was later implemented by Security Council Resolutions 1730 and 1735 of 19 and December 22, 2006, which enhanced the rights of the individuals and entities on the lists. They established a coordinating office – the "focal point" – and put in place a more sophisticated delisting procedure. An affected party can now request to be delisted either directly at the focal point or through his or her state of residence or citizenship. The request is then passed to the government that submitted the name for listing and to the governments of the states of residence and citizenship. If one of these recommends delisting, the request is passed on to the Sanctions Committee. A positive decision then requires unanimity, that is, *a single negative vote is enough to block the delisting*.

If, after consultation with the focal point, the government that originally issued the listing request or the state of residence refuses to support the delisting request, the Sanctions Committee is informed of the fact and is not required to consider the case. In such a case, the affected individual or entity cannot be removed from the list.

The focal point is thus not a true review panel, as it possesses no powers to challenge decisions of the Committee. Furthermore, the procedure is carried out *in camera*. The individuals and entities subject to sanctions are provided with no information on the reasons for having been listed. They are also required to prove their innocence without seeing the incriminating material, which frequently consists of information gathered by the intelligence services that, even in the Sanctions Committee, can only be narrated to the other member states in general terms.

Since its establishment, the focal point has received 24 requests for delisting from affected individuals or entities. Of these, 15 are still being processed, 20 names have been removed from the list, and 7 requests have been rejected (UN Security Council 2007a). All in all, 27 persons or organizations have been delisted for various reasons. While a list of persons and organizations that have been delisted is available on the website of the Sanctions Committee, it does not contain details of why they were removed (United Nations 2008b).

Since the new provisions still did not satisfy the critics, Michael Bothe, an expert on international law, was asked by Germany, Switzerland, and Sweden to make new suggestions on how listing and delisting could be improved. At the heart of his recommendations is the notion of a Review Mechanism, run by an independent agency, that would carry out a proper examination of the requests and the evidence, quickly come to a decision, and publish the results (cf. figure 2) (Bothe 2007, 2008).

Additional recommendations also emerged from discussions in the fields of international law and politics. For instance, the central recommendations made by Thomas Meerpohl were, first, that delisting requests should be approved by a majority vote (instead of consensus); second, that entries on the list should be deleted automatically after two years unless the Sanctions Committee were to consider the case again and resolve to renew them (Meehrpohl 2008, 299).

Apart from this procedure, in which those affected are entirely dependent on the judgment of political actors, there is currently no judicial authority at the UN level through which individuals may challenge their listing status. Many proposed improvements therefore mention a potential role for international courts. However, only states may be parties in cases before the International Court of Justice (ICJ).[5] However, the General Assembly can request a nonbinding opinion from the ICJ (Meehrpohl 2008, 36), but doing so would concern the whole process of listing and delisting rather than a single case.

Another relevant proposal is that of a World Court for Human Rights, whose proponents include Manfred Nowak, the UN Special Rapporteur on Torture. This aims to close a key gap in the UN human rights protection system, which is still lacking 60 years after the Universal Declaration of Human Rights (Schneider 2002, 321; Nowak 2008, 205ff).

Further progress in introducing legal procedures for listing and delisting is particularly opposed by the permanent members of the UN Security Council, who are frightened of seeing both their power and their ability to combat terrorism diminish. The role of vetoes in the Security Council and the requirement for unanimity in the sanctions committees give them considerable political influence over the imposition and execution of sanctions – influence they do not wish to surrender to other institutions.

The lack of engagement of many UN members is also a consequence of the antipathy of a number of key members of the UN Security Council toward weakening the Security Council's authority in the antiterrorism system. This is apparent, for instance, in the ineffective way smart sanctions are applied by the member states. Finally, it has so far proven impossible to reach an agreement on a general convention against terrorism that would unite the numerous individual measures in a coherent whole while closing the gaps that continue to exist. This is a consequence of an inability to agree on either a definition of terrorism or how best to combat both it and its root causes (Martinez 2008, 320ff.).[6]

The ECJ's judgments

The ECJ's[7] appeal decision of September 3, 2008 concerned the implementation of UN Sanctions in European Community law. The decisive element of the judgment is that, in the opinion of the court, the Community courts are entitled to review EC regulations that give effect to UN Security Council resolutions.

In its judgments of September 21, 2005, the European Court of First Instance (CFI) had rejected the cases brought by *Jassin Abdullah Kadi* and the *Al Barakaat International Foundation* against EC Regulation No. 881/2002 of May 27, 2002, which gave effect to UN Security Council Resolution 1267 from 1999. The complainants had applied for the regulation to be annulled on the grounds that the Council of the European Union had no competence to adopt the regulation, which also infringed several of their fundamental rights.

On appeal, the ECJ found for the appellants. In its judgment of September 3, 2008, it annulled the regulation in question as it applied to them. However, before the annulment took effect, the Council was given a three-month period during which the regulation would continue to apply. This was to enable the Council to remedy the infringements found.

It was first necessary to consider whether a court of the European Community has jurisdiction to review a regulation adopted in order to give effect to a UN Security Council resolution. The European Community is not a formal member of the UN (Heun-Rehn 2008, 329). Therefore, only the member states of the EC owe an immediate obligation to the UN under international law. The European Community is only under an indirect obligation (Meerpohl 2008, 190f.), which arises because community loyalty requires the EC to observe its member states' obligations under international law.

The ECJ decided that the UN Security Council resolution was not in itself subject to the jurisdiction of the European Community, but that the regulation effecting its mandate certainly was. The ECJ thus opened the way to a substantive review of the resolution with regard to the fundamental rights contained in Community law.[8] The CFI had restricted the right to review peremptory norms of international law (*jus cogens*).

The judgment further states that, in this specific case, the right to respect for property (only in relation to Mr *Kadi*) and the right to be heard and to effective judicial review (in relation to both plaintiffs) had been infringed. The reexamination procedure described above, the court held, was not sufficient to ensure effective judicial review and could not lead to a general rejection of the jurisdiction of the Community courts.[9]

The subjects affected by the sanctions were not informed as to why the sanctions had been imposed. However, the court recognized that, while the affected persons and organizations cannot be informed before they are put on the list, they must be after their assets have been successfully frozen. In addition, the plaintiffs were not informed of how they could defend themselves against the sanctions.

To provide the plaintiffs a remedy with regard to the regulation, the Council of the European Union would have to acknowledge that regulations whose purpose is to give effect to obligations under international law are not exempt from judicial review, and, furthermore, considering the right to property, to grant Mr *Kadi* the right to submit his concerns to the appropriate bodies. The restriction of his right to property can be justified in general, just not in this particular case.

The press[10] was right to stress the far-reaching consequences of this judgment. Although the court only annulled the regulation in so far as it affected the plaintiffs, it opened the way to further suits in European courts brought by anyone affected by these kinds of UN sanctions. That is because the court declared itself to be competent, ruling that regulations that give effect to UN sanctions are not exempt from review. The judgment marks the first time that those affected by such sanctions have been granted effective legal protection.

The ECJ judgment is likely to have an impact on the UN (Weinzierl 2008). A particular problem is entailed by the fact that (at least some) confidential knowledge possessed by Security Council members would have to be presented to the courts and the complainants. While virtually every independent legal system requires the evidence to be presented and the burden of proof to be fulfilled, confidential information from the security services that is released into the public domain may not survive the scrutiny of judicial review, as it is seldom of the standard required by the courts. Information held by the UN on individual terrorist organizations comes from various legal systems and is ultimately political in nature. The requirement for evidence to be made publicly available could lead to restrictions in the exchange of information between states while also providing states that are unwilling to implement the decisions with an argument or even a pretext (where politically or economically disadvantageous) for refusing to implement them at the national level, thereby endangering the system of international law (Heun-Rehn 2008, 333ff.).

The three-month period of grace granted to the Council by the ECJ ended at the start of December 2008. On November 28, 2008, the European Commission issued a regulation[11] confirming the listing of Mr *Kadi* and the *Al Barakaat International Foundation*. The regulation explained that a summary of the grounds for the listing of both parties, as provided by the Al Qaida and Taliban Sanctions Committee, had been passed to those affected to give them an opportunity to comment on them. The regulation further stated that the Commission had received these comments, examined them and decided that links with the Al Qaida network meant that the listing was nonetheless justified. No proceedings against the regulation have yet been brought before the CFI. Whether the Commission's actions comply with the ECJ judgment thus remains to be seen and we must await further developments.

The EU terrorist lists

The UN Security Council's terrorist blacklist must be distinguished from the lists kept by the EU. In Resolution 1373 of September 28, 2001, the UN Security Council called upon its members to supplement the UN Sanctions Committee's list by developing lists of their own for the freezing of funds belonging to people and organizations that could be linked with terrorist activities.[12] The EU complied with this on

December 27, 2001, in the form of a Common Position (2001/931/CFSP) and EC Regulation 2580/2001.

The Council's Common Position includes a list of individuals and organizations who were allegedly involved in terrorist acts. The most recent list, issued on December 22, 2009, contains 25 names of individuals and 29 organizations (2009/1004/CFSP). However, of those names that appear on the list, only those not appended with asterisks are subject to financial sanctions. Latter ones were also placed on a second list (2009/62/EC). On January 26, 2009, there were 28 individuals and 29 organizations on this list, including the PKK (Kurdish Workers' Party), the Palestinian Liberation Front (PLF), and Hamas.[13]

The EC regulation also states that the competent authorities of the relevant state may be granted specific authorizations to use the frozen funds to fulfill the essential human needs of a person on the list or a member of his or her family, as long as these are fulfilled within the Community. Those entered on the list are informed of the fact and provided with a statement containing the reasons for their being listed.[14] Any EU member state can apply to have a person or entity added to the list, as can non-EU member states. Those affected can submit a request for delisting with the appropriate authorities.

Yet this entire procedure often takes place on the edges of or outside the rule of law and the EU courts have therefore revoked sanctions several times. In contrast to the case of the UN list, here there is no problem with the competency of the courts. Among other things, the courts have criticized listing on the basis of insufficient grounds. On December 4, 2008, the CFI ruled that the inclusion of the *People's Mujahedin of Iran* (PMOI) on the list was incorrect. The PMOI is an opposition group in exile that works to oppose the current Iranian government. The suspicion therefore arose that its continuing classification as a terrorist group only came about as a result of pressure from Iran (Schweda 2007).

The PMOI had been campaigning for years to have its name removed and the CFI had already ruled three times in its favor. Despite this, the Council of the European Union had left it on the EU terror list. It justified this inaction by noting that the court had only admonished the fact that the PMOI had been granted no opportunity for a hearing or defense. Since the organization had since been provided with the reasons for its listing, the Council argued, it could still be considered a terrorist organization (Deutscher Bundestag 2007). After each of the various CFI decisions, the reasoning continued, new versions of the list were adopted in a Common Position. The judgment was therefore interpreted by the EU member states to no longer apply (Runner 2008). This makes a mockery of effective legal protection. It was only on January 26, 2009, a way out of this seemingly endless loop was found. It was agreed at a meeting of EU foreign ministers, in response to the ruling of the CFI, to finally strike the PMOI from the list.[15]

The EU terror list is regularly contested before the courts and was the subject of an action recently on May 12, 2010, during the public hearings before the Grand Chamber of the ECJ (preliminary ruling C-550/09). Doubts are especially voiced with regard to the establishment of an enemy criminal law. This is used to justify certain sanctions, similar to punishments, which have weak demands to proof and judicial rights. Although the ECJ attaches great importance to these questions, a comprehensive ruling on the EU terror list has not been forthcoming.

The ECHR and the Council of Europe

Besides the proceedings before the European Community courts, a case concerning an entry on the EU list had already come before the European Court of Human Rights (ECHR)[16] in May 2002 regarding the organizations *Segi* and *Gestoras Pro-Amnistia*.[17] The ECHR rejected the complaint, since the organization had only been classified as a terrorist entity by the EU but had not frozen its funds. As a result, none of its rights had been infringed. The ECHR also ruled that if the organization's rights had been infringed, there would be nothing stopping it from turning to the European Community courts. The ECHR thus declared that it was not competent for this or other claims related to the EU list.[18]

The Parliamentary Assembly of the Council of Europe, which had already condemned the abduction and secret imprisonment of terror suspects, has passed a resolution, Recommendation 1824 (2008), calling for better human rights protection in listing and delisting. The Assembly considers the members of the Council of Europe, particularly those that are also EU member states or permanent members of the UN Security Council, to have a responsibility to stand up for the observation of basic legal standards in the listing and delisting of terror suspects.

Complaints brought before national courts

It is doubtful whether the opportunity exists to appeal a listing by the UN Security Council before a national court. This is only indirectly possible, for instance, if a listed person were to bring a civil action against the bank for refusing to release the person's funds, and the bank were to invoke the national legislation giving effect to the UN Resolution

(Meerpohl 2008, 19). In the European Community there is an additional problem, as UN Security Council resolutions are given effect by means of pan-European regulations. Acts of European legislation are under the jurisdiction of the European courts, as recognized by Germany's constitutional court, for instance, in the *"Solange-II"* decision (cf. Decision of the Constitutional Court – BverfGE – 73, 339). According to this ruling, the Constitutional Court's review power is reactivated if the EC systematically fails to uphold the expectations the court has of it with regard to the protection of fundamental rights (Schmahl 2006, 570). At least as long as the Community courts had not seen themselves as competent, Stefanie Schmahl considered the implementation of Security Council resolutions for which there was no possibility of legal protection on any level, as problematic:

> In general, however, it cannot be acceptable for the Federal Republic of Germany to hand the power to implement Security Council resolutions over to the EC, and yet for the Community to contract out of its responsibility for the implementation of Security Council decisions by passing the main responsibility on to the United Nations, which offers no effective legal protection. (Schmahl 2006, 574)

National courts have far more experience in dealing with terror suspects than the courts of the European Community (Hörmann 2007, 133). It has therefore been recommended, purely on pragmatic grounds, that those seeking legal protection turn to the jurisdiction where most of the measures have their origin, the United States. It is the United States that has both proposed most names for the UN list and ensured that they were added to it (without informing the other Sanctions Committee members of the key facts of the cases (Schaller 2006, 28). Appealing to US courts has the practical advantage that US intelligence agencies need only reveal their information to US courts (Ley 2007, 292).

On May 13, 2009, according to the Monitoring Team of the UN Sanctions Committee, there were 30 pending cases related to the terror lists altogether – in the EU, Pakistan, Switzerland, the United States, and Turkey (United Nations 2009). A decision by Turkey's highest administrative court on July 4, 2006 was a sensation. The court decided in favor of Jassin A. *Kadi*, who had failed to have his listing undone by the European Court of First Instance in September 2005. The court did not examine his innocence, but based its decision on the fact that documents and materials upon which the Sanctions Committee had based its judgment could not be produced in court. An appeal was withdrawn following a political intervention by Turkish Prime Minister *Erdogan*, who presented the press with an image of *Kadi* as a credible philanthropist (Meehrpohl 2008, 288f.).

Conclusion

In summation, it is important to note that we are dealing with three different lists on two different levels. The ECJ judgment of September 2008 criticized the UN list implemented at the EU level. The court declared itself competent, thereby establishing the reviewability of EU regulations giving effect to UN sanctions. As a result, those affected are provided with effective legal protection, at least within the EU.

Consideration has also been made of the EU's own lists, which it creates independently of the UN list. One list consists of individuals and organizations involved in terrorist activities, but only those whose names appear on the second list have their assets frozen. The competence of the EU courts does not pose a problem in this case, but there are concerns regarding whether the procedure of the Council of the European Union infringes fundamental principles of the rule of law.

The concept of listing individuals under the auspices of the "smart sanctions regime" imposed after 9/11 offers the opportunity to sanction specific individuals, potentially weakening the human rights regime, as these individuals may be partially denied some of their human rights. This, however, is only the case if there is insufficient opportunity to challenge the listing by lawful means. Every listed individual or organization must have the possibility and means to challenge the accusations and be consequently delisted, if the evidence presented proves their innocence. Only then will the "smart sanctions" potentially strengthen the Human Rights Regime, as they offer a precise tool to combat illegal financial transactions. Nevertheless, this is only the case if the listing process is based on the "presumption of innocence." This implies that the individual or organization is only listed if conclusive evidence is presented and the accused has had the chance to be heard *before* the listing takes place.

The EU should therefore also resolve to pay more heed to the rule of law. It needs to comply immediately with the judgments of the ECJ. The action taken against the PMOI was and remains unacceptable, even though the delisting that has finally come about should be welcomed. Combating terrorism at the EU level not only needs institutional procedures that can enable more intense cooperation on security policy, but also requires confidence-building as a prerequisite (Bendiek 2006, 40f.). Only if these procedures are subject to parliamentary or judicial control can the confidence of the member states and their citizens be strengthened, thereby contributing to deepening the European integration process.

The Security Council needs considerable room to maneuver if it is to fulfill its task of safeguarding security and peace. At the same time, it needs to respect an overall core of norms. This is also laid down in Article 24 of the UN Charter, which states that the Security Council must "act in accordance with the Purposes and Principles of the United Nations." As long as there is no effective mechanism for reviewing the legitimacy of Security Council resolutions, it will fall short of fulfilling certain fundamental obligations, particularly the right to effective remedy, according to Article 8 of the Universal Declaration of Human Rights.

Where no such procedure is in place, the danger also exists that resolutions of the Security Council and its sanctions committees will become increasingly weakened as courts in member states subject ever more listing decisions to review. In the relevant literature, this is increasingly being seen as a legitimate last resort as a means of protecting human rights (Payandeh 2006, 65f.).

The ECJ has now decided to support this position – and with good reason. Listing and delisting need to be reviewable. The danger that individuals might find themselves on a terror blacklist as a result of political considerations that simply do not fulfill the defined criteria for the categorization of terrorist organizations is too great. As Feinäugle has correctly pointed out: "... the Sanctions Committee... remains a political body driven by the individual States' interests" (Feinäugle 2010, 127).

States can deliberately abuse these lists by proposing their "archenemies," such as opposition movements, while allowing each other to proceed unhindered in the name of "honor among thieves." This makes it too easy to impose sanctions upon the innocent. In addition, the possibility of false accusations, as a result of intelligence failures, for instance, or simply the misidentification of names, makes the establishment of a legal procedure with several levels of review a matter of urgency. The same applies to the listing procedure, as the public accusation of an individual or an organization stigmatizes them, which can not only damage them commercially[19] but can also have an irreparable negative impact in the personal sphere (Schmahl 2006, 568).

Transferring the task of reviewing sanctioning decisions to national courts is, however, very problematic. It carries the danger that individuals and organizations could be exempted from sanctions, for instance for cooperating with the national authorities, even if this contradicts the spirit and purpose of the sanctions. How can it be guaranteed that countries such as Pakistan, Egypt, Saudi Arabia, or Libya make their rulings based only on considerations of the legitimacy of a delisting procedure without regard to political considerations?

The consequence of the ECJ judgment must therefore be the accelerated development of a listing and delisting procedure that is consistent with fundamental human rights standards. While a review mechanism, for example, judicial review, would certainly uncover mistakes made by the Sanctions Committee in individual cases, it would not damage the overall authority of the Security Council.

An opportunity for more general supervision of the Security Council – not only with regard to the terror list – is considered by many to be desirable in view of the way its tasks have multiplied and its powers have grown over the years. Campaigning for the rule of law is an imperative. Despite all the problems these plans reveal, they need to be kept in view as long-term goals for UN reform.

If the UN offered adequate legal protection, future cases brought to the ECJ would in all likelihood collapse. The only sensible course is to continue to insist that a neutral review mechanism be introduced at the UN level. If it becomes clear that the latest changes in the sanctions regime are meeting with rejection and are not being implemented by the member states (including as a result of court decisions), it should be possible to bring Security Council members to agreement by means of political pressure, and the European countries and other democracies should be obliged to fulfill their moral duty in this regard. Another possibility is that the Security Council dreads the judicial review of its decisions – no matter how indirect – so much that it gives up the listing and delisting procedure altogether.[20] This would be one way to abolish the dilemma between the two columns of international law: the functioning of the UN system and international human rights obligations. Such a course, however, would certainly not lead to a satisfying solution, as, on the one hand, it would weaken the civil instruments in the fight against terrorism and, on the other, it would not address the phenomenon of UN actions increasingly affecting individuals' civil rights directly.

Notes

1. Article 103 of the UN Charter also states: "In the event of a conflict between the obligations of the Members of the United Nations under the present Charter and their obligations under any other international agreement, their obligations under the present Charter shall prevail."
2. "*The Security Council ... [d]ecides further that ...* all States shall ... [f]reeze funds and other financial resources, including funds derived or generated from property owned or controlled directly or indirectly by the Taliban, or by any undertaking owned or controlled by the Taliban, as designated by the Committee established by paragraph 6 below, and ensure that neither they nor any other funds or financial resources so designated are made available,

by their nationals or by any persons within their territory, to or for the benefit of the Taliban or any undertaking owned or controlled, directly or indirectly, by the Taliban, except as may be authorized by the Committee on a case-by-case basis on the grounds of humanitarian need." Excerpt from Resolution 1267, October 15, 1999.

3. *"The Security Council ... [d]ecides* to establish, in accordance with rule 28 of its provisional rules of procedure, a Committee of the Security Council consisting of all the members of the Council to undertake the following tasks and to report on its work to the Council with its observations and recommendations." Excerpt from Resolution 1267, October 15, 1999.

4. Fifty-six states are said to have indicated in 2005 that they could not effectively implement the sanctions under the given conditions. For details of the activities of the General Assembly, the Secretary-General and the Secretariat, see Meehrpohl 2008, 24ff.

5. With its headquarters in The Hague, the ICJ is the main judicial organ of the United Nations. All members of the UN are simultaneously parties to the ICJ statute. The affected states must agree before the ICJ can accept a case. They may either accept the court's jurisdiction generally, with reservations, or on a case-by-case basis.

6. The conflict over the definition of terrorism revolves mostly around two questions: How acts of terrorism can be distinguished from acts of violence carried out legitimately in pursuit of the right to self-determination, and whether measures taken by the military forces of a state can be considered to be acts of terror.

7. Based in Luxembourg, the ECJ is the highest court for European law. It has already made fundamental contributions to promoting European integration on many occasions. The enforcement of its judgments is problematic, as no means exists by which European institutions may be forced to put judgments by European courts into effect. A "CFI" was created in 1989 to take some of the ECJ's burden.

8. "It follows from the foregoing that the Community judicature must, in accordance with the powers conferred on it by the EC Treaty, ensure the review, in principle the full review, of the lawfulness of all Community acts in the light of the fundamental rights forming an integral part of the general principles of Community law, including review of Community measures which, like the contested regulation, are designed to give effect to the resolutions adopted by the Security Council under Chapter VII of the Charter of the United Nations." Extract from the ECJ judgment of September 3, 2008.

9. "321 In any event, the existence, within that United Nations system, of the re-examination procedure before the Sanctions Committee even having regard to the amendments recently made to it, cannot give rise to generalized immunity from jurisdiction within the internal legal order of the Community.

322 Indeed, such immunity, constituting a significant derogation from the scheme of judicial protection of fundamental rights laid down by the EC Treaty, appears unjustified, for clearly that re-examination procedure does not offer the guarantees of judicial protection." Extract from the ECJ judgment of September 3, 2008.

10. Cf. *Süddeutsche Zeitung* "EU erhält Rüge von höchster Stelle"; *taz*, "EuGH stärkt Terror-Verdächtige"; *FAZ*, "Gericht verlangt Rechtsschutz bei Kontoeinfrierungen," all from 3 September 2008.
11. See Commission Regulation (EC) No. 1190/2008 at http://eur-lex.europa.eu/ (accessed January 8, 2009).
12. "*The Security Council ... decides* that all States shall:
    a) Prevent and suppress the financing of terrorist acts; ...
    c) Freeze without delay funds and other financial assets or economic resources of persons who commit, or attempt to commit, terrorist acts or participate in or facilitate the commission of terrorist acts; ..." Excerpt from Security Council Resolution 1373 from September 28, 2001.
13. The Council updates the lists regularly, for which unanimity is a requirement. Article 2 Section 3 of EC Regulation 2580/2001: "The Council, acting by unanimity, shall establish, review and amend the list of persons, groups and entities to which this Regulation applies ..."
14. Cf. European Union, "The EU list of persons, groups and entities subject to specific measures to combat terrorism, January 27, 2009.
15. Cf. the latest CFSP/EC lists of January 26, 2009, on which the PMOI does not appear: 2009/67/CFSP, 2009/62/EC.
16. Sitting in Strasburg, the ECHR monitors compliance with the European Convention on Human Rights, to which all signatory states of the Council of Europe are subject. The Council of Europe was founded in 1949 in an effort to drive forward European integration and secure peace on the continent. It currently has 47 member states. The Convention, which entered into force in 1953, contains a catalog of fundamental and human rights. Both individuals and states may petition the ECHR.
17. Cf. ECHR Ruling of May 23, 2002.
18. Excerpt from the ECHR Judgment of May 23, 2002: "However, the applicants are not concerned by that regulation since, according to the list in the annex to the common position, they are subject only to Article 4. And even if they were affected, they could always apply to the Court of Justice of the European Communities."
19. One example concerns one of Somalia's largest companies, which was driven to bankruptcy without any evidence being produced that would have stood up in court; Vlcek 2006, 497ff.
20. Some experts consider this to be implicitly the most feasible option right now. This is based on the reluctant attitude of the permanent Security Council members toward proposals to introduce some kind of judicial review to the listing/delisting procedure. On the other hand, the list of "[i]ndividuals, groups, undertakings and entities that have been removed from the Consolidated List pursuant to a decision by the 1267 Committee," which dated from September 26, 2008, was updated as recently as 2 October 2009: this does not signal a political will to introduce a judicial review in the near future.

9
Human Rights and Counterterrorism: The Case of the Netherlands

Peter R. Baehr

Has the commitment to human rights shifted after the attacks on the World Trade Center in New York on September 11, 2001? The answer would at first sight seem to be negative, if one looks at statements delivered on behalf of governments such as that of the Netherlands.

The Foreign Minister of the Netherlands, Maxime Verhagen, has been quite outspoken in his commitment to human rights:

> Tradition, culture or religion must never be used to justify the violation of human rights. Equally, there can be no special circumstances in which human rights violations may be condoned. A simple example is our duty to protect people from torture. The fight against terrorism has sparked a debate on where there are circumstances in which torture may be acceptable. I have a very simple answer to that: no. Torture is not acceptable in any circumstances. (Statement by Maxime Verhagen, Minister of Foreign Affairs of the Netherlands, at the 7th Session of the Human Rights Council, Geneva, 3 March 2008)

In his paper on a strategy for human rights, the Foreign Minister stated: "The rules that have been set down in international treaties on the respect for human rights, are valid under all circumstances and therefore also in the fight against terrorism" (Netherlands Ministry of Foreign Affairs 2007, 63).

That is what the Netherlands government had to say. In the following, we will discuss whether and to what extent the commitment to human rights still has undergone changes since the events of September 11, 2001, commonly known as 9/11. The site of analysis will be the Netherlands. This means that we will focus on a small Western European democracy that has always put great emphasis on the development and maintenance of international law in general and human rights law in particular. It is a party to most international human rights treaties and has taken the lead in the development of some of them such as the prohibition of torture (Burgers and Danelius 1988; Reiding 2007, 75–127). As a cofounder of the North Atlantic Treaty Organisation (NATO) in 1949, the Netherlands is a firm member of the Western alliance. It is also a cofounder of the United Nations (UN), which it has always strongly supported. However, the events in the Bosnian enclave of Srebrenica in 1995, when under the very eyes of Dutch peacekeepers, more than 7,000 Bosnian Muslims were killed by Bosnian Serb forces, have been a traumatic experience for the Netherlands. It meant a challenge to both its commitment to human rights and its faith in the UN (Baehr, forthcoming).

This chapter provides an analysis of how the Netherlands has responded to the threat of terrorist activities after 9/11, raising some critical questions over the way in which the traditional emphasis on human rights has given way to what are considered necessary measures to counterterrorism – a tension that is not necessarily recognized by government officials.

Terrorism

The threat of terrorism and the means taken to combat terrorist attacks (the "war on terrorism") are nowadays often cited as threats to the maintenance of international human rights standards, "implying that the usual legal restraints and checks and balances [do] not apply" (Forsythe 2006, 471; see also Forsythe 2008, 25–33).

Terrorism is an assault on human rights. It constitutes "… any action … if it is intended to cause death or serious bodily harm to civilians or non-combatants with the purpose of intimidating a population or compelling a Government or an international organization to do or abstain from any act" *(In Larger Freedom. Towards Development Security and Human Rights for All.* Report by the UN Secretary-General in the Follow-Up to the Millennium Summit, UN Doc. A/59/2005, March 21, 2005, par. 91). Although this is what then UN Secretary-General Kofi Annan has proposed, there does not yet exist a universally accepted definition of terrorism (Van Ginkel 2009, 149). Another proposal is the draft comprehensive convention on international terrorism, which is stalled because there are differences between the West and the members of the Organization of Islamic conference (http://cns.miis.edu/pubs/inven/pdfs/intlterr.pdf; accessed April 15, 2010; see also Wilson 2005, 2, note 2; Schrijver and van den Herik 2007, 573–5). Such acts violate the *right to life* of civilians.

The terminology used in the current debates such as "the fight against international terrorism" suggests that we are dealing with a recognizable, uniform and new phenomenon – with its own ideology, organizational structure, and so on – that regards the West as its enemy and wishes to cause it harm ("jihadist terrorism," Al Qaeda). However, historical examples of the 19th and early 20th century and the separatist terrorism of the IRA and ETA and various groups in Kashmir show that it is not an entirely new phenomenon. There will always be people who wish to attack their enemies and who accept – or even aim for – innocent casualties (Advisory Council on International Affairs 2006, 7).

What is relatively new, however, is that today's transnational terrorism focuses on "the West," thereby trying to change power relations in Middle Eastern countries such as Saudi Arabia and Egypt. The governments of these countries are seen by revolutionary groups as being subservient to "the West," more in particular the United States of America. Hurting or bringing down these governments would help the revolutionary cause, which is, however, not necessarily explicitly stated. Also new is the effectiveness of the attacks and the scale on which they occur as well as the degree to which perpetrators are willing to risk their own lives for the cause. As the UN Special Rapporteur on the Promotion and Protection of Human Rights and Fundamental Freedoms while Encountering Terrorism, Martin Scheinin, has noted: "[W]hat turns a suicide attack into terrorism, even during an armed conflict, is the targeting of civilians as victims" (Report of the Special Rapporteur on the promotion and protection of human rights and fundamental freedoms, while countering terrorism, (UN Doc. A/HRC/4/26 (January 29, 2007), par. 69).

In his report to the Human Rights Council over 2006, he warned against the increasing practice by states of terrorist "profiling" based on certain physical, behavioral, or psychological characteristics, including "race," ethnicity, national origin, and/or religion. This practice he considered both ineffective and a disproportional interference with human rights such as the right to privacy, freedom of movement, personal liberty, and nondiscrimination (ibid., 6–7). He also warned against disproportionate measures against suicide attacks: "Combined with shoot-to-kill policies or other forms of relaxing the standards related to the use of firearms, 'profiling' can have lethal consequences for totally innocent individuals" (25).

In a policy paper that was sent to Parliament in early March 2008, the Dutch Minister of Foreign Affairs stated that the promotion and protection of human rights should be an integral part of an effective antiterrorism strategy. "The protection of human rights is essential in preventing extremism and violent political opposition" (Netherlands Ministry of Foreign Affairs 2008, par. 62). In conversations with US government representatives, the Minister had repeatedly criticized the juridical foundations of the detention of terrorism suspects in Guantánamo Bay. The paper also stated that the dialogue with the United States about the antiterrorism activities would be continued, both bilaterally and through the European Union (EU). The Foreign Minister added, not without a touch of realism: "This will be a long-winded process" (par. 68). It should be added that recent research has revealed that the instructions to the Dutch delegation to the UN Commission on Human Rights for the period 2001–3 remained silent on the new US detention policy since 9/11, "while Amnesty and Human Rights Watch regarded them as priorities" (Malcontent 2008, 205).

Antiterrorism in the Netherlands

In the Netherlands, various measures have been taken to counter terrorist activities that would seem at odds with basic human rights (Peters and van der Laan 2007, 127–32). Such measures include the right of the General Intelligence and Security Service, Algemene Inlichtingen- en Veiligheidsdienst (AIVD) to tap the telephone conversations of journalists under certain conditions. Evidence can be withheld from court proceedings if the AIVD objects and information can be withheld from the accused for up to two years. Administrative measures can be taken by the government to restrict persons in their freedom of movement by prohibiting them from visiting certain areas or being in the vicinity of certain other persons. Stalking by the police is allowed, even if such actions may lack a specific legal basis. For many years, Dutch citizens were not required to carry any identification. Proposals to that effect were always rejected on the basis of the experience with such measures under German occupation during the Second World War. However, shortly after 9/11 the measure was introduced purportedly with the aim of combating terrorism, but it has been criticized for not achieving what it was supposed to achieve (Jebbink 2008). Peters and van der Laan argue that one should be aware of the risk that governments may try to expand their powers under the pretext of fear: "The question may be asked if the fear instilled by governments is not greater than any terrorist could achieve" (Peters and van der Laan 2007, 132).

After 9/11 several measures were taken in the Netherlands to increase the possibilities for the authorities to combat what they saw as the threat of terrorism. These entailed in particular measures of a preventive nature, such as a heightened level of information-gathering, information-analysis as well as guarding and securing vulnerable sectors of society and individual persons (Bron 2008, 492). These included judicial and administrative measures at the national and local level. The public prosecutors and the police were given additional authority for tracing persons suspected of terrorist activities and/or plans (De Hoog 2008, 594–7). A National Coordinator to Combat Terrorism (NTCb) was appointed to facilitate communication about possible terrorist activities (Bron 2008, 481–3).

Though often criticized by human rights organizations, these measures were generally upheld by the courts. In one case, in 2006, The Hague Court of Appeals decided that the general security service (AIVD) had, under certain conditions, the right to wiretap telephone conversations of journalists. In another case, the Supreme Court decided that information collected by the security service can be used in criminal procedures as "start-up information" (Peters and van der Laan, 2007, 127).

The nature of antiterrorist measures in the Netherlands received international attention in 2008 during the Universal Periodic Review by the UN Human Rights Council. In a report submitted in 2008 to the Council, the Netherlands government stated that the terrorist threat had thrown up new dilemmas in recent years (National Report Submitted in Accordance with Paragraph 15 (a) of the Annex to Human Rights Council Resolution 5/1, 2008, 18). Protecting the public from security threats has traditionally been a duty of the government, but measures to ensure security can conflict with human rights. The Netherlands government stated that it was mindful of the concerns expressed by NGOs and when taking counterterrorism measures it tried to strike a balance with the classic fundamental rights of individuals that might be curtailed by these measures. In seeking to protect fundamental values, it tried to avoid compromising these values that included the right to privacy, personal freedom, safety, the right to a fair trial, and freedom of expression. A number of checks were built into the legislative process to assess the compatibility of new legislation with fundamental rights. After these checks in the legislative process, it was the task of an independent court in specific cases to assess the application of legislation in the context of counterterrorism activities (ibid.).

In a compilation prepared by the UN Office of the High Commissioner for Human Rights reference was made to concern expressed in 2007 by the UN Committee against Torture that persons in police detention in the Netherlands did not have access to legal assistance during the initial period of interrogation. It recommended that the Netherlands review its criminal procedures so that access to a lawyer is guaranteed to persons in police custody from the very outset of their deprivation of liberty (Compilation Prepared by the Office of the High Commissioner for Human Rights in Accordance with the Annex to Paragraph (B) of Resolution 5/1 of the Human Rights Council, The Netherlands, 7).

In a report under the Universal Periodic Review, submitted to the UN Human Rights Council, the Netherlands State Secretary for Justice noted that respect and attention for human rights and the rule of law were starting points. She indicated that the Netherlands combated radicalization that preceded terrorist activities and highlighted the importance of promoting the rule of law, which is conducive to the delegitimization of the use of violence by groups of citizens. This included countering the instigation of violence on the Internet, other media, in education, and religious institutions. The Netherlands was building an effective mechanism to counter terrorism in the earliest possible stages. While this might mean that certain persons and organizations had to be "observed more closely," measures for combating terrorism were defined by law and enforced under legal supervision. The Netherlands respected the absolute nature of the prohibition of torture in expulsion cases of terrorist suspects. This meant that no one liable to Netherlands jurisdiction would ever be knowingly subjected to treatment contrary to the provisions dealing with the right to life and the prohibition of torture (Universal Periodic Review: Report of the Working Group on the Universal Periodic Review. The Netherlands, 2008, pars. 7–9).

During the Universal Periodic Review, Cuba and Switzerland expressed concern about counterterrorism measures in the Netherlands. Cuba asked how the Netherlands government reconciled counterterrorism measures with the respect of human rights obligation and recommended that it consider revising all antiterrorism legislation to bring it in line with the highest human rights standards (ibid., par. 29). The Netherlands State Secretary of Justice said that the possible effects of legislative measures on human rights are taken into account in new lawmaking processes, in particular how such measures addressed sensitive issues such as the prevention of terrorism. Parliament would use all means and instruments to examine the compatibility of new legislation with human rights. She said that "therefore" the legislation met international human rights standards (par. 37). Switzerland, taking note of the new antiterrorism legislation, which extended the scope of maneuver of services in charge, recommended that measures be implemented in respect of international human rights obligations, including the right to a fair trial and the right to freedom and security of the person (par. 70).

In its response the Netherlands government said that it supported the recommendations of Cuba and Switzerland, which had already been implemented. The government strongly believed that even the most threatening forms of terrorism should be fought against within the framework of the constitutional rights and freedoms of individuals. A number of checks were built into the legislative process at various stages to assess the compatibility of new legislation with fundamental rights. The Kingdom of the Netherlands considered the antiterrorism legislation to be in full compliance with the "standards of international human rights law" (Universal Periodic Review, Report of the Working Group on the Universal Periodic Review: The Netherlands, Addendum, par. 29).

Not quite though. The recommendations of the UN Committee against Torture mentioned before have not yet fully been implemented. So far, the Netherlands government has started a "pilot" study in two regions, where a lawyer may consult with his client during the half hour before the police examination. The lawyer is then invited to be present during the examination of a suspect by the police. This pilot study is intended to last until May 2010 after which the situation will be evaluated. Depending on the outcome of this evaluation, it will be decided whether and to what extent the Code of Criminal Procedure will be changed in this respect (Jebbink 2008).

In 2009, the Council of Europe's Commissioner for Human Rights, Thomas Hammarberg, has added his voice to the expressions of concern about antiterrorist measures taken by the Netherlands. He expressed his concern over various criminal and administrative measures to combat terrorism and recommended an evaluation with a view to ensure full compliance with international human rights standards (Report by the Commissioner for Human Rights Mr Thomas Hammarberg on his Visit to the Netherlands September 21–5, 2008, Strasbourg, March 11, 2009).

In reacting to these expressions of concern by UN and Council of Europe bodies, the government of the Netherlands has been at pains to state that it was as much concerned as these international agencies about the need to respect international human rights standards. The question can of course be raised to what extent it was sincere in these expressions of concern or merely paying lip service. What seems clear is that the government has been trying to sail a middle course whereby it takes the measures it deems necessary for combating terrorism, while at the same time maintaining fundamental human rights standards. This sometimes creates a dilemma where on the one hand domestic critics try to have it adopt strong antiterrorist measures, while human rights activists, both at home and abroad, warn against the danger of transgressions of classical human rights standards. There would seem, however, no reason to doubt the government's sincerity, when it claims its adherence to those international human rights standards.

Torture

The Netherlands has a tradition of being strongly opposed to torture practices. Together with Sweden, it took the lead in bringing about the International Convention against Torture and Other Cruel, Inhuman or Degrading Treatment or Punishment of 1984 (Reiding 2007, 75–127). A well-known professor of international law (and later Foreign Minister and member of the International Court of Justice), Peter Kooijmans, was from 1985 till 1992 UN Special Rapporteur on Torture. So was Theo van Boven, another professor of international law. The Dutch opposition to torture is unquestioned.

Acts of torture are prohibited under all circumstances and 147 states are party to the International Convention against Torture and Cruel, Inhuman or Degrading Behaviour or Punishment. A few years ago, it looked as if the prohibition of torture was on its way to becoming a human rights standard that was universally accepted. That seems no longer to be the case. More and more voices are being heard in many parts of the world that "methods of intensive interrogation" that are akin to torture, or at least cruel, inhuman or degrading treatment or punishment, may be necessary to obtain vital information, for example from alleged terrorists (Advisory Council on International Affairs 2005, 6; Wilson 2005, 17; Twiss 2007, 346–67).

In 2006, the Amsterdam daily newspaper *de Volkskrant*, under the headline "Dutch Military Tortured in Iraq" ("Nederlandse Militairen Martelden in Irak,") reported that three years earlier Dutch military serving in Iraq had committed acts of torture against Iraqi detainees. This news caused a great deal of commotion in Dutch political circles and forced the Minister of Defense to order an investigation by an independent commission (in actual fact, two such commissions conducted inquiries independently of each other). In June 2007, the two commissions reported that no acts of actual torture had been committed, but questioned some of the interrogation methods ("Inquiry Interrogations in Iraq" 2007 and "Summary of Inquiry Military Information and

Security Services" 2007). The findings of the two commissions caused a great deal of relief in official Dutch circles.

However, since then, Herman Burgers, a former official at the Ministry of Foreign Affairs who was closely involved in the drafting of the 1984 International Convention on the Prohibition of Torture, having examined the two reports and having attended the subsequent debate in the Standing Committee on Defense of the Second Chamber of the Dutch parliament, has made the following points (Burgers 2007):

- The two commissions did not question the victims of the alleged acts of torture.
- The commissions accepted too easily the motivations for their questionable practices mentioned by the Dutch military involved. A striking example was the electrical sticks that had been taken to Iraq allegedly to keep vagrant dogs at a distance.
- No witnesses were allowed to attend the questionings, including the legal adviser of the Dutch military battalion.
- The detainees were blindfolded to prevent them from recognizing their interrogators, who also wore blackened ski-glasses.
- The detainees were exposed to "white noise," a loud sound when a radio is tuned to a high volume, not on but close to a broadcasting station, allegedly to prevent the detainees from communicating with each other and from listening to the conversations of their interrogators.
- The reports did not mention the UN Convention against Torture and Cruel, Inhuman or Degrading Treatment or Punishment ("CAT") to which the Netherlands is a party.

Burgers did not question the conclusion of the two commissions that no torture was committed by the Dutch military, but concluded that the combination of exposing the detainees to "white noise," the deprivation of sleep, the fact that they were kept handcuffed and blindfolded during the interrogations, and that they were sprinkled with cold water, amounted to cruel treatment prohibited by CAT, which could lead to torture. Torture as well as cruel, inhuman, or degrading treatment or punishment is under international law under no circumstances allowed (see also Advisory Council on International Affairs 2006, 10).

If one accepts Burgers' findings (as I do), one must conclude that the prohibition of torture was maintained both qua standard and in practice. However, the reactions by the Dutch public and political opinion tended to stress their relief over the fact that there were no findings of torture, but showed relatively little concern over the practice by Dutch military of cruel, inhuman, or degrading treatment or punishment – which is equally prohibited under international human rights law. Forsythe has made the point that there is no clear scientific or legal distinction between torture and lesser forms of mistreatment. Given that the international legal definition of torture hinges on the intentional infliction of *intense* pain, physical or mental, the dividing line is subjective (Forsythe 2007, note 45).

In the chapter on terrorism in his recent paper on a human rights strategy, the Dutch Foreign Minister points out that "under extraordinary circumstances," within a clearly delineated juridical framework, derogation from certain human rights standards is possible: "Therewith the principles of proportionality, non-discrimination and limited duration are valid. The fight against terrorism cannot offer a license to suspend certain human rights *ad infinitum*" (Netherlands Ministry of Foreign Affairs 2007, 53). It would have been helpful, if he had also mentioned that certain rights such as the prohibition of torture and cruel, inhuman, or degrading treatment or punishment may not be suspended under any circumstances. In the words of the Advisory Council on International Affairs: "The ban on torture is absolute and may not be compromised in any situation whatsoever" (Advisory Council on International Affairs 2005, 11).

However, in 2007, the European Committee on the Prevention of Torture expressed its concern about the placement in the Netherlands of terrorism suspects in special high-security "terrorist departments." The conditions governing these departments were considered so strict that they amounted to *de facto* isolation. The Committee recommended that the decision to hold people in these departments be based on a comprehensive individual risk assessment and be reviewed regularly. It also said the criteria for these placements should be specified by law. Security measures should be reviewed in the terrorist departments with respect to contact between prisoners and their lawyers "in order to ensure that they are not having an unduly negative impact on the quality of their legal defence" (Report to the Authorities of the Kingdom of the Netherlands on the visits carried out to the Kingdom in Europe, Aruba and the Netherlands Antilles by the European Committee for the Prevention of Torture and Inhuman or Degrading Treatment or Punishment (CPT) in June 2007; report published by the Netherlands government on January 30, 2008).

In a reaction, the Minister of Justice informed the Second Chamber of Parliament that the criteria for placing a person in a terrorist department were the following: (1) to be suspected of a terrorist crime; (2) to be condemned for a terrorist crime, and (3) spreading messages of radicalization before or during detention. The first two criteria did not need a periodic evaluation, while decisions based on criterion (3) were evaluated every 12 months. The minister further stated that he had decided to have windows installed in the facade of the cells. Both the ventilation and lighting would be improved: "The section for terrorists is located in a unit in an old building that carries certain restrictions with it. Therefore the development of a unit in a new building has begun. It is expected that this new unit will be ready in 2009." The minister remarked further that point of departure was that the terrorist unit did not involve long time solitary detention. "If well-founded, the detainees will be enabled to participate in communal activities" (*"Justitiële Inrichtingen"* ["Judicial Institutions,"] 24587 245 Letter of the Minister of Justice to the Chairman of the Second Chamber, January 29, 2008, 7). Similar information was contained in the formal response of the Netherlands to the Council of Europe's Committee for the Prevention of Torture (Response of the Authorities of the Kingdom of the Netherlands to the report of the CPT) on its visits to the Kingdom in Europe, Aruba, and the Netherlands Antilles, February 4, 2009, 4–6; www.cpt.coe.int/ documents/nld/2009–07-inf-eng-htm, accessed on April 15, 2010).

Renditions

Rendition refers to the extrajudicial transfer of individuals (including suspected terrorists) to countries where the person is wanted for trial, to countries where the individual can be adequately interrogated or prolonged detained. In a recent report (Intelligence and Security Committee 2007) a British Parliamentary Committee distinguished five different forms of such rendition:

> "Rendition": Encompasses any extrajudicial transfer of persons from one jurisdiction or State to another.
> "Rendition to Justice": The extrajudicial transfer of persons from onejurisdiction or State to another, for the purposes of standing trial within an established and recognized legal and judicial system.
> "Military Rendition": The extrajudicial transfer of persons (detained in, or related to, a theatre of military operations) from one State to another, for the purposes of military detention in a military facility.

"Rendition to Detention": The extrajudicial transfer of persons from one jurisdiction or State to another, for the purposes of detention and interrogation outside the normal legal system.

"Extraordinary Rendition": The extrajudicial transfer of persons from one jurisdiction or State to another, for the purposes of detention and interrogation outside the normal legal system, where there is a real risk of torture or cruel, inhuman or degrading treatment. (ibid. 6, par. 7; see also Report of the Special Rapporteur on the Promotion and Protection of Human Rights and Fundamental Freedoms while Countering Terrorism, UN Doc. A/62/263; Weissbrodt and Berquist 2006)

Obviously, it is especially the latter two types of rendition that cause the greatest concern if looked at from a human rights point of view. In his recent paper on a human rights strategy, the Dutch Foreign Minister strongly rejected the practice of extraordinary renditions: "Such matters as 'extraordinary renditions' and secret detention facilities, that are in violation of international law, will be explicitly condemned" (Netherlands Ministry of Foreign Affairs 2007, 51). Since 2001, hundreds of terror suspects are alleged to have been transferred by the United States to states, such as Pakistan and Egypt, where physical and psychological brutality and coercion feature prominently in interrogations. Many detainees are alleged to have been subjected to enforced disappearance, a crime under international law. European states such as Germany, Italy, the Netherlands, Spain, Sweden, Turkey, and the United Kingdom are reported to have if not participated then at least condoned this practice of rendition by not sufficiently controlling flight movements and being less than interested in clarifying reports of such flights. Between 2003 and 2005 the CIA ran secret detention sites in Poland and Romania (Council of Europe, Parliamentary Assembly, Committee on Legal Affairs and Human Rights, *Secret Detentions and Illegal Transfers of Detainees involving Council of Europe Members: Second Report, Explanatory Memorandum, Rapporteur Mr Dick* Marty, Switzerland, ALDE, June 7, 2007, 4). In February 2008, the EU's European Commission accused Poland and Romania of dodging its requests for clarifying their possible role in the United States extraordinary rendition program ("EU Accuses 2 Members of Delay on Renditions," *International Herald Tribune* (Paris), November 13, 2007).

Diplomatic guarantees concerning the treatment of such persons by the country of destination should be tested for compatibility with the peremptory *non-refoulement* principle in order to assess the practicability and moral acceptability. In light of the numerous promises that have been broken, there is a body of authoritative opinion that categorically rejects the diplomatic guarantee system, because it is no more than a means of undermining or circumventing the *non-refoulement* principle. The UN Special Rapporteur on Torture, in his report of 2006, reiterated that such diplomatic assurances are not legally binding and undermine state obligations to prohibit torture, are ineffective and unreliable in ensuring the protection of returned persons, and therefore should not be resorted to by states (Report of the Special Rapporteur on Torture and Other Cruel, Inhuman or Degrading Treatment or Punishment, UN Doc. E/CN.4/2006/6 (2006)). The UN Special Rapporteur urged, in his recent report to the General Assembly, "restraint" in respect of so-called diplomatic assurances by the receiving state not to subject a person to torture and other inhuman treatment, "as this can never replace the receiving State's obligation to carry out an individual assessment of whether a real risk of torture or cruel, inhuman or degrading treatment or punishment exists in respect of the person" (UN Doc. A/62/263, August 15, 2007, par. 82 (c)). An ad hoc working group of the Council of Europe has also dealt with this subject (see Heinz 2007, 14 ff.).

In 2007, Amnesty International came out with a report on a very special kind of extraordinary rendition, saying that the International Security Assistance Force in Afghanistan (ISAF), particularly those from Belgium, Britain, Canada, the Netherlands, and Norway, had transferred detainees to Afghanistan's intelligence service, the National Directorate of Security (NDS), despite consistent reports of torture and other ill-treatment by the NDS (Amnesty International 2007). Amnesty put forward a number of recommendations, including:

- ISAF must temporarily suspend all transfer of detainees to Afghan authorities and hold them in their custody until effective safeguards are in place.
- ISAF contributing countries should promote the reform of the Afghan detention system and explore the feasibility of placing international staff within Afghan detention facilities in order to train new Afghan detention officials.
- The Afghan government must publish the secret Presidential decree governing the operation of the NDS and take steps to separate the current functions of detention, investigation and prosecution.
- The Afghan government should ratify the Optional Protocol to the Convention against Torture and invite the UN Special Rapporteur

on Torture to visit Afghanistan, including detention facilities under their control.

* Independent monitors should be given unrestricted and unhindered access to all detention centers and unsupervised access to all detainees.

This report had obvious consequences also for the Netherlands, as a member of ISAF. Repeatedly there were items in the Dutch newspapers that Dutch military had transferred Afghan detainees suspected of being members of the Taliban to either the Afghan authorities or the US military. In both cases it was unclear as to what was happening to these detainees. These incidents led to repeated questioning of the Minister of Defense in parliament. The cabinet has decided that the Dutch military, who are stationed in the unruly southern province of Uruzghan, will remain there until August 2010. However, it remains unclear whether the Dutch will only give up their present leading military role or depart from Afghanistan altogether.

Conclusion

This chapter has focused on the role of the Netherlands in the maintenance of human rights standards, while countering terrorist activities. For many years after the Second World War, the adherence of the Netherlands to international human rights standards was beyond question. A greater percentage of its Jewish inhabitants had been killed during the German occupation than in any other Western European country. There was a generally shared conviction that "this should never happen again" and that the basic standards as laid down in the Universal Declaration of Human Rights should be maintained under all circumstances. This is less so today, in the wake of the events of 9/11.

The Netherlands finds itself in an exposed geographical position, for instance with regard to the location of its principal entries for international transportation such as the seaport of Rotterdam and the international airport near Amsterdam. That, in addition to its small territory, makes it potentially extremely vulnerable to terrorist attacks. This explains why the government has taken a number of measures, as described in this chapter, that would seem to be at odds with the respect for human rights. Specific measures originally taken to combat terrorism tend to become part and parcel of ordinary criminal law. If not only individuals but also entire groups, such as

Muslims, are seen as security risks, this jeopardizes their political and social integration. The head of the Council of State, the supreme advisory body in the Netherlands, has rightly warned against the possible consequences:

> The democratic state, with its rule of law, its fundamental rights, its diversity and its tolerance, is *not* among the root causes of terrorism. On the contrary, democracy and the rule of law are the most effective weapons against it. So democracy and the rule of law must not be restricted to protect them against terrorism. Far from it, they must be deployed to the full in the fight against terrorism, both nationally and internationally. (Tjeenk Willink 2007, 26)

The murders of politician Pim Fortuyn and filmmaker Theo van Gogh (the latter by a Muslim activist) in 2002 were unprecedented in the Netherlands and have greatly affected the Dutch political scene. The 9/11 attack on the Twin Towers in New York led to anti-Muslim feelings among major segments of the Dutch population. The politician Geert Wilders, who runs on a strongly anti-Muslim platform, would, according to recent public opinion polls, gather as many as 20 parliamentary seats (out of 150) if elections were held today. Together with the assaults in Bali (2002), Madrid (2004), London (2005), and other places, it has contributed to a feeling of jitteriness among public officials, translated into strong antiterrorist legislation and administrative measures. Some of these measures would seem to be at odds with fundamental principles of human rights and even the rule of law. This means that there has clearly been a change in the focus on and continuity of human rights after 9/11. Although it is now over nine years since 9/11 took place and no major terrorist attacks have occurred in the Netherlands, the authorities – if not the public at large – remain very much concerned about what might happen in the Netherlands. That concern often takes precedence over an emphasis on human rights.

According to an academic study, the Netherlands has become less outspoken on the subject of human rights during the last quarter of the 20th century than before that time. Four reasons are offered by way of explanation: (1) the "political climate of the time"; it would seem that the political climate of the late 1970s was more geared to human rights than that of the early 21st century; (2) while in the late 1970s the human rights situation in most parts of Latin America and in Eastern Europe as well as parts of Asia and of course South Africa was of the utmost concern, later the scene shifted to Africa, which was seen by many as a "lost continent" where it was extremely hard to apply human rights considerations; (3) the Netherlands government's freedom of operation in the field of foreign policy is increasingly restricted by its membership of the EU, where human rights considerations take a less prominent place; (4) there has been a renewed emphasis on the notion of Dutch "national interests," usually interpreted as Dutch economic interests, which tend to go at the expense of an emphasis on human rights (Baehr et al. 2002, 233). A more recent study, however, has challenged those findings as being "not completely convincing" (Malcontent 2008, 201). At the Netherlands Institute of Human Rights (SIM) a current research project deals with the role of the Netherlands within the EU in the field of human rights.

Degrading treatment or punishment or – another topic – extraordinary renditions should never be resorted to, not even when combating terrorists. It is clear that the government keeps insisting on its commitment to human rights standards. Yet it is also clear that the fight against terrorism has put that commitment into danger – a fact that is not necessarily recognized or admitted by government officials. The use of torture, while out of the question until a few years ago, has come under serious consideration, if not actual practice. In the case of the Netherlands, at least, the use of cruel, inhuman, and degrading treatment or punishment by some of its military has been admitted. Whether or not the Netherlands was involved in facilitating "extraordinary renditions" by the United States has never been fully clarified. The least one can say is that there is a considerable amount of tension between the maintenance of international human rights standards on the one hand and the struggle against terrorist activities by the security forces on the other hand. The views and criticisms expressed by human rights experts expounded in this chapter should be carefully considered by all concerned.

The UN Special Rapporteur on the Promotion and Protection of Human Rights and Fundamental Freedoms While Countering Terrorism has repeatedly pointed out that antiterrorism measures should not go at the expense of the promotion and protection of human rights. His warnings would seem to have been insufficiently heeded by governments, including the Netherlands. Similarly, the Netherlands must pay proper attention to the concerns raised by the Council of Europe's Committee on Torture. The Committee has tried to call attention to the general way in which persons suspected of terrorist activities are being dealt with. A reaction by the government to the Committee's recommendations was not yet available at the time of writing, It stands to reason that this reaction should pay proper attention to all of these recommendations and to the spirit in which they were made.

Some of these issues were raised during the first Universal Periodic Review by the UN Human Rights Council in 2008. It was admittedly somewhat odd that, next to Switzerland, it was Cuba – a country not known for its commitment to civil and political human rights – that raised questions about antiterrorism measures in the Netherlands that were supposedly at odds with its commitment to the promotion and protection of human rights. Nevertheless it was a good thing that the issue was raised and responded to by the Netherlands government. Dutch nongovernmental human rights organizations will undoubtedly see to it that the Netherlands government is continually reminded of its expressed commitment to human rights and the consequences this entails.

The promotion and protection of human rights is of special importance in difficult times, when the survival of the state is under attack. It is understandable that governments in general, and their security services in particular, want to do everything in their power to prevent and to counter terrorist attacks. Such attacks, as we said before, are themselves an onslaught on the human rights of innocent civilians. Yet, at the same time, human rights are intended to protect these very civilians. The authorities should always remember that the maintenance of the rule of law and human rights is one of the important matters that distinguishes them from their terrorist adversaries. That is one of the main reasons why such practices as torture and cruel, inhuman, or degrading treatment or punishment or – another topic – extraordinary renditions, should never be resorted to, not even when combating terrorists.

10

Caught in the Storm: Middle Powers as Barometers for the West's Changing Attitude toward Security and Human Rights after 9/11

Yan St. Pierre

For many, the end of the Cold War was the victory of "good" liberalism against the "evil" socialism/communism, the "end of history" as Francis Fukuyama famously put it. What really ended was the ideological, strategic, and agenda-setting straitjacket that shackled aligned countries for over 40 years. With the ideological umbrella now gone, less prominent countries – middle powers – like Canada, Australia, or the Netherlands could play a more important role on the international stage, most notably for the human rights regime. So as the 1990s unfolded, Western states took to promoting the triad of modern liberalism – free market, democracy, and human rights – with middle-power countries not only in the vanguard of agenda-setting and policy-making, but also in the application of these humanitarian policies. By their actions, middle-power countries confirmed the tendencies of major powers and therefore legitimized the discourse, setting new tones in policy and establishing domestic and international precedents that translated into interventions in the Balkans and Africa. Middle powers thus established themselves as the barometer, reflecting the atmosphere of big power politics and the realpolitik tendencies of major Western powers. However, the terrorist attacks of September 11, 2001 brought the focus back to more basic security priorities and human rights were deemed a luxury. With a declaration of "war on terror" and a policy of retaliation and regime change being set, middle powers, historically strongly committed to the human rights regime, faced the strict choice of complying to the new policies or being labeled as supporters of terrorism. As their commitment to the new security regime began, this not only reasserted the role of middle powers as barometers for international regime changes and tendencies, but buried the human rights legacy of the 1990s under the World Trade Center rubble.

Of course, reprisal and deterrence has always been the policy of states being threatened or attacked. But on the other hand, middle-power countries have in modern times been the levelheaded counterparts to such actions, favoring compromise, diplomacy, and the importance of principles and the rule of law. Based on this historical approach, must middle-power countries like Canada enact and use strong, coercive measures out of solidarity with their allies? Should they not offer a more flexible response in light of their policy history? If not, do counterterrorism policies enacted since 2001 in numerous middle-power states represent a shift in their attitude toward human rights, both domestically and internationally? What factors could explain this turnaround and what are the larger consequences of such a shift in policy? Moreover, does middle-power credibility legitimize the actions and policies of more powerful, more aggressive states, because they now appear to follow suit instead of counterweighing the latter's excesses?

Using Canada as a case study, in light of its human rights reputation and its experience with terrorism, I will argue that the middle powers' use of counterterrorism measures and methods that parallel those of the major powers establish and legitimize post-9/11 standards toward security and human rights, thereby providing an accurate microcosm of Western trends and attitudes when dealing with terrorism as well as on Western states' handling of human rights. To properly understand the influence of middle-power security policies after 9/11 on the international human rights regime, I will first establish for analytical purposes Canada's historical human rights profile and its experience with terrorism. This will then be compared to the country's counterterrorism attitudes and measures prevailing since September 2001, a profile which will then be set within the larger security framework at play, that is, Western counterterrorism tendencies, particularly those of the United States, United Kingdom, France, and Germany. The question is then to determine if Canada's experience with terrorism justifies its shift in attitude toward security, both nationally and internationally, or if outside factors bear greater influence on the matter. Consequently, middle powers may be used as a barometer to assess the impact of such policy changes on its broader scale and determine how middle-power attitudes embody the scope of Western tendencies in attitudes toward human rights and security in the first years of the 21st century, a view consistent with Peter Baehr's findings in his contribution to this volume.

Canada's historical approach toward human rights

In the postwar years, while in need of a defining identity, Canadian policies focused on their capacity for dialogue and respect, on both domestic and international levels. Internationally, John Humphrey co-drafted the UN's Universal Declaration of Human Rights while former Prime Minister Lester B. Pearson – the country's lone Nobel Peace Prize recipient – implemented the organization's "Blue Helmet" structure, a pledge to peace often renewed. Domestically, this could be observed through the implementation of open immigration policies, defining multiculturalism as a state policy and reasserting the primacy of human rights. More than values, human rights have become part of the Canadian identity.

Canada's role and stature in world politics increased dramatically in the 1990s, as the end of the Cold War opened up the space for an international politics centered around human rights. On the humanitarian aspect, the country was a huge contributor to the peacemaking/peacekeeping missions in the Balkans, under General Lewis MacKenzie in Sarajevo, and in Rwanda, under Lt-General Roméo Dallaire. The latter's efforts to stem the genocide, his failure to do so, and his ensuing plight have made him a stern defender of international human rights policies. As a member of NATO, Canada was also part of the bombing campaign carried out by the organization in the spring of 1999 in response to the Serbian campaign of genocide against ethnic Albanians in Kosovo, and is currently a major player in the organization's mission in Afghanistan, where Canadian troops are responsible for the region of Kandahar.

In terms of agenda-setting, Canadian human rights policy played a key role in establishing the International Court of Justice and the International Criminal Court, while the 2001 report, *The Responsibility to Protect*, was groundbreaking in pursuing a greater state commitment to humanitarian intervention and human rights. It also instigated the 1997 Convention on the Prohibition of the Use, Stockpiling, Production and Transfer or Anti-Personnel Mines and on Their Destruction, known as the Ottawa Treaty, set out to eliminate the use of landmines in conflicts. As will be shown, it is this historically positive international involvement for human rights that has given way, domestically as well, since 2001, to a more negative policy and a less dissident stance toward the security attitudes of other Western powers.

Human rights as a national policy

Canada's commitment to human rights became a national priority in the 1960s with the recognition of minority rights for Québécois and First Nations members. Provinces set the tone in the 1970s (Alberta in 1973, Québec in 1977) by enacting Rights and Freedoms charters, nationally followed in 1982 with the Canadian Charter of Rights and Freedoms.

The charter grants everyone four fundamental rights, none of which are the right to life or physical integrity: (1) freedom of conscience and religion; (2) freedom of thought, belief, opinion, and expression, including freedom of the press and other media of communication; (3) freedom of peaceful assembly; and (4) freedom of association (Canada, 1982). The right to life, physical integrity and security are "Legal Rights," a technical aspect that appears to be of importance in the methods used by law enforcement agencies. Although the fundamental rights list is short, the charter provides excellent protection for its inscribed rights and freedoms, as they are constitutional rights, making them basic for all.

A first look at empirical studies confirms the country's high respect for human rights and the charter's enforcement. Amnesty International's annual report on human rights has little devoted to the Canadian case while Human Rights Watch's report does not even mention the country in its 2007 and 2008 reports – an indication of its excellent performance. Statistically, the analysis provided by the Cingranelli-Richards (CIRI) Human Rights Data Project rates Canada a perfect 10 on its Empowerment Rights Index, which measures respect for Freedom of Movement, Freedom of Speech, Workers' Rights, Political Participation, and Freedom of Religion indicators (Cingranelli and Richards 2007).

Intriguingly, however, Canada consistently scores comparatively poorly on the *Physical Integrity* index, another additive index measuring respect for rights against Torture, Extrajudicial Killing, Political Imprisonment, and Disappearance (Cingranelli and Richards 2007). This difference is surprising, especially for a country with a very low crime rate of 7,513/100,000 (STATCAN 2007). Canada's recent human rights performance is summarized in Figure 10.1.

Canada's record is quite similar to that of other middle-power countries such as the Netherlands, Belgium, or Austria (see Figure 10.2) (Cingranelli and Richards 2007).

Based on the data seen in Figure 10.2, it is perhaps too soon to appropriately evaluate whether the impact of the post-2001 counterterrorism measures on the Canadian domestic approach to human rights

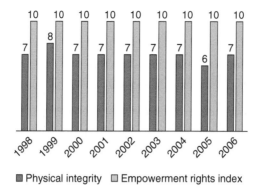

■ Physical integrity □ Empowerment rights index

Figure 10.1 Level of respect for human rights, Canada (1998–2006)

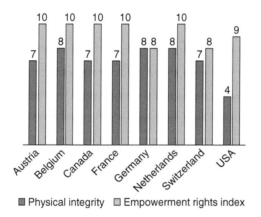

■ Physical integrity □ Empowerment rights index

Figure 10.2 Level of respect for human rights, Western comparison

is merely incidental or actually due to the consistency of the ratings. However, it must be noted that the Cingranelli-Richards (CIRI) Human Rights Data Project does not contain data pertaining to privacy issues such as surveillance and data mining. Here, Canada is one of only nine states where "safeguards against surveillance are still adequate but these are nonetheless weakened" (Privacy International 2008), but despite the top-tier position, this represents a fall in the rankings. In 2006 it was one of only two countries where privacy protection standards were continuously upheld, the other being Germany, which also stumbled in the 2007 rankings (Privacy International 2008). This decrease in terms of privacy protection for Canadians is consistent with the shift in national security policy that can be observed after 9/11, in line with the changes in Western security policies in this period. Furthermore, the data does not reflect the use of a political discourse that constantly focuses on security – the 2009 budget grants $630 million (CAN) to improving security structures – despite the lowest crime rate in 32 years and a negligible history of political violence (Castonguay 2008). Internationally, the shift in prioritizing the human rights agenda is clearer, as the relation between a change in attitudes toward human rights and the country's involvement in post-9/11 responses to terrorism can be observed through the country's actions in Afghanistan and in a variety of terrorism-related cases. Indeed, the government's passivity in defending the rights of its citizens or those under its jurisdiction, and in the outright collaboration of its security services in dismissing those rights, confirms an alignment to the security regime put in place by major Western powers since 2001.

The Canadian experience with terrorism

In the history of terrorism, countries like Canada are seldom mentioned. However, statistics compiled on the subject since 1968 indicate that 34 terrorist attacks[1] have occurred in Canada (MIPT 2008). The vast majority of these incidents was perpetrated by foreign nationals on foreign nationals and had more to do with targeted assassinations than actual terrorism. In fact, the country's only real experience with terrorism stems from the community-terrorism campaign (1963–70) staged by the pro-independence *Front de Libération du Québec*, a group responsible for 60 bomb attacks and two kidnappings that resulted in three deaths and 42 injuries (Gaudette 2005).

Prior to late 1970, the Quebec Liberation Front (FLQ) attacks had been limited to destroying symbols of "British" occupation – that is, the Canadian government – essentially causing material damage, although one unintentionally led to the death of a night watchman. But on October 5, 1970, the FLQ kidnapped British diplomat James R. Cross, followed five days later by the kidnapping of then Québec Labor minister Pierre Laporte. These FLQ successes and their potential to invigorate the nationalist movement in the province prompted then Canadian Prime Minister Pierre-Elliott Trudeau to declare, at the request of the Québec government, a state of exception under the War Measures Act. Consequently, the army was sent in to assist law enforcement officials in bringing the crisis to an end. As of 16 October all civil liberties were suspended and security officials were granted unlimited stop and search as well as arrest and detention powers, a measure seemingly justified hours later by the discovery of Laporte's body in the trunk of a car.

What is known as the October Crisis ended with the rescue of Cross on 3 December; 487 people were arrested and held without charge, and the FLQ was disbanded (Gaudette 2005).

Today the issue of terrorism in Canada concerns its status as a terrorist breeding ground, as exemplified by the plot of the "Toronto 18,"[2] who were preventively arrested in 2006, or by the case of "Millennium Bomber" Ahmed Ressam, arrested in December 1999. Although the threat posed by the Toronto group has yet to be fully ascertained, Ressam's case has been fully documented. An Algerian immigrant who lived in Montreal for four years, he was caught trying to smuggle explosives across the American border to bomb Los Angeles airport on New Year's Eve 2000. His arrest also led to that of his accomplices, but more importantly, raised questions about sleeper agents in Canada, notably among the country's diverse Muslim population.

Beyond the plot itself, it was Ressam's ease in manipulating the Canadian citizenship and immigration system that caused concern. Ahmed Ressam was able to obtain a Canadian passport, driver's license, and social security card (Campos 2006), giving him the mobility necessary to plan the attack. Worse, he had been held in 1995 by immigration agents for entering the country with a false passport before being unconditionally released because "carrying a false passport is not a major offense, a lot of asylum seekers possess false passport and are not criminals" (Campos 2006). This careless approach was made obvious in April 1999 when French chief antiterror judge Jean-Louis Bruguière submitted a formal request to the Canadian government that Ressam be brought in for questioning and his Montreal apartment searched, on the grounds that he was involved in a terrorist plot. Despite knowing that Ressam was using an alias, the request was delayed for seven months, by which time the suspect had already fled (Campos 2006).

This case gave a black eye to the Canadian government. It won the country a reputation as a point of entry and staging ground for sleeper terrorists and therefore as a security threat. It also created a determination within Canadian security circles to prevent such a lapse from ever recurring – a determination heightened in the wake of 9/11. The event thus provided a pretext for updating Canada's counterterrorism laws.

Shifting the stance: the post-9/11 approach to human rights and terrorism

That powerful states with considerable experience with terrorism felt the need to reassert their counterterrorism policies in light of the Al Qaida attacks is both cautious and normal. But when a country with no history of aggressive international policy and a negligible experience of terrorism overhauls its domestic and international security policies, its reveals the extent of the realpolitik applied by the tenants of the "war on terror" in order to bring more reluctant countries in line with their new regime.

Canada had earned a solid reputation for the participation of its soldiers in humanitarian missions throughout the 1990s. This hard-won respect was jeopardized by the Canadian involvement in operation Enduring Freedom in Afghanistan. Indeed, several organizations, including Amnesty international, condemned the country's lack of concern for prisoner safety,[3] especially when they are handed over to Afghan authorities (Amnesty International 2008). Because Afghan authorities allegedly condone the use of torture on captured insurgents/ terrorists, Canadian authorities have been criticized for proceeding with the transfer of prisoners despite being aware of their potential fate. The basis for this lies in the notion that prisoners captured by a foreign nation are subject to that state's laws, including basic human rights. Furthermore, numerous countries, including Canada, have laws that forbid them to expel or extradite individuals that may be submitted to torture or other forms of physical violence. Therefore, Canada is in this case deemed to be failing in its responsibilities to protect the human rights of its prisoners (Amnesty International 2009), contrary to country's reputation.

This problem is also compounded by the cases of Maher Arar, Canada's contribution to the US *Extraordinary Renditions Program*, and that of Guantanamo detainee Omar Khadr. Mr. Arar was arrested as a terrorist suspect during a stopover in New York and sent to Syria where he spent a year in jail, regularly subjected to torture. He had been arrested and detained based on erroneous information obtained by the Royal Canadian Mounted Police (RCMP) that was sent to US authorities. Though the error was later recognized, the Canadian government took its time resolving the issue. An inquiry commission was eventually set up and Maher Arar was financially compensated, but he remains blacklisted as a terrorist in the United States (Canadian Press 2008a).[4]

What is revealing in these cases is the government's inaction. The United Kingdom, Australia, and Germany have all demonstrated at least a modicum of effort when it came to the rights of their detainees at Guantánamo, and other European states, such as Portugal and Spain, have agreed to take in released prisoners or initiated prosecution against human rights violations by the United States. Canada, on the other hand, has systematically refused even to comment on the

Omar Khadr situation, all the while dancing around the prisoner transfer issue in Afghanistan and washing its hands of the Arar case once a financial settlement was reached.

Canada's domestic counterterrorism profile

Prior to December 24, 2001, Canada did not have a particular counterterrorism law. Classically, infractions stipulated within the United Nations' 12 terrorism-related conventions were integrated within the criminal code. The measures and methods that were normally used to deal with organized crime were also applied in terrorism cases when necessary (Canada 2001). Two particular measures were used: provisions of the 1996 *Criminal Law Improvement Act*, including many surveillance and data mining measures (Canada, 1996), and the 1976 (1978) security certificate included in the *Immigration Act*, that are basically an expulsion order issued by the Immigration or Public Safety minister against a permanent resident or immigrant deemed to be a serious threat to national security (Canada, 1978).

Like many of its Western counterparts, Canada limits a number of rights when its legal system is handling terrorism-related cases, such as the right to confront one's accuser, the presumption of innocence, and freedom of movement.[5] As in the military tribunals set up by the George W. Bush Administration for the Guantánamo detainees, if the information used to issue a security certificate is deemed to be dangerous to national security or that of a foreign country, it can be kept from the defendant and thus remain confidential at all times (Canada 1978). However, a 2007 Supreme Court ruling found this to be unconstitutional (Canada 2007) and gave the government one year to amend the law.[6] Under the c-3 amendment to the Immigration and Refugee Protection Act, the defendant is still refused access to confidential information, but a special advocate is assigned to argue the confidential nature of the information and to cross-examine governmental witnesses on the defendant's behalf, thus indirectly allowing the defendant to contest the charges (Canada 2008).

As Canadian immigration and security policies were sharply criticized, most notably from US senators Charles Schumer and Hillary Clinton and more recently Secretary for Homeland Security Janet Napolitano, who claimed that terrorists use Canada as a point of entry to the United States in order to carry out attacks (SRC 2009), and at the time 18 months removed from the "Millennium Bomber" fiasco, Canadian politicians deemed it necessary to elaborate and enact a specific antiterror law, one adapted to the new challenges posed by the terrorist threat and growing concerns for national security (Canada 2001). Hence the enactment on December 18, 2001 of the Anti-Terror Law, ratified shortly prior to the signature of the US imposed Smart Border Accords, and amended four times over a five-year span (Canada 2002–6). This law was complemented by the National Security Program, the aim of which was to upgrade national security structures, officially completed in mid-January 2008.

In essence, the Canadian Anti-Terror Law specifies terrorism-related infractions and significantly increases preexisting law enforcement powers. *Any type* of participation in terrorist actions is subject to ten years in prison without possibility of parole, and these charges are additional to any other criminal offenses that the terrorist attack may have incurred (Canada 2001).

More precisely, the aim of the law is to focus on prevention rather than consequence (Canada 2001). Hence, police officers now possess preventive arrest powers that are in fact arbitrary, as they rely on the officer's assessment of the urgency of the situation, which is analogous to the powers granted to British officers by the Terrorism Act 2000. In any case, the suspect is to be brought before a judge within 24 hours of the arrest but must nonetheless provide DNA samples to be stored in a databank (Canada 2001). The "last resort" motive, the necessity to prove to a judge that electronic surveillance is the only means to properly collect information on an alleged suspect, is no longer necessary if used for counterterrorism purposes. Also, the validity of the authorization period for electronic surveillance is extended from 60 days to a year in order "to grant law enforcement agencies sufficient time to gather information" (Canada 2001). Finally, any individual subject to surveillance by the authorities will only be informed three years after the fact, compared to the previously stipulated one year (Canada 2001).

It is important to bear in mind that this antiterror law is an amalgam of different preexisting measures included in different laws registered in the criminal code and that, in many ways, it is an upgrade perhaps designed to respond to political pressure rather than a proactive security measure, especially when analyzed in light of the prevailing attitude up to 9/11. However, the increased margin for maneuver given to security personnel with these laws make the measures equivalent to those in countries who have had to deal with terrorism and have either been overturned by human rights courts or sharply criticized. More importantly, this newfound latitude, more than the measures themselves, is not in line with the country's historical approach toward human rights or counterterrorism but rather in line with the counter-terrorism approaches taken by major powers in the aftermath of 9/11, the draconian aspects of which were made obvious by the discourses pertaining to the "war on terror."

In light of the spectacular aspect of the terrorists' attacks of September 11, it was hardly surprising that states, especially the United States, reacted forcefully to the aggression. Combined with a discourse advocating the presence of a new, more deadly type of terrorism, responses have included the establishment of the "unlawful combatants" prison at Guantánamo Bay and a more forceful Extraordinary Renditions Program. Wrongful detention cases have increased along with the use of electronic surveillance and data mining, creating more concern of human rights abuses by Western powers.

Although research shows that counterterrorist legislation and methods have remained practically unchanged in the West since the 1970s, the strength of the counterterrorism discourse and emphasis placed by Western politicians on terrorism has put their draconian aspects into light, notably when it comes to the use of guilt by association, preventive detention and surveillance. Consequently, the ugly side of Western states' approach to human rights was revealed, thereby damaging their credibility and accentuating the gap in attitude with more moderate powers such as Canada.

One example is policies related to "guilt by association." Historically a legal tightrope, the "guilt by association" approach aims to eliminate or deter all the possible links in a terrorist network by using loose definitions for support or participation. For example, the United States' Patriot Act defines material support to terrorism as "irrespective of any nexus between the individual's support and any act of violence, much less terrorism" (Cole and Dempsey 2006, 198). This is an extension of the same "material support" provision included in the 1996 Anti-terrorism and Effective Death Penalty Act, which, in its section 303, "made it a crime for citizens and non-citizens alike to provide any material support to the lawful political or humanitarian activities of any foreign group designated by the Secretary of State as 'terrorist'" (Cole and Dempsey 2006, 135).

Germany and the United Kingdom have similar laws. The German penal law (Strafgeseztbuch) §129, enacted in 1976, clearly stipulates that any form of support, including promotion through graffiti, for example, can lead to financial penalty and/or up to five years in prison (Weigend 2006, 75). As for the United Kingdom, §57 of the Terrorism Act 2000 states that a terrorist offence is committed if a person "possesses an article in circumstances which give rise to reasonable suspicion that his possession is for a purpose connected with the commission, preparation or instigation of an act of terrorism"(UK 2001).

The major issue with guilt by association is that it applies to the weakest of connections to an alleged suspect, creating a network of suspicion that rapidly has no relevance to the case. Although it has been used as a common legal tool for several decades, it nonetheless severely undermines the basic right to the presumption of innocence and poor interpretation, as in the case of Samina Malik. Arrested on November 8, 2007, Malik, also known as the "Lyrical Terrorist," was found guilty of owning terrorist material, although she was found not guilty of terrorism support under §57. She possessed books on terrorism and wrote in her diary that she sometimes dreamt of being a martyr, although she had no ties to any terrorist organization. Such cases are usually the exception but as they became more common since 9/11, the fear of a "Big Brother" state that monitors thoughts and opinions has increased and contributed to the perception that powers like the United States or Germany are dismissive of human rights.

Another area of concern is the use of preventive detention. This, like its military counterpart presumes that someone could be or is planning a crime or an attack, based on circumstantial evidence. Seldom used domestically in the West prior to 9/11, it has since then become increasingly popular, particularly in Europe, where several police operations have culminated in preventive arrests. Moreover, France has come under further scrutiny for both the duration and intransigence of its preventive detention. In 1986, the *Pasqua* law, created the *14e section spéciale du parquet de Paris*, a special judicial branch composed of six antiterror judges that handle all terrorism-related cases (France 1986). This law, further amended in 2006, states that anyone suspected of terrorism may be arrested and held without charge for four days, with a possible extension of 48 hours if a terrorist act is deemed imminent (France 2008). Additionally if a judge states *intent* to prosecute, the suspect may be held indefinitely, in some cases numerous years (Lerougetel 2006), a breach of the basic right of *habeas corpus*.

As for the United Kingdom, preventive action also includes conditional freedom, embodied by the Control Orders. Included in the Terrorism Act 2005, these orders "... impose obligations on him [the suspect] for purposes connected with protecting members of the public from a risk of terrorism" (UK 2005). Therefore, despite release, the suspect remains under surveillance, and this for a period of 12 months (UK 2005). Despite undergoing slight modifications – a reduction of curfew hours – after being determined to be a violation of human rights, the control orders remain a problem, to the extent that a second ruling on human rights violation was handed down, pertaining to the use of secret evidence (Jones and Rozenberg 2006; Travis 2009). This ruling is obviously analogous to the one Canada's Supreme Court made concerning the Security Certificates.

Although the majority of post-9/11 counterterrorism measures are actually slight updates of preexisting laws, they are depicted by politicians and experts as being novel and appropriate to counter the threat of terrorism.[7] Combined with a more malign depiction of terrorists, this discourse creates a climate of fear that appears to legitimize the laws, and more importantly justifies the greater latitude given to interpretation and application of these laws by security forces. Hence these measures seem harsher and enhance the perception of infringing on human rights, further deepening the gap between the human rights discourse of the 1990s and that of the post-9/11 period.

Again, such discourses and changes might be warranted in countries with significant experience with terrorism, but are dissonant in middle powers that appear to have no justification for it, thereby accurately reflecting a changing climate for human rights.

International influences on policy change

It is difficult to find domestic sources for Canada's recent policy changes, given its microscopic crime rate and lack of external terrorist threats. Much of the shift in policy seems to have been influenced by external actors. The international response to 9/11 sanctioned through UN resolutions 1368 and 1373 certainly played a significant role, especially as the country's involvement in Afghanistan has made it a target for terrorists, but I believe the main factors lie in the American security discourse and its policies.

Following 9/11, the American-Canadian border immediately became a security issue. The border's length, combined with the cordial relationship between the two countries and the North American Free Trade Agreement (NAFTA) border permissions, made circulation between the two states easy. Therefore, surveillance had to be increased and tighter controls at the main crossing points had to be implemented. But, as seen above, American policymakers also had an issue with Canada's own borders, which many deemed too lax and consequently unsafe for the United States.

From an American perspective, these arguments make sense. The Ahmed Ressam case had immediately resurfaced. He had obtained easy entrance into Canada and received official citizenship documents;

warnings about him from foreign security agencies had been dismissed. Had it not been for the vigilance of the American customs agents in Seattle, Ressam's plot to blow up LAX might well have been successful. September 11 exposed US vulnerabilities, and the immigration policies of its northern neighbor was one of them. Additionally, the United States has always sought to export its borders in order to protect its interests and security against external threats. Thus, following the first ever attack on its mainland since obtaining its independence, it was normal for the United States to reinforce its historical stance on security and insist that its external vulnerabilities be dealt with adequately. Consequently, it became state policy to put pressure on its partners to enhance security, as described in the 2002 *National Strategy for Homeland Security.* The document states that

> Internationally, the United States will seek to screen and verify the security of goods and identities of people before they can harm [*sic*] to the international transportation system and well before they reach our shores and land borders ... The United States will work with other countries and international organizations to improve the quality of travel documents and their issuance to minimize their misuse by smugglers and terrorist organizations. We will also assist other countries, as appropriate, to improve their border controls and their coordination with us. (DHS 2002, 7)

How does this international pressure related to homeland security apply to Canada? Following the signing in December 2001 of the Smart Borders Accord, this being a 30-point program whose aim was

> to secure the border and facilitate the flow of low-risk travelers through (1) coordinated law enforcement operations; (2) intelligence sharing; (3) infrastructure improvements; (4) the improvement of compatible immigration databases; (5) visa policy coordination; (6) common biometric identifiers in certain documentation; (7) pre-screening of air passengers; (8) joint passenger analysis units; and (9) improved processing of refugee and asylum claims. (Seghetti 2004)

Canada implemented in 2004 its first *National Security Program* and the creation of the *Department of Public Safety and Emergency Preparedness,* whose goal was to upgrade security measures and personnel in government buildings and in each one of the country's points of entry

(Radio-Canada 2008). This measure includes a background security check for every employee, something that prior to 2004 was done only for law enforcement agencies. In terms of law enforcement, the *Integrated Border Enforcement Teams*, a joint Canada/US program, was created to increase the chances of capturing the illegal flow of individuals between the two states, focusing in particular on drug dealers, illegal immigrants and terrorists (Canadian Press 2008b). Financially, $930 million have been invested in the program, with an extra $145 million planned in the 2008 budget (Castonguay 2008).

More revealing about the program however, are its three core interests, most notably "ensuring Canada is not a base for threats to our allies" (Canada 2004). I specified earlier that Canada's main problem with terrorism is not the terrorism itself but rather its capacity as a breeding ground for terrorists. This "core interest" not only responds to that problem but the "base for threats to our allies" is also a clear indication of the pressure exerted by the United States.

US influence does have its limits, however. If Canada did not hesitate to contribute troops to *Operation Enduring Freedom*, as part of its commitment to NATO and to resolutions 1368 and 1373, it categorically refused take part in the invasion of Iraq despite strong US pressure.

Although the bulk of foreign pressure comes from the United States, the measures and policies of other states or groups, such as the European Union, may also have a role in the policy turnaround of middle-power states. The US may lead the way in implementing biometrical travel documents, but they are increasingly required by other Western countries such as Germany or the United Kingdom, which creates secondary pressure to implement such programs and devices, in other words to comply with emerging standards. Another crucial factor in Canada's evolving policies is the pressure deriving from its presence in Afghanistan, which makes it a potential target for terrorism, exemplified by the case of the Toronto 18.

Given the spectacular circumstances of 9/11, it is difficult to imagine that the Canadian government would not have enhanced its security measures even if the American government had not demanded such changes through the Smart Borders Accord and the joint security declaration of December 3, 2001. However, the extent of the measures, as well as the urgency of their implementation, is most certainly the result of outside pressure, consequently affecting domestic attitudes and priorities, an influence perhaps increased by the election of a pro-American, Conservative government in early 2006.

Canada as a barometer for international trends on security and human rights

We have examined throughout this chapter the prevailing tendencies before and after 9/11 in Canada in terms of terrorism, counterterrorism and human rights as well as the impact of post-9/11 bilateral and multilateral relations. We have seen that despite the country's lack of experience with terrorism or of an actual threat, it vigorously responded to the 9/11 attacks, like its Western counterparts, by enacting a counterterrorism law and implementing a set of programs aimed at improving national security. More importantly, we have seen that although the domestic level of human rights abuses has remained steady in the past 11 years, the abuses and blatant disregard for legal responsibility toward these rights at the international level has either increased or become far more prominent since September 2001. Cases of complicity to torture or inaction toward human rights abuses have defined Canada's international involvement during the first decade of the 21st century, a situation dissonant with both the country's historical stance on human rights and its strong humanitarian involvement.

This of course severely undermines the country's hard-won reputation as a human rights leader and protector as well as its credibility as a viable, neutral mediator in conflicts. But if this is the price of policy alignment, why would Canadian policymakers do this? As we have seen, the answer is that international pressure, essentially from the United States, greatly outweighs any domestic misgivings about international policy-making. This is not to say that Canadian governments would have kept a security status quo, especially when one considers the swiftness and intransigence with which it handled its own domestic terrorism issues in 1970, a response which is to this day unique among postwar Western countries. But because Canadian borders and transport infrastructures were deemed by the world's most powerful country to be a threat to their security, American pressure on Canadian authorities for security reforms is perhaps the greatest factor explaining the reversal.

That being said, when a country that based its international identity on humanitarian issues and human rights, like Canada or the Netherlands, becomes, in less than a decade, infamous for its abuses and abandons its role as guardian, it becomes quite emblematic of the extent of post-9/11 Western attitudes toward human rights and security. Therefore, Canada, not unlike the Netherlands and other middle powers, is demonstrating that it is merely a barometer of the international political climate, simply reflecting the stronger policy changes imposed by major powers. Rather than demonstrating leadership in striving to maintain human rights policies and agendas, middle-power countries merely embody the atmosphere of international regimes, gloomy or bright, depending on the tone set by stronger voices.

The problem, however, is one of credibility and legitimacy. Because the credibility of middle powers lends, via collaboration or inaction, a certain legitimacy to human rights abuses in the name of security, a formal recognition of draconian attitudes in terms of national security, consequently setting new security management standards, one with little regard for human rights, confirms the barometer's accuracy. The broader consequences of this weakness in terms of policy-setting may very well be that the international human rights regime itself may be deemed superfluous, a luxurious tool branded by major powers when it serves their purpose. If so, this severely undermines the already precarious value of the international human rights regime, as countries that built their international reputation on it dismiss its importance when pressured by the interests of more powerful states. We are therefore left to wonder, if not them, who else?

Notes

1. Terrorist attacks are extremely difficult to assess, as data and definitions vary widely from one country to the next. I rely on the statistical data compiled by MIPT, which, although not without problems, is perhaps the most reliable source on the subject.
2. On May 5, 2009, one of the suspects, Saad Khalid, pleaded guilty to accusations of plotting a terrorist act, aimed at destroying various Canadian landmarks.
3. On June 9, 2009, a military inquiry commission established that Canadian military personnel did not abuse Afghan prisoners but had rather treated them humanely. However, some questioned the narrowness of the inquiry and called for a more general review.
4. This decision was twice appealed by the Canadian government. The decision was upheld by the first federal court of appeals while the Supreme Court, without invalidating the decisions of the lower courts or denying the wrongdoings of the government's attitude in the case, stated in its judgment of January 29, 2010 that it would "leave it to the government to decide how best to respond to this judgment in light of current information, its responsibility for foreign affairs and in conformity with the charter." Using this margin of maneuver, the government refused to undertake the repatriation process for Khadr (Austen 2010).

5. This also includes a media blackout for the duration of the trial.
6. That the provisions of this law were not contested prior to 2007, 29 years after its enactment, demonstrates how the use of the certificates has become an issue after 2001.
7. Following the second ruling on the control orders, UK Home Secretary Alan Johnson declared that the "judgment made his task of protecting the public harder" (Travis 2009).

Part IV
Continuity? Global Trends

11
Transnational NGOs and Human Rights in a Post-9/11 World

Hans Peter Schmitz

The September 11, 2001 attacks and the subsequent military response by the administration of George W. Bush had significant consequences for the work of US-based nongovernmental organizations (NGOs) working on human rights-related issues around the world. NGOs active in the fields of humanitarian aid, development, and human rights faced challenges ranging from increased security threats to their staff, more governmental restrictions and violations of civil and political rights, and pressures to align themselves with foreign policy objectives of the United States. While the global environment for their operations deteriorated as a consequence of the terrorist attacks and violent state responses, transnational NGOs proved resilient and became a key defense for the international human rights regime. Transnational activists led by organizations such as Amnesty International (AI) and Human Rights Watch (HRW) succeeded in halting a rapidly deteriorating respect for human rights in the United States and elsewhere. In the development and humanitarian sector, human rights ideas continued to flourish and gave rise to significant organizational and strategic innovations strengthening advocacy strategies in defense of explicit rights claims. The strength of the global human rights regime was tested by 9/11, but its power remains largely intact and its reach continues to expand.

While 9/11 and the subsequent US-led wars in Afghanistan and Iraq had important and often negative consequences for NGOs, the events were not a major turning point for NGOs or the international human rights regime. Continuity and change of transnational human rights activism is best understood not in the context of 9/11, but in the context of how the specific model of nongovernmental mobilizing against human rights violations emerged during the 1960s and 1970s and experienced a profound crisis during the early 1990s, when this model of "shaming" primarily state perpetrators for violations became increasingly outdated. Well before 9/11, NGOs across different sectors of transnational activism had begun to develop more proactive and preventative strategies whose aims were to overcome the inherent limitations of a reactive activist model. Despite facing different kinds of challenges in the post-9/11 world, many development, human rights, and humanitarian groups were joined in a focus on improving the legitimacy and accountability of Northern-based advocacy, a desire to move beyond defending a narrow set of civil and political rights, and a need to adopt new networking and mobilization strategies as a basis for recruiting supporters and organizing campaigns.

States responding to terrorism with violence and restrictions on civil rights and political freedoms made it more difficult for NGOs to expand advocacy efforts and temporarily forced them to spend resources on preventing further backsliding on basic civil rights in established democracies. As it turned out, NGOs were successful in defending basic human rights protections under threat in many democratic societies, while also continuing to innovate with regard to pushing into areas of social and economic justice. A well-established global human rights treaty system certainly aided NGOs in their efforts and has provided additional support in favor of increasing respect for these norms (Simmons 2009).

This chapter begins with a brief history of the transnational human rights movement, primarily focused on US and European-based activist groups. This section will highlight how the creation of human rights institutions at the global and regional levels facilitated a peculiar type of transnational activism represented by AI and HRW which was focused on *ex post* "shaming" and mass media strategies targeted at governments. The 1970s represent the key period when human rights became the central frame of global activism, such as the struggles against colonialism and Apartheid or the movements challenging authoritarian rule in Southern Europe and Latin America. But it also represented a period where human rights advocacy became largely separated from development and humanitarian efforts.

The next section will then describe in what ways the end of the Cold War exposed some of the limitations of transnational activism (Rodio and Schmitz 2010). Questions about the effectiveness and accountability of NGOs multiplied following the atrocities committed in Rwanda and the former Yugoslavia, the subsequent humanitarian crises in the Great Lakes region, and the perceived failures of the development aid model. The experiences of the 1990s crystallized for many NGOs ongoing discussions about how intensified advocacy efforts, increased focus on prevention, and intensified collaboration across sectors may strengthen the transnational NGO sector as a whole.

The third main section then elaborates why 9/11 was not a major turning point for transnational NGOs in the United States. Based on extensive interviews with leaders of selected US-based transnational NGOs, conducted between 2005 and 2008, the section shows that fundamental challenges to the transnational activist model emerged well before 9/11 and became particularly apparent in the post-Cold War period. To be sure, the wars in Afghanistan and Iraq, as well as the global focus on terrorism and sectarian violence had significant repercussions for transnational NGOs. But 9/11 neither resulted in a significant erosion of support for the global human rights regime nor did it slow down the previously set in motion intensified cross-sectoral collaborations between human rights, humanitarian, environmental, and development organizations.

In a post-9/11 world, human rights NGOs mobilized effectively against efforts to limit basic civil and political rights, while activists in other sectors implemented lessons learned during the 1990s and earlier. For humanitarian organizations, the Rwandan genocide and other humanitarian crises of the 1990s led to a fundamental questioning of the norms of impartiality and independence (Anderson 1999). An increased focus on the consequences and effectiveness of humanitarian aid as well as greater accountability to those receiving aid became central to reform efforts expressed in the adoption of codes of conduct. After 9/11, when aid groups faced efforts by the US military to take over humanitarian aid in Afghanistan and Iraq, individual organizations already had experience in dealing with the inevitable politicization of the humanitarian model (de Torrente 2004; O'Brien 2004). In the development sector, a profound sense of crisis also preceded 9/11 and focused primarily on the failures of development aid and the "charity" model. During the 1990s, development NGOs increasingly looked towards human rights ideas as a key to regaining legitimacy. A rights-based approach (RBA) to development (Uvin 2004) emerged as NGOs explored more sustainable ways of supporting economic development. Finally, human rights groups began well before 9/11 to question the success of *ex post* "shaming" strategies and develop more sustainable efforts to prevent abuses. Post-9/11, the already established focus on violence committed by non-state armed groups aligned with new concerns about terrorism and sectarian violence.

Initiated in the 1990s, the significant strategic shifts within sectors of transnational activism were accompanied by increased collaboration among transnational activist groups. The rights-based development agenda, the broad support for the International Criminal Court (ICC), the landmines ban, and the INGO Accountability Charter of 2006 represent a few examples of joint efforts to increase the effectiveness and accountability of transnational activist groups. The events following 9/11 offered nothing more than a reminder about the inadequacies of a reactive and ameliorative activist model which had been in crisis for some time and had failed to effectively address fundamental injustices causing poverty, ethnic divisions, and discrimination.

Transnational human rights activism: from the Cold War to the post-9/11 world

While the systematic transnational promotion of norms reaches back to the 19th century and Christian missionary movements (Hirono 2008), a sustained secular and transnational movement focused on the idea of universal human rights only emerged with the formation of the United Nations and the adoption of the Universal Declaration of Human Rights (UDHR) in 1948. The UDHR codified for the first time a state-led consensus on human rights and legitimated the activities of organizations such as AI or HRW. Understanding the successes (Keck and Sikkink 1998) and challenges (Rieff 1999; Tarrow 2005) of this new type of transnational activism represents the crucial backdrop to assessing continuity and change after 9/11.

The first section here focuses on how the Cold War shaped the organization and strategies of transnational human rights activism. Three prominent effects stand out: The narrowed focus on civil and political rights, the focus on "information politics" (Keck and Sikkink 1998, 18) and shaming strategies, and the explicit avoidance of partisan politics. The second section then turns attention to how the practices emerging in the 1970s and 1980s became a liability in responding to a changed post-Cold War period. The professionalization and media-driven character of transnational campaigns perpetuated a widening North-South gap (Jordan and Van Tuijl 2000), limited cooperation across the advocacy/service divide within the nongovernmental sector, and demobilized the grassroots level by privileging elite-driven strategies (Kennedy 2004). The limits of transnational activism were exposed by the atrocities committed in the former Yugoslavia and Rwanda and led to significant changes in the practice of transnational activism prior to 9/11. The final section then presents a contemporary view of selected leaders of transnational human rights groups based in the United States on the opportunities and challenges of transnational activism in the post-9/11 world.

The evolution of modern transnational human rights activism

The adoption of an expanding list of global and regional human rights accords undergirds the emergence and legitimization of transnational human rights activism. During the 1960s and 1970s, human rights groups established their moral authority based on strategies of "bearing witness" and "shaming" the perpetrators through meticulous research and publication of violations (Hopgood 2006, 14). This particular strategy was first developed by AI in the 1960s and 1970s and later modified by a new crop of advocacy groups such as HRW (founded in 1978) which further professionalized the campaign-style approach with an expanded focus on mass media and lobbying efforts.

As a coalition of authoritarian states began in the 1960s to target NGOs within the United Nations (Korey 1998, chapter 3), activists concluded that their "principal efforts would need to be focused for a long time *outside* the UN" (Sidney Liskofsky, cited in Korey 1998, 139). With a predominant focus on civil and political rights as well as state agents perpetrating violations, those activists developed a distinct nonpartisan and transnational human rights movement. Unlike their predecessors, represented by the generation of Eleanor Roosevelt, the type of activism strove to establish a more independent and transnational network dedicated to the collection and dissemination of human rights-related information. Combining the power of new communication technologies, reliable information, and the sacred symbolism created by an organization such as AI (Hopgood 2006), popular support for the idea of human rights as a universal value spread primarily in Western Europe and North America.

The 1977 Nobel Peace Prize awarded to AI and the creation of Helsinki Watch in 1978 marked the early success of this new type of transnational human rights organization. While AI had already become a global player during the 1970s, the emergence of Helsinki Watch and Americas Watch (in 1981) represented a crucial step "to subject the State Department's annual country reports [on human rights] to close and critical scrutiny" (Korey 1998, 342). From the 1980s onward, AI and HRW would dominate the human rights discourse with their "shaming" strategies, developing a largely reactive model of exposing human rights violations after they took place. This model became increasingly outmoded with the end of the Cold War and the realization that it had little appeal among citizens in the Global South and failed to address many of the root causes of persistent patterns of violations.

Amnesty International's membership base, its parallel structures of professional and volunteer organization, and its refusal to solicit any funding sources other than membership dues, represent an outlier in the NGO world. HRW is a more typical example of an NGO without an individual membership base which relies more heavily on larger donations by foundations. The trade-offs between the two types of transnational organizing became apparent when HRW quickly rose during the 1980s to become the main competitor of AI and was able to respond more quickly to new human rights issues favored by large donors (e.g. child soldiers). The broader support and legitimacy AI enjoyed as a result of representing close to 2 million members organized in close to 50 national sections also represented a core limitation making the organization less nimble and driven by tensions between the professionals (International Secretariat) and the volunteers organized in the national sections. During the 1990s, AI moved only very slowly in convincing its membership and supporters that fundamental change was inevitable and required a more overtly political approach leaving behind the singular focus on principles and symbolic "idolatry" (Ignatieff 2001). By 2001, AI embarked on a trial period of abandoning its mandate in favor of broader campaign themes, including the promotion of social and economic rights.

The emergence of HRW and its success in challenging AI created a more competitive environment among human rights groups and led to some innovation, but it did not prevent the profound crisis of the movement during the 1990s. This crisis was largely the result of a failure to take seriously the human rights issues of the Global South as well as a blindly principled view[1] that was ill-prepared for developing more sophisticated analyses of the social and political root causes of many human rights violations. The professionalization of human rights activism also created growing complacency on the part of (liberal) states and the general public. As the visibility and mass media efforts of human rights groups increased, the general public became content with delegating these tasks to an elite group of activists. The membership of AI peaked in the late 1980s, indicating a crisis in popular support well before the post-Cold War challenges to the transnational "shaming" model of human rights activism.

With the end of communism in 1989/90 human rights groups not only lost one of the cornerstones of their principled, nonpartisan strategy, but also realized that traditional state-sponsored repression became less important in accounting for global patterns of violations. As patterns of ethnic and communal violence as well as global economic inequality became more prominent, the limits of a reactive "shaming" model came into sharp relief since human rights groups largely lacked political strategies designed to address the structural causes of these violations. Efforts to address poverty or ethnic divisions as root causes for many human rights violations force human rights groups to become more overtly political, join alliances with like-minded groups, and debate the relative merits of different conflict resolution and poverty reduction programs.

Transnational human rights activism has evolved since the end of the Second World War from a limited lobbying effort by committed individuals to a transnational movement led by professionals, heavily reliant on campaigns and media attention. AI's system of adopted political prisoners created a powerful link between victims and their defenders abroad, while HRW was at the forefront of developing campaign-style mass media strategies. The very success of this emphasis on exposing violations left the human rights movement unprepared for the challenges of the post-Cold War period. As human rights NGOs became more prominent and successful, the attention of the general public waned and its Northern bias solidified. The "shaming" strategy born in the 1970s and aided by advances in technology and communication was less effective in preventing violations in the first place, failed to move perpetrators immune to reputational costs associated with committing atrocities, and could not effectively be used to address structural causes of violations which defied the model of linking a specific perpetrator and action to a violation.

The post-Cold War period: crisis and innovation

Transnational activists witnessed in the early 1990s the disappearance of many authoritarian regimes as familiar sources of human rights violations while facing new challenges emerging as a result of ethnic conflict, the increasing prominence of violent non-state actors, and the failures of the state community to respond effectively to humanitarian crises in Rwanda, the former Yugoslavia, Zaire/Democratic Republic of Congo, Sudan, and elsewhere. A profound experience of crisis not only affected human rights groups, but also other areas of transnational activism where an expressed apolitical, neutral approach to improving people's lives was dominant. Humanitarian organizations faced the paradox of well-intentioned aid contributing to more violence (Terry 2002) and development groups began to understand how their increasing role "to fill the vacuum left by nation states" (Lindenberg and Bryant 2001, 1) slowed democratization and the emergence of domestic accountability patterns between rulers and ruled.

The post-Cold War period is marked by a growing realization that effective responses to persistent abuse patterns required a shift away from a primarily reactive activism towards prevention and addressing root causes of violations. As a result, human rights activism has moved well beyond the state as the main target and has also challenged the sectoral separation between advocacy and service groups. As early adopters within the development sector began in the mid-1990s to develop a RBA to their work (Uvin 2004), the human rights discourse now expanded into the humanitarian, development, and environmental sectors of transnational activism.

Three notable developments set the post-Cold War period apart and can be understood as a response to new challenges and the crisis of the particular model of principled activism emerging in the 1960s and 1970s. First, humanitarian and development NGOs primarily focused on service delivery began to expand their advocacy role (Lindenberg and Bryant 2001) and adopted human rights frameworks in their activities. Second, new types of advocacy groups emerged which sought to move beyond the focus on civil and political rights to address structural causes of abuses, including resource conflicts and ethnic divisions. At the same time, traditional human rights organizations began in the early 1990s to shift attention away from state governments and explicitly address violations committed by non-state actors (Andreopoulos et al. 2006). Third, the same groups played a significant role in the accelerated establishment of international institutions designed to address human rights issues (e.g. the International Criminal Court, the International Convention to Ban Landmines, or the Kimberley Agreement on Conflict Diamonds).

Humanitarian aid and rights-based approaches to development

Growing cooperation across the advocacy/service divide, primarily in the humanitarian, development, and human rights sectors, represents a distinct response to the limitations of activism within each of these sectors. Following an increased awareness of the failures of foreign aid and humanitarian/development efforts, service-oriented organizations became more aware of the political consequences of their work and developed greater advocacy capacities (Lindenberg and Bryant 2001; Rugendyke 2007) designed to support local development interventions by targeting national level and international causes of inequality and stunted development.[2] These shifts were most pronounced in the humanitarian and development sectors.

For humanitarian aid groups, the core value of neutrality and non-discrimination (Leebaw 2007, 227) was fundamentally challenged during their operations in refugee camps following the Rwandan genocide in 1994. As some Hutus "genocidaires" used the aid to reorganize in the camps and sustain the violence, humanitarian groups faced accusations that their aid "strengthened the power of the very people who had caused the tragedy" (Terry 2002, 2). Beyond the cases of possibly doing harm by enabling continued violence, humanitarian aid frequently violated the dignity of those receiving aid as increased professionalization and technical capabilities to deliver aid were not matched by adequate concerns for the basic rights of those affected by natural or human-made disasters. As humanitarian groups faced increasing criticisms, fundamental norms of neutrality, impartiality, and independence were weighted against the possible negative consequences of short-term aid (Barnett and Weiss 2008). In response, aid groups developed a number of codes of conduct (Hilhorst 2005) specifically designed to regulate humanitarian relief activities and increase the legitimacy of organizations previously only focused on the moral imperative to aid the suffering.

After 9/11, those codes played a significant role in helping many humanitarian groups to formulate a common response to efforts by the United States and allied military forces blurring the lines between combat and humanitarian aid in Afghanistan and Iraq (O'Brien 2004). In Iraq shortly after the US invasion, humanitarian NGOs faced the dilemma of maintaining independence and neutrality while at the same time receiving funding from Western governments as well as relying on US-led coalition forces for their security. In this situation, the bombing of the ICRC headquarters on October 27, 2003 and the murder of Margaret Hassan, the director of CARE (Iraq) in October 2004 caused many humanitarian groups to leave Iraq (Sunga 2007, 114). As neutrality and independence as core elements of humanitarian legitimacy were severely undercut by coalition forces and terrorist attacks, debates about the future of humanitarianism proliferated (de Torrente 2004; O'Brien 2004). But NGOs were already familiar with the basic contours of this conundrum and Iraq presented a case where humanitarian principles had to be married with a more pronounced effort of political advocacy challenging the behavior of belligerents. These debates had emerged long before 9/11 and have ultimately been resolved by strengthening human rights as core principles for legitimate action.

The dignity of those receiving aid has also become a greater concern in the area of more long-term development aid. Here, the main cause pushing the shift away from neutrality and charity was precipitated by a widespread perception of failure of development aid overall. Human rights ideas became central to closing the gap between organizations working in traditional development areas of education or health care and advocacy NGOs primarily focused on "shaming" strategies. Many of the major development NGOs, including CARE, Oxfam, and ActionAid, adopted some version of a rights-based approach to development and supplemented their service activities with expanded advocacy efforts. A similar, if slower movement in the opposite direction emerged among traditional human rights groups. As aid groups moved into advocacy, organizations such as AI experimented with campaigns on social and economic rights and began to develop tentative ideas about how to broaden their legitimacy and take seriously the challenge of how a "more acutely political, as opposed to moral activism might be more attentive to the question of whom activists represent" (Ignatieff 2002, 10).

Addressing root causes of human rights violations

Based on growing awareness of the limits of apolitical, professional-ized activism across the humanitarian, development, and human rights sectors, transnational NGOs also began in the 1990s to devote more resources to understanding better the causes of poverty, systematic abuses, and their own frequent failures to contribute to a sustainable improvement of the conditions motivating their interventions in the first place. In many cases, a better understanding of what causes atroci-ties led to the creation of new types of transnational NGOs, including the International Crisis Group (founded in 1995) and Global Witness (founded in 1998) whose focus include competition for resources (e.g. diamonds, timber, oil) and/or an emphasis on predicting imminent crises and alerting the global public. More traditional human rights NGOs, such as AI or HRW, have also increased their efforts to address complex and varied sources of human rights violations, for example by supporting stricter controls of arms sales and UN efforts to limit the availability of small arms.

Addressing root causes of gross violations and seeking new alliances with humanitarian and development NGOs reflect efforts by traditional human rights groups to move from a reactive to a preventive human rights strategy. For decades, AI sustained an explicit policy of only holding governments accountable for human rights violations committed on the territory of a state. The core strategy of letter-writing campaigns mobilized AI members and targeted government officials in defense of individuals deemed worthy of the designation "prisoner of conscience." With HRW emerging during the final years of the Cold War as a key challenger to AI's global leadership on human rights issues (Korey 1998, 340), both organizations experienced periods of crises before 1989, but faced even more competition from new groups in an increasingly crowded field of transnational activism. With the end of the Cold War, both organizations' original purpose of primarily targeting state repression within the context of superpower competition had lost relevance.

One of the first significant changes to the methodology of transnational human rights activism after the end of the Cold War was to explicitly target violent and nonviolent non-state actors implicated in gross violations. In 1991, AI adopted its new policy of targeting non-state actors primarily within the context of failed states, ethnic violence, and atrocities committed by warlords. The human rights violations were familiar to its traditional mandate (extrajudicial killings, torture, disappearances), but required different strategic and tactical responses. Multinational corporations also became targets of human rights groups either because of their explicit or implicit support of state repression (e.g. Royal Dutch/Shell in Nigeria or UNOCAL in Burma/Myanmar) or because of their direct control over workers in their own or their suppliers' factories. By shifting the target of mobilization away from states, human rights groups not only abandoned the fiction of state sovereignty over a given territory and population, but also moved into new issue areas, including conflict resolution, social and economic rights, and economic development.

Strengthening international institutions

The participation of advocacy networks in the creation and evolution of global human rights institutions has become a major focus of scholarly research (Martens 2005). During the 1970s, a coalition of states across ideological divides tried (and failed) to revoke the consultative status of many human rights organizations and inadvertently confirmed the rising power of nongovernmental participation (Shestack 1978, 91). The expansion of UN human rights institutions offered new opportunities for human rights groups (1) to use the proceedings of the UN human rights institutions for their shaming efforts exposing state violations

(Korey 1998: ch. 11; Martens 2006); (2) to further strengthen international human rights institutions (Clark 2001; Khagram et al. 2002; Joachim 2007); and (3) to lobby for mandate changes in international institutions lacking an explicit focus on human rights (Nelson 2000; Oestreich 2007).

After much internal debate, AI decided in the early 1970s to launch its first single-issue campaign focused on torture and to lobby the United Nations for a separate convention to ban the practice under any circumstances. Although the AI Secretariat ultimately rejected the 1984 UN torture convention, the organization played a central role in establishing strengthened international agreements on core mandate issues, including torture, disappearances, and capital punishment. Transnational groups also played prominent roles in the creation and adoption of the UN anti-landmines treaty (Price 1998), the establishment of the ICC (Glasius 2002), the inclusion of sexual violence in the definition of war crimes (Spees 2003), the adoption of the Kimberley Agreement to end the sale of conflict diamonds, and more generally, in giving human rights a more prominent position in global governance (signified in the creation of the UN High Commissioner for Human Rights in 1993). Despite the formal limits on the participation of NGOs in intergovernmental institutions (Friedman et al. 2005), transnational activists have used the post-Cold War period to establish human rights concerns across mandates of international institutions, reflecting a belief that strengthened international institutions are central to sustainable human rights change.

After 9/11: interviews with US-based human rights groups

The events following the attacks of September 11, 2001 have had a profound effect on transnational NGOs, but those effects are best understood in the context of changes taking place during the 1990s. This history can be written as a smashing success measured in organizational growth as well as increased influence and power, but it also reveals episodes of profound crisis of the professionalized model across all sectors of activism. Success and crisis created during the 1990s conditions facilitating fundamental organizational reforms and strategic reorientation within many organizations, but also across the main sectors of humanitarian relief, human rights, development, and environmental protection. These reforms helped the global NGO community, and in particular US-based groups, to respond in a more concerted fashion to the events following the attacks of 9/11 and specifically the policies of the Bush Administration. This section presents evidence from

12 interviews with the leadership of selected US-based human rights conducted between 2005 and 2008. While the semi-structured interviews covered issues of governance, effectiveness, accountability, networking, and leadership, the primary focus here is on evidence speaking to the NGOs' responses to the events of and subsequent to 9/11. The broader study[3] included interviews with 152 leaders of transnational NGOs based in the United States (Hermann et al. 2010). A basic population of transnational NGOs was determined based on organizations rated for financial health by Charity Navigator (www.charitynavigator.com). The sample for the study was then determined based on criteria of size, financial efficiency, and main area of activity, including organizations active in conflict resolution (13 organizations), human rights (21), humanitarian relief (32), environmental activism (22), and sustainable development (64). The interviewers typically travelled to the headquarters of the organization and the interviews took between 90 and 120 minutes. Confidentiality was promised to all organizations included in this study.

The events of 9/11 and the subsequent military response by the Bush Administration had significant repercussions for US-based and international NGOs. Organizations relying on funding from the United States Agency of International Aid (USAID) faced increased pressures to align themselves with US foreign policy goals (Sunga 2007, 107) and to refrain from any advocacy critical of US policies. Naomi Klein summarized the Bush Administration's views in 2003, writing: "NGOs should be nothing more than the good hearted charity wing of the military, silently mopping up after wars and famines. Their job is not to ask how these tragedies could have been averted or to advocate for policy solutions" (Klein 2003). Following the 9/11 attacks, counterterrorism laws were broadened in many developed nations, affecting overseas funding for development and civil society support (Sidel 2008). While this "disciplining" of civil society (Howell et al. 2008, 92) across the world should not be underestimated, the interviews with TNGO leaders show little evidence that 9/11 was a major watershed for transnational activism.

The interviews reveal that NGOs active in the development, humanitarian, and human rights sectors consistently focused on how to address shortcomings in their own effectiveness and accountability. While there is evidence that issues of terrorism-related state repression as well as specific US policies (e.g. renditions, Guantánamo) garnered greater attention relative to other advocacy topics, NGOs have not changed their missions as a result of any material pressure that may have been applied. Shifts in funding opportunities implemented by the newly incoming administration prior to 9/11 as well as the wars in Afghanistan and Iraq shaped the focus of US-based NGOs, especially for humanitarian and development organizations with substantial US government contracts.[4] But many of these organizations also took this opportunity as a challenge to diversify funding sources and ease their dependency on USAID or other governmental donors.

For the advocacy sector, the interviews reveal consistent evidence suggesting a continued strong role of transnational human rights groups in the US policy process. In one example of early 2005, NGOs lobbied successfully against a US veto in the United Nations Security Council referring the situation in Darfur/Sudan to the ICC. In this case, NGOs effectively challenged the Bush Administration's initial argument for an "African solution" by pointing to the strong support of African nations for the ICC and by using statements from African leaders in support of a referral to the ICC.[5] Human rights groups did not change their views on the inviolability of human dignity even after the attacks on US soil, and much of their internal debates reflect a desire to overcome the limits of the reactive model of transnational mobilizing which had become apparent during the 1990s.

For the service delivery sector, the interviews with humanitarian organizations offer additional evidence about how current thinking about strategic and organizational change is primarily driven by experiences dating back to the 1990s. While 9/11 and its consequences, in particular the wars in Afghanistan and Iraq, had a major impact on humanitarian groups, the concomitant challenges to the traditional humanitarian model of impartiality had emerged well before 2001 and most prominently during the 1990s. Following the Rwandan genocide, humanitarian organizations had already developed codes of conduct and addressed some of the political consequences of their interventions. The US policies after 9/11, and particularly the challenge of operating alongside belligerents, reignited a debate between those activists advocating for a return to the principles of neutrality and impartiality, and others claiming that such an option no longer existed and would do more harm than good.

A representative of one humanitarian organization interviewed for our study pointed out that in a post-9/11 world "independent, neutral, impartial organizations ... are being marginalized" and governments are now looking for organizations to "help them implement their political goals."[6] This development is particularly pronounced in the US-led post-9/11 wars, but the interviewee identified a larger trend that began with the end of the Cold War. "But that kind of the West going in as to solve crisis and having a military, political, and aid presence, that's something that we see not just in Afghanistan and Iraq." In response, some humanitarian activists see a return to impartiality and neutrality as the best option for the future. This view reflects a desire to return to the original mission of humanitarianism which focuses primarily on short-term survival and does not concern itself with long-term questions of conflict resolution or development (Rieff 2002).

Others within the humanitarian community have challenged this perspective and argued that humanitarian aid has always been political and should explicitly address "not only the tragic symptoms of conflict, but also its root causes. Not all wars are inevitable. Nor is global poverty inevitable" (O'Brien 2004, 38). To some degree, the two positions are not necessarily incompatible, since capabilities vary across individual organizations and those responding immediately following a disaster may find that the traditional humanitarian creed provides sufficient guidance for their efforts. The wars in Afghanistan and Iraq presented a new context for the debate on the consequences of humanitarian activism, but the basic issues had arisen well before 9/11.

Finally, in the sustainable development sector, the interviews confirm an ongoing shift away from the traditional donor model of transferring resources from rich to poor nations. An increasing number of development organizations are using a rights-based understanding of poverty to justify their increased efforts in advocacy and a relative decline of providing direct aid which may only create and sustain dependencies. These trends emerged well before 9/11 and show strong similarities to debates with the humanitarian and human rights sectors. As is the case elsewhere, there are development organizations which have moved much more quickly in embracing a RBA as well as more extensive advocacy strategies, while others express skepticism about such changes and fear that donors or members will punish such profound changes in mandate and strategy. Just as AI struggled with abandoning its letter-writing model and shifting towards broader campaigns, child sponsorship organizations in the United States and elsewhere face a tension between developing broader strategies empowering local communities and maintaining the traditional focus on transferring funds to a child and family in need. In both cases, the singular link between an individual or a group of sponsors in the North and someone in need in the Global South proved to be a successful business model, but its limitations became increasingly visible in the 1990s.

One interviewee of a development organization explained that "what we really struggle with is how can you incorporate structural change deep into an organizational business model that has historically been founded on a philanthropic basis ... If, and so we wanted to get, we wanted to depart from the charitable model, and move toward a structural model. The second thing we decided we wanted to do is we wanted to anchor all of that work and structural social change in a rights based approach."[7] This profound shift currently taking place in the development sector creates unique challenges and tensions. While barriers between different sectors of transnational activism are disappearing, individual organizations struggle with developing the appropriate organizational structures and capabilities to accomplish much more complex tasks and mandates. Across all three sectors discussed here, acknowledging the fact that neutral and impartial activism has always been a fiction creates extensive challenges not only in maintaining donor support but also for recruitment and training of staff. The interviews show across all sectors that NGO leaders see organizational learning and increasing their own impact as the key challenge.

Conclusion

The 9/11 attacks and the subsequent reassertion of state power in nations around the world has profoundly shaped the environment within which US-based NGOs with human rights mandates operate. But those effects need to be placed in the context of a broader understanding of the evolution of transnational human rights activism as well as the developments in the post-Cold War period of the 1990s. A significant number of NGOs across major areas of transnational activism were for some time engaged in a fundamental review of their activities and focused on increasing their impact as individual organizations and in cooperation with other civil society groups. Looking beyond the traditional human rights sector dominated by organizations such as AI or HRW, it is particularly instructive to observe that human rights ideas became central to this reform process within the humanitarian and development sectors.

A key paradox emerging from this analysis is the simultaneous strengthening of the global human rights discourse occurring alongside the profound crisis and weakness of transnational activism overall. During the past decades, humanitarian, human rights, and development NGOs have perfected addressing symptoms rather than root causes. Violations are reported and aid is handed down to victims of disasters and poverty, but only rarely are the root causes of these conditions addressed. While many organizations across these three sectors began in the 1990s to explore what a more proactive, preventive (and effective) strategy would look like, 9/11 highlighted the limitations of the reactive model and increased the urgency to create more effective strategies and coalitions with the ability to address structural conditions of discrimination, poverty, and exclusion. In this context, the US-led military response represented a more challenging global environment since many NGOs were at the same time experimenting with new and more overtly political strategies while also facing increased pressures from governments using security arguments as an excuse for increased repression. While the majority of transnational NGOs interviewed for this study were capable of mitigating such pressures, smaller and local NGOs were more likely to respond by avoiding controversial issues.

Human rights groups based in the United States (or elsewhere) were largely unable to prevent or end any of the policies implemented by the Bush Administration in response to the terrorist attacks. Governmental secrecy combined with a lack of public attention and support severely undercut the effectiveness of NGOs relying primarily on information dissemination through mass media and shaming efforts. But this research also shows that human rights groups were not powerless during the Bush years. After 9/11, US-based NGOs continued to lobby successfully on many human rights-related topics, for example on the ICC referral of the Darfur situation. The creation of the offshore detention facility Guantánamo Bay and the extraordinary efforts to manipulate the definition of torture certainly exposed the weaknesses of law and transnational activism, but those efforts also confirm that the presence and vigilance of human rights groups limits the range of options available to governments.

In the humanitarian sector, the debate about the future of impartiality and neutrality began well before 9/11. The military interventions in Afghanistan and Iraq added the challenge of a military taking over humanitarian tasks in order to "win the hearts and minds" of those occupied. Unlike the human rights area, there is no clear-cut case for all organizations to shift away traditional, principled behavior, in this case impartial and neutral aid to those suffering. As the presence of aid agencies becomes more permanent, the fiction of being neutral disappears and organizations need to weigh the long-term consequences of their presence. A more permanent transnational presence usually distinguishes the activities of sustainable development organizations from humanitarian or human rights groups. Here, the widespread adoption of a rights-based approach is unrelated to 9/11 and represents the most remarkable transformation of a transnational sector. Yet, the motives for this shift are very similar to other sectors, where organizations have also been primarily driven by an increased awareness of their own limitations and a desire to affect sustainable impact that relies less and less on their presence.

The analysis of transnational human rights activism today can no longer be limited to the activities of organizations such as AI and HRW. The continued diffusion of the human rights discourse has not only contributed to lowering barriers between different types of transnational NGOs, but has also led to the articulation of profound challenges to traditional practices within various sectors of NGO activism. Human rights may not be the only promising basis for facilitating social and political change, but they are increasingly seen by many as a framework broadly conducive to local empowerment and government accountability. While 9/11 exposed once again the weaknesses of a reactive model of transnational activism, many organizations have begun well before 2001 to reflect on their mandates and strategies and a few have implemented extensive reforms designed to overcome longstanding challenges such as the gap in capacity between Northern and Southern organizations or the lack of strategies designed to address the actual causes of the conditions transnational NGOs have sought to address for decades. It is a whole different issue to evaluate whether those changes in transnational organizing and strategy are effectively implemented and actually make the difference suggested by their proponents.

Notes

1. The failure of AI to adequately address the South African apartheid regime and its refusal to adopt Nelson Mandela as a prisoner of conscience are an example for the limitations of a principled view that failed to recognize structural patterns of abuse.
2. Examples include more explicit efforts to lobby national governments to support neglected regions and local communities as well as campaigns against agricultural subsidies in Europe and the United States.
3. This research was partly supported by National Science Foundation Grant No. SES-0527679 (Agents of Change: Transnational NGOs as Agents of Change: Toward Understanding Their Governance, Leadership, and Effectiveness) and the TNGO Initiative at the Moynihan Institute of Global Affairs at Syracuse University. For more information on the methodology and results, please visit www.maxwell.syr.edu/moynihan_tngo.aspx.
4. Broadly in line with the general argument of this chapter, the organization CARE had begun well before 9/11 to adopt a rights-based approach and to expand its advocacy activities. As a result of 9/11, a prior advocacy focus

on "countries in conflict" became largely reduced to Afghanistan, partially reflecting funding priorities of USAID, a major donor of CARE.

5. Interview 1 with a representative of a human rights organization.
6. All quotes in this section from Interview 2 with a representative of a humanitarian organization.
7. All quotes in this section are from Interview 3 with a representative of a development organization.

12
Disaggregating the Effects of 9/11 on NGOs

Lena Barrett

The earth shook with the collapse of the Twin Towers, in more ways than one. The tremors would be felt for most of the first decade of the 21st century, reaching halfway around the world to devastate Iraq and Afghanistan, and bringing old certainties about security and freedom tumbling down. Things changed, less as a result of the attacks themselves, horrifying though they were, and more as a result of how states altered their behavior in response, in the context of the so-called war on terror. Then UN High Commissioner for Human Rights Mary Robinson (2006) reported that an Ambassador said bluntly to her in 2002: "Don't you see, High Commissioner? The standards have changed." Nearly a decade later, however, as the tremors die down and the dust finally clears, the world that emerges is beginning to look rather familiar once more.

After 9/11, the powerful felt threatened. The relationship between governments and human rights nongovernmental organizations (NGOs) involves a challenge to power, by which the powerful are called to account for their actions. It is therefore not surprising that a new note of tension could be discerned in government/NGO relationships in the wake of 9/11. Howell et al. (2008) went as far as to call it "a sombre backlash against civil society on many levels and fronts... [which] threaten[s] the spaces for civil society to flourish and act." It is the contention of this chapter that in the past few years, the backlash has passed its peak, and something closer to equilibrium has been reestablished.

It is, however, necessary to qualify this broad statement. States vary greatly, and so do NGOs. Depending on their focus and geographic location, NGOs have experienced 9/11 and its aftermath very differently: the encounter has variously been catastrophic, sobering, strengthening or largely irrelevant. To judge the impact properly, it is necessary to disaggregate NGOs into three categories:

(1) NGOs working on issues that are generally not perceived as related to terrorism have usually escaped direct harm, regardless of the nature of the state, although some have found themselves struggling with the challenge of the diversion or the politicization of aid. The organizations in this category tend to be local and international organizations working on economic and social rights (Oxfam, CARE).

(2) NGOs working in authoritarian states, particularly on sensitive issues such as ethnic conflict, have been damaged by the fallout from 9/11. They may not face increased risk from the authorities, but these authorities have been able to better disguise their repression by calling it counterterrorism. This disguise has made it harder to find international allies (the Human Rights Society of Uzbekistan). With the change of regime in the United States, however, there is room for hope that counterterrorism will no longer function as such an effective smokescreen for repression at international level.

(3) NGOs working on sensitive issues in states that are generally not repressive have experienced some harm from certain state-imposed counterterrorism measures. They have also succumbed to a degree of self-censorship at various times (such as immediately post-9/11) and on various issues (such as the treatment of noncitizens with criminal records). Larger NGOs with considerable political clout such as Amnesty International have ultimately suffered little long-term harm, while smaller ones with militant sympathies, real or suspected, have faced more significant challenges. The travails of Interpal, a Palestinian support group based in the UK, is a good illustration of this latter category.

NGOs working in democratic states may also have received an unexpected benefit in the wake of 9/11. By holding fast to their principles in the face of powerful challenges, they have been able to demonstrate their relevance and establish moral authority.

NGOs working on issues unrelated to terrorism

Not all NGOs work on issues that are perceived as threatening by state authorities. An organization working on the rights of disabled children, for example, while it may criticize state provision for its clients, is unlikely to be a serious target for state repression. Such organizations have tended to escape direct harm. Reporting from Pakistan, the director of the Green Economics and Globalization Initiative found that "women's NGOs that restrict themselves to unthreatening health and literacy initiatives, for example, are left alone" (Sadeque 2007). The years since 2001 have in some ways been years of growth and expansion for NGOs, particularly in terms of an increased focus on economic and social rights, which from a counterterrorism perspective are generally less threatening than civil and political rights. Development agencies have increased their use of rights-based approaches, and human rights agencies have become more interested in framing economic and social problems as rights violations (Nelson and Dorsey 2008).

While relatively safe from direct harm, however, at least some NGOs in this category have suffered from the diversion of international aid to areas that support the security interests of major donors. The development assistance mandates of the United States and other countries have been altered to address their security concerns, with the result that development cooperation assistance in respect of many poor countries has been "sidelined for aggressive military intervention in Afghanistan and Iraq and their neighbours" (Reality of Aid Management Committee 2006).

As well as the problem of diversion of aid, NGOs have also faced difficulties arising from the politicization of aid, a trend that predates the "war on terror" but was exacerbated by it. In Afghanistan, the United States in particular directed funding toward Afghan reconstruction as "political appeasement – the price that had to be paid for a failed foreign policy" (O'Brien 2005). Both the United States and the next largest donor, the EU, imposed conditions on the organizations they funded, insisting they remain at arm's length from the Taliban. O'Brien argues that using a rights-based approach helped NGOs, notably CARE, to move from an apolitical stance that was no longer appropriate in a politicized context toward advocacy that was political in a very positive sense. In his view, from 2003, CARE successfully encouraged the Afghan government to reconfigure its relationship to donors toward a model based not on charity but on assisting the government to meet its responsibilities to its citizens. In this case, the post-9/11 context ultimately resulted in positive strategic adjustments by NGOs.

NGOs working on terrorism-sensitive issues in authoritarian states

By contrast, for NGOs working on issues deemed by hostile authorities to be relevant to terrorism, the "war on terror" has been deeply harmful, at least in the short-term. Whether an issue is "relevant to terrorism" is very much in the eye of the beholder, in this case the state, but would include regional conflicts where terrorist activities have been used. Islamic groups may also fall into this category, such as the nonviolent Hizb-ut-Tahrir (Party of Liberation) in Uzbekistan.

Without strong international support, NGOs working in hostile states have very little ability to safely carry out effective human rights work. Authoritarian regimes have quite cynically used counterterrorism as a smokescreen for outright repression of all dissent. Robinson (2006) described witnessing "undemocratic regimes using the tragedy ... to pursue their own repressive policies, secure in the belief that their excesses would be ignored ... The extension of security policies in many countries has been used to suppress political dissent and to stifle expression with political violence."

As the UN Special Rapporteur on the Promotion and Protection of Human Rights and Fundamental Freedoms has pointed out, this is made easier by the fact that there is no common international definition of terrorism. He comments

> First of all, the very old trend of States resorting to the notion of "terrorism" to stigmatize political, ethnic, regional or other movements they simply do not like, is also very much a new trend. What is new is that, since September 2001, the international community seems to have become rather indifferent to the abuse of the notion of terrorism. The result is that calls for and support for counter-terrorism measures by the international community may in fact legitimize oppressive regimes and their actions even if they are hostile to human rights. (Scheinin 2005)

A prime example of this dynamic is Uzbekistan. The events of 9/11 did not herald a change in Uzbek domestic policy: the state targeted NGOs before that date, and it continued to do so afterwards, particularly in the wake of the Andijan massacres in 2005. What changed is the fact that as Uzbekistan styled itself an ally of the United States in the "war on terror," allowing American airbases on its territory, international criticism of its problematic human rights record became much more muted (Human Rights First 2005). The EU imposed an arms embargo after the 2005 massacres and Uzbekistan's failure to mount an independent inquiry, but withdrew it in October 2009 at the insistence of Germany, which uses an airbase in Uzbekistan to supply its troops in Afghanistan (Rettman 2009).

Members of NGOs have been subject to surveillance, have faced restrictions on their right to freedom of speech, assembly, and movement, and have suffered physical assault and imprisonment without fair trial (Frontline 2008; Human Rights Watch 2009b). In December 2008, the Human Rights Society of Uzbekistan appealed for the release of nine of its members, who had been imprisoned (in one case in a psychiatric hospital) along with six other individuals who were either themselves human rights defenders or the family members of defenders. Held in cruel, inhuman, and degrading conditions in prison, several were reportedly also subject to torture and ill-treatment (Frontline 2008).

While it is obviously local NGOs that suffer by far the greatest persecution, even well-known international NGOs have not been exempt from problems: in July 2008, the Uzbek government banned the Tashkent representative of Human Rights Watch. This move built on a long history of delaying or denying visas and accreditation to the organization's staff (Human Rights Watch 2008c).

While the US State Department decided to decertify foreign assistance funds of $18 million in 2004 as a result of continuing Uzbek persecution of NGOs and human rights abuses more generally, the US Department of Defense undermined the message by shortly afterwards announcing $21 million in separate funding for bioterrorism defense. The Pentagon increased its aid package in the same year, "demonstrating that despite the concerns of the U.S. State Department the strategic and military partnership would continue to trump human rights concerns in the bilateral relationship" (Human Rights First 2005).

Another state that has seized upon the terrorism label to disarm criticism of its human rights policies is the Russian Federation. The real motivation for a clampdown on NGOs seems to have been Western support for the so-called color revolutions in Georgia, Ukraine, and Kyrgyzstan, but as in Uzbekistan, the language used to justify the clampdown is that of the "war on terror." In 2005, the Russian Duma passed legislation aimed at restricting the activity of NGOs by subjecting them to increased state oversight and regulation, based on the logic that such monitoring was necessary to combat terrorism. The Russian Chechen Friendship Society is one NGO that had to close its office after being accused of links to terrorism because of its work in Chechnya (Frontline 2009).

It is instructive to pay attention to the timeline of these events, which indicates that the impetus for state crackdowns on dissent did not come from the 9/11 attacks in themselves: as noted above, the heightened repression in Uzbekistan followed the Andijan massacre in 2005, while Russian restrictions on NGOs increased in the wake of the color revolutions in neighboring countries that took place between 2003 and 2005. The "war on terror" provided the vocabulary to make state repression appear almost respectable; it was not a driver of the repression in and of itself.

Despite normative restrictions on granting aid to human rights abusers, Uzbekistan and the Russian Federation are far from the only states to have received US financial assistance in return for support in the "war on terror." The United States has also provided financial help to states with such dubious human rights records as Armenia, Azerbaijan, Ethiopia, Georgia, Indonesia, Jordan, Kazakhstan, Kenya, Nepal, Pakistan, the Philippines, Tajikistan, and Yemen (Federation of American Scientists 2003). Howell et al. identify similar trends in China and in African states such as Uganda, Nigeria, Zimbabwe, and Benin, where again "the legitimating discourse of terrorism" provides a cover for state efforts to eliminate dissent and political opposition (Howell et al. 2008).

Since the change in administration in the United States, authoritarian states are less able to hide their human rights abuses behind the excuse of terrorism. US Coordinator for Counterterrorism Daniel Benjamin has made it clear that "counterterrorism efforts can best succeed when they make central respect for human rights and the rule of law" (Benjamin 2010). In July 2009, President Obama addressed a civil society summit in Russia, calling for:

what many of you have dedicated your lives to sustaining – a vibrant civil society; the freedom of people to live as they choose, to speak their minds, to organize peacefully and to have a say in how they are governed; a free press to report the truth; confidence in the rule of law and the equal administration of justice; a government that's accountable and transparent.

While it is too early to say how effective this change in direction will be in practice, this is a powerful message of encouragement to civil society in authoritarian states. Much of the harm caused to NGOs in this category was due less to 9/11 than to the problematic interaction of their own state's authoritarianism with Bush-era foreign policy; with the end of the Bush era, their situation looks rather closer to that which obtained prior to 9/11. While they still face serious repression from their own governments, they can hope for more international support, at least in so far as permitted by the kind of cynical realpolitik that saw the EU dropping its arms embargo relating to Uzbekistan in 2009.

NGOs working on terrorism-sensitive issues in democratic states

Even in mature democracies, NGOs found themselves operating in a new political climate post-9/11. The changes were both internal, such as NGOs resorting to self-censorship in the immediate wake of the attacks, and external, with relationships between NGOs and states becoming more contentious. In this latter regard, 9/11 did not so much mark a complete departure from previous trends as a heightening of them: Howell et al. (2008) argue that relationships between states and civil society organizations were already cooling since the high point of their relationship in the mid-1990s; the 9/11 attacks turned the existing growing state disquiet into what they categorize as a full-scale backlash against civil society.

Internal impact

In the initial period after the attacks, the internal reaction of at least some NGOs was to fall into a stunned silence. Four months after 9/11, Kinsley (2002) noted that there was little formal smothering of dissent in the United States, but pointed out that this Swas largely because there was very little dissent to smother. Social norms rather than political demands resulted in a kind of self-censorship: there was less public tolerance of aberrant views, which could be construed as disloyal or hurtful to the families of victims or simply in bad taste. Those who could normally be relied on to be critical of state policy were silenced by "listening to [their] inner Ashcroft."

Such silence was never likely to last long, of course. Protests became less muted over the course of 2002, louder again with the proposed attack on Iraq in 2003, and they became a positive roar at the revelations of the Abu Ghraib abuses in 2004. The ultimate impact was that NGOs would thrive under the Bush Administration as their role was so demonstrably necessary.

While the larger high-profile NGOs show little sign of censoring themselves at the time of writing, there does perhaps remain a legacy of caution for certain smaller NGOs working on particularly sensitive issues, such as migrant rights:

> Even immigrant rights advocates were less willing to advocate for more reasoned policies regarding noncitizens with criminal records, because that might jeopardize the tenuous rights of "innocent" noncitizens... It was and is a seriously short-sighted strategy to distinguish

between "good" and "bad" immigrants, because policies that arise from demonizing one sector of immigrants will ultimately hurt all immigrants. (Nguyen 2006)

In the United Kingdom, there was less of an imperative toward self-censorship out of consideration toward the victims, but some British NGOs were impelled to self-censor out of self-protection, due to the lack of clarity over the reach of antiterrorism legislation:

> While the larger charities such as Liberty and Amnesty International can campaign on their issues, smaller charities that work with Kurds or Egyptians find their freedom of expression is considerably restricted as their normal publications come under the [UK Terrorism] Act... [E]ven the larger well known charities had become concerned about restrictions on campaigning and had, in effect, begun policing themselves. (Economic and Social Research Council 2006)

External impact

NGOs found themselves operating in a very different political environment post-9/11. Some observers feel that there was a narrowing of the political space in general – a "general querying of the probity of civil society organizations" (Howell et al. 2008). States were not cynically attempting to suppress all dissent as in the previous category, yet persisted in imposing counterterrorism measures regardless of the fact that the harm they caused to NGOs (and others) was disproportionate to the risk in question (McMahon 2007). In particular, those advocating on behalf of terrorist suspects or noncitizens with criminal records or Muslim communities found themselves fighting a rearguard action to establish the legitimacy of their work, which was harmful to their perception by the public and by the state. The necessity of defending their reputation risked becoming a distraction from the real substance of their work.

The United States, and to some extent the United Kingdom, make for fascinating case studies in this regard. One must beware the temptation to overstate the case: NGOs in both the United States and the United Kingdom were and are free to criticize state policy without facing persecution. This is a freedom that should be appreciated. However, it cannot be ignored that state/NGO relations became more contentious than previously, and that NGOs often found themselves operating in a more difficult environment.

It is clear that governments have a legitimate interest in devising measures to protect the security of their citizens – indeed they have an obligation to do so. These measures might involve some degree of infringement of civil liberties. Privacy rights and freedoms such as the freedom of expression and association are not absolute. However, when states take such measures, they must ensure that these restrictions are justified, lawful, and proportionate. To go too far is to inhibit democracy: "too much control threatens to stifle healthy debate and lead to fear, alienation and self-censorship, which are all antithetical to democratic governance" (Howell et al. 2008). Many commentators have argued that the state overstepped constitutional boundaries and started to interfere in an unacceptable manner with privacy rights.

An administration that imposes rights-restricting measures should be subject to the scrutiny of the legislative and judicial branches of government. These are necessary checks and balances on the power of the executive arm of the state. However, Lauren Regan of the US Civil Liberties Defense Center argues that the "war on terror" allowed the Bush Administration to overrule constitutional provisions on the balance of power, allowing the executive to exercise more power than the legislature and judiciary (Regan 2006).

Discussing post-9/11 measures in the United States and the UK, Donohue (2008) points out that the "single most defining feature of counterterrorist law is hypertrophic executive power." She explains the process as follows:

> In the aftermath of a terrorist attack... [t]he executive branch... seeks broader powers. And the political stakes are high: legislators are loath to be seen as indifferent to the latest atrocity or, worse, as soft on terror. Accordingly, the legislature grants the executive broader authorities, often under abbreviated procedures and without careful inquiry into what went wrong. Government officials claim that the new powers will be applied only to terrorists. To make the most extreme provisions more palatable, the legislature appends sunset clauses. But in the rush to pass new measures, legislators rarely incorporate sufficient oversight authorities. New powers end up being applied to nonterrorists – often becoming part of ordinary criminal law. And temporary provisions rarely remain so – instead, they become a baseline on which future measures are built. At each point at which the legislature would otherwise be expected to push back – at the introduction of the measures, at the renewal of the temporary provisions, and in the exercise of oversight – its ability to do so is limited. The judiciary's role, too, is restricted: constitutional structure and cultural

norms narrow the courts' ability to check the executive at all but the margins. (p. 2)

It is not argued that the United States was attempting to suppress the human rights sector in its entirety; nonetheless, the Bush Administration, already suspicious of international institutions and laws, succumbed to a degree of paranoia regarding individuals and organizations with any kind of antiestablishment views. In the initial period after 9/11, the administration was able to indulge this paranoia without encountering the challenges that would usually be expected from legislature and judiciary.

Many commentators have noted the "erosion of trust" between governments and NGOs (Donohue 2008). Amnesty International Secretary General Irene Khan reported in the 2002 Annual Report that a senior government official said to Amnesty International delegates: "Your role collapsed with the collapse of the Twin Towers" (Amnesty International 2002). In its 2005 National Security Strategy, the US Department of Defense explicitly equated those who attempted to claim internationally recognized human rights with terrorists: "Our strength as a nation state will continue to be challenged by those who employ a strategy of the weak using international fora, judicial processes, and terrorism." For NGOs, which generally believe in the value of international fora and judicial processes, this sentence reveals a deeply alarming mindset. "In more than a decade of studying US policy I have never read a more frightening sentence," according to one commentator (LeVine 2005). It indicated a pervasive hostility to NGO goals, methodology, and even their very existence on the part of the executive. David Scheffer, former US ambassador at large for war crimes issues, argued in the *Financial Times* that "Europeans and human rights organisations are waging 'lawfare' against the US" in the context of the human rights violations in Abu Ghraib prison. He said they seek to "constrain the use of US military power worldwide through the 'soft' weapon of international law and its 'sovereignty-bashing' treaties, as well as anti-US interpretations of principle of customary international law" (Scheffer 2004).

This increased antipathy to NGOs resulted in increased levels of monitoring and surveillance of NGOs' financial dealings and activities by state authorities. The US Treasury introduced voluntary guidelines that attempted to ensure that US-based charities did not inadvertently finance terrorist activities (US Department of the Treasury 2002; updated guidelines 2006). Some NGOs objected that the requirements for investigation and reporting set out in the Guidelines effectively turned them into government agents, undermining their relationship with Southern counterparts (McMahon 2007). While transparency and accountability are important goals, overly onerous requirements relating to data collection place a significant burden on NGOs, leading to a diversion of already limited resources.

Given that the 9/11 attacks were framed in terms of Islamic fundamentalism, Muslim organizations have tended to be the most prone to state and public suspicion. Some potential donors, both institutional and individual, have been deterred from funding Muslim charities out of fear that this might be construed as supporting terrorist activities (Lönnqvist 2007). The largest US Muslim Foundation, the Holy Land Foundation for Relief and Development, was proscribed and had its assets seized. In the subsequent trial of five of its officers, the official public records of the indictment included a list of 300 unindicted coconspirators, including such prominent organizations as the Council on American-Islamic Relations. One Muslim commentator in the United States said of attempts to link Islamic charities to terrorism:

> the damage of trying to do so will outlive the historical legal precedents of freezing charities' assets, of naming Muslim organizations as un-indicted co-conspirators, and of assuming that individuals are guilty by association.
>
> American Muslims now face the ongoing dilemma of where to give their charitable dollars. Although Muslim advocacy groups ... are calling on Washington to develop regulations that clearly define what constitutes an illegal donation, so far there are no guarantees that a donation made to a "legitimate" cause one day will be deemed illegal the next day. (Benlafquih 2008)

This heavy-handed approach by the US authorities to the finances of NGOs extended beyond its own borders. The UK-based organization Palestinian Relief and Development Fund, also known as Interpal, channels humanitarian aid to partner organizations working with Palestinians. In August 2003, the United States deemed Interpal to be a "Specially Designated Global Terrorist" based on allegations that some of its partner organizations supported Hamas, a proscribed terrorist organization in both the United States and the UK. The UK Charity Commission had previously investigated similar allegations and found no evidence for them. Nevertheless, it froze their bank accounts while waiting for waiting the United States to submit its evidence. When the United States failed to submit any credible evidence, and its own investigation found no links with Hamas, the Charity Commission unfroze the accounts, allowing Interpal to carry on its work once more (Lönnqvist 2007).[1]

Besides the increased regulation, activists have complained of reduced political space for protest and dissent. An environmental activist said that instead of free speech, activists now have only "pay-as-you-go" speech, "which basically means that payment for your free speech comes in the form of bogus charges, lawsuits, police attending your events, writing down your license numbers, being followed, etc., etc." (Regan 2006).

Until 9/11, the secret monitoring of events where people expressed their opinions was among the most tightly limited of police powers. This quickly changed: in some cases the laws limiting those powers were amended – for example, in New York, the administration of Mayor Michael R. Bloomberg persuaded a federal judge in 2003 to enlarge the Police Department's authority to conduct investigations of political, social, and religious groups (Regan 2006). In other cases, the changes were more covert: then President Bush acknowledged in 2005 that he secretly permitted the National Security Agency to eavesdrop without a warrant on international telephone calls and e-mail messages in terror investigations (Regan 2006). In 2005, the *New York Times* came into possession of videotapes showing police conducting covert surveillance of people protesting the Iraq War, bicycle riders taking part in mass rallies and a march of homeless and poor people (Dwyer 2005). Undercover police officers were shown infiltrating the demonstrators and recording events.

Regan also identified the problem of local authorities enacting quick legislation to ban mass gatherings and protests – for example, ordinances banning activists from certain areas or the imposition of curfews. Because they were enacted in such a way that the organizers did not have the opportunity to go to court to get an injunction, activists were, in her view, left with little recourse other than to break the law, submit to arrest, and then challenge the law in question, which they in many cases successfully did (Regan 2006). Getting permits for large demonstrations became more difficult: in the lead up to the 2003 antiwar protest in New York City, the city authorities and the Second Circuit Court of Appeals refused the right of anyone to march anywhere in the city, and in a brief, the Department of Justice urged the court to give significant weight to security issues arising from the 9/11 attacks. Demonstrators were permitted only a stationary rally, although in the event an unplanned march did take place, complete with allegations of inappropriate and violent police behavior toward protestors.

Regan also raises concerns about activists being harassed by private actors, with the complicity of police and federal government, giving the example of police passing the names of activists to corporations to allow them to purse lawsuits against the individuals (Regan 2006).

When it comes to prosecution of activists, "[w]e are definitely seeing more severe sentences post-9/11, no doubt about it," said Heidi Boghosian, the director of the National Lawyers Guild, referring to a 22-year jail sentence handed down to environmental militant Marie Mason in February 2009. "We have seen a trend of using the terrorist label and federalising a lot of criminal activities that would have gotten a far less stringent sentence before" (Goldenberg 2009).

As time passed and public panic abated, the executive did begin to encounter some resistance from the judiciary. Notably in *Hamdan v. Rumsfeld (2006)*, the US Supreme Court limited the power of the executive to create a military commission to try a terrorism suspect, marking an important step in the reestablishment of judicial oversight of government action.

With the inauguration of President Obama, with his personal history of commitment to civic engagement, many activists hoped to see an end to the Bush-era counterterrorism measures that caused them so much difficulty. Despite these hopes, however, most of the security-related framework remains in place. In January 2010 the *New York Times* noted that Obama was continuing Bush's surveillance program and embracing the Patriot Act. It quoted the executive director of the American Civil Liberties Union, Anthony Romero, as saying that Obama was demonstrating the "hubris" of wishing to retain the extended executive powers in the belief that he would wield it more wisely (Baker 2010).

While the UK response to 9/11 was less radical than the United States in terms of expansion of executive powers, significant changes did take place. While such measures were not taken in a deliberate bid to harm NGOs, they undoubtedly have a chilling factor on all activism. Often the problem is that new powers are used in ways that were not originally envisaged – for example, the use of the UK Terrorism Act by police in 2005 to briefly hold Walter Wolfgang, an elderly supporter of the Campaign for Nuclear Disarmament, after he had been ejected from the Labour Party Conference for heckling the Foreign Secretary Jack Straw's speech on Iraq. The House of Lords ruled that the use by police of antiterror laws to stop-and-search demonstrators at an east London arms fair was valid, a decision that was overturned in January 2010 by the European Court of Human Rights in the case of *Gillan and Quinton v. UK*. It held that the use by police of arbitrary stop-and-search powers against peace protestors and photographers under terrorism legislation was a breach of their rights under Article 8 of the European Convention on Human Rights. In a separate case in the High Court, also in January 2010, Kent police accepted that they had acted unlawfully in searching demonstrators – including 11-year-old children – at an environmental protest. In April 2010, well-known activist Mark Thomas was awarded compensation from the police after they searched him during a protest against an arms fair in London on the grounds that he looked "overconfident" and was "believed to be an influential individual." The checks and balances on power necessary to a democracy were properly functioning once more.

Challenges: opportunities turned inside out?

It would be rather distasteful to tell a human rights defender locked in a prison cell in an authoritarian state to look on the bright side of the post-9/11 world. It is hard to see any real advantages that may have emerged for NGOs in this position. However, for NGOs working in more democratic states, a silver lining can be discerned. Despite the prevailing wisdom that 9/11 and the "war on terror" has been an enormous setback for civil liberties and the NGOs that advocate for them, NGOs have also experienced a few positive consequences.

Human rights organizations have been forced to go back to the basics on many issues. After 9/11, human rights took center stage in a new and pressing way. The US response to the attacks, in particular the war in Iraq, had a revitalizing effect on the global antiwar movement, with unprecedented numbers of demonstrators turning out in Britain, Italy, and Spain, as well as large numbers in the United States and elsewhere (Sieff 2003).

Many citizens were appalled by their own government's complicity in human rights violations, and human rights NGOs provided a forum in which they could locate their resistance. In some cases, NGOs found themselves taking positions that were not popular with the general public – for example, that suspected terrorists are still entitled to due process of the law. The UK Charity Commission noted that "media coverage is not always helpful as it is hard to convey the complexities of human rights situations in 'sound bites' for news stories" (Charity Commission 2007). It required a certain degree of courage to take unpopular stances, but over time, this has paid off, adding to the moral stature of NGOs.

By the willingness of many Western NGOs to criticize their own governments (once past the initial period of self-censorship), they have demonstrated a lack of bias. When states could no longer be trusted to adhere to such basic norms as the prohibition on torture, human rights organizations grew in moral authority by their adherence to fundamental principles. Arcane issues about due process and the definition of combatants in humanitarian law became front-page news. The views of NGOs were sought by the media on topics such as torture and extraordinary rendition: after 9/11, NGOs were seen as more relevant than ever before. Only some human rights issues benefited from this new public fascination, however. NGOs found it more difficult than ever to draw attention to human rights crises that were not linked to the "war on terror." In fact, as their agendas came to be dominated by Abu Ghraib, Guantánamo Bay, Iraq, Afghanistan, and similar topics, there was a real risk of unfashionable crises dropping off the radar of the NGOs themselves. In 2003, for example, Human Rights Watch published three reports on the Democratic Republic of Congo, against 17 reports on Iraq. By 2007, however, it was back to releasing equal numbers of reports on both countries.

Winston points to a core positive message emerging from the debates of the past few years: instead of the Bush Administration delegitimizing the international human rights regime by its reliance on torture and secret prisons and the like, the reverse happened: the international human rights regime delegitimized the Bush Administration's tactics, thus demonstrating the robustness of the international consensus on human rights (Winston 2008).

NGOs did not emerge unscathed from 9/11, far from it. Some faced great difficulties, which are not over yet. But as the specter of terrorism begins to lose some of its power to distort legal and political processes, the world is once more recognizable as the world that existed back when the Twin Towers still stood.

Note

1. Interpal was again the subject of allegations that its partner organizations promoted terrorism in a BBC program in 2006. The Charity Commission launched a new investigations (its third), deciding in February 2009 that there was not sufficient evidence to conclude that Interpal's partners were supporting terrorism. However, it directed Interpal to improve its due diligence and monitoring procedures in relation to its partners (Charity Commission 2009).

13
Business As a New Actor in the Human Rights Regime

Brigitte Hamm

The international commitment to peace and human rights is laid down in the Charter of the United Nations (UN) of 1945. Based on this foundational contract and on the Universal Declaration of Human Rights of 1948, a considerable number of international human rights treaties has been adopted, above all the International Covenant on Civil and Political Rights (ICCPR) and the International Covenant on Economic, Social and Cultural Rights (ICESCR). These treaties build the fundament of the human rights regime with – in theory – political rights and civil liberties at the same level as social, economic, and cultural rights.

The implementation of human rights has always been affected by political interests and double standard policies. These had been partly justified by the ideological dispute between Western and socialist countries thereby confronting political rights and civil liberties with social, economic, and cultural rights. The end of this Cold War era in the early 1990s was considered to be an eminent chance for the promotion of all human rights as ranking on an equal level and being interdependent. Such a differentiated approach had been proposed at the Second World Conference on Human Rights 1993 in Vienna (Hamm 2001). However, the euphoria of the early 1990s quickly faded away as the neoliberal course of economic globalization tended to disregard social and economic human rights. Moreover, the terrorist attacks of 9/11 in 2001 meant a backlash to political rights and civil liberties with the prohibition of torture and the right to privacy being at stake.

While looking only at 9/11 and the "war on terror," one could assume that social, economic, and cultural rights took a back seat again. However, this is not true for the overall discourse on human rights, because more or less simultaneously to the end of the Cold War and as part to the above described holistic approach to human rights, a discourse on business and human rights had evolved in the early 1990s. This sub-discourse takes a strong focus on social and economic rights and remains separate and unaffected by the human rights debates in the context of 9/11 for predominantly two reasons, namely an issue-specific and an actor-related shift. Thus, while the human rights debate in the context of 9/11 revolves around concerns of national security, the debate on business and human rights is a response to challenges of the neoliberal course of economic globalization. Demands toward business activities in countries of the South include that social and economic rights, but also political rights, such as freedom of association, should be realized at worksites and within affected communities. General topics in this debate are the human rights responsibility of business as well as the need to define the sphere of influence of business and the complicity with human rights violations (Ruggie 2008b). In contrast to the 9/11 debates which have been state dominated, the discourse on business and human rights has developed as a multi-stakeholder process, including above all, nongovernmental organizations (NGOs) and business.

The debate on an explicit responsibility of business for human rights intensified in the context of the 2003 Norms on the Responsibilities of Transnational Corporations and Other Business Enterprises with regard to Human Rights (UN Norms), which were presented by the former UN Sub-Commission on the Promotion and Protection of Human Rights. As is argued in the following, one important outcome of this debate is a stronger institutionalization of the discourse by means of the nomination of John Ruggie as the Special Representative of the Secretary-General on the issue of human rights and transnational corporations and other business enterprises (SRSG) in 2005 and Ruggie's policy framework for the human rights responsibility of business which was presented in 2008.

To discuss the consequences for the regime of also holding the private sector responsible for human rights, this chapter pursues three questions: (1) What kind of human rights responsibility is the private sector supposed and willing to assume? (2) How is this human rights responsibility of business received by human rights institutions and how will it become integrated into the human rights regime? (3) What are possible impacts in respect to changes of the human rights concept and to the regime itself? In order to answer these questions, the first section will briefly outline the economic and political background for this debate and thereby also point to specifics of the human rights regime that may be challenged. The second section will reconstruct the discourse on business and human rights, thereby looking at major actors involved, underlying ideas and institutional frames. The third section will discuss the policy framework of the SRSG which represents a widely shared understanding of this topic. Following this, the implications for the human rights regime will be summarized.

States' human rights duties under conditions of economic globalization

Like other international agreements human rights treaties are based on the principle of reciprocity, meaning that the states acceding to a treaty are supposed to benefit mutually from fulfilling the contract. Nevertheless, human rights treaties constitute " ... a rather specific category of treaties," because the implementation and fulfillment of human rights is considered to be territorially bound and an inner affair of states (Shaw 2003, 885). This view of human rights as a feature of national sovereignty leads to an absence of effective reciprocity for human rights contracts (Shaw 2003, 360).

Already in 1980, Henry Shue had distinguished between the duties of avoidance, protection and aid. He underlined that " ... it is impossible for any basic right – however 'negative' it has come to seem – to be fully guaranteed unless all three types of duties are fulfilled" (Shue 1980, 53). This trilogy of state duties to respect, protect, and fulfill became accepted for all human rights which, to some extent, reflects the model of the welfare state with governments willing to and capable of providing public goods.

The state duty to protect is perceived as the duty to ensure that no third party – be it individuals or companies – takes steps that affect or contribute to the violation of human rights. However, at the conceptual level there is an overall lack of precision of this state duty, and the various committees in charge of monitoring human rights conventions only slowly begin to further specify it. In spite of such efforts, many governments lack the political will for a consistent enforcement of human rights, and conflicting interests often lead to double standards in national human rights policies. This weakness is also valid for the duty to protect against corporate misbehavior as governments of developing countries may try to attract foreign direct investments at the cost of an appropriate regulation of these investors that would include a coherent human rights policy.

The discourse on business and human rights means a reaction to these deficiencies and to the overall challenges of neoliberalism and the impacts of globalization. The growing permeability of national borders through global production systems and global trade challenges the territorial limitation of human rights, and increasingly extraterritorial state obligations of home states of transnational corporations (TNCs) are becoming discussed. Moreover, as part of the discourse on business and human rights, the states' obligations for human rights have become an element of debate, partly because state functions are changing. Often mentioned signs are the ongoing privatization of public services (including public security as a major realm of state power) and a reduction of public goods allocation as part of the decline of the welfare state.

Thus, structural changes in the world economy and cutbacks in state competence together with the blurring of the public and private domains raise questions about the overall state responsibility for human rights. This comes along with the perception of business actors, especially TNCs, not only as powerful actors in the economic sphere, but increasingly as holding political authority (Cutler et al. 1999). The assumption that the state has withdrawn from its functions in national and international arenas supports the perception of the soaring power of business (for example Held et al. 1999). This power is also virulent at the discursive level, as the following section reveals.

Discourse on business and human rights

Discourse can be understood as a process in which ideas are constituted and become generalized as dominant ones, thereby power being "...a function of norms, ideas, and societal institutions. It is reflected in discourse, communicative practices, and cultural values and institutions..." (Fuchs 2005, 83). Such a dominant idea that frames the discourse on business and human rights is the emphasis on self-regulation combined with the commitment of business to corporate social responsibility (CSR) on a voluntary basis. This view reflects the power of "...the dominant forces of contemporary globalization...constituted by a neo-liberal historical bloc that practises a politics of supremacy within and across nations" (Gill 2003, 120). The following two subsections analyze the process and the underlying ideas of the discourse on business and human rights.

Process: business's quest for self-regulation

The discourse on business and human rights can be perceived in the context of two broader debates, namely that on regulation and self-regulation as well as that on the private sector's commitment to internationally recognized standards on a voluntary basis. These debates historically follow and reinforce each other. The first one took place within the United Nations and was concerned with the regulation of the global economy and binding rules for TNCs. It was part of the dispute over a New Economic World Order in the early 1970s. In 1974, the UN Commission on Transnational Corporations was established " ...with the mandate to negotiate an international code of conduct for transnational corporations" (Haufler 2003, 236). Affiliated to the commission was the UN Centre on Transnational Corporations (UNCTC), which was dissolved in 1992 by the then Secretary-General, Boutros Boutros-Ghali, under pressure from the US government and international business associations (Paul 2001, 111). As part this discourse neoliberal ideas of privatization, deregulation and flexibility came to the fore.

The second debate revolves around the business sector's commitment to CSR which partly was meant to soothe criticism toward the neoliberal course of economic globalization. Also because of strong opposition, the private sector's quest for self-regulation more and more became related to the commitment to CSR. Analysts consider the 1992 UN Conference on Environment and Development (UNCED) in Rio de Janeiro, Brazil, as an important catalyst for this trend (for example, Haufler 2003, 242). UNCED was the first UN world conference where business had a strong representation and one of the first significant efforts of TNCs to shape international negotiations by directly participating in the meetings, instead of predominantly acting behind the scenes.

Until the 1990s, core topics in the discussion on CSR were the environment and ecology, and private commitment was partly due to threats of binding regulation in this policy field. While the concern for environmental and sustainability standards is perceived as being widely accepted, from 2000 onward one can spot a shift in the CSR debate toward social and human rights standards with the discussion on business and human rights understood as being part of the overarching discourse on CSR. The private sector sees the specific topic of human rights as universal norms as an important source to build up reputation and a license to operate. Due to specific scandals and to pressure from human rights organizations acting as norm entrepreneurs (Florini 1996, 375) this discourse gained a dynamic of its own.

Scandals can be considered as an opportunity for norm entrepreneurs to exert political pressure, to encourage discussion and to enforce specific norms (Adut 2004). Similar to Virginia Haufler (2003), who takes corporate scandals as events for tracing the process of corporate self-regulation, here scandals are perceived as important events in the discourse on business and human rights. Thus, the execution of Ken Saro-Wiwa in 1995 in Nigeria and the entanglement of Shell are understood as catalysts for the intensification of the debate. The broad reception of the scandal not only led Shell to install a human rights branch at its management level, but raised public awareness of the possible complicity of big corporations in human rights abuses. The scandal supported demands by civil society organizations that TNCs especially should accept responsibility for human rights within their sphere of influence. Partly as reactions to this public pressure, in 2000 the fifth revision of the OECD Guidelines for Multinational Enterprises for the first time was undertaken with the participation of NGOs, and the Global Compact between the United Nations and the private sector was launched. Today, the latter can be considered to be the most important official dialogue forum for business on CSR issues with national and regional networks worldwide.

A discussion on the relationship between the enforcement of human rights and the activities of TNCs also got under way within the United Nations, including three background papers presented by the Secretary-General between 1995 and 1998 (Nowrot 2003, 7). In 1998, the UN Sub-Commission had installed the Sessional Working Group on the Working Methods and Activities of Transnational Corporations, made up of five experts that elaborated on the issue, finally leading to the UN Norms. The presentation of the UN Norms in 2003 initiated a boom time in the debate during 2004 and 2005.

The strong reaction to the UN Norms and the pressure of civil society organizations resulted in a new form of institutionalization, namely the appointment of John Ruggie as Special Representative of the Secretary-General on the issue of human rights and transnational corporations and other business enterprises[1] on July 28, 2005. Until April 2008 he had submitted three reports.[2] Ruggie's views reflect structural conditions of the neoliberal course of globalization, above all privatization and deregulation as well as the influence of powerful stakeholders, most notably business and civil society actors. Ruggie's mandate has been extended until 2011 in order to "operationalize" his policy framework.[3]

Content: the responsibility of business for human rights

Human rights are the normative fundament of the discourse on business and human rights. However, human rights treaties do not address the private sector in an explicit manner, but only in the context of the state duty to protect against abuses of third parties. When emphasizing a human rights responsibility of business, most often reference is made to the preamble of the Universal Declaration of Human Rights, where it is laid down that "...every individual and every organ of society...shall strive by teaching and education to promote respect for these rights and freedoms and by progressive measures, national and international, to secure their universal and effective recognition and observance."[4] Within the normative and legal framework of human rights the quest for greater responsibility of the private sector is discussed in manifold ways, emphasizing either the state or the company. One focus is on extraterritorial state obligations, meaning that the competence for ensuring private compliance with human rights abroad lies with the state where a company has its headquarters.

Other views directly address the private sector: One thread of the debate concerns individual liability for committed crimes under international and national law. Thus, the 2002 Rome Statute of the International Criminal Court assesses individual responsibility, inter alia, for genocide and crimes against humanity. In addition, corporate liability for international crimes is more and more brought to national courts; one important example is the Alien Tort Claims Act (ATCA) in the United States of America. Another thread concerns the single company's responsibility in the form of voluntary codes of conduct and initiatives. Here, important examples are the already mentioned OECD Guidelines for Multinational Enterprises and the Global Compact. In a rather general manner, the first two (out of ten) principles of the Compact emphasize the human rights responsibility of business:

- Businesses support and respect the protection of internationally proclaimed human rights.
- Businesses make sure they are not complicit in human rights abuses.

The UN Norms may be taken as the first attempt to present an independent and comprehensive official UN instrument for the human rights responsibilities of business. They not only highlight best practices and various modes of monitoring and enforcement but also emphasize state obligations for human rights and transfer these to private actors. The UN Norms have been disparaged especially because of the supposed simple transmittance of state duties to business. In addition, they have been criticized for their unclear definition of "sphere of influence" and "complicity" with human rights abuses as well as for the inclusion of general obligations for consumer and environment protection in a human rights document. Further criticism expressed by the private sector and many governments refers to provisions of implementation stating that "[t]ransnational corporations and other business enterprises shall be subject to periodic monitoring and verification by

United Nations... "[5] Critics point out that such requests for monitoring and verification would render companies subjects under international law and weaken national governments in their control of the private sector; commentators also contend that the UN Norms would lead to binding regulations for the global economy. Here one can see how the discourse on the human rights responsibility of business is part of the overarching discourse on CSR with the focus on voluntary commitments and self-regulation as an expression of the dominance of neoliberal thinking. In spite of fierce criticism, caveats and even broad denial, the UN Norms laid ground for the further debate, and became an important criterion for future endeavors in this field. One may even hypothesize that the content and comprehensiveness of Ruggie's policy framework is only intelligible in the light of the preceding debate on the UN Norms.

Similar to these, the SRSG's concept relies on the existing human rights system by emphasizing state obligations. However, the UN Norms draw a closer parallel between state obligations and business responsibilities while Ruggie clearly distinguishes between the State duty to protect and a corporate responsibility to respect. Ruggie also points to the relevance of monitoring and verification, but in contrast to the UN Norms he does not insist on external mechanisms. A further distinction to the UN Norms is Ruggie's emphasis on companies' responsibility to respect *all* human rights.

Actors involved in the discourse

In general, the discourse on business and human rights is dominated by four groups of actors, namely states, international organizations, human rights NGOs, and business. The different actors vary in their access to resources. Among these are expertise, legitimacy, capital, and position, as well as access to media and to institutions. Power potentials in the discourse may thus differ, resulting in the emergence of new institutional settings with specific power constellations. Depending on these resources, (collective) actors may execute different discursive practices and take over particular roles in the debate. Cox and Jacobsen (1974, 3–4) propose an actor's typology of how influence is exercised in international organizations, namely as initiators, vetoers, controllers and/or brokers. Drawing on this view for the debate on business and human rights roles as leaders, hardliners, compromisers, and facilitators are distinguished in the following.

Hardliners

Broadly speaking, two discourse communities with conflicting positions can be identified, above all in respect to the quest for binding regulations for the private sector, including the implementation clause in the UN Norms described above. From an ideal type point of view, these two communities – the business sector and human rights activists – assume the roles of hardliners. They more or less adhere to their traditional views and roles in respect to regulation: business as principled disclaimer using stonewalling strategies (Haufler 2003) and NGOs who follow a command and control path (Utting 2004) applying blaming and shaming strategies (Liese 2006). Thus, on one side, there is the bulk of business and respective associations, above all the ICC, also the United States Council for International Business (USCIB) or the Bundesverband Deutscher Industrie (BDI) in Germany, on the other side civil society actors, such as the British NGO Coalition on Corporate Responsibility (CORE).

With respect to content, these two competing patterns of interpretation (for example, Mark-Ungericht 2005) can be described as: *first* a more conservative and reluctant position of large parts of the private sector. Based on a neoliberal background, it is predominantly characterized by the following views:

- Focus on state responsibility
- Human rights by market liberalization
- Voluntariness of business commitment beyond national laws
- No obligation to transparency and external monitoring.

Second, on the side of civil society, the ideal type hardliner position is asking for:

- Enforceable regulation on the international level
- Obligatory minimal standards
- Costs and sanctions for noncompliance
- Transparency and external monitoring
- Participation of persons concerned (stakeholders).

Compromisers and facilitators

Within both positions, important differences open up the debate, and actors may stick to a hardliner position in respect to binding regulation at the same time as they opt for dialogue concerning concrete measures for the human rights responsibility of business.

On the business side, one actor that has adopted such a proactive role has been the Business Leaders Initiative on Human Rights (BLIHR). The initiative was founded in 2003 by six companies and one foundation – ABB Ltd, Barclays PLC, MTV Networks Europe, National Grid plc, Novo Nordisk, The Body Shop International and the Novartis Foundation for Sustainable Development (NFSD) – in cooperation with two NGOs, Respect Sweden and Realizing Rights: The Ethical Globalization Initiative (EGI). In later years a few other companies joined the initiative. Following an official statement, the inspiration for BLIHR "... came from the *Business Leaders Initiative on Climate Change* and the fact that no similar objective and universal framework existed for the social responsibility of business... "[6] As intended from the beginning, BLIHR has dissolved in its existing form during 2009. Various tasks will be pursued by newly created institutions and initiatives. Among them is the Institute for Human Rights and Business, based in London.

BLIHR has adopted the role of a compromiser when stating that the "... polarization of views on the respective merits of voluntary and regulatory approaches has been regrettable. For us it is a false dilemma, human rights have always required a combination of both voluntary and mandatory efforts in order to achieve sustainable change and to raise the minimum standard of acceptable behaviour. As businesses, we believe there is a 'minimum' or 'essential' level of behaviour below which no business should be allowed to fall. In many countries this is already regulated by national laws" (BLIHR 2004, 5). BLIHR expresses a strong commitment to human rights, demonstrates knowledge of the existing human rights regime, and combines its role as a compromiser with the economic rationale of its members' long-term interests. The initiative claims a leadership role, among other things, by proposing a definition of both sphere of influence and complicity that has become more or less mainstreamed in the discussion. With its presentation of a human rights matrix and its commitment to road-testing the UN Norms in practice, BLIHR has presented itself as a role model, building up trust among all discourse parties.

On the NGO side, organizations such as Amnesty International, Christian Aid, Greenpeace, Human Rights Watch, Oxfam, and the World Wide Fund for Nature – beyond demanding binding rules – stand for compromise and dialogue when it comes to concrete measures for strengthening the human rights responsibility of business. For example, already in 1991 in the United Kingdom, Amnesty International established a specific Business Group to work on the human rights responsibility of the private sector which, inter alia, has supported companies in designing internal human rights guidelines.[7] The preparedness for dialogue enables mutual learning and the reduction of ideological biases. One may describe these compromisers as a kind of transient or temporary discourse community. Many of them cooperate in multi-stakeholder initiatives, such as the Global Compact. However, the compromisers will belong to their discourse communities when for example symbolic events allow for a more fundamental critique and thus offer an opportunity to emphasize one's genuine role as norm entrepreneur or business enterprise, respectively. An example for such a shift in position is an open letter of more than 200 human rights organizations and activists –among them Amnesty International and Human Rights Watch, who, in the light of the 60th anniversary of the Universal Declaration of Human Rights, asked the SRSG to be more critical about the limitations of voluntary standards (Joint open letter 2007).

Important for driving the compromising position are prominent individuals. With their symbolic capital (Bourdieu 1996) and legitimacy, they can further enhance the preparedness for dialogue, and thus strongly affect on the discourse. One prominent person is Mary Robinson, former president of Ireland and the second UN High Commissioner for Human Rights (between 1997 and 2002). In 2002, she founded the NGO EGI. Robinson has also been the Honorary Chair of BLIHR. Another outstanding person in the debate is Sir Geoffrey Chandler, a former director of Shell and founding Chairman of *the Amnesty International UK Business Group*. He criticized the – from his point of view – confrontational approach in the just mentioned open letter of NGOs by stating that " ... if we wish to see human rights prevail in the world, we will not do so without the positive involvement of companies."[8]

The dominance of the compromiser discourse community is also reflected by the role of intergovernmental actors. They not only contribute through statements to the debate but provide expertise, legitimacy to the discourse, and a forum for debate, and thus act as facilitators. Most important is the United Nations, with various branches involved, above all the Office of the High Commissioner on Human Rights, and the Global Compact Office,[9] as well as the SRSG. In the beginning, human rights activists vehemently disputed the nomination of Ruggie, because they saw him as the intellectual father of the Global Compact, standing for soft agreements, and because he has harshly criticized the UN Norms for putting state obligations for human rights on a par with business responsibilities. Nevertheless, considering demands from the various sides addressed to him, he was able to give the debate shape and direction. Despite criticism, his leadership role in the process of discourse formation has become broadly accepted and after presenting the 2008 report, Ruggie's concept and language has quickly become mainstreamed.

In this report, he presents his policy framework with the three dimensions of protection, respect, and access to remedies. Although denying binding rules, Ruggie's concept is not just an adoption of a business hardliner position, but has the potential to put pressure both on states and businesses so that they follow their duties as well as commitments and take human rights seriously. The overall acceptance of Ruggie's framework reflects and at the same time shapes the dominant ideas in the discourse. This consent may also be supported by the legitimacy and authority that the United Nations possesses among the discourse communities. Thus, to reach consensus, it was important that the United Nations provided the institutional forum for the discourse and by means of the position of an SRSG for the topic gave direction to the discourse.

One important outcome of the discourse on business and human rights is the further institutionalization of the idea of a business responsibility for human rights. Here, institutionalization refers not only to forms of institution building but also to order through dominant views. The rather heated debates since 2003 on a voluntary or obligatory instrument for business and human rights have toned down after it became clear to human rights activists that binding rules are neither on the agenda of the UN bodies nor of governments. The dominance of the rejection of binding rules at the international level is also reflected by soft law measures and by further development of national and international legal and nonlegal mechanisms for prosecuting human rights abuses (Ruggie 2007). Thus, in respect to the issue of binding rules the discursive power of business prevails.

The following section discusses Ruggie's concept in more detail in order to get a deeper understanding of the ideas that have emerged from discourse and of the concept's relevance in the overall human rights regime.

Ruggie's policy framework

Characteristic for Ruggie is his pragmatic and outcome-oriented approach: "My bottom line is that the last thing victims need is more unenforced declarations; they need effective action" (Ruggie 2006, 2). In his report of April 2008, Ruggie elaborates his policy framework for shaping the human rights responsibility of business with the aim to reflect " ... the complexities and dynamics of globalization [and] to reduce or compensate for the governance gaps created by globalization, because they permit corporate-related human rights harm to occur even where none may be intended" (Ruggie 2008a, 5).

Ruggie's three pillars – protect, respect, access to remedies – implicate three major actors in the human rights responsibilities of business. The state is mainly involved through its duty to protect, business through its corporate responsibility to respect, and civil society, through its role as an advocate providing access to remedies. Civil society also has a key role as watchdog with respect to the first two pillars. Ruggie charges the state and business mainly with improving the prevention of human rights abuses. By including the dimension of remedy, he acknowledges that human rights abuses by business occur and victims need improved access to judicial and nonjudicial grievance mechanisms. Here, he intends civil society to play an important role as advocate, because civil society organizations frequently prepare and file cases of complaint.

States' duty to protect

With the focus on the state duty to protect individuals from human rights abuses of third parties, Ruggie relies on the existing human rights regime. He sees a broad array of policy domains in order to fulfill the state duty to protect. His proposals cover the need for disclosure by improved and obligatory reporting mechanisms and the development of more coherent policies in host as well as in home states. He proposes peer learning among states and assistance among host and home governments to enforce basic compliance with human rights standards. As many developing countries are not willing or able to fulfill their state duty to protect, the SRSG emphasizes extraterritorial state obligations especially of OECD member countries where most TNCs are seated. Furthermore, Ruggie addresses the need to include human rights considerations into agreements such as bilateral investment treaties (BITs) and the allocation of export credits. With such proposals Ruggie sets longstanding civil society demands onto the international agenda, thereby increasing their chance of implementation.

At the international level, Ruggie asks human rights treaty bodies to scrutinize the state duty to protect in respect to business more carefully and to incorporate human rights more explicitly into the OECD Guidelines, a request that is taken up in the actual revision process of the guidelines. He also demands that the Security Council considers sanctions if corporations are directly responsible for the aggravation of conflicts.

Corporate responsibility to respect

Beyond compliance with national laws, the SRSG emphasizes the need for business to respect all human rights. In his opinion this reflects the social expectations of stakeholders and is the basis for a company's social license to operate (Ruggie 2008a, 17).

The SRSG argues that companies – in order not to become exposed to public criticism, and even to charges in courts – need to develop an internal human rights policy which defines the impact of their activities to ensure to do no harm. As a condition for the realization of the business responsibility to respect human rights, Ruggie introduces the concept of due diligence, meaning the steps a company should take in order to become aware of, to prevent, and to address negative human rights impacts. For such a process of due diligence a company has to consider three main factors: (1) The analysis of the context of the country, which means that a company must be aware of the human rights situation where it does business; (2) The consideration of the impact of its own activities should include all relevant groups such as employees, communities, and consumers; (3) A company should also ensure that it does not get involved in human rights abuses through its relationships with other parties. Thus, the concept of due diligence basically is the quest for a company-based human rights policy, including a feasible human rights impact assessment (HRIA).

Access to remedies

The third dimension of Ruggie's policy framework – access to remedies – is meant to complement and enforce both the state duty to protect and the corporate responsibility to respect. Improved access to remedies implies the creation and strengthening of the corresponding institutional structures both at the state and at the corporate level. While corporations are asked to install in-house complaint mechanisms for workers as well as communities afflicted, the focus is on the state level. Here, access to remedies may be achieved in the form of litigation as well as nonjudicial complaint and mediation mechanisms such as national human rights institutions or the National Contact Points (NCPs) of the OECD Guidelines for Multinational Enterprises. The strengthening of these NCPs by means of institutional independence is an important demand of Ruggie. An important element of access to remedies is also the execution of international criminal law by ICC member states and the ICC itself. Access to remedies in its legal form is a longstanding demand from civil society organization as it allows for sanctioning corporate human rights abuses, and thus asks for action by the state. Especially, this third dimension grants Ruggie's policy framework the potential to turn into a strong instrument with the capability to bare its teeth. Using judicial means for access to remedies can be perceived as being part of the state duty to protect emphasizing binding laws for companies. The threat of litigation is an important condition for taking the corporate responsibility to respect human rights seriously as financial and reputational costs are at stake.

Implications for the human rights regime

Above all, the demand for a human rights responsibility of business means a particular challenge to the traditional human rights concept. The latter originally defines the relationship between the state and the individual in the public sphere and embraces the overall state's obligations to respect, protect, and fulfill political, as well as social, economic, and cultural rights. In spite of the international commitment to human rights, the state competence for human rights and thus their territorial ties are a prevalent characteristic of the human rights concept.

The debate on business and human rights reaffirms this view when emphasizing the state duty to protect, and in his latest interim report the SRSG offers some specification in respect to the implementation of this duty (Ruggie 2010). At the same time, the actual debate on business and human rights expresses a tension between the territorial orientation and the need for a stronger international and transnational response for human rights. This leads to a modification of perspective as states no longer are the only addressees for taking over responsibility for human rights. In addition, concerns related to the process of globalization express the need for specifying state obligations. Above all two trends have to be mentioned: one is the watering down of national borders, thereby weakening the principle of territoriality; the other is the trend of privatization that affects states' capacities for steering and for the provision of public goods.

The reconstruction of the discourse on business and human rights indicates a mainstreaming of human rights within the overall discourse of CSR, and in order to answer the first question – what kind of responsibility the private sector is supposed and willing to assume – it is a responsibility on a voluntary basis. The private sector takes up the human rights language and uses it to construct a positive image of corporations in order to counter threats of vulnerability by blaming and shaming as well as to protect corporate reputation under conditions of globalization. This common ground may weaken blaming and shaming as one traditional action of human rights NGOs, which has been an important impetus for change and willingness for dialogue within parts of the private sector. Thus, the discourse may create a shift in power potentials among discourse communities. Ruggie's policy framework with the focus on a voluntary basis reflects this discursive shift at the institutional level.

However, the commitment to human rights also creates ground for making business accountable and thus more vulnerable to public criticism. The positive attitude of business toward human rights opens up debate and dialogue, enabling learning and contributing to further norm internalization within business. Typical for this trend are multistakeholder initiatives and discourse communities that act as compromisers.

In spite of such overall commitments there is not yet a clear understanding of how the business responsibility for human rights should be realized in practice. As part of his policy framework, the SRSG has made important proposals for a corporate human rights policy including due diligence and HRIAs. However, such instruments are not mainstreamed yet. Companies that are not an active part of the CSR debate still have to be convinced. The same is true for TNCs of emerging economies such as China, India, and Malaysia who increasingly compete with Western companies in the global economy. Western corporations criticize the ignorance toward internationally recognized standards as a competitive disadvantage vis-à-vis these "newcomers" and the lack of public pressure on them. In spite of progress, the voluntary character of Ruggie's framework might be one reason that the discourse on business and human rights is still a niche matter. Efforts are necessary to create a level playing field for all businesses by strengthening and scaling up the business and human rights concerns and instruments.

The second question dealt with the integration of the human rights responsibility of business into the existing human rights regime. With the nomination of John Ruggie as SRSG, the United Nations tried to give direction to the debate and to underline the organization's dominant role for human rights. The overall consent by non-state and state actors to Ruggie's policy framework with the emphasis of the state duty to protect in addition to the corporate responsibility to respect and access to remedies may turn this concept into an internationally agreed standard. Although on a voluntary basis, the proposed instruments such as due diligence and HRIAs carry the potential of becoming common standard and thus may contribute to the improvement of the human rights situation of people concerned, above all workers, small-scale producers and communities affected by business activities. Moreover, Ruggie's approach carries the potential of strengthening the existing human rights regime as – by emphasizing the state duty to protect – he focuses on the major actor for human rights in the regime. The adaptation of the state duty to protect to the conditions of globalization implies the inclusion and further discussion of extraterritorial state obligations. Another important dimension will be the emphasis of access to remedies which may be understood as being inter alia part of state duties. At the same time, access to remedies puts pressure on both states and companies.

The third question addressed possible impacts on the human rights concept. First of all there is the potential that the existing human rights regime may be strengthened by sharpening and specifying the state duty to protect, including extraterritorial state obligations. However, there are also possible changes induced by the discourse on business and human rights. Klaus Leisinger, president and CEO of the NFSD talks about the historic relativity of the human rights concept as an agreement of states in 1948, " … when nobody would have thought to compare the influence of nation states with that of business" (NFSD 2007, 2). He sees the need to adjust the human rights " … concept … into the language of the world of business" (NFSD 2007, 5). Such adjustments may be understood as being part of the discourse. But there is also a risk that the historic legal character of human rights will become undermined by these efforts, especially by focusing only on the business case for a human rights responsibility. Even though proactive initiatives such as BLIHR contribute to mainstreaming human rights in the private sector, the overall discourse on business and human rights only rarely addresses human rights as enforceable rights. Concrete human rights abuses by TNCs or complicity with such, for example land evictions or intellectual property rights as opposed to indigenous rights, are scarcely touched on in the discussions. Instead, a positive relation of business and human rights is brought to the fore. Such redirection underlines the importance of access to remedies as the third dimension of Ruggie's policy framework.

Conclusion

Since the early 1990s, a debate on business and human rights has evolved, asking for a business responsibility for all human rights. It reflects not only a holistic view on human rights, but also the need to adjust the human rights regime to the challenges of economic globalization. During the following years, the attacks of 9/11 and the war against terror have meant the most severe threat to such a holistic approach, and especially governments started to question achievements anchored in the human rights regime, for example the ban on torture and the rights to privacy for the supposed benefits of national security. However, 9/11 had no observable impact on the discourse on business and human rights, predominantly because of different topics and actors involved. Instead, this discourse gained momentum leading to a stronger institutionalization and a specific impact of its own on the existing human rights regime.

Although not legally binding, Ruggie's policy framework of protect, respect, and remedy may become further elaborated and accepted as guiding principles, and thus part of the international human rights regime. This perspective as well as the diverging human rights debates proposes that one should not perceive of the human rights regime as a more or less closed system, but as consisting of different streams and discourses that respond to varying demands.

Notes

1. Commission on Human Rights (2005),
   www.reports-and-materials.org/UN-Commission-resolution-business-human-rights-Apr-2005.doc, date accessed March 18, 2008.
2. The interim report of 2006 (E/CN.4/2006/97), the second report of 2007 (A/HRC/4/035), and – based on his initial mandate – his final report to the UN Human Rights Council (A/HRC/8/5).
3. Human Rights Council (2008) Resolution 8/7. Mandate of the Special Representative of the Secretary General on the issue of human rights and transnational corporations and other business enterprises,
   http://ap.ohchr.org/documents/E/HRC/resolutions/A_HRC_RES_8_7.pdf, date accessed May 10, 2010.
4. See United Nations (n.d.) www.un.org/Overview/rights.html, date accessed March 19, 2008.
5. See chapter H of the UN Norms.
6. BLIHR has been the second initiative created in 2003 by Respect Table, which is a business network that has been initiated by the consultancy Respect Europe. The first initiative of Respect Table, the Business Leaders Initiative

on Climate Change (BLICC), has focused on a stringent Climate Policy. (See BLIHR 2003).
7. The group dissolved itself in October 2007, with no reason given.
8. The *Economist*, 2007, 74.
9. The latter abstained from a clear position in favor of the UN Norms in the beginning. Among civil society actors this was perceived as an underlying sense of competition within the United Nations.

Conclusion

Michael Goodhart and Anja Mihr

The contributors focus on what we have collectively referred to as "the international human rights regime." Any general assessment of how that regime has fared, however, proves difficult – less because of empirical disagreement than because of interpretive and analytical differences among the contributors. The problem is like the one in the old story about a group of blind sages who come upon an elephant. Encountering this enormous and unfamiliar creature, each of the sages investigates a different part of it – trunk, tusks, ear, body, leg, tail – and each reaches a different assessment of the beast (it is like a snake, a spear, a fan, a wall, a tree, and a rope, respectively).

This parable illustrates the difficulty of studying complex systems from a single point of view. Like these proverbial sages, each contributor to this volume has focused on that part of the regime she or he knows best. Unlike them, we are keenly aware of the restricted scope of our individual inquiries and their limited explanatory power when considered in isolation. Indeed, we have consciously assembled scholars with dissimilar approaches and areas of expertise in an attempt to avoid the mistake of the sages. Accordingly, our aim in this conclusion is not merely to *summarize* the findings of the various contributors regarding the international human rights regime since 9/11 but to *juxtapose* and ultimately to try to *synthesize* them, in hopes of gaining a better understanding of the whole animal.

We begin with some broad and quite general evaluations of continuity and change in the regime. Next, we consider evidence from the regime's various "layers," drawing some conclusions about how they have fared, individually and jointly, in the new century. We then turn to two important, related questions that emerged repeatedly throughout the chapters and in our discussions: whether, and in what sense,

9/11 constituted a turning point for the international human rights regime, and what to make of developments in the regime during the 1990s. We consider both the substantive and the analytic dimensions of each of these questions.

Assessing the international human rights regime

Following Donnelly,[1] we understand the international human rights regime as comprising all the multilateral governance institutions and practices dealing with human rights. Donnelly notes that this definition might be considered too narrow, and his overview of the regime since 9/11 also considers the key roles of national implementation, of transnational non-state actors such as human rights organizations (HROs), of bilateral foreign policy arrangements, and of genocide and humanitarian law. In addition, many of the contributors see the human rights discourse itself as an important element in the regime, or at least in understanding it. All of these elements, then, jointly make up the regime.

From this definition it is immediately obvious that to speak of *the* international human rights regime is in certain respects problematic (see Hamm). The regime is the sum of its many disparate parts. Each of these parts has its own rules, norms, institutional machinery, and surrounding politics and discourse. There is no reason to expect each to be affected similarly, or affected at all, by even severe shocks like 9/11 and the events and policies that followed it. Similarly, there is no reason to assume that there will be a single or succinct reply to questions about the resilience or deterioration of the regime as a whole. Indeed, such a general assessment – while crucially important – is only one of many important levels of analysis for scholars and practitioners concerned with understanding and learning from the experience of (various elements of) the regime after 9/11.

Nonetheless, a general assessment is essential for getting to grips with the widespread impression or assumption that "everything changed" after September 2001. This is – at least on a first cut – an empirical question, one concerning changes in laws and policies; alterations in institutional procedures and mechanisms; activities undertaken by various transnational and international actors; and violations of established human rights law, norms, and principles. Donnelly presents striking and persuasive evidence that, measured on these criteria, the regime as a whole has been quite resilient. The other contributors largely concur in this finding: certain worrisome exceptions notwithstanding, we find that the regime has fared well, perhaps surprisingly so, since 9/11. Norms related to counterterrorism, including interrogation and detention policies and the use of torture, have been seriously eroded in some prominent cases (especially but not only in the United States); there have also been related and troubling shifts in the policies of some formerly stalwart defenders and leaders in the human rights regime (see Baehr; St. Pierre). In addition, some HROs have found it more difficult to conduct their work. Yet this backsliding is for the most part contained at the level of national implementation. International arrangements, including the definitions of torture and other laws and norms connected to counterterrorism and related policy domains, have not been compromised – and should perhaps be regarded as strengthened by having weathered the storm (see Donnelly; Winston). Likewise, HROs have maintained and even increased their already historically unprecedented levels of access and influence internationally (see Barrett; Hamm; Schmitz).

Contrary to widespread assumptions, the international human rights regime as a whole has suffered little deterioration as a consequence of 9/11 and the "war on terror." This is a welcome and significant finding. Still, it can provide only a partial and provisional understanding of the impact of 9/11 on the regime. Many other questions important to scholars, policymakers, and practitioners concerned with human rights are left unaddressed by such a broad assessment. More detailed analysis is also required to identify and assess localized problems or warning signs. Such investigations provide valuable insight into how the regime functions and what its weak points might be. Moreover, closer examination reveals that the regime's various components often work at cross-purposes, complicating the picture of unity and coherence conveyed by broad assessments. Understanding these tensions and vulnerabilities is crucial for efforts to understand and ultimately strengthen the regime. In this chapter we assess the international human rights regime itself, focusing on its multiple layers, including international and national institutions and practices, discourses, and transnational civil society activity. We then turn to questions of change and continuity, with a particular focus on the importance of the 1990s as a period for comparison.

A multilayered regime

It makes sense to conceptualize the international human rights regime as "multilevel" or "multilayered." We prefer the latter term, as the idea of levels is inappropriately hierarchical and implies a degree of neatness of separation that the regime clearly lacks. Layers can be of varying expanse and thickness; they can merge together at some places and come apart in others. They thus describe the regime's complexity better than the idea of levels.

International institutions

For instance, the international human rights regime in Europe has more and thicker layers than that in North America. In Europe the UN system is complemented by the Council of Europe (CoE)'s human rights arrangements (especially the European Court of Human Rights (ECHR)) as well as by the human rights-related activities of the Organization for Security and Cooperation in Europe (OSCE) and the European Union (EU). Especially the ECHR provides much thicker – more extensive and more binding – institutionalization than do the comparable institutions of the Organization of American States. As Mayerfeld, Mihr, and Schneider all show, these additional layers have a significant effect on the functioning and the performance of the regime.

Schneider and Mihr both demonstrate how the various European institutions – including treaties and regional supranational courts – can push back against the UN system, even when the institutions in question are not in the first instance human rights institution (e.g. the European Court of Justice (ECJ)). Formal procedures as well as more informal checks have helped in preventing erosion of international human rights norms and standards as well practice in Europe (Mihr). But as Schneider shows, the ECJ decisions on terrorism lists also pose a much broader potential challenge to the UN system, whose supremacy vis-à-vis national laws and policies in the fight against terrorism it calls into question. The very idea of checks and balances, so vital to constitutional government, is largely absent internationally. With respect to human rights this is a double-edged sword. Greater accountability can help to check abuses; it also risks reinstating a kind of national veto that echoes the claims of sovereignty advanced by states eager to shield their treatment of their own citizens from international scrutiny.

In contrasting US and European policies and practices regarding torture, Mayerfeld shows that among the key factors explaining why the United States moved so quickly to implement torture policies is the lack of international institutionalization, oversight, and enforcement. European arrangements helped to advance the criminalization of torture and also created social and political pressures for compliance that proved resistant to the rapid and disturbing erosion witnessed in the United States. This case clearly demonstrates how one norm, subject to the same global laws and procedures, can be very differently protected by different states and regional groupings of states. Institutions matter – and international institutions seem, at least in this case, to have been particularly important in upholding the relevant human rights norm. Additional layers of institutionalization do seem to provide additional safeguards – even when any of those layers, taken singly, might appear weak or ineffective.

The question of torture also helps to illustrate some of the limits of general assessments about the health of the regime. The regime's good general health can distract us from the presence of a malignancy within it. In the case of torture, the pathology is particularly disturbing, as it infected one of the most highly institutionalized issue domains within international human rights. That the existing norms and mechanisms have emerged relatively unscathed only underscores the extent to which, despite comparatively strong monitoring, the regime proved unable to prevent significant backsliding in the period immediately after 9/11. It would be cold comfort, for obvious reasons, to reply that we shouldn't worry much about this failure because the regime has never been 100 percent effective in reducing or stopping torture or abuses of personal freedoms. The important point is that better institutions are more effective, as Mayerfeld shows. He suggests improvements such as closing legal loopholes, establishing judicial oversight, creating international inspection mechanisms, and emphasizing criminalization of torture and ill-treatment. This reminds us that, however robust existing international arrangements might remain after 9/11, they are nonetheless in need of significant adjustment if they are to be effective and progressive in the future.

States

States form an important, if problematic, layer of the international human rights regime. From its inception the United Nations and European human rights systems were predicated on state enforcement of human rights. Many scholars and activists lament that that this amounts to asking the wolf to watch the sheep when it comes to respecting, protecting, and fulfilling most human rights. Further, the UN system is notoriously underdeveloped with respect to enforcement, however, and recent reforms – including the creation of the UN Human Rights Council to replace the weak, ineffective, and highly politicized Commission on Human Rights – have done little to improve things in this respect.

While the UN system depends on states for implementation, it is much more than the sum of states' behavior. Clearly, there is wide variance in state performance on human rights, and changes in the policies or practices of a particular state do not necessarily alter or affect the regime as such. At the same time, however, significant changes in patterns of compliance among several or many states would signal an important shift in the regime, though it is difficult to specify precise indicators of such a shift. This ambiguity probably helps to explain the widespread view that a general deterioration has befallen the regime since 9/11: the enormous attention given to a small number of very high-profile examples of worsening state practice has perhaps exaggerated perceptions of the extent and severity of the actual changes that have occurred. Not surprisingly, the weaker a regime's monitoring standards and institutions prior to 9/11, the less effective it was in protecting human rights norms in the respective member states. Another important factor is the extent to which member states embrace its norms and use them in self-regulatory ways. In this respect, Donnelly's finding that state human rights practices, including practices related to the civil and political freedoms most centrally threatened by new counterterrorism and detention policies, show little change or even a slight improvement since 9/11 is comforting. On a variety of measures, there seems to have been no broad deterioration of state human rights practices – high-profile exceptions notwithstanding.

Once again, however, while the general outlook on state practices is encouraging, worrisome signs are evident in the details. One concerns the so-called middle powers, countries like Canada and the Netherlands, which have long been the mainstays of the international human rights regime. The regime derives a great deal of its legitimacy and global credibility from the active support of these middle powers, which are widely seen as independent of the great powers and genuinely committed to promoting human rights through multilateral cooperation – both politically and with boots on the ground in UN peacekeeping and humanitarian missions. The great powers are often suspected – and sometimes guilty – of using the rhetoric of human rights to advance their own aims and interests, to provide rhetorical cover for other ambitions. Middle powers' support of the regime commands immense respect (and invites less suspicion) because of the reputations they have cultivated for leadership and integrity on human rights issues (see Baehr; St. Pierre) and because they are too small to provoke fear about their ulterior motives.

In this respect it is worrisome that both Baehr and St. Pierre find evidence of erosion in the policies and practices of the Netherlands and Canada. Both attribute this erosion in part to outside (US) pressure, though this appears stronger in the case of Canada, whose proximity to and long, open border with the United States make its immigration policies of special interest to its southern neighbor. The deterioration in Canada and the Netherlands, like any backsliding on human rights, is unfortunate, though the evidence from the studies here suggests that it is probably too soon to say that any kind of permanent or structural deterioration has occurred. The politics of such changes – as is also evident in the United States – can take a long time to play out. But these cases of state policy and practice raise two important questions about the regime. First, if middle powers are the anchors of the international human rights regime, do they have enough weight to keep the great powers from drifting off course on human rights issues? The evidence here raises serious doubts: Canada and the Netherlands were unable – or unwilling – to resist the strong security pressures arising after 9/11. Indeed, perhaps especially in the Netherlands, it seems that domestic political calculations about how to deal with an increasing, and perhaps increasingly radicalized, Muslim population place the willingness of the government to push back against American pressure in question. Indeed, that pressure perhaps provided a useful pretext for actions already envisioned by political elites. Schneider sees some signs that the EU was able to check the United States on some issues – or at least, to limit the extent of the changes the American were seeking – but both Baehr and Winston remain skeptical about the overall short-term prospects for countering the United States from Europe.

A second, and much broader, question is whether the general cooperation or acquiescence of middle powers in the American-led "war on terror" has compromised the legitimacy and credibility of the human rights regime more generally. Whether, as St. Pierre suggests, we should see middle powers less as anchors than as "barometers" indicating changes in the international regime is a provocative and important question – as is the related question of how we differentiate changes in weather from changes in climate (to which we return below). Such qualitative aspects of change in the international human rights regime, arising from state practice, need to be better conceptualized and more deliberatively investigated.

Another trend in state human rights practice that demands more attention is the adoption by states of a security discourse that effectively seeks to legitimize human rights violations in the name of protecting against terrorist threats. Mälksoo's chapter on Russia offers an important perspective on this phenomenon, in part because Russia's invocation of a "terrorist" threat from "radical Islamic" separatists in Chechnya to justify its harsh military, police, and political tactics there predates the 9/11 attacks – which triggered a strikingly similar reaction in the United States of America. Russia sees its practices as vindicated by the American responses to 9/11 and to the threat posed by Al Qaeda, and feels aggrieved in so far as a double-standard is applied to condemn its wars in Chechnya while giving the Americans a fairly easy pass in Iraq and Afghanistan. At the same time, however, Mälksoo observes that the rulings of the ECHR are beginning to shape Russia's policy on Chechnya and on human rights more broadly. This is a crucial case to watch, both with respect to Russia and the ECHR. Russia is a great power with a unique historical and cultural perspective on human rights as well as an axe to grind over American hypocrisy and double standards; at the same time, it is a member of the CoE seeking greater integration into European political forums. Whether Russia is willing and able to conform its behavior to international standards will be an important test. The ECHR, by contrast, has often been criticized as being effective only because it isn't needed – that is, of appearing to work only because its members are already predisposed to respect, promote, and fulfill human rights. Following a major expansion after the end of the Cold War, the CoE now comprises some 46 countries, many of which, like Russia, differ profoundly from the core group of founding states. If the CoE proves effective in modifying Russian behavior and moderating Russian attitudes, it will represent a major endorsement of that regime's principles and mechanisms.

The human rights discourse after 9/11

The rise of the "security discourse" as a rival to human rights discourses in global politics is a theme taken up by several contributors. Mälksoo, again, shows how Russia views the American-led "war on terror," in both its discursive and practical dimensions, as a validation of its own approach to dealing with separatists in Chechnya. This is hardly an isolated example: some central Asian states, notably Uzbekistan, as well as China, dealing with its Muslim Uighir minority, have quickly adopted the language of antiterrorism, seeking rhetorical cover for abusive practices in long-running struggles with internal political opponents. Indeed, if one scans the headlines of the past nine years, one is quickly overwhelmed by examples of governments labeling their domestic challengers "terrorists" and using that designation to rationalize and excuse a range of indefensible policies. (This practice helps to explain why the seemingly technical issue of terrorism lists, taken up by Schneider, is so politically charged and has such wide repercussions.)

This new tactic was licensed and encouraged, as Mälksoo and Goodhart demonstrate in quite different ways, by the dramatic shift in American rhetoric and practice following the 9/11 attacks. While Mälksoo focuses on the practical implications, Goodhart is more concerned with the long-term effects of what he sees as a broader shift toward a security discourse that presents human rights discourse with its first serious post-Cold War rival. Some potential negative effects of such a shift can be detected in the NGO sector where, as Barrett shows, organizations working on issues or in countries closely connected to the "war on terror" have found their political environment dramatically worsened and their freedom of action in some cases sharply curtailed.

Goodhart is concerned that this discursive shift interrupts progress in the regime and threatens to erode the moral status of human rights. Winston is less concerned, seeing the global (and now also apparently domestic) rejection of the "war on terror" paradigm as a good indication of the regime's robustness. This difference stems in part from their divergent views of the relationship between human rights discourse and the international human rights regime itself: Goodhart views the discourse as itself (partially) constitutive of the regime, while Winston seems to see it as epiphenomenal. This question is further complicated by Hamm's analysis, which points to the existence of "different streams and discourses that respond to varying demands."

Transnational civil society

Several contributors – Hamm, Barrett, and Schmitz – are all concerned with how discursive changes have created and closed off possibilities for human rights organizations. Both Barrett and Schmitz, in different ways, find that the disconnect between human rights discourse and political power has become highly salient since the 9/11 attacks. Hamm, by contrast, finds that the discourse of human rights and business ethics has remained essentially unaffected by the "war on terror," proceeding according to a separate logic and rhythm.

Barrett, looking at the daily operations of HROs, usefully disaggregates them according to the contexts in which they work (authoritarian or democratic states) and the issues which with they are primarily concerned (terrorism-sensitive or not). She finds that while HROs working on non-terrorism sensitive issues have seen little change since 9/11, their counterparts in terrorism-sensitive issue domains have faced severe repression in authoritarian states and a more fraught political atmosphere in democratic ones. She notes that in authoritarian states repressive measures against HROs are often justified by appeals to counterterrorism (again illustrating how discursive change can impact the regime across various layers). In democratic states, relations with governments have become increasingly tense as HROs become more critical. In some instances, however, this tension has helped to increase the relevance and moral authority of these organizations.

Schmitz focuses more on the structural predicament of HROs, arguing that while the "war on terror" triggered a sharp upturn in interest in and activism around traditional civil and political liberties, its primary effect was to highlight the overall weakness of transnational human rights activism. This weakness, in his view, can be traced to the systemic changes brought on by the end of the Cold War. The "name and shame" model of reactive activism had been quite effective in pressuring repressive governments on civil and political rights. That model proved less amenable to the political context of the 1990s, in which poverty and ethnic strife, often involving non-state actors and often in the context of humanitarian emergencies, emerged as the central issues of concern for HROs. The events of 9/11 and the "war on terror" underscored, in his view, the need to expand the range of rights on which HROs focus, to shift from a reactive to a proactive strategy focused on preventing human rights violations, and on the need to move away from a Northern-based framework of advocacy to one with greater global legitimacy and accountability. We might say that Schmitz's study points to the need for transnational human rights groups to find a way to (re)connect with politics – and thus with power.

Barrett notes that it is only because HROs have historically been effective that we are concerned with how the changing political and discursive landscapes effects their activities. This question of effectiveness proves quite difficult, however, in assessing the work of HROs since 2001. While there was a good deal of sometimes vocal opposition to many terrorism-related policies in democratic countries and beyond, it is hard to gauge whether HROs were "effective" in resisting these policies or whether their advocacy made a significant difference in shaping outcomes. This difficulty arises because it involves the assessment of counterfactuals – what might have happened in the absence of criticism from HROs and civil society. The findings suggest that comparative studies of the strategies and successes of civil society actors in different national contexts might provide some valuable insights.

Overall assessment

Our overall assessment of the international human rights regime since 9/11 must be, in light of the contributors' findings, a nuanced one. We find many reasons to be optimistic about the overall condition and resilience of the regime, as there is little evidence to suggest any widespread or systematic deterioration. We want to stress this point: the issues we raise in the remainder of this section are areas of concern, areas where greater research, activism, and institutionalization might help to strengthen the regime going forward. We do not mean, in emphasizing them, to detract from the overall sense among the authors that, important exceptions notwithstanding, the regime has survived a major shock largely intact. That said, in the issue domain most directly affected by this shock – torture – the record is much more mixed. Despite comparatively high levels of institutionalization through the UN system, the regime had little effect in limiting abuses related to torture and detention. It is nonetheless encouraging that regional arrangements in Europe do seem to have had a positive effect in deterring backsliding in this area. Institutionalization, through monitoring and implementation mechanisms, does seem to help protect human rights.

The latent weakness of the international regime on counterterrorism after 9/11, especially in matters surrounding torture and detention, suggests that the mere existence of laws and related oversight and compliance mechanisms is inadequate – even when these laws and mechanisms are strongly embedded in what appears to be a dominant global normative discourse. States are always in danger of backsliding when faced with serious threats or shocks, and greater enmeshment in international arrangements has the potential to help limit or even prevent the decline. One conclusion, then, is that creating more, and thicker, layers of institutionalization should be a priority. This is an area of structural development where HROs might play a potentially significant role. It provides an opportunity for these organizations to (re)connect to domestic politics by organizing to build political support for greater international institutionalization. The failure of HROs in the United States, in the wake of widespread public disgust with former administration officials who devised and authorized programs of torture, to mount a campaign for their prosecution shows just how wide the gulf between advocacy and political mobilization remains.

Whether the deterioration of human rights discourse (at least in issue domains sensitive to terrorism) proves to be lasting might well depend on how much time passes before another monumental attack takes place. It is also a question of political leadership. The present debates in the United States between the Obama Administration and its predecessor show that the relative standing of human rights and security concerns remains a bitterly contested political issue. Further attacks will surely influence this debate. Calls for harmonizing security and human rights concerns, while potentially constructive (and conceivably complementary to efforts by HROs to encourage rights-based approaches to problems like development), must avoid the danger of composing the harmony in such a way that security takes precedence over human rights in times of crisis. Another important question is whether greater enmeshment in international human rights arrangements could help to restrain American exceptionalism. Evidence from Europe is encouraging on this point. Indeed, European arrangements, while flawed in important ways, do provide general support for the idea that institutionalization makes a positive difference (at least when all participating states perceive some benefit from participation).

In sum, there is evidence of important and reassuring continuity in the international human rights regime, as well as of – mostly quite worrisome – change. In the remaining pages we consider two related epistemological questions about how change should be assessed: the baseline for comparison and 9/11 as a turning point.

Changes and baselines: the 1990s

Most of our contributors implicitly adopt the 1990s as their baseline for assessing change in the 21st century. This makes sense chronologically. But many of the authors also see the 1990s as an era of important progress and development within the international human rights regime – and perhaps even more so in the development of regional human rights regimes, particularly in Europe. Following the end of the Cold War, human rights became more widely institutionalized, internationally and domestically – most notably in Europe, with the expansion of the EU and the CoE, but not only there. Human rights norms proliferated widely, and their universality was affirmed in the Vienna Final Declaration in 1993 and in the emergence of human rights as a global normative standard of political legitimacy. The 1990s also saw a veritable explosion in transnational civil society activity around human rights and related issues – so much so that transnational civil society and human rights are often (dangerously) conflated. There can be no doubt that the human rights regime grew tremendously throughout the 1990s.

Whether that expansion translated into greater respect for and protection of human rights is another, and more vexing, question. As many of the authors here observe, the 1990s were also a period of shocking human rights violations – genocide and ethnic cleansing erupted throughout the world, terrorism metastasized, and poverty remained stubbornly entrenched across much of the planet. These failures are hardly attributable to the regime, yet they raise an uncomfortable question about the relationship between the status of the regime and the status of human rights around the world.

Nearly all of the authors are united in seeing the end of the Cold War as a significant milestone for human rights. Some see this event as inaugurating a period of welcome expansion and progress. Some see it as unleashing the tremendous potential of transnational civil society while others see it precipitating a crisis in that quarter. Some see it as a period of renewed US leadership, or at least of greater cooperation and support, while others see merely a continuation of American exceptionalism and double standards. While Europe leapt ahead in domesticating human rights law and expanding international mechanisms of compliance, America remained largely separate and aloof. As we have seen, the institutionalization of human rights standards in Europe throughout the 1990s changed not only the baseline but the institutional background against which change unfolded. Where such institutionalization did not occur, more, and more serious, backsliding was evident.

How we assess the 1990s is a crucial question. The reasons for the expansion of the regime, its growing effectiveness, and its limitations are all important factors in assessing what came afterwards and in molding the lessons we learn from the period following 9/11. Thus what we should make of the 1990s is one element in a larger puzzle confronting anyone interested in assessing the effects of 9/11 on the international human rights regime. That puzzle is how to determine a baseline for comparison. Perhaps we are interested in the regime itself, its formal arrangements and characteristics – such as the number of conventions, signatories, reservations, oversight mechanisms, special rapporteurs, etc. Perhaps we are interested in levels of compliance – numbers or rates of violations, or vectors of change in compliance levels, either in the aggregate or in specific countries and regions. Perhaps we are interested in discursive shifts – in how the dominant discourse(s) have changed, what they allow and foreclose, how they are contested. Perhaps we are concerned with the strength of transnational civil society actors and their ability to pressure governments and shape the human rights agenda. All of these questions are interesting and important, but each must be approached differently. Careful attention to the elements of the regime in which the analyst is interested and to the baseline for comparison are essential, as becomes clear when we ask whether and to what extent 9/11 represents a turning point for human rights.

9/11: change and continuity

Donnelly finds little or no deterioration in the regime, but he nonetheless entertains the possibility that one important consequence of 9/11 and the "war on terror" is "lost momentum" or "progress interrupted." If we view the 1990s, as Donnelly and Goodhart do, as a period of important – if also importantly limited – progress, then a loss of momentum or a shift in the discursive context might themselves represent significant losses of a kind. (This also raises the question of whether we view the 1990s or the Cold War period as the baseline: Were the 1990s abnormal or "the new normal"?) Winston, by contrast, is both less sanguine about the 1990s and more optimistic about the positive effects that the shake-up after 9/11 might have on the regime. Hamm sees little discernible change in the part of the regime she assesses, again reminding us of the difficulty of sweeping general assessment of "the regime" and "the impact" of 9/11.

The "n of 1" problem plagues attempts to assess the regime as a whole. Assessing counterfactuals – what would have taken place if 9/11 hadn't happened – is fraught with complications. Schmitz, for instance, dates the challenges confronting HROs to the early 1990s. Disaggregation and careful comparative analysis hold a great deal of promise for making solid empirical assessments of the regime. Cross-sectional comparisons of states and regional arrangements (Barrett; Mayerfeld; Schneider; St. Pierre) and time-series assessments of single countries, sectors, or mechanisms (Baehr; Mälksoo; Mihr; Schmitz; St. Pierre) are essential. Yet some of the questions in which we are rightly interested – including questions about discourse, about leadership, about HRO strategies, and many others – are, at least in part, judgment calls.

Yet for all its disparate parts and complex, overlapping layers, the regime remains somehow a whole. Given the profound nature of the shock delivered on 9/11, and the magnitude of the responses it triggered, the urge and the urgency to draw general conclusions are intense, and, we believe, justified. We have suggested that the regime remains resilient but that the "war on terror" has exposed some important weaknesses and vulnerabilities nationally and internationally. In short, the international human rights regime has been affected at all levels. We have seen that these effects are highly variable and uneven, depending significantly on the number and thickness of the regime's layers in any particular area; differently situated actors – states, HROs – have been affected and have responded differently to similar stimuli. Another important factor is how closely an actor, issue, or discourse is linked to terrorism and counterterrorism; the further one gets from terrorism, the less the impact of 9/11. This is perhaps unsurprising, but it is also an important indicator of how functional institutional design can help to contain damage and threats to other elements of the regime and facilitate necessary adjustments. The regime's fragmentation has, in this respect at least, proven to be a strength.

The overall prospects for human rights in the 21st century are in large part contingent on whether the regime can adapt to new challenges and the new demands to which they give rise. A regime that cannot adapt, that cannot remain useful and relevant to solving the problems of member states and other participating entities, seems likely to lose its meaning; a regime that provides a forum through which international actors can address new and urgent concerns in mutually beneficial ways is likely to fare much better. In this respect, empirical evidence regarding the state of the international human rights regime, such as the number of treaties signed or the levels of NGO activity, might prove less important to its long-term survival and flourishing than its flexibility and creativity in acting as a mechanism for tackling new concerns after 9/11.

What does seem clear is that 9/11 is an unavoidable starting point for any systematic analysis of continuity and change in human rights – at least for the moment. Much more could be said; we expect that this volume's contribution is to be among the first rather than the last words on this subject.

Note

1. All citations in this Conclusion refer to chapters in this volume.

Bibliography

Abu-Lughod, L. (2002), "Do Muslim Women Really Need Saving? Anthropological Reflections on Cultural Relativism and Its Others," *American Anthropologist*, 104/3, 783–90.

Adut, A. (2004), "Scandal Norm Entrepreneurship Strategy: Corruption and the French Investigating Magistrates," *Theory and Society*, 33/5, 529–78.

Advisory Council on International Affairs (2005) (tr), "Advisory Letter Counterterrorism in a European and International Perspective: Interim Report on the Prohibition of Torture," No. 11 Ministry of Foreign Affairs, The Hague.

Advisory Council on International Affairs (2006) (tr), "Advisory Report Counterterrorism from an International and European Perspective," No. 49 Ministry of Foreign Affairs, The Hague.

Afghanistan Independent Human Rights Commission, UNAMA (2009), Joint Monitoring of Political Rights Presidential and Provincial Council Elections Second Report 16 June – 1 August 2009. Afghanistan Independent Human Rights Commission (AIHRC) and the United Nations Mission to Afghanistan (UNAMA), http://unama.unmissions.org/Portals/UNAMA/human%20rights/3rd%20PRM%20report%2022%20oct%20ENG.pdf, accessed September 2010.

Afghanistan Independent Human Rights Commission, UNAMA (2010), Joint Monitoring of Political Rights Presidential and Provincial Council Elections Third Report August 1 – 21 October 2009, Afghanistan Independent Human Rights Commission (AIHRC), http://unama.unmissions.org/Portals/UNAMA/human%20rights/3rd%20PRM%20report%2022%20oct%20ENG.pdf, accessed June 2010.

Alcoff, L. M. (1998), *Epistemology: The Big Questions* (Malden, MA: Wiley Blackwell).

Alexander, M. (2008), *How to Break a Terrorist: The U.S. Interrogators Who Used Brains, Not Brutality, to Take Down the Deadliest Man in Iraq* (New York: Free Press).

American Civil Liberties Union [ACLU] (2006), Enduring Abuse: Torture and Cruel Treatment by the United States at Home and Abroad, http://www.aclu.org/national-security/enduring-abuse-torture-and-cruel-treatment-united-states-home-and-abroad-executive, accessed September 2010.

Amnesty International (1999), Women in Afghanistan: Pawns in Men's Power Struggles, November 1, 1999. http://web.amnesty.org/library/index/ENGASA110111999, accessed september 2010.

Amnesty International (2002), Amnesty International Report 2002, 26 May 2002, http://www.amnesty.org/en/library/asset/POL10/001/2002/en/b2589d8e-d8a8-11dd-ad8c-f3d4445c118e/pol100012002en.pdf, accessed October 2010.

Amnesty International (2006), Partners in Crime: Europe's Role in u.s. Renditions, 14 June 2006, http://www.amnestyusa.org/document.php?lang=e&id=ENGEUR010082006, accessed September 2010.

Amnesty International (2007), Afghanistan: Detainees Transferred to Torture: ISAF Complicity?, http://www.amnesty.org/library/print/ENGASA110112007, accessed January 2010.

Amnesty International (2008), Les Détenus en Afghanistan, http://www.amnistie.ca-/content/view/10900/56, accessed September 2008.

Amnesty International (2009), Women in Afghanistan: Pawns in Men's Power Struggles, 1 November 2009, http://web.amnesty.org/library/index/ENGASA110111999, accessed June 2010.

Amnesty International EU Office (2005), "Human Rights Dissolving at the Borders? Counter-Terrorism and EU Law," Amnesty International Report, IOR 61/013.

Amor, M. and Estébanez, M. (1998), "The OSCE and Human Rights," in Hanski, R. and Suksi, M. (eds), *An Introduction to the International Protection of Human Rights, A textbook* (Turku: Abo Akademi University), 265–82.

Anderson, C. (2003), *Eyes Off the Prize: The United Nations and the African American Struggle for Human Rights, 1944–1955* (Cambridge: Cambridge University Press).

Anderson, M. B. (1999), *Do No Harm. How Aid Can Support Peace – or War* (Boulder, CO: Lynne Rienner).

Andersson, H. (2010), "Red Cross Confirms 'Second Jail' at Bagram, Afghanistan," *BBC News*, May 11, 2010.

Andreopoulos, G., Kabasakal Arat, Z. F., and Juviler, P. (2006), *Non-State Actors in the Human Rights Universe* (Bloomfield, CT: Kumarian Press).

Anonymous, (2007), Interrogation Video from Omar Khadr, http://www.youtube.com/watch?v=aQHFFbD_-Pg, accessed June 2009.

Archer, C. (2000), *The European Union. Structures and Process* (London/New York: Continuum).

Aust, H. Ph. and Naske, N. (2006), "Rechtsschutz gegen den UN-Sicherheitsrat durch europäische Gerichte? Die Rechtsprechung des EuG zur Umsetzung 'gezielter Sanktionen' aus dem Blickwinkel des Völkerrechts," *Zeitschrift für öffentliches Recht*, 61, 587–623.

Austen, I. (2010), "Canada's Supreme Court Says Inmate's Rights Were Violated at Guantánamo," *New York Times*, http://www.nytimes.com/2010/01/29/world/americas/30canada.html, accessed March 2010.

Ayotte, K. J. and Husain, M. E. (2005), "Securing Afghan Women: Neocolonialism, Epistemic Violence and the Rhetoric of the Veil," *NWSA Journal*, 17/ 3, 112–33.

Ayres, J. and Tarrow, S. (2002), "The Shifting Grounds for Transnational Civic Activity," After September 11 Archive, Social Science Research Council, http://www.ssrc.org/sept11/essays/ayres.htm, accessed March 2009.

Baehr, P.R. (2010), "Accountability of the United Nations: The Case of Srebrenica," in Wouters, J., Brems, E., Smis, S. and Schmitt P. (eds), *Accountability for Human Rights Violations by International Organisations* (Antwerp/Portland/Oxford: Intersentia), 269–286.

Baehr, P. R., Castermans-Holleman, M., and Grünfeld, F. (2002), *Human Rights in the Foreign Policy of the Netherlands* (Antwerp/Oxford/New York: Intersentia).

Bailyn, B. (1992), *The Ideological Origins of the American Revolution* (Cambridge, MA: Belknap Press Harvard).

Baker, L. (2009), "Lawyer Says Guantánamo Abuse Worse Since Obama," *Reuters*, February 25, 2009.

Baker, P. (2010), "Obama's War Over Terror," *New York Times*, January 4, 2010.

Barnett, M. and Weiss, T. G. (2008), *Humanitarianism in Question: Politics, Power, Ethics* (Ithaca, NY: Cornell University Press).

Barstow, D. (2008), "Message Machine: Behind TV Analyst's, Pentagon's Hidden Hand," *New York Times*, April 20, 2008.

Bellah, R. N. (1975), *The Broken Covenant: American Civil Religion in Time of Trial* (New York: Seabury).

Bellamy, R. and Warleigh, A. (2001), *Citizenship and Governance in the European Union* (London/New York: Continuum).

Bendiek, A. (2006), "Europäische Union: Netzwerke bilden, um Netzwerke zu bekämpfen," in Schneckener, U. (ed.), *Chancen und Grenzen multilateraler Terrorismusbekämpfung*. SWP-Study (Berlin: Stiftung Wissenschaft und Politik), 31–41.

Benjamin, D. (2010), International Counterterrorism in the Obama Regime: Developing a Strategy for the Future, Speech to the International Peace Institute, 1 March 2010, http://www.state.gov/s/ct/rls/rm/2010/137865.htm, accessed April 2010.

Benlafquih, C. (2008) *Muslim Charities, Unfairly Eyed with Suspicion*, Arabisto, July 2, http://www.arabisto.com/article.cfm?articleID=974, accessed March 2009.

Benoit-Rohmer, F. (2005), "Members and Special Status," in Benoit-Rohmer, F. and Klebes, H. (eds), *Council of Europe Law. Towards a Pan-European Legal Area* (Strasbourg: Council of Europe Publishing), 33–46.

Berdyaev, N. (1955), *The Origin of Russian Communism* (London: Geoffrey Bles).

Biersteker, Th. J. and Eckert, S. E. (2006), "Strengthening Targeted Sanctions Through Fair and Clear Procedures," Watson Institute for International Studies. Brown University, http://www.watsoninstitute.org/pub/Strengthening_Targeted_Sanctions.pdf, accessed July 2009.

BLIHR (Business Leaders Initiative on Human Rights) (2003), Report 1: Building Understanding. http://www.bhrseminar.org/2004%20Documents/BLIHR%20Report%20I.pdf, accessed November 2010.

BLIHR (Business Leaders Initiative on Human Rights) (2004), "Report 2: Work in Progress," London, http://www.blihr.org/Reports/BLIHR%20Report%202004.pdf, accessed March 2008.

Blitz, B. K. (2006), *War and Change in the Balkans. Nationalism, Conflict and Cooperation* (Cambridge: Cambridge University Press).

Blumenthal, D. (1997), *Women and Soap Opera: A Cultural Feminist Perspective* (Westport, CT: Praeger Publishers).

Bojkov, V. (2004), "National Identity, Political Interest and Human Rights in Europe. The Charter of Fundamental Rights of the European Union," *Nationalities Papers*, 32/2, 323–53.

Bonner, D. (2007), *Executive Measures, Terrorism and National Security* (London: Ashgate).

Bothe, M. (2007), "Targeted Sanctions and Due Process Initiative. Discussion Paper on Supplementary Guidelines for the Review of Sanctions Committee's Listing Decisions. Explanatory Memorandum," Permanent Mission of Liechtenstein to the United Nations (New York), http://www.liechtenstein.li/en/fl-aussenstelle-newyork/fl-aussenstelle-newyork-dokumente/fl-aussenstelle-newyork-dokumente-verbrechensbekaempfung.htm, accessed July 2009.

Bothe, M. (2008), "Security Council's Targeted Sanctions against Presumed Terrorists. The Need to Comply with Human Rights Standards," *Journal of International Criminal Justice*, 6/3, 541–55, http://jicj.oxfordjournals.org/cgi/content/abstract/6/3/541, accessed July 2009.

Bourdieu, P. (1996), *Die feinen Unterschiede: Kritik der gesellschaftlichen Urteilskraft* (Frankfurt am Main: Suhrkamp).

Bowring, B. (2008), *The Degradation of the International Legal Order? The Rehabilitation of Law and the Possibility of Politics* (London: Routledge).

Bradbury, S. (2005), Memo Re: Application of United States Obligations Under Article 16 of the Convention against Torture to Certain Techniques That May Be Used in the Interrogation of High Value Al Qaeda Detainees, Office of the Principal Deputy Assistant Attorney General, 30 March 2005.

Brett, R. (1996), "Human Rights and the OSCE," *Human Rights Quarterly*, 18/2, 668–93.

Bron, R. P. (2008) (tr), "Organisatie en Structuur Terrorismebestrijding: Wetgeving en Beleid," ["Organisation and Structure of Combating Terrorism: Legislation and Policy,"] in Muller, E. R., Rosenthal, U., and Wijk, R. de (eds) (trs), *Terrorisme: Studies over Terrorisme en Terrorismebestrijding* (Deventer: Kluwer), 471–506.

Brown, C. (2003) (ed.), *Lost Liberties: Ashcroft and the Assault on Personal Freedom* (New York: The New Press).

Buergenthal, T., Shelton, D., and Stewart, D. (2002), *International Human Rights in a Nutshell* (St. Paul: West Group).

Bullard, A. (2008) (ed.), *Human Rights in Crisis* (Beurlington: Ashgate).

Bunch, C. (2010), Whose Security?, *Women's World*, http://www.wworld.org/archive/archive.asp?ID=298, accessed June 2010.

Burgers, J. H. (2007) (tr), "Dissenting Opinion: Geen Deuren Open Laten Staan Naar Marteling," ["Not to Leave Doors Open Towards Torture,"] *NJCM Bulletin*, 32, 958–66.

Burgers, J. H. and Danelius, H. (1988), The United Nations Convention against Torture: A Handbook on the Convention against Torture and Other, Cruel, Inhuman and Degrading Treatment or Punishment (Dordrecht/Boston/London: Martinus Nijhoff Publishers).

Bush, G. W. (2001), Address to a Joint Session of Congress and the American People, 20 September 2001, http://www.whitehouse.gov/news/releases/2001/09/20010920-8.html, accessed November 2009.

Bush, G. W. (2002), Second State of the Union Address, January 29, 2002, http://en.wikisource.org/wiki/George_W._Bush%27s_Second_State_of_the_Union_Address, accessed October 2010.

Bush, G. H. W. (1991), Address Before a Joint Session of Congress on the End of the Gulf War, March 6, 1991, http://millercenter.org/scripps/archive/speeches/detail/3430, accessed November 2010.

Bush, L. (2001), Radio Address by Mrs. Bush, The American Presidency Project, 17 November 2001, http://www.presidency.ucsb.edu/ws/index.php?pid=24992, accessed November 2009.

Bykova, V. and Stepanov, A. (2007) (eds), *Sekretnye tjurmy CIA* (Moscow: Evropa).

Campos, E. (2006), L'affaire Ahmed Ressam: parcours d'un terroriste, http://www.erta-tcrg.prg/ahmedressam/ressam.htm, accessed March 2007.

Canada (1978), Immigration Act, 1976, http://www1.canadiana.org/citm/specifique/immigration_e.html#1976, accessed November 2010.

Canada (1982), Canadian Charter of Rights and Freedoms, http://laws.justice.gc.ca/en/charter/, accessed March 2007.

Canada (1996), Criminal Law Improvement Act, 1996, http://www2.parl.gc.ca/HousePublications/Publication.aspx?DocId=2329437&Language=e&Mode=1&File=16#1, accessed March 2007.

Canada (2001), Anti-Terrorism Act, 2001, http://www2.parl.gc.ca/HousePublications/Publication.aspx?pub=bill&doc=C-36&parl=37&ses=1&language=E, accessed March 2007.

Canada (2007), Charkaoui vs Canada, accessed February 2007.

Canada (2008), Statutes, http://www2.parl.gc.ca/HousePublications/Publication.aspx?Docid=3300375&file=4, accessed May 2008.

Canadian Press (2008a), Nouveau rapport fédéral – Les douaniers canadiens et américains ont les mains liées, http://www.ledevoir.com/2008/02/11/175661.html, accessed May 2008.

Canadian Press (2008b), "Affaire Arar: le Canada et les États-Unis sont dans l'impasse," *Le Devoir*, 4 February 2008, http://www.ledevoir.com/2008/02/04/174615.html?sendurl=t, accessed February 2008.

Cassese, A. (1996), *Inhuman States: Imprisonment, Detention and Torture in Europe Today*, J. Greensleaves (tr) (Cambridge: Polity).

Castonguay, A. (2008), "La loi, l'ordre et la sécurité restent des priorités conservatrices," *Le Devoir*, February 27 2008, http://www.ledevoir.com/2008/02/27/177974.html, accessed February 2008.

Ceyhan, A. (2002), "Terrorisme, immigration et patriotisme. Les identités sous surveillance," *Cultures & Conflits*, 44, www.conflits.org, accessed February 2005.

Charity Commission (2007), Report on Charities Working in the Field of Human Rights, December 2007, http://www.charitycommission.gov.uk/publications/rs16.asp, accessed March 2009.

Charity Commission (2009), Charity Commission Publishes Interpal Inquiry Report, 27 February 2009, http://www.charity-commission.gov.uk/news/printerpal.asp, accessed March 2009.

Charlesworth, H. and Chinkin, C. (2002), "Sex, Gender and September 11," *The American Journal of International Law*, 96/3, 600–5.

Charlesworth, H., Chinkin, C., and Wright, S. W. (1991), "Feminist Approaches to International Law," *American Journal of International Law*, 85, 613–645.

Cheney, D. (2003), "Transcript of Meet the Press," *NBC News*, September 14, 2003.

Chenoy, A. M. (2002), "Forever Victims," in Hawthorne, S. and Winter, B. (eds), *After Shock: September 11, 2001, Global Feminist Perspectives* (Vancouver: Raincoat Books), 229–31.

Chomsky, N. (1998), "The United States and the Challenge of Relativity," in Evans, T. (ed.), *Human Rights Fifty Years On: A Reappraisal* (Manchester: Manchester University Press), 24–57.

Cingranelli, D. and Richards, D. (2007), The Cingranelli-Richards Human Rights Dataset Version 2007.11.29, http://www.humanrightsdata.org, accessed February 2008.

Clark, A. M. (2001), *Diplomacy of Conscience. Amnesty International and Changing Human Rights Norms* (Princeton, NJ: Princeton University Press).

Clinton, H. (2010), "Afghan Women: We Will Not Abandon You," *The Associated Press*, Friday, May 14, 2010, http://www.nydailynews.com/news/politics/2010/05/14/2010-05-14_secretary_of_state_hillary_clinton_to_afghan_women_we_will_not_abandon_you.html, accessed June 2010.

CNN 10.09.2002, 9/11 a "Turning Point" for Putin, http://archives.cnn.com/2002/WORLD/europe/09/10/ar911.russia.putin/, accessed on September 2010.

Cole, D. (2009) (ed.), *Torture Memos: Rationalizing the Unthinkable* (New York: New Press).

Cole, M. (2009), "Officials: Lithuania Hosted Secret cia Prison to Get 'Our Ear'," *ABC News*, August 20, 2009.

Cole, D. and Dempsey, J. (2006), *Terrorism and the Constitution* (New York: The New Press), 198.

Commissie van Onderzoek naar de Betrokkenheid van Nederlandse Militairen bij Mogelijke Misstanden bij Gesprekken met Gedetineerden in Irak, (2007) (tr), "Onderzoek Ondervragingen in Irak" ["Inquiry Interrogations in Iraq. Report of the Commission of Inquiry into the Involvement of Dutch Military in Possible Abuses in Talks with Detainees in Iraq,"] The Hague, June 18, 2007.

Commissie van Toezicht Betreffende de Inlichtingen- en Veiligheidsdiensten (2007) (tr), "Samenvatting inzake het Onderzoek naar het Optreden van MIVD-medewerkers in Irak bij het Ondervragen van Gedetineerden" ["Summary of the Inquiry into the Actions of Stafmembers of the Military Information and Security Service in Iraq During the Interrogation of Detinees,"] CTIVD, nr. 15, June 18, 2007.

Commission on Human Rights (2005), Resolution 2005/69, UN Doc. E/CN.4/2005/L.87, http://www.reports-and-materials.org/UN-Commission-resolution-business-human-rights-Apr-2005.doc, accessed February 2009.

Compilation Prepared by the Office of the High Commissioner for Human Rights (2008), in Accordance with the Annex to Paragraph 15 (B) of Resolution 5/1 of the Human Rights Council, The Netherlands, A/HRC/WG.6/NDL/2, March 19, 2008.

Conquest, R. (1990), *The Great Terror. A Reassessment* (Oxford: Oxford University Press).

Correa, C. (2007), "Waterboarding Prisoners and Justifying Torture: Lessons for the U.S. from the Chilean Experience," *Human Rights Brief*, 14/12, 21–5.

Council of Europe (1999), *A Visit by the CPT – What's It All about? 15 Questions and Answers for the Police* (Geneva: Council of Europe Publications).

Council of Europe (2002) (ed.), "Guidelines on Human Rights and the Fight against Terrorism," Adopted by the Committee of Ministers on 11 July 2002 (Strasbourg: Council of Europe Publishing).

Council of Europe (2005) (ed.), "European Convention on Prevention of Terrorism," Treaty Series 196, Warsaw 15.V.2005 (Strasbourg: Council of Europe Publishing).

Council of Europe (2007) (ed.), "Memorandum of Understanding between the Council of Europe and the European Union," 117th Session of the Committee of Ministers (Strasbourg: Council of Europe Publishing).

Council of Europe (2008), Parliamentary Recommendation of Assembly of the Council of Europe 1824: United Nations Security Council and European Union Blacklists, http://assembly.coe.int/main.asp?Link=/documents/adopt-edtext/ta08/erec1824.htm, accessed July 2009.

Council of Europe, Committee of Experts on Terrorism (2009), CODEXTER, http://www.coe.int/gmt, accessed January 2009.

Council of Europe, Directorate of Communication (2007) (ed.), *800 Million Europeans* (Strasbourg: Council of Europe Publishing).

Cox, R. W. and Jacobsen, H. K. (1974), "The Framework for Inquiry," in Cox, R. W. and Jacobsen, H. K. (eds), *The Anatomy of Influence. Decision Making in International Organizations* (New Haven, CT: Yale University Press), 1–36.

Cubilie, A. (2005), *Women Witnessing Terror* (New York: Fordham University).

Cutler, C. A., Haufler, V., and Porter, T. (1999), *Private Authority and International Affairs* (New York: State University of New York Press).

Danner, M. (2004), *Torture and Truth: America, Abu Ghraib, and the War on Terror* (New York: New York Review Books).

Davis, J. (2008), *Justice across Borders: The Struggle for Human Rights in U.S. Courts* (Cambridge: Cambridge University Press).

Davis, Y. N. (2002), "Forum: The Events of 11 September 2001 and Beyond," *International Feminist Journal of Politics*, 4/1, 102.

Davis, T. R. and Lynn-Jones, S. M. (1987), "City Upon a Hill," *Foreign Policy*, 66, 20–38.

Dayan, C..(2007), *The Story of Cruel and Unusual* (Cambridge, MA: MIT Press).

De Hoog (2008) (tr), "Politiële Terrorismebestrijding in Nederland: Inrichting en Uitdagingen van een Bijzondere Politietaak," ["Combating Terrorism by the Police: Institution and Challenges of a Special Task of the Police,"] in Muller, E. R., Rosenthal, U., and Wijk, R. de (eds) (trs), *Terrorisme: Studies over Terrorisme en Terrorismebestrijding* (Deventer: Kluwer), 579–612.

Department of Homeland Security (2002), *National Strategy for Homeland Security* (Washington, DC: USG printing).

Department of Justice, Canada (2004), http://www.justice.gc.ca/en/anti_terr/context.html.

Der Derian, James (2003), "The Question of Information Technology in International Relations," *Millennium: Journal of International Studies*, 32, 3, 441–56.

Deutscher Bundestag (2007) (*June 13*): Regierung: EU listet Volksmudschahedin zu Recht als Terrorgruppe, in: Meldung, Deutscher Bundestag, unter: http://www.bundestag.de/aktuell/hib/2007/2007_159/01.html, accessed November 2008.

Dietrich, J. W. (2006), "U.S. Human Rights Policy in the Post-Cold War Era," *Political Science Quarterly*, 121/2 ,269–94.

Doehring, K. (1997), "Unlawful Resolutions of the Security Council and their Legal Consequences," *Max Planck Yearbook of United Nations Law*, 1, 91–110.

Donnelly, J. (2004), "International Human Rights: Unintended Consequences of the War on Terrorism," in Weiss, T. G., Crahan, M. E. and Goering, J.(eds), *Wars on Terrorism and Iraq: Human Rights, Unilateralism and U.S. Foreign Policy* (New York: Routledge, 98–112).

Donohue, L. K. (2008), *The Cost of Counter-Terrorism: Power, Politics and Liberty* (Cambridge: Cambridge University Press).

Drzewicki, K. and Graaf, V. de (2007), "The Activities of the OSCE High Commissioner on National Minorities," *European Yearbook of Minority Issues*, 5, 315–37.

Dwyer, J. (2005), "Police Infiltrate Protests Videotapes Show," *New York Times*, December 22, 2005.

Ebadi, S. A. H. G. (2005), "The Human Rights Case Against Attacking Iran," *New York Times*, February 8, 2005.

Economic and Social Research Council (2006), The Role of Civil Society in the Management of National Security in a Democracy, Seminar Report on Seminar Four: The Role of Civil Society, March 8, 2006, http://www.lse.ac.uk/collections/humanRights/articlesAndTranscripts/ESRC_seminar4_civil_society. pdf, accessed March 2009. The *Economist* (2007), "Doing the Wrong Thing," 385, 74.

European Center for Constitutional and Human Rights [ECCHR] (2009), "cia 'Extraordinary Rendition' Flights, Torture and Accountability – A European Approach," 2nd edn, January 2009.

European Commission (2004), *Eurobarometer 62, Report* (Brussels: European Commission Publishing).

European Commission (2005), *Eurobarometer 64, Report* (Brussels: European Commission Publishing).

European Commission (2008), *Eurobarometer Standards 69, Values of Europeans* (Brussels: European Commission Publishing).

European Commission (2009), *Eurobarometer 70, First Results* (Brussels: European Commission Publishing).

European Commission External Relations (1998) (ed.), Declaration of the European Union on the Occasion of the 50th Anniversary of the Universal Declaration on Human Rights. Vienna December 10, 1998. Brussels.

European Commission External Relations (2007) (ed.), *The European Union. Furthering Human Rights and Democracy across the Globe* (Brussels: Publication Office).

European Community (2001a), Council Common Position of 27 December 2001 on the Application of Specific Measures to Combat Terrorism, http://eur-lex. europa.eu/LexUriServ/LexUriServ.do?uri=OJ:L:2001:344:0093:0096:EN:PDF, accessed April 2009.

European Community (2001b), Council Regulation (ec) No 2580/2001 of 27 December 2001 on Specific Restrictive Measures Directed against Certain Persons and Entities with a View to Combating Terrorism, http://eur-lex. europa.eu/LexUriServ/LexUriServ.do?uri=OJ:L:2001:344:0070:0075:EN:PDF, accessed July 2009.

European Community (2002a), Council Regulation (ec) No 881/2002 of 27 May 2002 Imposing Certain Specific Restrictive Measures Directed against Certain Persons and Entities Associated with Osama Bin Laden, the Al-Qaida Network and the Taliban, and Repealing Council Regulation (ec) No 467/2001 Prohibiting the Export of Certain Goods and Services to Afghanistan, Strengthening the Flight Ban and Extending the Freeze of Funds and Other Financial Resources in Respect of the Taliban of Afghanistan, http://eur-lex. europa.eu/LexUriServ/LexUriServ.do?uri=OJ:L:2002:139:0009:0022:EN:PDF, accessed April 2009.

European Community (2002b), Council Framework Decision of 13 June 2002 on Combating Terrorism (2002/475/jhi), http://eur-lex.europa.eu/LexUriServ/ LexUriServ.do?uri=OJ:L:2002:164:0003:0007:EN:PDF, accessed April 2009.

European Community (2007), Acts Adopted Under Title v of the eu Treaty Council Common Position. 2007/448/cfsp of 28 June 2007 Updating Common Position 2001/931/cfsp on the Application of Specific Measures to Combat Terrorism and Repealing Common Positions 2006/380/cfsp and 2006/1011/ CFSP, http://eur-lex.europa.eu/LexUriServ/LexUriServ.do?uri=OJ:L:2007:169: 0069:0074:EN:PDF, accessed July 2009.

European Community (2008a), *The EU List of Persons, Groups and Entities Subject to Specific Measures to Combat Terrorism. European Union Factsheet* (Brussels: Press), http://www.consilium.europa.eu/uedocs/cmsUpload/080715_combat%20terrorism_EN.pdf, accessed July 2009.

European Community (2008b), Council Decision of 15 July 2008 Implementing Article 2(3) of Regulation (ec) No 2580/2001 on Specific Restrictive Measures Directed against Certain Persons and Entities with a View to Combating Terrorism and Repealing Decision 2007/868/ec, 2008/583/ec, http://eur-lex. europa.eu/LexUriServ/LexUriServ.do?uri=OJ:L:2008:188:0021:0025:EN:PDF, accessed April 2009.

European Council (2002) (ed.), *Council Framework Decision of 13 June 2002 on Combating Terrorism (2002/474/JHA), L 164/3* (Brussels: European Council).

European Council (2005) (ed.), *The European Union Counter-Terrorism Strategy. Prevent, Protect, Pursue, Respond. The European Union's Strategic Commitment. To Combat Terrorism Globally while Respecting Human Rights, and Make Europe Safer, Allowing its Citizens to Live in an Area of Freedom, Security and Justice* (Brussels: European Council).

European Court of Human Rights (1999), *Selmouni v. France* no. 25803/94.

European Parliament (2007), *European Parliament Resolution on the Alleged Use of European Countries by the CIA for the Transportation and Illegal Detention of Prisoners 2006/2200(INI)* (Strasbourg and Brussels), htp://www.europarl. europa.eu/comparl/tempcom/tdip/final_ep_resolution_en.pdf, accessed January 2009.

European Union (2008), Commission Regulation (ec) No 1190/2008 of 28 November 2008 Amending for the 101st Time Council Regulation (ec) No 881/2002 Imposing Certain Specific Restrictive Measures Directed against Certain Persons and Entities Associated with Usama Bin Laden, the Al-Qaida Network and the Taliban, http://eur-lex.europa.eu/LexUriServ/LexUriServ.do? uri=OJ:L:2008:322:0025:0026:EN:PDF, accessed April 2009.

European Union (2009a), "Preliminary Statement, 'Afghan Elections Take Place in a Reasonably Well-organised Manner, Amid Widespread Violence and Intimidation', European Union Election Observation Mission, Islamic Republic of Afghanistan, Presidential and Provincial Council Elections 2009," Kabul August 22, 2009, http://www.reliefweb.int/rw/RWFiles2009. nsf/FilesByRWDocUnidFilename/MUMA-7V742E-full_report.pdf/$File/full_report.pdf, accessed September 2010.

European Union (2009b), eu Fight against Scourge of Terrorism, http://ec.europa. eu/justice_home/fsj/terrorism/fsj_terrorism_intro_en.htm, accessed January 2009.

European Union (2009c), Factsheet. the eu List of Persons, Groups and Entities Subject to Specific Measures to Combat Terrorism, http://www.consilium. europa.eu/uedocs/cmsUpload/090127_EU_terrorist_list_EN.pdf, accessed July 2009.

European Union (2009d), Preliminary Statement of the European Union Observation Mission to the Islamic Republic of Afghanistan, Presidential and Provincial Council Elections 2009, http://www.europarl.europa. eu/meetdocs/2009_2014/documents/droi/dv/droi_20090910_47/ droi_20090910_47en.pdf, accessed October 2010.

European Union (2009e), "Updating the List of Persons, Groups and Entities Subject to Articles 2, 3 and 4 of Common Position 2001/931/cfsp on the Application of Specific Measures to Combat Terrorism," COUNCIL DECISION 2009/1004/CFSP, http://eur-lex.europa.eu/LexUriServ/LexUriServ.do?uri=OJ: L:2009:346:0058:0060:EN:PDF, accessed May 2010.

Evans, R. and Lewis, P. (2010a), "Comedian Wins £1,200 Over Police Search," *The Guardian*, April 20, 2010.

Evans, R. and Lewis, P. (2010b), "Police Admit Stop and Searches on 11-Year-Olds at Kingsnorth Protest," *The Guardian*, January 12, 2010.

Evans, M. D. and Morgan, R. (1998), *Preventing Torture: A Study of the European Convention of the Prevention of Torture and Inhuman Or Degrading Treatment Or Punishment* (Oxford: Oxford University Press).

Fain, N. (2003), "Human Rights Within the United States: The Erosion of Confidence," *Berkeley Journal of International Law*, 21, 607–30.

Farall, J. M. (2007), *United Nations Sanctions and the Rule of Law* (Cambridge: Cambridge University Press).

Farer, T. J. (2008), "Un-Just War Against Terrorism and the Struggle to Appropriate Human Rights," *Human Rights Quarterly*, 30/2, 356–403.

Federation of American Scientists (2003), The "War on Terrorism" and Human Rights: Aid to Abusers, http://www.fas.org/terrorism/at/docs/Aid&Humanrights. html accessed April, 2009.

Feeley, M. M. and Rubin, E. L. (1998), *Judicial Policy Making and the Modern State: How the Courts Reformed America's Prisons* (Cambridge: Cambridge University Press).

Feinäugle, C. A. (2010), "The UN Security Council Al-Qaida and Taliban Sanctions Committee: Emerging Principles of International Institutional Law for the Protection of Individuals?," in Bogdandy A. von, Wolfrum, R., Bernstorff, J. von, Dann, P. and Goldmann, M. (eds), *The Exercise of Public Authority by International Institutions* (Heidelberg: Springer), 101–31.

Ferrero-Waldner, B. (2005), "EU and OSCE Strong Partnership. European Commissioner for External Relations and European Neighbourhood Policy," 13th OSCE Ministerial Meeting, Ljubljana.

Ferrero-Waldner, B. (2007), "European Commissioner for External Relations and European Neighbourhood Policy," OSCE Ministerial Council, November 29, 2007.

Fischer, H., Lorion, S., and Ulrich, G. (2007), *Beyond Activism. the Impact of the Resolutions and Other Activities of the European Parliament in the Field of Human Rights Outside* (Venice: Marsilio).

Flaherty, M. S. (2006), "Judicial Globalization in the Service of Self-Government," *Ethics and International Affairs*, 20, 477–503.

Florini, A. (1996), "The Evolution of International Norms," *International Studies Quarterly*, 40/3, 363–89.

Forman, J. Jr. (2009), "Exporting Harshness: How the War on Crime Has Made the War on Terror Possible," *New York University Review of Law and Social Change*, 33, 331–74.

Forsythe, D. P. (2006), *Human Rights in International Relations* 2nd edn (Cambridge: Cambridge University Press).

Forsythe, D. P. (2006), "United States Policy toward Enemy Detainees in the 'War on Terrorism'," *Human Rights Quarterly*, 28, 465–91.

Forsythe, D. P. (2007), "The United States: Protecting Human Dignity in an Era of Insecurity," in Brysk, A. and Shafir, G. (eds), *National Insecurity and Human Rights: Democracies Debate Counterterrorism* (Berkeley, CA: University of California Press), 37–55.

Forsythe, D. P. (2008), "The United States and International Humanitarian Law," *Journal of Human Rights*, 7, 25–33.

France (1986), LOI 86–1020 (1986). §17–19.

France (2008), Code Pénal §706–88.

Franke-Ruta, G. (2009), "Layoffs Hit NARAL, ACLU," *The Washington Post*, January 28, 2009.

Friedman, E. J., Hochstetler, K., and Clark, A. M. (2005), *Sovereignty, Democracy, and Global Civil Society. State-Society Relations at UN World Conferences* (Albany: State University of New York Press).

Frontline (2008), Letter to Ms.Margaret Sekaggya, Special Rapporteur on the Situation of Human Rights Defenders, December 12, 2008, http://www.frontlinedefenders.org/files/en/Letter%20to%20Margaret%20Sekaggya.pdf, accessed April 2009.

Frontline (2009), Europe and Central Asia, http://www.frontlinedefenders.org/europe-central-asia, accessed March 2009.

Fuchs, D. (2005), *Understanding Business Power in Global Governance* (Baden-Baden: Nomos).

Fukuyama, Francis. *The End of History and the Last Man*, New York: Free Press, 1992.

Gall, C. (2009), "Intimidation and Fraud Observed in Afghan Election," *New York Times*, August 22, 2009, http://www.nytimes.com/2009/08/23/world/asia/23afghan.html, accessed October 2010.

Gaudette, É. (2005), Les réseaux felquistes, http://www.independance-quebec.com/flq/recherche_reseaux.php#4, accessed February 2008.

Gawande, A. (2009), "Hellhole: Is Solitary Confinement Torture?," *New Yorker*, March 30, 2009, 36–45.

Gearty, C. (2007), "Terrorism and Human Rights," *Government and Opposition*, 42/3, 340–62.

Geyer, F. (2007), "Fruit of the Poisonous Tree: Member States' Indirect Use of Extraordinary Rendition and the eu Counter-terrorism Strategy," Centre for European Policy Studies Working Document No. 263.

Gill, S. (2003), *Power and Resistance in the New World Order* (Basingstoke: Palgrave Macmillan).

Gillan and Quenton v. The United Kingdom (App no 4158/05) (2010).

Gilligan, E. (2010), *Terror in Chechnya: Russia and the Tragedy of Civilians in War* (Princeton, NJ: Princeton University Press).

Gillis, S., Howie, G., and Munford, R. (2005/2007) (eds), *Third World Feminism*, 2nd edn (New York: Palgrave).

Gilman, D. (2007), "Calling the United States' Bluff: How Sovereign Immunity Undermines the United States' Claim to An Effective Domestic Human Rights System," *Georgetown Law Journal*, 95, 591–652.

Glasius, M. (2002), "Expertise in the Cause of Justice. Global Civil Society Influence on the Statute for an International Criminal Court," in Glasius, M., Kaldor, M., and Anheier, H. (eds), *Global Civil Society*, 137–68, http://www.lse.ac.uk/Depts/global/Publications/Yearbooks/2002/2002chapter6.pdf, accessed September 2010.

Goede, Marieke de (2008), "The Politics of Preemption and the War on Terror in Europe," *European Journal of International Relations*, 14/1, 161–85.

Goldenberg, S. (2009), "Serving 22 Years: The Environmentalist Who Fell Foul Victim to us Anti-terror Laws," *The Guardian*, London March 24, 2009.

Goldhaber, M. D. (2007), *A People's History of the European Court of Human Rights* (New Brunswick, NJ: Rutgers University Press).

Gready, P. and Ensor, J. (2005), *Reinventing Development? Translating Rights-Based Approaches from Theory into Practice* (London: Zed Books).

Greenberg, K. J., Dratel, J., and Lewis, A. (2005) (eds), *The Torture Papers: The Road to Abu Ghraib* (New York: Cambridge University Press).

Greer, S. (2006), *The European Convention on Human Rights* (Cambridge: Cambridge University Press).

Guelke, A. (2006), *Terrorism and Global Disorder* (London/New York: I.B.Tauris & Co. Ltd).

Hamdan v. Rumsfeld, Secretary of Defense et al, 548 U.S. 557 (2006).

Hamm, B. (2001), "A Human Rights Approach to Development," *Human Rights Quarterly*, 23 /4, 1005–31.

Hansen-King, J. (2009), "Human Rights and Solitary Confinement: The American Story," Senior Honors Thesis, University of Washington.

Harbury, J. (2005), *Truth, Torture, and the American Way* (Boston: Beacon Press).

Hartsock, N. C. M. (1998), *The Feminist Standpoint Revisited and Other Essays* (Boulder, CO: Westview Press).

Haufler, V. (2003), "Globalization and Industry Self-Regulation," in Kahler, M. and Lakes, D. A. (eds), *Governance in a Global Economy: Political Authority in Transition* (Princeton, NJ: Princeton University Press), 226–52.

Heinz, W. (2007), *Terrorismusbekämpfung und Menschenrechtsschutz in Europa* (Berlin: German Institute for Human Rights Publishing).

Heinz, W. and Arnd, J. -M. (2005), *The International Fight against Terrorism and the Protection of Human Rights, With Recommendations to the German Governments and Parliament* (Berlin: German Institute for Human Rights Publishing).

Held, D., McGrew, A., Goldblatt, D., and Perraton, J. (1999), *Global Transformations: Politics, Economic and Culture* (Stanford: Stanford University Press).

Henkin, L. (1995), "u.s. Ratification of Human Rights Conventions: The Ghost of Senator Bricker," *American Journal of International Law*, 89, 341–50.

Hersh, S. (2004), *Chain of Command: The Road from 9/11 to Abu Ghraib* (New York: HarperCollins).

Heun-Rehn, S. L. -Th. (2008), "Kadi und Al Barakaat – Der EuGH, die Gemeinschaft und das Völkerrecht," *European Law Reporter*, 10, 322–37.

Heupel, M. (2008), "I've Got a Little List. UN and EU Terrorist Blacklists," *The World Today*, August 2008, 27–28.

Hilhorst, D. (2005), "Dead Letter or Living Document? Ten Years of the Code of Conduct for Disaster Relief," *Disasters*, 29/4, 351–69.

Hirono, M. (2008), *Civilizing Missions. International Religious Agencies in China* (Houndmills: Palgrave Macmillan).

Hirschmann, N. J. (1992), *Rethinking Obligation: A Feminist Method for Political Theory* (Ithaca, NY: Cornell University Press).

Hoffmann, S. (1968), "The American Style: Our Past and Our Principles," *Foreign Affairs*, 46/2, 362–76.

Hoffman, P. (2004), "Human Rights and Terrorism," *Human Rights Quarterly*, 26/4, 932–55.

Holsti, O. R. (1962), "The Belief System and National Images: A Case Study," *The Journal of Conflict Resolution*, 6/3, 244–52.

Hook, S. and Spanier, J. (2000), *American Foreign Policy Since World War II*. 15th edn (Washington D.C.: CQ Press).

Hopgood, S. (2006), *Keepers of the Flame. Understanding Amnesty International* (Ithaca, NY: Cornell University Press).

Hörmann, S. (2007), "Die Befugnis der EG zur Umsetzung von Resolutionen des UN-Sicherheitsrates zur Bekämpfung des internationalen Terrorismus," *Europarecht*, 1, 120–33.

Horsbrugh-Porter, A. (2009), *Created Equal: Voices on Women's Rights* (New York: Palgrave Macmillan).

Hobsbawm, E. (1989), *The Age of Empire: 1875–1914* (New York: Vintage Books).

Hobsbawm, E. (1996), *The Age of Revolution: 1789–1848* (New York: Vintage Books).

Howell, J. and Lind, J. (2010), "Securing the World and Challenging Civil Society: Before and After the 'War on Terror'," *Development and Change*, 41, 2.

Howell, J., Ishkanian, A., Obadare, E., Seckinelgin, H., and Glasius, M. (2008), "The Backlash against Civil Society in the Wake of the Long War on Terror," *Development in Practice*, 18/1, 82–93.

Human Rights Council (2008) Resolution 8/7. Mandate of the Special Representative of the Secretary General on the issue of human rights and transnational corporations and other business enterprises, http://ap. ohchr.org/documents/E/HRC/resolutions/A_HRC_RES_8_7.pdf, accessed May 2010.

Human Rights First (2005), Karamov's War, http://www.humanrightsfirst.info/ pdf/05119-hrd-uzbek-rep-karimov.pdf, accessed March 2009.

Human Rights First (2008), Command's Responsibility: Detainee Deaths in u.s. Custody in Iraq and Afghanistan, February 2008.

Human Rights Watch (2004), Eradicating Torture in Turkey's Police Stations, September 2004.

Human Rights Watch (2008a), Afghanistan: World Report, http://www.hrw.org/englishwr2k8/docs/2008/01/31/afghan17600.htm, accessed June 2010.

Human Rights Watch (2008a), Not the way forward. The UK's Reliance on Diplomatic Assurances, October 2008.

Human Rights Watch (2008b), Preempting Justice: Counterterrorism Laws and Procedures in France, July 2008.

Human Rights Watch (2008c), Uzbekistan: Human Rights Watch Representative Banned, July 25, 2008.

Human Rights Watch (2008d), *World Report 2008* (New York: Human Rights Watch).

Human Rights Watch (2009a), Cruel Britannia: British Complicity in the Torture and Ill-treatment of Terror Suspects in Pakistan, November 24, 2009.

Human Rights Watch (2009b), Uzbekistan: Human Rights Defender Attacked, Threatened, April 16, 2009, http://www.hrw.org/en/news/2009/04/16/uzbekistan-rights-defender-attacked-threatened, accessed April 2009.

Human Rights Watch (2010) Campaigning Against Fear: Women's Participation in Afghanistan's 2005 Elections, http://www.hrw.org/backgrounder/wrd/afghanistan0805/index.htm, accessed October 2010.

Hunt, K. (2002), "The Strategic Co-option of Women's Rights," *International Feminist Journal of Politics*, 4/1, 116–21.

Hunt, K. (2006), "Embedded Feminism and the War on Terror," in Hunt, K. and Rygiel, K. (eds), *(En)gendering the War on Terror: War Stories and Camouflaged Politics* (Ashgate: Aldershot), 51–70.

Iacopino, V., Rasekh, Z., Yamin, A.E., Freedman, L., Burkhalter, H., Atkinson, H. and Heisler, M. (1998), "The Taliban's War on Women: A Health and Human Rights Crisis in Afghanistan," Physicians for Human Rights, Boston, 1998.

Ignatieff, M. (2001), *Human Rights as Politics and Idolatry* (Princeton, NJ: Princeton University Press).

Ignatieff, M. (2002a), "Is the Human Rights Era Ending?," *New York Times*, February 5, 2002, A25.

Ignatieff, M. (2002b), "No Exceptions? The United States' Pick-and-Choose Approach to Human Rights is Hypocritical. But That's Not a Good Reason to Condemn It," *Legal Affairs*.

Ignatieff, M. (2005a) (ed.), *American Exceptionalism and Human Rights* (Princeton, NJ: Princeton University Press).

Ignatieff, M. (2005b), "American Exceptionalism and Human Rights: Introduction," in Ignatieff, M.(ed.) *American Exceptionalism and Human Rights*, manuscript on file with author Cambridge, MA.

Intelligence and Security Committee (2007), Rendition, Presented to Parliament by the Prime Minister by Command of Her Majesty, http://www.cabinetoffice.gov.uk/intelligence.

International Committee of the Red Cross (2007), ICRC Report on the Treatment of High Value Detainees' in cia Custody, February 14, 2007, http://www.nybooks.com/icrc-report.pdf.

Ivleva, V. (2010), "Karina Moskalenko: Otvetit li pravitel'stvo Rossii za 'Nord-Ost'?," *Novaya Gazeta*, April 9, 2010.

Jebbink, W. H. (2008) (tr), "Wat de Schiedammer Parkmoord Niet Leert," ["What the Schiedam Park Murder Does Not Teach Us,"] *Nederlands Juristen Blad*, 1, 564–8.

JEHT Foundation (2008), Statement of Robert Crane, President of the JEHT Foundation, on Behalf of the Foundation's Board of Directors, December 15, 2008, http://www.jehtfoundation.org/news/ accessed March 2009.

Joachim, J. (2007), *Agenda Setting, the UN, and NGOs. Gender Violence and Reproductive Rights* (Washington, DC: Georgetown University Press).

Joint open letter to UN Special Representative on Business and Human Rights (2007), http://www.escr-net.org/usr_doc/OpenLetter_Ruggie_FinalEndorsements.pdf, accessed February 2009.

Jones, A. (2009), "Afghanistan: Remember the Women?," *The Nation*, October 21, 2009.

Jones, G. and Rozenberg, J. (2006), "Human Rights Ruling Leaves Anti-terror Law in Tatters," *Telegraph online*, www.telegraph.co.uk, accessed June 2006.

Jordan, L. J. and Hess, P. (2008), "Cheney, Others ok'd Harsh Interrogation," *Associated Press*, April 10, 2008.

Jordan, L., and Tuijl, P. van (2000), "Political Responsibility in Transnational NGO Advocacy," *World Development*, 28/12, 2051–65.

Jordan, P. A. (2003), "Does Membership Have Its Privileges? Entrance into the Council of Europe and Compliance with Human Rights Norms," *Human Rights Quarterly*, 25/3, 660–88.

Kandiyoti, D. (2009), Gender in Afghanistan: Pragmatic Activism, November 2, 2009, http://www.opendemocracy.net/deniz-kandiyoti/gender-in-afghanistan-pragmatic-activism, accessed June 2010.

Kaplan, M. B. (2008), "'Criminal Justice' and the Politics of Punishment," Lecture Delivered to the Greater Philadelphia Philosophy Consortium, 12 April 2008, (Philadelphia).

Karzai Administration, (2004–6), Afghanland Online, http://www.afghanland.com/history/cabinetkarzai.html, accessed November 2009.

Kateb, G. (2007), "Punishment and the Spirit of Democracy," *Social Research*, 74, 269–306.

Katherine, M., Darmer, B., Baird, R.M. and Rosenbaum, S.E. (2004) (eds), *Civil Liberties vs. National Security in a Post-9/11 World* (Amherst: Prometheus Books).

Keck, M. E. and Sikkink, K. (1998), *Activists beyond Borders: Advocacy Networks in International Politics* (Ithaca, NY: Cornell University Press).

Kennedy, D. (2004), *The Dark Sides of Virtue. Reassessing International Humanitarianism* (Princeton, NJ: Princeton University Press).

Khagram, S., Riker, J. V., and Sikkink, K. (2002), *Restructuring World Politics: Transnational Social Movements, Networks, and Norms* (Minneapolis, MN: University of Minnesota Press).

Kinsley, M. (2002), *Listening to Our Inner Ashcroft*, Slate, 3 January, http://www.slate.com/id/2060339/, accessed March 2009.

Klein, N. (2003), "Bush to Ngos: Watch Your Mouths," *Globe and Mail*, June 24, 2003.

Koh, H. H. (2003), "Foreword: On American Exceptionalism," *Stanford Law Review*, 55, 1479–1527.

Koh, H. H. (2007), "The Future of Lou Henkin's Human Rights Movement," *Columbia Human Rights Law Review*, 38, 459.

Korey, W. (1998), *NGOs and the Universal Declaration of Human Rights. A Curious Grapevine* (Houndmills/Basingstoke: Macmillan).

Krashennikova, V. (2007), *Amerika-Rossija: kholodnaya voina kul'tur* (Moscow: Evropa).

Krasner, S. D. "Structural Causes and Regime Consequences: Regimes as Intervening Variables," *International Organization*, 36/2 (1982): 185–205.

Lawyers Committee for Human Rights (2003), *Assessing the New Normal: Liberty and Security in the Post-September 11 United States* (New York: Lawyers Committee for Human Rights).

Leebaw, B. (2007) "The Politics of Impartial Activism. Humanitarianism and Human Rights," *Perspectives on Politics*, 5/2, 223–39.

Leino, P. (2002), "A European Approach to Human Rights? Universality Explored," *Nordic Journal of International Law*, 71/4, 455–95.

Lepgold, J. and McKeown, T. (1995), "Is American Foreign Policy Exceptional? An Empirical Analysis," *Political Science Quarterly*, 110/3, 369–84.

Lerougetel, A. (2006), France: Le juge Bruguière – de l'utilisation de l'anti-terrorisme comme instrument politique, http://www.wsws.org/francais/News/2006/janvier06/260106_JugeBruguiereprn.shtml, accessed September 2006.

Levin, C. (2008), Inquiry into the Treatment of Detainees in U.S. Custody, Report of the Committee on Armed Services, United States Senate, December 11, 2008.

LeVine, M.A. (2005), The New Axis of Evil: International Fora, Judicial Processes and Terrorism, 18 April 2005, http://hnn.us/blogs/comments/11397.html, accessed March 2009.

Levinson, S. (2004) (ed.), *Torture: A Collection* (Oxford: Oxford University Press).

Ley, I. (2007), "Legal Protection Against the UN-Security Council. Between European and International Law: A Kafkaesque Situation?," *German Law Council*, 3, 279–94.

Liese, A. (2006), *Staaten am Pranger. Zur Wirkung internationaler Regime auf die innerstaatliche Menschenrechtspolitik* (Wiesbaden: VS Verlag).

Lieven, D. (2000), *Empire: The Russian Empire and Its Rivals* (New Haven, CT: Yale University Press).

Lindenberg, M. and Bryant, C. (2001), *Going Global: Transforming Relief and Development NGOs* (Bloomfield, CT: Kumarian Press).

Lipset, S. M. (1996), *American Exceptionalism: A Double-Edged Sword* (New York: W.W. Norton).

Lissack, M. R. (2004), "The Redefinition of Memes: Ascribing Meaning to an Empty Cliché," *Journal of Memetics – Evolutionary Models of Information Transmission*, 8, http://cfpm.org/jom-emit/2004/vol8/lissack_mr.html accessed June 2010.

Lobel, J. (2008), "Prolonged Solitary Confinement and the Constitution," *University of Pennsylvania Journal of Constitutional Law*, 11, 115–38.

Lönnqvist, L. (2007), UK-Based NGOs: Stigma and Labelling at Interpal, *Intrac Newsletter*, no. 35, January, available for download via www.intrac.org.

Lourie, R. (2002) *Sakharov – A Biography* (Hanover, NH: Brandeis University Press).

Lukasheva, E. A. (2009) (ed.), *Prava Cheloveka*, 2nd edn (Moscow: Norma).

Kammen, M. (1993), "The Problem of American Exceptionalism: A Reconsideration," *American Quarterly*, 45/1, 1–43.

Madsen, D. L. (1998), *American Exceptionalism* (Jackson, MS: University Press of Mississippi).

Malcontent, P. (2008), "The European Union's Influence on the Character and Effectiveness of Dutch Conduct in the UN Commission on Human Rights," in Boerefijn, I. and Goldschmidt, J. (eds), *Changing Perceptions of Sovereignty and Human Rights: Essays in Honour of Cees Flinterman* (Antwerp/Oxford/Portland: Intersentia), 199–231.

Mälksoo, L. (2001), "Soviet Genocide? Communist Mass Deportations in the Baltic States and International Law," *Leiden Journal of International Law*, XIV, 757–87.

Mälksoo, L. (2008), "The History of International Legal Theory in Russia: A Civilizational Dialogue with Europe," *European Journal of International Law*, XIX, 211–32.

Manuel Dias das Almas v. Portugal (App no 12979/87) (1990) (ECHR), http://cmiskp.echr.coe.int/tkp197/viewhbkm.asp?sessionId=9266860&skin=hudoc-en&action=html&table=F69A27FD8FB86142BF01C1166DEA398649&key=25 544&highlight accessed July 2009.

Mark-Ungericht, B. (2005), "MenschenrechteundinternationaleGeschäftstätigkeit," *Zeitschrift für Wirtschafts- und Unternehmensethik*, 6/3, 324–42.

Martens, K. (2005), *NGOs and the United Nations: Institutionalization, Professionalization and Adaptation* (Houndmills/Basingstoke: Palgrave Macmillan).

Martens, K. (2006), "Professionalized Representation of Human Rights NGOs to the United Nations," *The International Journal of Human Rights*, 10/1, 19–30.

Martinez, L. M. H. (2008), "The Legislative Role of the Security Council in its Fight Against Terrorism: Legal, Political and Practical Limits," *The International and Comparative Law Quarterly*, 27, 333–59.

Marty, (Senator) D. (2007), Secret Detentions and Illegal Transfers of Detainees Involving Council of Europe Member States, Second Report to the Parliamentary Assembly of the Council of Europe, June 7, 2007.

Mayer, J. (2008), *The Dark Side: The Inside Story of How the War on Terror Turned into a War on American Ideals* (New York: Doubleday).

Mayer, J. (2009), "The Secret History: Leon Panetta's c.i.a. Challenge," *New Yorker*, June 22, 2009, 50–9.

Mayerfeld, J. (2007), "Playing by Our Own Rules: How u.s. Marginalization of Human Rights Law Led to Torture," *Harvard Human Rights Journal*, 20, 89–141.

Mayhall, S. L. (2009), "Uncle Sam Wants You to Trade, Invest and Shop! Relocating the Battlefield in the Gendered Discourses of the Pre- and Early post-9/11 Period," *NWSA Journal*, 21/1, 29–50.

McCoy, A. W. (2006), *A Question of Torture: CIA interrogation, from the Cold War to the War on Terror* (New York: Metropolitan Books).

McEvoy-Levy, S. (2001), *American Exceptionalism and US Foreign Policy: Public Diplomacy at the End of the Cold War* (London: Palgrave).

McGeary, J. (2003), "Dissecting the Case," *Time*, 161/6, 56.

McMahon, J. (2007), Counter-Terrorism Measures for NGOs: The Letter of the Law, *INTRAC Newsletter* no. 35, January, available for download via www.intrac.org,

Medvedev, D. (2008), Address to the Federal Assembly of the Russian Federation, November 5, 2008, http://www.kremlin.ru/eng/speeches/2008/11/05/2144_t ype70029type82917type127286_208836.shtml accessed on.

Meerpohl, Th. (2008), *Individualsanktionen des Sicherheitsrates der Vereinten Nationen. Das Sanktionsregime gegen die Taliban und Al-Qaida vor dem Hintergrund des Rechts der VN und der Menschenrechte* (München: Herbert Utz Verlag).

Mertus, J. (2003), "Improving the Status of Women in the Wake of War: Overcoming Structural Obstacles," *Columbia Journal of Transnational Law*, 41, http://www.aupeace.org/files/ImprovingStatusofWomen.pdf, accessed October 2010.

Mertus, J. (2003), "Shouting From the Bottom of the Well," *International Feminist Journal of Politics*, 6, 1, 110–28.

Meyer, Karl E. (1999), "Enforcing Human Rights," *World Policy Journal*, 16, 3, 45–51.

Mihr, A. (2008a), "Human Rights in Europe: Origins, Institutions, Policies and Perspectives," in Seidelmann, R. and Vasilache, A. (eds), *European Union and Asia: A Dialogue on Regionalism and Interregional Cooperation* (Baden-Baden: Nomos), 197–220.

Mihr, A. (2008b), "The Role of Human Rights NGOs Since 9/11: New Policies Or Just Necessary Changes?," The International Human Rights Regime Since 9/11: Trans-Atlantic Perspectives, University Centre for International Studies, University of Pittsburgh, Pittsburgh, April 17–19, 2008, http://www.ucis.pitt. edu/euce/events/conferences/HR-PDF/Mihr.pdf, accessed March 2009.

Miller, P. (1956a) (ed.), *The American Puritans: Their Prose and Poetry* (New York: Columbia University Press).

Miller, P. (1956b), *Errand Into the Wilderness* (Cambridge, MA: Belknap Press, Harvard).

Mills, M. A. and Kitch, S. L. (2006), "Afghan Women Leaders Speak: An Academic Activist Conference, Mershon Center for International Security Studies, Ohio State University, November 17–19, 2005," *NWSA Journal*, 18/3, 91–100.

MIPT (2008), Country Profile Canada, *http://www.tkb.org/Country.jsp?country Cd=CA*, accessed February 2008.

Mommsen, M. and Nußberger, A. (2007), *Das System Putin* (München: C.H.Beck).

Moravcsik, A. (2000), "The Origins of Human Rights Regimes: Democratic Delegation in Postwar Europe," *International Organization*, 54/2, 217–52.

Muller, E. R., Rosenthal, U., and de Wijk, R. (eds) (trs) (2008), *Terrorisme: Studies over Terrorisme en Terrorismebestrijding* ["Terrorism: Studies about Terrorism and Combating Terrorism"] (Deventer: Kluwer).

Murdie, A. (2007), "Boomeranging Betterment: The Impact of Human Rights NGO Activity on Human Rights Practices," International Studies Association, 48th Annual Convention Chicago, February 28, 2007, http://www.allacademic.com/meta/p_mla_apa_research_citation/1/7/9/7/6/p179767_index. html accessed April 2009.

Murdoch, J. (2006a), "Tackling Ill-treatment in Places of Detention: The Work of the Council of Europe's 'Torture Committee'," *European Journal of Criminal Policy Research*, 12, 121–42.

Murdoch, J. (2006b), *The Treatment of Prisoners: European Standards* (Strasbourg: Council of Europe Publishing).

Naples, N. (2000), "A Standpoint Epistemology and the Use of Self-reflection in Feminist Ethnography: Lessons for Rural Sociology," *Rural Sociology*, 65/2, 194–214.

Narayan, U. (1997), *Dislocating Cultures: Identities, Traditions, and Third World Feminism* (New York: Routledge).

National Report Submitted in Accordance with Paragraph 15 (a) of the Annex to Human Rights Council Resolution 5/1: The Netherlands, AHRC/WG.6/1/NLD/1, March 7, 2008.

Nayak, M. (2006), "Orientalism and 'Saving' US State Identity after 9/11," *International Feminist Journal of Politics*, 8/1, 42–61.

NDI (2009), Preliminary Statement of the NDI Election Observer Delegation to Afghanistan's 2009 Presidential and Provincial Council Elections, National Democratic Institute, Kabul, August 22, 2009, *http://www.ndi.org/files/Afghanistan_EOM_Preliminary_Statement.pdf*, accessed June 2010.

Nelson, P. J. (2000), "Heroism and Ambiguity. NGO Advocacy in International Policy," *Development in Practice*, 10/3–4, 478–90.

Nelson, P. J. and Dorsey, E. (2008), *New Rights Advocacy: Changing Strategies of Development and Human Rights NGOs* (Georgetown: Georgetown University Press).

Netherlands Ministry of Foreign Affairs (2007) (tr), Naar een Menswaardig Bestaan: Een Mensenrechtenstrategie voor het Buitenlands Beleid ["Towards a Dignified Existence: A Human Rights Strategy for Foreign Policy,"]The Hague.

Netherlands Ministry of Foreign Affairs (2008) (tr), Actieplan voor Implementatie van de Notitie "Naar een Menswaardig Bestaan – een Mensenrechtenstrategie voor het Buitenlands Beleid" ["Plan of Action for the Implementation of the Paper'Towards a Decent Existence – A Human Rights Strategy for Foreign Policy,"] The Hague.

Newberg, P. R. (2004), "Missing the Point: Human Rights in U.S.-Pakistan Relations," in Liang-Fenton, D. (ed.), *Implementing U.S. Human Rights Policy: Agendas, Policies, and Practices* (Washington, DC: United States Institute of Peace Press).

NFSD (Novartis Foundation for Sustainable Development) (2007), "Business and Human Rights – Advancing the Debate," *Newsletter Express* 11, *http://www.novartisstiftung.org/platform/apps/Publication/getfmfile.asp?id=214&el2056&se=883554036&doc=150&dse=5*, accessed March 2008.

Nguyen, T. (2006), *We Are All Suspects Now: Untold Stories from Immigrant America after 9/11* (Boston: Beacon Press).

Ní Aoiláin, F. (2004), "The European Convention on Human Rights and Its Prohibition on Torture," in Levinson, S. (ed.), *Torture: A Collection* (Oxford: Oxford University Press).

Nikitinski, L. (2010), "Strasburg trebuet peremen. Intervju s Anatoly Kovlereom," *Novaya Gazeta*, April 16, 2010.

Nordstrom, C. (2007), *A Different Kind of War Story: Ethnography of Political Violence* (Philadelphia, PA: University of Pennsylvania Press).

Nowak, M. (2002), *Einführung in das internationale Menschenrechtssystem* (Wien/Graz: Neuer Wissenschaftlicher Verlag).

Nowak, M. (2006), "What Practices Constitute Torture? US and UN standards," *Human Rights Quarterly*, 28/4, 809–41.

Nowak, M. (2008), "Ein Weltgerichtshof für Menschenrechte. Eine utopische Forderung?," *Vereinte Nationen*, 5, 205–11.

Nowrot, K. (2003), "Die un-Norms on the Responsibility of Transnational Corporations and Other Business Enterprises with Regard to Human Rights – Gelungener Beitrag Zur Transnationalen Rechtsverwirklichung Oder Das Ende Des Global Compact?," Beiträge zum Transnationalen Wirtschaftsrecht, 21, http://www.telc.uni-halle.de/Heft21.pdf, accessed March 2008.

Nußberger, A., Schmidt, C., and Morščakova, T. (2009) (eds), *Verfassungsrechtsprechung in der Russischen Föderation. Dolumentation und Analyse der Entscheidungen des Russischen Verfassungsgerichts 1992–2007* (Kehl am Rhein: N.P. Engel Verlag).

O'Brien, P. (2005), "Rights-based Responses to Aid Politicization in Afghanistan," in Gready, P. and Ensor, J. (eds), *Reinventing Development? Translating Rights-Based Approaches from Theory into Practice* (London: Zed Books 201–32).

Oates, L. (2009), "A Closer Look – The Policy and Law-Making Process Behind the Shiite Personal Status Law," Afghanistan Research and Evaluation Unit (AREU), September 30, 2009, http://www.reliefweb.int/rw/rwb.nsf/db900sid/MYAI-7WD9PX?OpenDocument, accessed June 2010.

Obama, B. (2009), "Remarks by the President at Parallel Civil Society Summit," Office of the Press Secretary, The White House Moscow, Russia, July 7, 2009, http://www.whitehouse.gov/the_press_office/Remarks-By-The-President-At-Parallel-Civil-Society-Summit accessed April 2010.

O'Brien, P. (2004), "Politicized Humanitarianism: A Response to Nicolas de Torrente," *Harvard Human Rights Journal*, 17, 31–40.

Oestreich, J. E. (2007), *Power and Principle. Human Rights Programming in International Organizations* (Washington, DC: Georgetown University Press).

Office of the High Commissioner for Human Rights (2009), *2008 Report: Activities and Results* (Geneva: Office of the High Commissioner for Human Rights).

Office of the High Commissioner for Human Rights (2009), *2010. High Commissioner's Strategic Management Plan 2010–2011* (Geneva: Office of the High Commissioner for Human Rights).

OSCE (2000), *OSCE Handbook 1975–2000 Helsinki Final Act* (Vienna: OSCE Publishing).

OSCE (2001), The Bucharest Plan of Action for Combating Terrorism, December 4, 2001, MC(9).DEC/1, http://www.unhcr.org/refworld/docid/47fdfb250.html, accessed April 2010.

OSCE (2004), ODIHR Legislations Line, http://www.legislationline.org, accessed January 2009.

OSCE (2005), Upholding Human Rights in the Fight against Terrorism, http://www.osce.org/item/17108.html, accessed March 2009.

OSCE (2009), odihr Activities to Combat Terrorism, http://www.osce.org/odihr/13373.html, accessed January 2009.

OSCE and Council of Europe Publishing (2007), *National Minority Standards. A Compilation of OSCE and Council of Europe Texts* (Strasbourg: Council of Europe Publishing).

Osiatyński, W. (2009), *Human Rights and Their Limits* (Cambridge: Cambridge University Press).

Paul, J. A. (2001), "Der Weg zum Global Compact. Zur Annäherung von UNO und multinationalen Unternehmen," in Brühl, T., Debiel, T., and Hamm, B.

(eds), *Die Privatisierung der Weltpolitik. Entstaatlichung und Kommerzialisierung im Globalisierungsprozess* (Bonn: Dietz), 104–29.

Payandeh, M. (2006), "Rechtskontrolle des UN-Sicherheitsrates durch Staatliche und überstaatliche Gerichte," *Zeitschrift für ausländisches öffentliches Recht und Völkerrecht*, 66, 41–71.

Peters, J. and Laan, L. van der (2008), "Conflicts of Rights and Today's Dilemmas in Combating Terrorism," in Boerefijn, I. and Goldschmidt, J. (eds), *Human Rights in the Polder: Human Rights and Security in the Public and Private Sphere* (Antwerp/Oxford/Portland: Intersentia), 113–36.

Peterson, S. V. (2000), "Rereading Public and Private: The Dichotomy Is Not One," *SAIS Review*, 20/2, 11–28.

Peterson, S. V. (2002), "Forum: The Events of 11 September 2001 and Beyond," *International Feminist Journal of Politics*, 4/1, 111.

Peterson, S. V. (2004), "Feminist Theories Within, Invisible to and Beyond International Relations," *Brown Journal of World Affairs*, 10/2, 35–46.

Petman, J. J. (2004), "Feminist International Relations After 9/11," *Brown Journal of World Affairs*, 2, 88.

Pfeiffer, K. and Schneider, P. (2008), "Menschenrechte gelten doch auch für Terrorverdächtige," *Hamburger Informationen zur Friedensforschung und Sicherheitspolitik*, 44.

Pipes, R. (1997), *Russia under the Old Regime*, 2nd edn (London: Penguin).

Pipes, D. and Garfinkle, A. (1991) (eds), *Friendly Tyrants: An American Dilemma* (New York: St. Martin's Press).

Pohjolainen, A. -E. (2006), *The Evolution of National Human Rights Institutions* (Copenhagen: Danish Institute for Human Rights).

Price, R. (1998), "Reversing the Gun Sights: Transnational Civil Society Targets Land Mines," *International Organization*, 52/3, 613–44.

Privacy International (2008), National Privacy Ranking 2007 – Leading Surveillance Societies around the World, www.privacyinternational.org, accessed February 2008.

Public Safety Canada (2004a), Facts about Organized Crime, http://ww2.ps-sp. gc.ca/policing/organized_crime/FactSheets/org_crime_e.asp, accessed March 2007.

Public Safety Canada (2004b), Securing an Open Society: Canada's National Security Policy, http://www.publicsafety.gc.ca/pol/ns/secpol04-eng.aspx accessed March 2007.

Public Safety Canada (2008), Security Certificates, http://www.publicsafety. gc.ca/prg/ns/seccert-eng.aspx, accessed February 2008.

Pushkarskaya, A. (2010), "Konstitutsionnyi sud ostavil prisyazhnykh ne u del svyazannykh s terrorizmom," *Kommersant*, April 20, 2010.

Rabkin, J. (1998), *Why Sovereignty Matters* (Washington, DC: The AEI Press).

Radio Canada (2008), Scrutés à la loupe, http://www.radio-Canada.ca/nouv-elles/National/2008/01/20/001-securite-ports.shtml, February 2008.

Radio Canada (2009a), Querelle diplomatique, http://www.radio-canada.ca/nouvelles/National/2009/04/21/004-terrrorisme-frontieres-canada.shtml, accessed May 2009.

Radio Canada (2009b), Omar Khadr doit revenir au pays, http://www.radio-canada.ca/nouvelles/National/2009/04/23/002-kadhr-cour-federale.shtml, accessed May 2009.

Ramazanoglu, C. (1989), *Feminism and the Contradictions of Oppression* (New York: Routledge).

Reality of Aid Management Committee (2006) (eds), *The Reality of Aid 2006: Focus on Conflict, Security and Development* (London: Zed Books).

Regan, L. (2006), Surveillance, Infiltration, and Harassment of Environmental Organizations, Part II, March 29, 2006, http://www.truthout.org/article/surveillance-infiltration-and-harassment-environmental-organizations-part-ii accessed March 2009.

Reiding, H., (2007), *The Netherlands and the Development of International Human Rights Instruments* (Antwerp/Oxford/Portland: Intersentia).

Rejali, D. M. (2007), *Torture and Democracy* (Princeton, NJ: Princeton University Press).

Rettman, A. (2009), eu Decision on Uzbekistan Appals Human Rights Groups, October 22, 2009, http://euobserver.com/9/28864 accessed April 2010.

Reuters (2009), "Obama team drops 'war on terror' rhetoric" 30 March 2009. <http://www.reuters.com.>

Rhodes, L. (2004), *Total Confinement: Madness and Reason in the Maximum Security Prison* (Berkeley: University of California Press).

Rieff, D.(1999), "The Precarious Triumph of Human Rights," *New York Times*, August 8, 1999, 36–41.

Rieff, D. (2002), *A Bed for the Night. Humanitarianism in Crisis* (New York: Simon and Schuster).

Risse, T., Ropp, S. C., and Sikkink, K. (1999) (eds), *The Power of Human Rights: International Norms and Domestic Change* (Cambridge: Cambridge University Press).

Robinson, M. (2006), Five Years on from 9/11 – Time to Re-Assert the Rule of Law, Justice Lecture, March 20, 2006, http://www.justice.org.uk/images/pdfs/Mary%Robinson%20lecture%2020%20March%202006.pdf, accessed March 2009.

Rodio, E. B. and Schmitz, H. P. (2010), "Beyond Norms and Interests: Understanding the Evolution of Transnational Human Rights Activism," *The International Journal of Human Rights*, 14/3, 442–59.

Rogers, J. M. (1999), *International Law and United States Law* (Aldershot, Hampshire: Ashgate).

Rose, D. (2009), "How mi5 Colluded in My Torture: Binyam Mohamed Claims British Agents Fed Moroccan Torturers Their Questions," *Daily Mail*, March 7, 2009.

Rosenberg, E. S. (1991), "Walking the Borders," in Hogan, M. J. and Paterson, T. G. (eds), *Explaining the History of American Foreign Relations* (New York: Cambridge University Press), 31–5.

Ross, D. (1995), "American Exceptionalism," in Fox, R. W. and Kloppenberg, J. T. (eds) *A Companion to American Thought* (Cambridge, MA: Blackwell).

Roth, K. (2010), "Empty Promises?," *Foreign Affairs*, 89/2, 10–16.

Roth, K. and Worden, M. (2005) (eds), *Torture: Does It Make Us Safer? Is It Ever OK? A Human Rights Perspective* (New York: The New Press).

Roy, A. (2001), *The Algebra of Infinite Justice. With a Foreword by John Berger* (London: Penguin Books).

Ruby, J. (2001), "Is This a Feminist War?," in Hawthorne, S. and Winter, B. (eds), *September 11, Feminist Perspectives* (North Melbourne: Spinifex), 148–50.

Rugendyke, B. (2007), *NGOs as Advocates for Development in a Globalizing World* (New York: Routledge).

Ruggie, J. (2006), Opening Statement to the United Nations Human Rights Council by the Special Representative of the Secretary-General for Business and Human Rights, of September 25, 2006, http://www.reports-and-materials.org/Ruggie-statement-to-UN-Human-Rights-Council-25-Sep-2006.pdf, accessed October 2008.

Ruggie, J. (2007), Business and Human Rights: Mapping International Standards of Responsibility and Accountability for Corporate Acts. Report of the Special Representative of the Secretary-General (srsg) on the Issue of Human Rights and Transnational Corporations and Other Business Enterprises, un Doc. A/HRC/4/035, http://documentsddsny.un.org/doc/UNDOC/GEN/G07/108/85/pdf/G0710885.pdf?OpenElement, accessed March 2008.

Ruggie, J. (2008a), Protect, Respect and Remedy: A Framework for Business and Human Rights. Report of the Special Representative of the Secretary-General (srsg) on the Issue of Human Rights and Transnational Corporations and Other Business Enterprises, un Doc. a/hrc/8/5, http://www.unhcr.org/refworld/docid/484d2d5f2.html accessed April 2008.

Ruggie, J. (2008b), Clarifying the Concepts of "Sphere of Influence" and "Complicity". Report of the Special Representative of the Secretary-General (srsg) on the Issue of Human Rights and Transnational Corporations and Other Business Enterprises, un Doc. a/hrc/8/16. Http://Www.Reports-and-Materials.Org/Ruggie-Companion-Report-15-May-2008.pdf, accessed October 2008.

Ruggie, J. (2010), Business and Human Rights: Further Steps toward the Operationalization of the "Protect, Respect and Remedy" Framework un Doc. A/HRC/14/27, http://198.170.85.29/Ruggie-report-2010.pdf, accessed May 2010.

Runner, Ph. (2008), eu Terror List Outpacing Court Rulings, EUobserver.com, http://euobserver.com/9/26990/?rk=1, accessed July 2009.

Rutherford, K., Brem, S., and Matthew, R. A. (2003), *Reframing the Agenda: The Impact of ngo and Middle Power Cooperation in International Security Policy* (Santa Barbara, CA: Praeger Publishers).

Sadeque, N. (2007), "The 'War on Terror' and Mutual Suspicions," *INTRAC Newsletter* no. 35, January 22, 2007.

Savage, C. (2008), *Takeover: The Return of the Imperial Presidency and the Subversion of American Democracy* (New York: Little, Brown).

Schaller, Ch. (2006), "Völkerrechtliche Rahmenbedingungen und die Rolle der Vereinten Nationen bei der Terrorismusbekämpfung," in Schneckener, U. (ed.) *Chancen und Grenzen multilateraler Terrorismusbekämpfung. SWP-Study* (Berlin: Stiftung Wissenschaft und Politik), 13–28.

Scheffer, D. (2004), "The Double Standards of Bush's War," *The Financial Times,* May 5, 2004.

Sheinin, M. (2005), Report of the un Special Rapporteur on the Promotion and Protection of Human Rights and Fundamental Freedoms, e/cn.4/2006/98, 28 December 2005, Geneva: United Nations, http://www.coe.int/t/e/legal_affairs/legal_co-operation/fight_against_terrorism/3_CODEXTER/Working_Documents/2006/Sheinin%20E-CN.4-2006-98.pdf, accessed September 2010.

Scheinin, M. (2007a), *Report of the Special Rapporteur on the Promotion and Protection of Human Rights and Fundamental Freedoms while Countering Terrorism* (United Nations: Human Rights Council).

Scheinin, M. (2007b) (tr), "Terrorism and Human Rights," *Zeitschrift fur Menschenrechte*, 1, 1, 11–18.

Scheppele, K. L. (2006), "The Migration of Anti-constitutional Ideas: The Post-9/11 Globalization of Public Law and the International State of Emergency," in Choudhry, S. (ed.), *The Migration of Constitutional Ideas* (New York: Cambridge University Press).

Schmahl, S. (2006), "Effektiver Rechtsschutz gegen 'targeted sanctions'des UN-Sicherheitsrats?, " *Europarecht*, 41/4, 566–76.

Schmitz, H.P., Mitchell, G.E., Raggo, P., and Hermann, M.G. (2010), *Transnational NGOs: A Cross-sectoral Analysis of Leadership Perspectives* (Syracuse: Moynihan Institute of Global Affairs).

Schneckener, U. (2007) (ed.), *Chancen und Grenzen multilateraler Terrorismusbekämpfung. SWP-Study* (Berlin: Stiftung Wissenschaft und Politik), http://swp-berlin.org/common/get_document.php?asset_id=4062, accessed July 2010.

Schneider, P. (2002), "Menschenrechte und ihr Schutz: Ein Fazit," in Müller, E.,

Schneider, P., and Thony K. Menschenrechtsschutz (2002) (eds), *Politische Maßnahmen, zivilgesellschaftliche Strategien, humanitäre Interventionen* (Baden-Baden: Nomos), 321–69.

Schrijver, N. and Herik, L. van den (2007), "Counter-Terrorism Strategies, Human Rights and International Law: Meeting the Challenges, Final Report Poelgeest Seminar," *Netherlands International Law Review*, LIV, 572–87.

Schulz, W. F. (2003), *Tainted Legacy: 9/11 and the Ruin of Human Rights* (New York: Thunder's Mouth Press/Nation Books).

Schulz, W. F. (2008) (ed.), *The Future of Human Rights: U.S. Policy for a New Era* (Philadelphia, PA: University of Pennsylvania Press).

Schweda, B. (2007), EU-Terrorliste auf dem Prüfstand. Das Parlament mit der Beilage, Aus Politik und Zeitgeschichte, 25, http://www.bundestag.de/dasparlament/2007/25/europawelt/16196023.html, accessed July 2009.

Seghetti, L. (2004), Border Security: U.S.-Canada Immigration Border Issues, CRS Report for Congress, http://www.ndu.edu/library/docs/crs/crs_rs21258_28dec04.pdf, accessed March 2005.

Shafer, B. E. (1991) (ed.), *Is America Different? A New Look at American Exceptionalism* (Oxford: Clarendon).

Shaw, M. (2003), *International Law*, 5th edn (Cambridge: Cambridge University).

Shestack, J. J. (1978), "Sisyphus Endures: The International Human Rights NGO," *New York Law School Law Review*, 24/1, 89–123.

Shue, H. (1980), *Basic Rights: Subsistence, Affluence & U.S. Foreign Policy* (Princeton, NJ: Princeton University Press).

Sidel, M. (2008), "Counter-terrorism and the Enabling Legal and Political Environment for Civil Society: A Comparative Analysis of 'War on Terror' States," *The International Journal of Not-for-Profit Law*, 10/3, 7–49.

Sieff, M. (2003), Giant Demonstrations Transform Europe, Washington Report on Middle East Affairs, April 2003, http://wrmea.com/archives/april03/0304038.html, accessed March 2009.

Simic, C. (2009), "Connoisseurs of Cruelty," *New York Review of Books*, March 12, 2009.

Simmons, B. A. (2009), *Mobilizing for Human Rights. International Law and Domestic Politics* (Cambridge: Cambridge University Press).

Slaughter, A. M. and Ratner, S. R. (1999), "The Method Is the Message," *American Journal of International Law*, 93, 410–23.

Smith, A. (2006), "The Unique Position of National Human Rights Institutions. A Mixed Blessing?," *Human Rights Quarterly*, 28/4, 904–46.

Spees, P. (2003), "Women's Advocacy in the Creation of the International Criminal Court: Changing the Landscapes of Justice and Power," *Signs: Journal of Women in Culture and Society*, 28/4, 1233–54.

Spiro, P. J. (2000), "The New Sovereigntists: American Exceptionalism and Its False Prophets," *Foreign Affairs*, 79/6, 9–16.

St. Pierre, Y. (2005), *Le 11 septembre et la réinterprétation du paradigme terroriste* (Paris: Université Paris 7), 105.

Statistics Canada (STATCAN) (2007), "Crime Statistics," *The Daily*, http://www.statcan.ca/Daily/English/070718/d070718b.htm, accessed February 2008.

Steans, J. (1998), *Gender and International Relations* (New Brunswick, NJ: Rutgers University Press), 5.

Steiner, H., Alston, P., and Goodman, R. (2007), *International Human Rights in Context, Law, Politics, Morals* (Oxford: Oxford University Press).

Sullivan, M. J. I. (2008), *American Adventurism Abroad: Invasions, Interventions, and Regime Changes Since World War II* (Malden, MA: Blackwell Publishing).

Sunga, L. S. (2007), "Dilemmas Facing NGOs in Coalition-Occupied Iraq," in Bell, D. A. and Coicaud, J. -M. (eds), *Ethics in Action. The Ethical Challenges of International Human Rights Non-Governmental Organizations* (Cambridge: Cambridge University Press), 99–116.

Suponitskaya, I. (2010), *Ravenstvo i svoboda. Rossia i SShA: sravnenie sistem* (Moscow: Rosspen).

Sylvester, C. (2002), *Feminist International Relations: An Unfinished Journey* (New York: Cambridge University Press).

Tarrow, S. (2005), *The New Transnational Activism* (Cambridge: Cambridge University Press).

Tawhida, A. and Butler, I. de Jesus (2006), "The European Union and Human Rights. An International Law Perspective," *European Journal of International Law*, 17/ 4, 771–80.

Taylor, J. K. (1992), *Reclaiming the Mainstream: Individualist Feminism Rediscovered* (New York: Prometheus).

Terry, F. (2002), *Condemned to Repeat? the Paradox of Humanitarian Action* (Ithaca, NY: Cornell University Press).

Thomas, D. C (2001), *The Helsinki Effect. International Norms, Human Rights, and the Demise of Communism* (Princeton, NJ: Princeton University Press).

Tickner, A. J. (2001), *Gendering Global Politics: Issues and Approaches in the Post-Cold War Era* (New York: Columbia University Press).

Tickner, A. J.(2002), "Feminist Perspectives on 9/11," *International Studies Perspectives*, 3/4, 333–50.

Tjeenk Willink, H. (2007), "To What Extent May in a Constitutional Democracy the Rule of Law be Limited in Order to Protect Her against Terrorism?," in

Review Committee on the Intelligence and Security Services (CTIVD) & Faculty of Law Radboud University, Nijmegen, Accountability of Intelligence and Security Agencies and Human Rights, The Hague.

Tocqueville, A. de (2003), *Democracy in America and Two Essays on America* (London: Penguin Books).

Tong, R. P. (1998), *Feminist Thought: A More Comprehensive Introduction* (Boulder, CA: Westview Press).

Torrente, N. de (2004), "Humanitarian Action Under Attack: Reflections on the Iraq War," *Harvard Human Rights Journal*, 17/1, 1–30.

Trochev, A. (2008), *Judging Russia: Constitutional Court in Russian Politics, 1990–2006* (Cambridge: Cambridge University Press).

Trunov, I. L. (2007) (ed.), *Terrorizm. Pravovye aspekty protivodeistvija. Normativnye i mezhdunarodnye akty s kommentarijami. Nauchnye stati*, 2nd edn (Moscow: Eksmo).

Twiss, S. B. (2007), "Torture, Justification, and Human Rights: toward An Absolute Proscription," *Human Rights Quarterly*, 29, 346–67.

Tzanou, M. (2002), "Case-note on Joined Cases C-402/05 P & C-415/05 P Yassin Abdullah Kadi & Al Barakaat International Foundation v. Council of the European Union & Commission of the European Communities," *German Law Journal*, 10/02, 123–54.

UN Security Council (1999), Security Council Resolutions 1999. Resolution 1267 on the Situation in Afghanistan, http://daccessdds.un.org/doc/UNDOC/GEN/N99/300/44/PDF/N9930044.pdf?OpenElement, accessed April 2009.

UN Security Council (2001), Security Council Resolutions 2001, Resolution 1371, http://ue.eu.int/uedocs/cmsUpload/UN%20Resolution%201371.pdf, accessed April 2008.

UN Security Council (2007a), "Focal Point for De-listing Established Pursuant To Security Council Resolution 1730," UN Security Council Sanctions Committees, http://www.un.org/sc/committees/dfp.shtml, accessed May 2010.

UN Security Council (2007b), Security Council Resolutions 2006, Resolution 1730, http://daccessdds.un.org/doc/UNDOC/GEN/N06/671/31/PDF/N0667131.pdf? OpenElement, accessed April 2009.

UN Security Council (2007c), Security Council Resolutions 2006, Resolution 1735, http://daccessdds.un.org/doc/UNDOC/GEN/N06/680/14/PDF/N0668014.pdf? OpenElement, accessed April 2009.

United Kingdom (2005), Prevention of Terrorism Act §1 (1), http://www.opsi.gov.uk/acts/acts2005/20050002.htm, accessed February 2005.

United Nations (2000), Report of the Special Rapporteur on Violence Against Women, Its Causes and Consequences: Addendum–Mission to Pakistan and Afghanistan (1–13 September 1999). Prepared by Radhika Coomaraswamy, http://www.un.org/womenwatch/ afghanistan/reports.htm, accessed April 2009.

United Nations (2007) (tr), UN-Sanktionsauschuss, Polixea Portal, http://www.polixea-portal.de/index.php/Lexikon/Detail/id/156864/%20name/UN-Sanktionsausschuss, accessed April 2009.

United Nations (2008a), Report of the Analytical Support and Sanctions Monitoring Team Pursuant to Resolution 1267 (1999) Concerning Al-Qaida and the Taliban and Associated Individuals and Entities, http://daccess-dds-ny.

un.org/doc/UNDOC/GEN/N09/255/17/PDF/N0925517.pdf?OpenElement, accessed April 2010.

United Nations (2008b), Individuals, Groups, Undertakings and Entities That Have Been Removed from the Consolidated List Pursuant to a Decision by the 1267 Committee, http://www.un.org/sc/committees/1267/docs/Delisted.pdf, accessed July 2009.

United Nations (2008c), The Consolidated List Established and Maintained by the 1267 Committee with Respect to Al-Qaida, Usama Bin Laden, and the Taliban and Other Individuals, Groups, Undertakings and Entities Associated with Them, http://www.un.org/sc/committees/1267/pdf/consolidatedlist.pdf, accessed April 2009.

United Nations (2009), Report of the Analytical Support and Sanctions Monitoring Team Pursuant to Resolution 1267 (1999) Concerning Al-Qaida and the Taliban and Associated Individuals and Entities, May 13, http://www.un.org/sc/committees/1267/monitoringteam.shtml, accessed April 2010.

United Nations General Assembly (1993), "Vienna Declaration and Programme of Action, World Conference on Human Rights," *Office of the United Nations High Commissioner for Human Rights* (Geneva, United Nations).

Universal Periodic Review: Report of the Working Group on the Universal Periodic Review: The Netherlands, A/HRC/8/31, May 13, 2008.

Universal Periodic Review: Report of the Working Group on the Universal Periodic Review: The Netherlands, Addendum, Response of the Kingdom of the Netherlands to the Recommendations it Received during the Universal Periodic Review on April 15, 2008, A/HRC/8/31/Add.1, August 13, 2008.

US Department of Defense (2005), National Security Strategy, http://www.defenselink.mil/news/Mar2005/d20050318nds1.pdf, accessed March 2009.

US Department of the Treasury (2006), Anti-terrorist Financing Guidelines: Voluntary Best Practices for US-Based Charities, http://www.ustreas.gov/press/releases/reports/0929%20finalrevised.pdf, accessed April 2010.

US Senate Armed Services Committee (2008), Inquiry into the Abuse of Detainees in us Custody, December 11, 2008.

Ustinov, V. V. (2008), *Rossija: 10 let borby s mezhdunarodnom terrorizmom* (Moscow: OLMA Media Grup).

Utting, P. (2004), "Neue Ansätze zur Regulierung transnationaler Konzerne. Potential und Grenzen von Multistakeholder-Initiativen," in Brühl, T., Feldt, H., Hamm, B., Hummel, H., and Martens, J. (eds), *Unternehmen in der Weltpolitik. Politiknetzwerke, Unternehmensregeln und die Zukunft des Multilateralismus* (Bonn: Dietz), 96–121.

Uvin, P. (2004), *Human Rights and Development* (Bloomfield, CT: Kumarian Press).

Van Ginkel, B. (2009), "How to Repair the Legitimacy Deficit in the War on Terror: a Special Court for Dealing with International Terrorism?," in Zwaan, J. de, Bakker, E., and Meer, S. van der, (eds), *Challenges in a Changing World: Clingendael Views on Global and Regional Issues* (The Hague: T.M.C. Asser Press), 145–62.

Vlcek, W. (2006), "Acts to Combat the Financing of Terrorism: Common Foreign and Security Policy at the European Court of Justice," *European Foreign Affairs Review*, 11, 4, 491–507.

Voz'zhenikov, A. V (2006), *Mezhdunarodnyi terrorizm. Bor'ba za geopoliticheskoe gospodstvo* (Moscow: Eksmo).

Webb, M. (2007), *Illusions of Security: Global Surveillance and Democracy in the Post-9/11 World* (San Francisco: City Lights Books).

Weeks, K. (1998), *Constituting Feminist Subjects* (Ithaca, NY: Cornell University Press).

Weigend, T. (2006), *Strafgeseztbuch 42. Auflage* (Munich: DTV).

Weinzierl, R. (2008), "Menschenrechtsschutz in der Europäischen Union," in Gareis, S. B. and Geiger, G. (eds), *Internationaler Schutz der Menschenrechte* (Opladen: Verlag Barbara Budrich), 65–80.

Weissbrodt, D. and Berquist, A. (2006), "Extraordinary Rendition: a Human Rights Analysis," *Harvard Human Rights Journal*, 19, 123–60.

Welch, C. E. (2001) (ed.), *NGOs and Human Rights: Promise and Performance* (Philadelphia, PA: University of Pennsylvania Press).

Whelehan, I. (1995), *Modern Feminist Thought* (New York: New York University Press).

Whitman, J. Q. (2003), *Harsh Justice: Criminal Punishment and the Widening Divide between America and Europe* (Oxford: Oxford University Press).

Wilson, R. A. (2005) (ed.), *Human Rights in the "War on Terror"* (Cambridge: Cambridge University Press).

Winston, M. (2007), "Human Rights as Moral Rebellion and Social Construction," *Journal of Human Rights*, 6/3, 279–305.

Winston, M. E. (2008), "Why 9/11 Was Good for Human Rights," in The International Human Rights Regime since 9/11: Trans-Atlantic Perspectives. Pittsburgh, April 17–19, 2008, http://www.ucis.pitt.edu/euce/events/conferences/HR-PDF/Winston.pdf, accessed March 2009 (quoted with the kind permission of the author).

Wittes, B. (2008), *Law and the Long War. The Future of Justice in the Age of Terror* (New York: Penguin Press).

Woods, L. (1998). "The European Union and Human Rights," in Hanski, R. and Suksi, M. (eds), *An Introduction to the International Protection of Human Rights. A textbook* (Turku: Abo Akademi University), 283–300.

World Public Opinion (2005), 21 Nation Poll on Bush's Re-Election, http://www.worldpublicopinion.org, Washington DC, accessed August 2010.

World Public Opinion (2006a), Americans Support Full Due-Process Rights for Terrorism Suspects, http://www.worldpublicopinion.org, Washington DC, accessed August 2010.

World Public Opinion (2006b), World Citizens Reject Torture, *BBC* Global Poll Reveals, accessed August 2010.

World Public Opinion (2007a), America's Image in the World, http://www.worldpublicopinion.org, Washington DC, accessed August 2010.

World Public Opinion (2007b), Americans Support Full Due-Process Rights for Terrorism Suspects, http://www.worldpublicopnion.org, Washington DC, accessed August 2010.

World Public Opinion (2007c), World View of US Role Goes from Bad to Worse, http://www.worldpublicopinion.org, Washington DC, accessed August 2010.

World Public Opinion (2008a), Americans Support Full Due-Process Rights for Terrorism Suspects, http://www.worldpublicopinion.org, Washington DC, accessed August 2010.

World Public Opinion (2008b), World Public Opinion and the Universal Declaration of Human Rights, http://www.worldpublicopinion.org, Washington DC, accessed August 2010.

Wouters, J., Basu, S., and Lemmens, P. (2007), *EU Human Rights Dialogues. Current Situation, Outstanding Issues and Resources. Policy Brief No. 1* (Leuven: Center for Global Governance Studies).

Wouters, J., Brems, E., Smis, S. and Schmitt, P. (eds) (2010), "Introductory Remarks," in Wouters, J., Brems, E., Smis, S. and Schmitt P. (eds), *Accountability for Human Rights Violations by International Organisations* (Antwerp/Portland/ Oxford: Intersentia), 1–20.

Youngs, G. (2004) "Feminist International Relations: A Contradiction in Terms? Or: Why Women and Gender Are Essential to Understanding the World 'We' Live in," *International Affairs*, 80/1, January 2004, 75–87, http://onlinelibrary. wiley.com/doi/10.1111/inta.2004.80.issue-1/issuetoc, accessed October 2010.

Zalewski, M. (1995), "What Is the Feminist Perspective on Bosnia?," *International Affairs*, 71/2, 339–56.

Zalewski, M. and Parpart, J. (1998) (eds), *The "Man" Question in International Relations* (Boulder: Westview Press).

Zorkin, V. (2008), *Konstitutsia i prava cheloveka v XXI veke. K 15-letiju Konstitutsii Rossiiskoi Federatsii i 60-letiju Vseobshei daklaratsii prav cheloveka* (Moscow: Norma).

Index

Abu Ghraib prison, 1, 37
ACLU, *see* American Civil
    Liberties Union (ACLU)
advocacy networks, 213–14
Afghanistan, 19
    Canadian presence in, 197
    presidential elections of
        2009, 58–60
    women, 53–61
African regimes, 15
airport security, 136
Alien Tort Claims Act (ATCA), 243
Al Masri, Khalid, 35
Al Qaeda, 152
American Civil Liberties Union
    (ACLU), 38, 58
American exceptionalism, 65–85
    high price of, 108
    international human rights
        regime and, 82–4
    messianic engagement and, 80–1
    political engagement and, 70–3
    Providential exceptionalism, 68–80
    varieties of, 66–8
American Service-Members
    Protection Act, 39
Amnesty International, 32, 37, 38,
    48n6, 114, 138, 178, 186, 203,
    207–8, 214, 231, 246–7
Angola, 43
antiterrorism, *see* counterterrorism;
    war on terror
Anti-Terror Law, 192–3
antiterror sanctions, 152–3
Arar, Maher, 35, 190
ATCA, *see* Alien Tort Claims Act
    (ATCA)
Atlantic Charter, 74
Australia, 19, 183

Baghram airbase, 35
behavioral exceptionalism, 67
Berlin Wall, 34, 75–6, 131

blacklists, 150–65
black sites, 111, 113
Blair, Tony, 46
BLIHR, *see* Business Leaders Initiative
    on Human Rights (BLIHR)
Boghosian, Heidi, 234
Bonn Agreement, 56
Boumediene v. Bush, 38
Bretton Woods institutions, 74
Bricker, John, 110
Brickerism, 43
Britain, *see* United Kingdom
Bucharest Plan of Action, 145–6
burqa, 54
Bush, G. H. W., 76
Bush Administration
    backlash against, 37
    human rights record of, 34–9, 44
    policies of, 30, 62
    torture and, 108, 111–17, 120, 123
    use of executive power by, 230–1
    war on terror and, 26–8, 81
    world public opinion on, 39–42
business
    see also corporate responsibility
    human rights and, 237–54
    responsibility of, for human rights,
        242–4, 251–3
    scandals, 241–2
    self-regulation by, 240–2
Business Leaders Initiative on Human
    Rights (BLIHR), 246

Canada, 19
    as barometer for trends in security
        and human rights, 198–9
    counterterrorism in, 189–95
    foreign policy of, 185
    human rights and, 184–8
    immigration policies, 191–2, 195–6
    international influences on, 195–7
    post-9/11 policies of, 189–91, 195–7,
        261–2

Canada – *continued*
    terrorism in, 188–9
    US and, 195–7
Canadian Charter of Rights and
        Freedoms, 186
CARE, 224
Carter Administration, 42, 77
Central Asia, 19, 24
Central Intelligence Agency (CIA),
        43, 111, 113
Chahal v. UK, 123
Chandler, Sir Geoffrey, 247
Chechnya, 91–4, 99, 102, 113, 263
Cheney, Dick, 13, 36
CIA, *see* Central Intelligence Agency
        (CIA)
Cingranelli-Richards (CIRI)
        Human Rights Data Project, 15,
        17, 186, 187
civil society, transnational, 4–5, 32,
        79, 264–5
Clinton Administration, 26
CoE, *see* Council of Europe (CoE)
coercive interrogation, 123,
        130n17
    see also torture
Cold War, 43, 73–5, 78, 132, 183, 206
color revolutions, 226
commercial peace, 80–1
Committee for the Prevention
        of Torture (CPT), 119–20,
        124–6, 175
Constitutional Court, 96–7
Control Orders, 194–5
Convention against Torture, 77
Convention on the Elimination of
        Racial Discrimination, 77, 110
Convention on the Rights of
        Persons with Disabilities, 13–14
Copenhagen Criteria, 138
corporate social responsibility (CSR),
        241, 244, 250
Council of Europe (CoE), 101, 109,
        137, 143–5, 159, 165n16, 259
counterterrorism, 6, 14, 35–6
    see also war on terror
    in Canada, 189–97
    Council of Europe and, 143–5
    in Europe, 46, 132–43

    in Netherlands, 166–82
    OSCE and, 145–6
    in Russia, 86–104
    terrorist blacklists, 150–65
CPT, *see* Committee for the
        Prevention of Torture (CPT)
Cross, James R., 188
Cuban Missile Crisis, 72
Cubilie, Anne, 52
cultural rights, 5

Darfur, 27
Declaration on the Rights of
        Indigenous Peoples, 14
democracy norm, 14–15
Dershowitz, Alan, 95–6
detainee treatment, 124–7
Detainee Treatment Act, 120
development, rights based approach
        to, 205, 210–12
discourse on business and human
        rights, 237–8, 240–8
    actors in, 244–8
    implications of, 251–3
    Ruggie's policy framework for,
        248–51
dissent, 35, 225–8, 229, 233
domestication, 31–3, 46
double standards, 67, 98, 99, 237

Ebadi, Shirin, 44
ECHR, *see* European Court of
        Human Rights (ECtHR)
economic rights, 5
Egypt, 24, 25, 168
Eighth Amendment, 117, 118, 120
Empowerment Rights Index, 15,
        17, 20–3
Ethical Globalization Initiative
        (EGI), 246
Europe
    counterterrorism in, 46, 133–43
    human rights laws and, 108–11
    human rights norms in, 33, 46–7
    Muslim community in, 134–5
    post-9/11 human rights regime in,
        131–49
    prisons in, 119
    torture and, 107–15, 115–29

European Convention on Human
  Rights, 89, 109
European Convention on the
  Prevention of Terrorism, 144
European Convention to Prevent
  Torture, 125
European Court of Human Rights
  (ECHR), 3, 4, 14, 109, 119, 128,
  159, 165n16, 259
  judicial oversight and, 121–2
  Russia and, 100–2
European Court of Justice (ECJ), 3,
  132, 150–1, 155–7, 162, 164n7, 259
European Fundamental Rights
  Charter, 138
European human rights regime,
  131–49
  in Netherlands, 166–7
European Instrument for
  Democracy and Human Rights
  (EIDHR), 138
European Prison Rules, 119, 120
European Union (EU), 137–43
EU terrorists lists, 157–9
exceptionalism
  American, 65–85
  Providential, 68–80
  types of, 66–7
executive power, 230–1, 234
exemptionalism, 67
Extraordinary Renditions
  Program, 193

feminism
  about, 50–3
  on war on terror, 49–62
Fifth Amendment, 117
FLQ, *see* Quebec Liberation
  Front (FLQ)
Foreign Intelligence Surveillance
  Act, 35
foreign policy, 26–7
  Canadian, 185
  US, 42–4, 70–3
Forsythe, David, 67
Fortuyn, Pim, 180
Fourteenth Amendment, 117
Free and Fair Elections in
  Afghanistan (FEFA), 60

Freedom in the World report, 15
Freedom of Information Act, 112
freedom of speech, 17
Fukuyama, Francis, 76

Geneva Conventions, 38–9
genocide, 27, 205, 211
Genocide Convention, 110
Georgia, 226
ghost prisoners, 125
Gilligan, Emma, 94
Global Compact Office, 247
globalization, 76–7, 239–40
Guantánamo Bay, 28, 35, 37, 40,
  45, 48n6, 113, 118, 125, 193
"guilt by association," 193–4

Haiti, 78
Hamdan v. Rumsfeld, 38,
  126–7, 234
Hamdi v. Rumsfeld, 38
Hammarberg, Thomas, 172
Helsinki Final Act, 46, 88
Helsinki Watch, 207
Hoffman, Paul, 37
Hoffman, Stanley, 70
humanitarian aid, 210–12
humanitarian missions, 79
human rights
  during 1990s, 75–80
  Bush Administration
    and, 34–9
  Canada and, 184–8
  Cold War and, 74–5
  globalization and, 239–40
  implementation of, 237
  public opinion on, 39–42
  terrorism and, 167–9
human rights activism, *see*
  transnational human rights
  activism
Human Rights Commission, 5
Human Rights Committee, 14
Human Rights Council, 6, 14, 82
human rights discourse, 237–8,
  263–4
Human Rights First, 38
human rights norms
  domestication of, 31–3, 46

human rights norms – *continued*
  institutionalization of, 33
  internalization of, 32
human rights organizations, 207–9,
  213–18, 264–5
  see also transnational human
    rights activism
human rights paradigm, 31–4
human rights practice
  national trends in, 15–18
  regional patterns, 18–26
  of Russia, 86–104
  war on terror and, 30–48
human rights regime. *See*
  international human rights
  regime
human rights treaties, 110, 239
human rights violations, 1
  mobilization against, 203–4
  root causes of, 212–13
  "shaming" strategy for, 203–4,
    207–9
Human Rights Watch, 32, 38, 48n7,
  138, 203, 207–8, 236

ICC, *see* International Criminal
  Court (ICC)
ICJ, *see* International Court of
  Justice (ICJ)
Ignatieff, Michael, 67
impeachment, 39
information politics, 206
institutionalization, 33
institutional reform, 5, 6
integrity rights, 17
Inter-American Commission on
  Human Rights, 14
International Convention for
  the Protection of All Persons
  from Enforced Disappearance,
  13–14
International Court of Justice (ICJ),
  154, 164n5
International Covenant on Civil
  and Political Rights (ICCPR), 77,
  110, 237
International Covenant on Social,
  Economic and Cultural Rights
  (ICSECR), 3, 237

International Criminal Court (ICC),
  5, 34, 39, 77, 110, 126
international human rights
  regime, 267–9
  during 1990s, 75–80, 267–9
  agenda of, 5–6
  American exceptionalism and, 82–4
  assessment of, 257–67
  business and, 237–54
  compliance and implementation,
    3–4
  definition of, 3–4
  impact of, 4–6
  impact of 9/11 on, 1–2, 13–29,
    256–70
  marginalization of, 108
  middle powers and, 183–4
  as multilayered, 258–67
  norms of, 13–15
  post-Cold War, 4–5, 17–18
  role of states in, 260–3
  transatlantic differences in
    approach to, 108–11
  US and, 77–80
  war on terror and, 30–48
international inspection, 124–6
international institutions, 259–60
international relations
  feminist perspective on, 51–3
International Security Assistance Force
  in Afghanistan (ISAF), 178–9
International Tribunals for
  Rwanda, 5
International Tribunals for
  Yugoslavia, 5
Interpal, 232–3, 236n1
interrogation techniques, 36–7,
  111–12, 120, 123, 130n17
Iran, 43
Iraq, 24, 25, 26
Iraq War, 108
Ireland v. UK, 122–3
isolationism, 73, 81
Israel, 24, 25

judicial oversight, 121–4

Kadyrov, Ramzan, 92
Khadr, Omar, 190

Khan, Irene, 48n6
Koh, Harold Hongju, 31, 34
Kull, Steven, 40
Kuwait, 24, 25

Laporte, Pierre, 188
Lebanon, 24, 25, 43
legal framework, 33
legal isolationism, 67, 81
liberalism, 183
liberty, 68, 70–1, 84n6
Lisbon Treaty, 136–7

Maastricht Treaty, 5, 138, 139, 140–1
Malik, Samina, 194
Marshall Plan, 74
McCarthyism, 43
messianic engagement, 71, 72, 73, 80–1, 83–4
Middle East, 168
middle powers
  see also Canada; Netherlands
  international human rights regime
    and, 183–4
migrant rights, 228–9
Military Commission Act (MCA), 38–9, 127
Miller, Doug, 40–1
Modified Empowerment Index, 17, 20–3
Mukasey, Michael, 120–1
multilateral institutions, 14
multinational corporations, 213, 240–4
  see also business
Muslim NGOs, 232
Muslim states, 134–5

national courts
  terrorist cases in, 159–61
national human rights practice
  global trends in, 15–18
National Security Agency, 35
National Strategy for Homeland Security, 195–6
Netherlands
  counterterrorism in, 166–82
  human rights in, 166–7
  post-9/11 policies of, 261–2

renditions and, 176–9
torture and, 173–6
NGOs, *see* nongovernmental
  organizations (NGOs)
Nicaragua, 43
nongovernmental organizations
  (NGOs), 4–5, 27, 47, 79, 132,
    138, 203–21
  categories of, 223
  discourse on business and human
    rights and, 245–7
  impact of 9/11 on, 203–6, 214–20,
    222–36
  Muslim, 232
  transnational, 203–21
  working on issues unrelated to
    terrorism, 223–4
  working on terrorism-sensitive
    issues in authoritarian states,
    224–7
  working on terrorism-sensitive
    issues in democratic states,
    228–35
non-refoulement principle, 177–8
non-self-executing declaration, 110,
  122–3, 130n17

Obama, Barack, 40, 234
Obama Administration, 26, 27, 28,
  45, 48n5
  international human rights regime
    and, 83
  torture and, 108, 111–12
Office for Democratic Institutions
  and Human Rights (ODIHR),
    137, 146
Office of the High Commissioner for
  Human Rights, 14, 79, 247
Organization for Security and
  Cooperation in Europe (OSCE),
    131, 145–6, 259
OSCE, *see* Organization for Security
  and Cooperation in Europe
  (OSCE)

Padilla, Jose, 35
Pakistan, 19, 26, 113
Palestinian Relief and Development
  Fund, 232–3, 236n1

Pasqua law, 194
Patriot Act, 18, 28, 234
People's Mujahedin of Iran
    (PMOI), 158–9
Peterson, Spike, 49
Physical Integrity Rights Index, 15,
    17–23, 186
Poland, 177
political engagement, 70–3
Pollit, Katha, 58
popular sovereignty, 84n6
Powell, Colin, 36, 53
pragmatism, 72
Predator drones, 35
preventive action, 194–5
preventive detention, 194
Prison Litigation Reform Act, 125
prisons
    EU, 119
    US, 118–19, 125
protests, 233–4
Providential exceptionalism,
    68–80
public opinion, 39–42
Puritans, 68–9
Putin, Vladimir, 91, 93, 96

Quebec Liberation Front
    (FLQ), 188–9

racism, 5
Rasul v. Bush, 38
Reagan, Ronald, 74
Regan, Lauren, 230, 233
rendition, 1, 27, 35, 40, 113, 133,
    141–2, 176–9, 193
Resolution 1267, 152
Ressam, Ahmed, 189, 195–6
Revolutionary Association of Women
    of Afghanistan, 56
Rice, Condoleezza, 36
rights based approach (RBA) to
    development, 205, 210–12
Robinson, Mary, 222, 247
Romania, 177
Romero, Anthony, 234
Rome Statute, 5, 6, 39, 77, 110
Roosevelt, Eleanor, 42, 207
Ruggie, John, 238, 247–51, 252–3

Russia
    compared with US, 87–8
    European Court of Human Rights
        and, 100–2
    human rights policies of, 86–104
    impact of 9/11 on, 92–100
    separatism in, 99–100
    terrorism in, 90–2, 262–3
    torture and, 113
    war on terror and, 226–7
Rwanda, 5, 77, 205, 206, 211

Saadi v. Italy, 123
sanctions regime, 151–3, 161–3
Saudi Arabia, 24, 25, 168
Scheffer, David, 231
Scheinin, Martin, 35–6, 168
Schulz, William, 13
Second World War, 73–4
security discourse, 82–3
September 11, 2001, 1
    European reaction to, 133–7
    impact on international human
        rights, 1–2, 4–6, 13–29, 256–70
    impact on NGOs, 203–6, 214–20,
        222–36
    impact on Russia, 92–100
"shaming" strategy, 203–4, 207–9
Shell, 241–2
Shiite Personal Status Law, 57
Shue, Henry, 239
Simmons, Beth A., 103
single-issue campaigns, 214
Smart Border Accords, 192, 197
smart sanctions, 150–65
social movements, 32–3
social rights, 5
solitary confinement, 118, 119
Somalia, 78
South Africa, 34, 43
South Asia, 19, 24
Soviet Union, 74
    see also Russia
    collapse of, 93
    human rights in, 88–9
Sri Lanka, 19
state duty to protect, 239, 249–50
state secret argument, 123, 130n19
Sullivan, Michael, 43

Suponitskaya, Irina, 88
Switzerland, 171–2

Tajikistan, 19
Taliban, 53–4, 60–1, 152, 163n2
Tamil Tigers, 19
Tenet, George, 36
terror blacklists, 150–65
terrorism
  in Canada, 188–9
  definition of, 138–40, 167–8
  in Europe, 133–7
  human rights and, 167–9
  in Russia, 90–2, 262–3
terrorist attacks, 1, 136
  see also September 11, 2001
Tocqueville, Alexis de, 87
Toronto 18, 189
torture, 1, 17, 28, 35–7, 40, 41, 107
  Bush Administration and, 108,
    111–17, 120, 123
  criminalization of, 126–7
  definition of, 116–17
  international inspection
    and, 124–6
  judicial oversight and, 121–4
  legal loopholes and, 115–21
  Netherlands and, 173–6
  Obama Administration and, 111
  prohibitions on, 116, 117
  renditions and, 176–9
  strengthening vs. weakening the
    prohibition of, 115–27
  transatlantic differences in, 107–15,
    115–29, 259–60
Torture Convention, 110, 116, 123,
  124, 126
transnational civil society, 4–5,
  79, 264–5
transnational corporations, *see*
  multinational corporations
transnational human rights activism
  9/11 and, 203–6, 214–18
  collaboration and, 206
  evolution of modern, 207–9
  history of, 206–10
  in post-Cold War period, 209–10
  single-issue campaigns, 214
  targeting of non-state actors in, 213

transnational institutions, 259–60
Turkey, 24, 25, 124

UDHR, *see* Universal Declaration of
  Human Rights (UDHR)
Ukraine, 226
UN Centre on Transnational
  Corporations (UNCTC), 241
Uniform Code of Military Justice, 38
United Kingdom, 46
  Control Orders, 194–5
  judicial oversight, 121–2
  NGOs in, 229
  response to 9/11 in, 234–5
  torture and, 113–14
United Nations
  antiterror sanctions, 152–3
  Charter of, 237
United States
  Canada and, 195–7
  compared with Russia, 87–8
  credibility of, 30, 42–4
  criminal justice system, 114
  exceptionalism and, 65–85
  foreign policy of, 26–7, 42–4,
    70–3
  human rights abuses by, 30
  human rights in, 18–19, 33
  human rights policy and, 27–8,
    34–9, 42–4
  international human rights regime
    and, 77, 108–11
  judicial oversight in, 122–4
  messianic engagement of, 80–1
  moral stature of, 45–7
  NGOs in, 229–35
  prisons in, 118–19, 125
  ratification of international treaties
    by, 109–11
  torture and, 107–15, 115–29
  world public opinion on, 39–42
United States Agency of International
  Aid (USAID), 215
United States Council for
  International Business
  (USCIB), 245
Universal Declaration of Human
  Rights (UDHR), 3, 41, 88, 116,
  206, 237, 242–3

universal periodic review, 14
unlawful enemy combatants, 35, 193
US-Canadian border, 195–6
US Constitution, 116, 117
US military, humanitarian aid by, 211
US Supreme Court decisions, 38–9, 234
Ustinov, Vladimir, 97–9
Uzbekistan, 19, 26–7, 225–7

van Gogh, Theo, 180
Verhagen, Maxime, 166
Vice and Virtue Patrol, 57
Vienna Declaration and Programme of Action, 78–9
Vienna World Conference on Human Rights, 5, 78–9
Vietnam War, 43, 72

war crimes, 5, 38–9, 126–7
War Crimes Act, 126–7

war on terror, 1, 6
    see also counterterrorism
    feminist lens on, 49–62
    human rights and, 30–48, 262–3
    human rights organizations and, 203–6
    impact of, 2, 17, 26–9
    NGOs and, 224–36
    Russia and, 86–104, 226–7
    as war against women, 57–61
    as war for women's human rights, 53–7
water-boarding, 116–17, 120
Western Asia, 24–6
Western democracies, 18–19
women, Afghan, 53–61
women's voices, 52–3
World Court for Human Rights, 154

Yugoslavia, 5, 77, 206

Zalewski, Marysia, 51
Zorkin, Valery, 95–6